The Oral and Beyond
Doing Things with Words in Africa

A note by Ruth Finnegan on the cover images

The cover images capture just two moments in Africa's rich and variegated experience of doing things with words.

On the front Funky Freddy of the contemporary Sierra Leonean group Jungle Leaders is recording vocals at the microphone in a Freetown studio. His lyrics criticise the political corruption which some Sierra Leoneans feel is preventing the country from progressing, and have been banned from airplay on the government owned broadcasting service. The Jungle Leaders, who have also performed overseas, contribute to a new genre combining rap, hip-hop rhythms and protest lyrics which has emerged in Sierra Leone following the brutal ten-year civil war and is widely regarded as representing the voice of the country's younger generation during its post conflict period.

Behind him, and on the back and spine, the expert poet Sangowemi is performing one of her brilliant praise chants in the town of Okuku, Nigeria. In her rapid fluid delivery she demonstrates her mastery of the long-established Yoruba *oríkì* (praise) genre of oral poetry, binding together what to outsiders may at first seem a conglomeration of fragments into a dazzling fluent performance (for more on Sangowemi and the *oríkì* genre, see Barber 1991, also p. 194 below).

Survey of the Limba people of northern Sierra Leone, Overseas Research Publication No.8, HMSO 1965

Limba stories and story-telling, Clarendon Press, Oxford 1967. Reprinted, Greenwood Press, Connecticut 1981

Oral literature in Africa, Clarendon Press, Oxford 1970. Reprinted (paperback) OUP, Nairobi 1976

Modes of thought. Essays on thinking in Western and non-Western societies (ed. with Robin Horton) Faber and Faber, London 1973

Oral poetry: its nature, significance and social context, Cambridge University Press 1977; 2nd edition, Indiana University Press 1992

The Penguin book of oral poetry (ed.), Allen Lane 1978. Also published as *A world treasury of oral poetry*, Indiana University Press 1978

Essays on Pacific literature (ed. with Raymond Pillai) Oral Tradition Series 2, Fiji Museum, Suva 1978

Conceptions of inquiry (ed. with Stuart Brown and John Fauvel) Methuen 1981

New approaches to economic life (ed. with Bryan Roberts and Duncan Gallie) Manchester University Press 1985

Information technology: social issues (ed. with G.Salaman and K.Thompson) Hodder and Stoughton 1987

Literacy and orality: studies in the technology of communication, Blackwell 1988/Allen and Unwin, Sydney. Italian translation as *La Fine di Gutenberg: Studi sulla tecnologia della comunicazione*, Sansoni, Firenze 1990

The hidden musicians: music-making in an English town, Cambridge University Press 1989; 2nd edition Wesleyan University Press 2007

Oral traditions and the verbal arts: a guide to research practices, Routledge 1992

From family tree to family history (ed. with Michael Drake) Cambridge University Press/Open University 1994

Sources and methods for family and community historians: a handbook (ed. with Michael Drake) Cambridge University Press/Open University 1994; 2nd edition 1997

South Pacific oral traditions (ed. with Margaret Orbell) Indiana University Press 1995

Tales of the city: a study of narrative and urban life, Cambridge University Press 1998

Communicating: the multiple modes of human interconnection, Routledge 2002. Italian translation, De Agostini forthcoming

(ed.) *Participating in the knowledge society: researchers beyond the university walls*, Palgrave-Macmillan 2005

Story of mom
who committed
son to demon
Son killed her out of
revenge

Limba reflected on artistries of languages (p.21)
clothed in literary formulations
Negative assumptions (22)
Commented through medium on social &
natural world around them

Not just morals, but how people behave

Speaking central to social action for Limba (25)
Central to identity →

The Oral and Beyond
Doing Things with Words in Africa

Through stories, Limba formulate + comment on the world (56)

RUTH FINNEGAN

Function of written docs in literate cultures (26)
performed by Limba through speech acts
"Non-literate societies are complex & reflective
on language + exegesis (28)

Speech-acts. Acceptance in words marking
final stage in transactions (30)
— pleading, thanking as act of commitment
& institutional act acknowledgement of
relationships + transactions (37)

Speech acts are recognitions of wider
situations + relationships (41)

Performance is
crucial to oral
stories (45)

+ role of
audience

music+
dance
had
priority
(49)

James Currey
OXFORD

The University of Chicago Press
CHICAGO

experts carried
art of Limba
culture (51)

University of KwaZulu-Natal Press
PIETERMARITZBURG

creativity
+ conventional
styles +
themes

Limba recognized dual nature of literary art:
of individuals and adherence to tradition
Taught "by the dead + by my own ears" (47-48)

James Currey Ltd
73 Botley Road
Oxford OX2 0BS
www.jamescurrey.co.uk

The University of Chicago Press
1427 E. 60th Street
Chicago, IL 60637
www.press.uchicago.edu

University of KwaZulu-Natal Press
Private Bag X01
Scottsville, 3209
www.ukznpress.co.za

British Library Cataloguing in Publication Data
Finnegan, Ruth H.
    The oral and beyond: doing things with words in Africa
    1. Sociolinguistics - Africa 2. Oral communication - Social
    Aspects - Africa 3. Folk literature, African - History and
    criticism 4. Limba (African people) - Languages - Social
    aspects 5. Sociolinguistics - Sierra Leone 6. Oral
    communication - social aspects - Sierra Leone
    I. Title
    306.4'4'096
        ISBN 978-1-84701-000-1 (James Currey cloth)
        ISBN 978-1-84701-001-8 (James Currey paper)

ISBN 978-1-86914-125-7 (University of KwaZulu-Natal Press paper)

Library of Congress Cataloging-in-Publication Data
Finnegan, Ruth H.
    The oral and beyond : doing things with words in Africa / Ruth Finnegan
        p. cm.
    Includes bibliographical references and index.
    ISBN-13: 978-0-226-24971-1 (cloth : alk. paper)
    ISBN-13: 978-0-226-24972-8 (pbk. : alk. paper)
    ISBN-10: 0-226-24971-9 (cloth : alk. paper)
    ISBN-10: 0-226-24972-7 (pbk. : alk. paper)
    1. Oral tradition—Africa. 2. Africa—Folklore. I. Title.
    GR350.F556 2007
    398.2096—dc22

        2007005768

Typeset in 9/11 pt Melior by Long House Publishing Services, Cumbria, UK
Printed and bound in Malaysia

Parry - Lord's *Singer of Tales*
- variability of oral poetry. No correct version
- rejection of memorization (97)
- uniqueness of each performance
- interplay of known themes + expressions.

Unity of some story
only ever brought
about by collator
(127)

mutual
interweaving (187)

(209-10)

(102)

To David

who has lived through
the many stages and experiences of this book
for nearly as many years
as I have

Questions identity of oral lit + radical diff. w/ written
- relative + overlapping
- writing as a visual aid for memory (102)

Once one knows something is oral
then one must ask
Oral in what sense? how far? in what circumstances
for whom? and when? and so on (105)

See e.110 - Oral comp. takes different forms + different cultures
and circumstances. Relationship b/w composition + performance varies
memorization + composition go hand + hand w/ performance
Repeated word patterns (formula) not enough.   Soliloquy
Also, emphasis on music, parallelism, f.y long.; state
Orality as multiform - (112)

One distinction - orality depends on performance + is
an event in time (115)   who interact
                    Interruptions - people + help set up event (126)
memorization in Hindu myths - Vedas,

Contents

Contents

Contents

Preface

This volume grew from my experience of reflecting on how the study of oral forms in Africa has changed since, nearly half a century ago, I first became interested in studying verbal arts in Africa. Looking back over the period I still relish the interpretations and insights that I and others formulated in earlier years. But in the light of the many developments since then I also value the chance to take a second look.

My aim here is not so much to reiterate earlier positions (though some restatement may serve to set aspects of the unfolding study of oral forms in Africa into some historical setting) but rather to extend, contextualise and in some respects qualify them from the perspective of later research and thinking. This is not intended as an 'update' of my 1970 survey of 'oral literature in Africa' – the amount of work that has appeared since then could in no way be captured, even in summary, within a single pair of covers – but as, to an extent, a balancing of it by some taste of issues and findings that have been emerging since that time. I have been fascinated by the enlargement of understanding and the new moves in the field, the more so that since my earlier Africa-focused research I have in the interim largely turned to more comparative issues and to fieldwork in an English context. From this perspective of slight detachment – a huge disadvantage compared to those insightful scholars so closely imbued with the arts they are studying, but perhaps with some minor compensations nonetheless – it has been a delight to return to the continuing work on African oral literature, performance and action. I remain convinced that the thriving interest in the wonderful ways with words in Africa is of relevance not just for Africanists but for all those concerned with the arts of language, the deploying of words, textuality, creativity, multimodal performance, and the seeping boundaries between written and unwritten – issues of fundamental import for humankind.

Africa is commonly known as the oral continent. A wealth of material exemplifies and testifies to this characterisation. It is expressed above all in the verbal artistries, vocally embodied genres and rich traditions of performed literature that rightly form the heart of this volume. Alongside this, concepts like 'orality', 'oral culture' and 'the oral' have been deployed across a range of disciplines to interpret both the past and the present, and used among other things to set Africa in comparative context and illuminate its verbal forms. Yet all these terms remain elusive and controversial, whether applied to Africa or elsewhere, and are often wielded with little regard for their complexities and loaded connotations. So, conjoined with its focus on 'doing things with words' in Africa, this volume at the same time traces something of the development of these terms, written from the viewpoint of someone who has lived through, and played some part in, the continuing debates since the 1960s. They reinforce the need, in my view, for a critical reassessment both of 'orality' and of the still-evocative image of 'Africa-the-oral'

Acknowledgements

This is the point at which, the work nearly done, authors luxuriate in at last being able to express their personal thanks, a dear moment. It is often said to be invidious to name just a few out of many – I agree, but all the same have usually, like many academic authors, happily gone on to do so anyway. But as my list of very special people grew from handfuls to armfuls to something like worldfuls (or so it felt) I finally had to accept this time that setting a bound would be impossible. Many of those whose work and insights I have found particularly inspiring over the years will of course be obvious from the references here, but there are so many others too. So let me merely give my global and heartfelt thanks to the multitude of those both in Africa and elsewhere whose contributions, sometimes nameless, have helped to shape these pages and to whom the creative work of words in Africa owes so much. Without them, and without the long intellectual companionship of my dear husband and colleague David Murray (one exceptional debt I do wish to record), this book could in truth never have been written.

At a more formal level – but nonetheless most sincere – let me thank the Faculty of Social Sciences at the Open University for its continuing support, together with those many libraries that have made their resources available to me both recently and over the years, especially that of the Open University (ever friendly, ever efficient), the British Library's St Pancras Reading Room and inter-library loan service, and the great library of the School of Oriental and African Studies in the University of London.

Some of the material here has appeared in earlier versions (detailed, together with an indication of the revisions, in a note to each chapter). A few chapters have been left more or less as products of their time (especially Chapter 6 and the more ethnographically based Chapters 2 and 3), with revisions mainly confined to the introductory or concluding paragraphs, a few updating footnotes and some minor stylistic changes. Chapters 7, 8 and 9 have been abridged and/or revised, and in part updated; certain sections in Chapter 9 in particular have been substantially extended in the light of more recent studies. Chapters 4 and 10 partially overlap with earlier papers but have been so extensively reworked as virtually to constitute new publications. The remaining chapters (1, 5, 11, 12) are previously unpublished.

Preface

It remains to list where earlier versions previously appeared and express my thanks to the publishers and institutions concerned: Chapter 2: *Odu. A Journal of West African Studies* NS 2, 1969, Institute of African Studies, University of Ile-Ife, Nigeria; Chapter 3: *Man* NS 4, 1969, Royal Anthropological Institute and Blackwell Publishing; Chapter 4: *Folklore* 105, 1994, Folklore Society, London and Taylor & Francis (http://www.tandf. co.uk/ journals); Chapter 6: *Oral Literature in Africa*, Clarendon Press/Oxford University Press, 1970 by permission of Oxford University Press; Chapter 7: B. A. Stolz and R. S. Shannon (eds), *Oral Literature and the Formula*, Center for the Coordination of Ancient and Modern Studies, University of Michigan, 1976; Chapter 8: *Short Time to Stay: Comments on Time, Literature and Oral Performance*, African Studies Program series (12th Annual Hans Wolff Memorial Lecture), Indiana University, 1981; Chapter 9: *Southern African Journal of African Languages*, 12, 2, 1992; Chapter 10 [mostly rewritten]: E. Sienaert, N. Bell and M. Lewis (eds) *Tradition and Innovation: New Wine in Old Bottles?*, University of Natal Oral Documentation and Research Centre, Durban, 1991 and (section 3) Peter France (ed.) *Oxford Guide to Literature in English Translation*, Oxford University Press, 2000. I also acknowledge with thanks permissions from Professor Ioan Lewis to reproduce the extract on pp. 107–8, Cambridge University Press for that on p. 193, and, with particular appreciation, Dr Peter Seitel for the typographical layout on pp. 130–31.

Ruth Finnegan
Bletchley

1

Introducing Words

This volume revolves around human ways with words – the deployment of language, and in particular oral language, as a form of action, of art and of reflection. The prime focus is on African examples and the ways these have been studied and conceptualised over the last decades. But this in turn links into the wider current interest in 'the oral' in both scholarly analysis and everyday practice, something not just of the past, or just of Africa, but with pervading presence across the world of today.

There is certainly no doubt of the importance of the subject for the study of Africa. For Africa is celebrated above all for the treasure of her voiced and auditory arts, and as the home of oral literature, orature and orality, and the genesis and inspiration of the voiced traditions of the great diaspora. Commentators from all sides concur on the significance of the oral and the spoken word. Africa has been termed 'the oral continent par excellence' with 'orality' as the means by which 'Africa made its existence, its history, long before the colonial and imperial presence of the west manifested itself' (Gunner 2004: 1). Christiane Seydou draws attention to 'the prevailing importance of the spoken word in [African] cultures' (2004: 117) and Philip Peek and Kwesi Yankah reiterate a widely accepted position when they emphasise 'the primacy of the human voice and of the exchange of life through words' (Peek and Yankah 2004: xii).

'Oral culture' and 'orality' also figure in the assessments that delineate African forms in global and contemporary perspective. Harold Scheub sees 'the oral experience' retaining its hold on the African imagination (Scheub 1985: 41) and studies of written and 'postcolonial' literatures relate them to the continuing significance of 'oral tradition', 'orality' or 'oral story-telling'. 'Orature ... is the root from which modern African literature must draw sustenance' (Chinweizu et al. 1985: 2), and 'oral literature ... the fundamental reference of discourse and of the imaginative mode in Africa' (Irele 2001: 11). The African inheritance was maintained and constituted by the oral tradition

1

carried, even in slavery, through the portable poetic voice, and many would follow Ngugi wa Thiong'o in seeing 'orature' as 'the great legacy of African life and languages ... our common well' (1998: 126).

Oral tradition, speech, the verbal arts, orality, voice, audition, words, Africa – the images and the experiences hang together. They have played a crucial role in the delineation not only of Africa but also, by their contrasts, of the 'modernity' of the west.

This volume follows up this far-reaching set of images, exploring and reflecting on the oral arts of Africa and their study. There is a wealth of material to refer to in the diverse performances, stories, literatures, texts and traditions, in the varying ways groups and individuals have marshalled these, in how scholars have collected and analysed them, and in the subtle uses of words in art, reflection and action.

Doing things with words

'Doing things with words' is a key notion behind this discussion. It is a broad phrase – more conceit than precise formulation – but gives a rough indication of the inclination of this volume.

It envisages words in the context of action. That is, it is more concerned with what people *do* with words than with language as an abstract, cognitive or somehow independent system. The perspective here is broadly in the pragmatist tradition, consonant with Malinowski's view of language as 'a mode of action and not an instrument of reflection' (Malinowski 1923: 306, 312) and with the philosopher Austin's famous analysis (1962) of 'performative utterances' (his 'how to do things with words' is echoed in the sub-title of this volume, as also in Chapter 3). It is similarly in accord with the view of language as process and exchange rather than finalised textual product which has become more widely recognised over the last generation. Though I am not endeavouring to stake out any demarcated theoretical position within this rather wide and variegated territory, this is the background out of which this volume arises and with which my ideas have over the years interacted.

The volume's prime focus is on people doing things with words *orally* – spoken, vocalised, unwritten. It is true that, contrary to some preconceptions, writing too is an established medium for doing things with words in Africa, and that in any case the apparent split between written and spoken, enscribed and performed, even verbal and non-verbal eventually dissolves. But 'the oral' has increasingly become a topic of interest and scholarship over the last half century or so and it is this which serves as the point of entry here.[1]

---

[1] Given its focus on 'the oral', the volume does not attempt to consider the practices of writing as such. That should not be taken to imply however that I believe writing in Africa to have been unimportant – indeed the opposite (this seemingly still needs saying given the continuing misconceptions in some quarters; I think for example of the assertion in an authoritative recent collection that 'there was no previous [i.e. pre-colonial] literate tradition ... in Sub-Saharan Africa' (Olson and Torrance 2001: 6)). Some relevant studies from a variety of viewpoints (mainly though not exclusively focusing on African-language writing) include Abu-Haidar 1997, Barber 2006, Barber

Within that general area the spotlight here is mainly (though not exclusively) on people using words in ways that could be classed under such heads as oral literature, verbal art, orature, oral performance, song, story, text. Not that such deployments of language form a clear-cut arena – a point that will come up again – but it would be fair to say that the discussion and examples are mostly directed not just to *any* kind of action with or in words, but to verbalised action somehow recognised as imbued with style: with art, one might say, or play, 'attitude', deliberation, display. Overlapping with that, the discussion here is also concerned with the ways people act with words to formulate and interpret the world – and a world that includes others' words too – whether as story-tellers, performers, audiences or scholars.

'Doing things with words' thus also extends into the ways that analysts and researchers have worked with words: gathering them together, transcribing, translating, publishing, defining, controlling, conceptualising, commenting, and much else. Recent years have seen a gathering interest in such processes and in the constructed nature of 'texts' – not just products already independently existent in the real word but created by human agents working within specific circumstances, ideologies and power relations. So how people have enscribed oral performances into written words becomes a question for study: how they have made collections of oral texts; speculated about their origins or symbolism; analysed their functions or meanings; or produced overviews and conceptualisations of them in terms, variously, of 'oral tradition', 'oral literature', 'folklore', 'myths', 'traditional narrative', 'oral poetry', 'verbal art', 'orature' – all these too involve doing things with words.

All this rather begs the question of what is meant by 'words'. So let me be frank that my aim is not to unpack the concepts of 'words' or 'language' in any technical or systematic way, far less to establish some new definition of either term. At this point I will say merely that within the array of human arts this volume is concerned with a roughly identified sector to do with the verbal, spoken, vocalised, but also that, as I have become increasingly aware over the years, it is a sector with notably fluid and contested boundaries. Both 'language' and 'words' are elusive and weighted concepts: in one way notably culturally specific (in recent western traditions often enough tied to conceptualisations and practices that privilege the *written* forms); in another to some degree cross-culturally recognisable and certainly commonly treated as such. In the final chapter I return to take up some issues about the arguably ethnocentric ideologies of language and communication which have often dominated the discussion and perhaps precluded a full appreciation of the multi-modal and multi-media constellation of human arts – and, in turn, of human words.

The prime theme of the volume then is people doing things with and to words in many ways and senses – performing them, entextualising them, playing with them at many levels, organising them in time, uttering them,

[1] (cont.) and Furniss 2006, Dalby 1967–9, Farias 2003a, Gérard 1981, 1990, 1996, Griffiths 1997, Hofmeyr 2004b, Hunwick 1974, Hunwick and O'Fahey 1994– , Krieger 2004, Lüpke 2004, Msiska and Hyland 1997, Newell 2002a,b, Ngandu Nkashama 1992, Pilaszewicz 1985, Ricard 2004, Tuchscherer 2005; see also Barber 1995b and relevant chapters in Andrzejewski et al. 1985, Irele and Gikandi 2004.

3

enscribing them in written forms, decorating them multi-modally, reflecting on and through them, interpreting them, perhaps even downplaying them compared to other media. In this my own words are both part of the process – presenting as they do examples and analyses of people's use of words – and also part of what the volume is designed to reflect on.

Changing arenas

There have been many changes in the study and practice of African verbal arts since, a long generation ago, I first become involved in the subject. This volume, especially in its later chapters, is partly an occasion to chart and reflect on some of these developments. I will not pre-empt that discussion here but merely start with a preliminary sketch of what I see as the major shifts in the overall landscape. They fall in three interrelated areas: the changing balance of power in relation to studies of Africa; the burgeoning interest in 'performance' and in language-as-action; and the rise of so-called 'orality' studies.

The first is perhaps the most obvious: the change over the latter half of the twentieth century from the colonial or recently colonial status of so many African countries to the independent nations of today. How radical this has actually been in either political power or cultural practice remains controversial of course, as do the earlier effects of imperial experience; but certainly many significant developments have gone along with it. When I wished to visit Africa in 1960 the major funding source was the Colonial Social Science Research Council and anthropologists were commonly pictured as going out to gather information about unknown tribes (that is, about areas hitherto unstudied by professional European researchers!) and bring it back for scholars at home. It was more or less taken for granted that the study of 'native' Africa was owned and defined by those from the colonising nations of Europe (less often, though occasionally, from America). That is not to say there were no African scholars either then or earlier, as well of course as an infinitude of local knowledge; but in European circles these were scarcely visible and carried little authority in the 'mainstream' scholarship controlled from outside the continent.

The situation is spectacularly different now. Innumerable African scholars are working on African genres and recognised to be so doing, including many trained in or working at African universities and building on first-language expertise. It is no longer the assumption that it is for foreign-educated scholars to take responsibility for interpreting and theorising the practices and arts of the continent. This goes along with a greater acknowledgement of the contribution of earlier African scholars and thinkers too, not excluding those from Islamic traditions, and a higher profile for the study and practice of African arts generally, now recognised as of value in their own right rather than merely derivative from, and marginal to, the European cultural canon. An immense amount of informed and sustained work has resulted, both in general terms and in relation to historically and socially situated specificities. Older preconceptions have been challenged, new terms developed, and a host of examples studied in the context of changing practices, both in Africa itself and within a more global frame.[2]

This shift has helped to counter the generalised image of Africa as the epitome of unchanging 'tradition', essentially opposed to the 'modernity' of the progressive west. As I go on to consider later, that view remains a persistent one, tied as it is into a set of widely accepted polarities between 'primitive' and 'civilised', 'traditional' and 'modern', 'African' and 'western'. But there has at least been a welcome reaction against its more extreme negative and racist formulations (at any rate as far as concerns Africa and Africans – nowadays the 'Islamic' world is perhaps in some circles drawing the fire). This has been further supported by changing intellectual fashions and some turn against both evolutionist and Enlightenment-based formulations of the modernity, and civilising mission, of the west. As Isidore Okpewho rightly points out we have come a long way from a period when Frobenius could call his *Volksmärchen und Volksdichtungen Afrikas* series (1921–8) by the title of *Atlantis,* 'an epitome of that ecstatic pursuit of vanished worlds and other exotica that may help European students of culture trace the stages of growth of human civilization' (Okpewho 2004a: 304). The basic paradigm may in some ways continue, partly through the lingering legacy of both scholarly and popular interpretation over the years, partly in recycled formulations in the present. But the tone and vocabularies through which it is expressed have to a degree shifted, linked no doubt to the changing power relations in the contemporary world both within and between nations and – in turn – to whose formulations are heard.

A second major set of developments over the last generation concerns the study of performance and of language. When I was starting out my supposition was that for scholars 'the text' was the thing. That was the prevailing flavour in my initial experience of classical studies, in philology, in folklore and in the established analyses of literary works as self-contained and decontextualised entities. The 'text', verbally constituted, was already there as an object for contemplation and analysis (and if it had perhaps got 'corrupted' in transmission then the aim had to be to track down its true

---

[2] The varied overviews or syntheses in relation to African words, oral texts etc. over the last generation or so (i.e. subsequent to works cited in my 1970 survey) are clearly too extensive to summarise here, but for a selection see Abrahams 1983, Andrzejewski 1985, Andrzejewski and Innis 1975, Andrzejewski et al. 1985, Barber 1997c, Barber and Farias 1989, Belinga 1977, Calame-Griaule 1989, Dorson 1972, Furniss and Gunner 1995, Görög-Karady 1982, Hale 1998, Haring 1994, Irele and Gikandi 2004, Jones et al. 1992, Kaschula 2002, Kesteloot 1993a, Kesteloot and Dieng 1997, Kubik 1977, Lindfors 1977, Mapanje and White 1983, Okpewho 1979, 1983, 1990, 1992, 2004a,b, Peek and Yankah 2004, Prahlad 2005, Scheub 1985, 2002, 2005, Seydou et al. 1997, Vail and White 1991, White et al. 2002, also the two monograph series *Classiques africains* (Paris 1963–) and 'Oxford Library of African Literature' (Oxford 1964–79) supplemented by the more comparative 'Cambridge Studies in Oral and Literate Culture' (1981–93); articles and/or special issues in such journals or series as *Research in African Literatures, Journal of African Cultural Studies, Cahiers de littérature orale,* and *African Literature Today;* and bibliographies in Görög-Karady 1981, 1992, Scheub 1977b. For further comment see Chapters 9–11 (note also that, apart from the very occasional addition during the production process of this book, references here and elsewhere go up to mid-2005 only).

original form). So it ran counter to such models when I found myself engaged with performance, audience and context, as a result first of my initial experience of story-telling in northern Sierra Leone villages, and then of oral literature more generally. My consequent reaction against the timeless autonomous view of 'text' was deepened and refined as I became further acquainted with the impressive analyses in oral-formulaic studies, with the developing interdisciplinary work on 'orality' and cognate notions, and with the influential 'performance approach' and 'ethnography of speaking' perspective of (mainly) American anthropologists and folklorists, followed later by the recent developments in linguistic anthropology and 'performance studies' more generally. In ways retraced in part in these chapters it has become increasingly accepted that to understand oral forms it is necessary to pay at least some attention to their performance and context.[3]

This is complemented by approaches to language as process and action. Though with longer roots, this was brought particularly to the fore by the philosopher J. L. Austin's influential *How to Do Things with Words* (1962)[4] and, as time has gone on, by a cluster of studies by sociologists, sociolinguists, folklorists and linguistic anthropologists that have intersected with the 'performance' analyses just mentioned. This broad, if also variegated, set of approaches has found expression in ethnomethodological micro-analyses of conversations, in accounts of the dramatic presentations of everyday life, in studies of the ethnography of speaking or of textualisation, and the expanding interdisciplinary work which emphasises the processual, contextualised, ideological and socially situated dimensions of language. Across many disciplines, from anthropology and sociology to history and sociolinguistics, the balance has been shifting from the study of idealised and/or self-existent object or structure towards less judgmental accounts of diverse actions and creative practices. In ways consonant with the overall perspective of this volume scholars are now interested not just in the finalised product or the apparently firm tradition but the processual and dialogic activities through which these are manipulated, constrained, used, contextualised, re-contextualised or transformed.[5]

This has turned the spotlight on the detailed processes by which people create, entextualise, transmit, perform, or reflect about a multiplicity of forms of verbalised action: something to be considered not just in relation to texts

[3] Earlier discussions on these lines that I found especially inspiring include Abrahams 1968, Bauman 1977, 1989, 1992, Bauman and Sherzer [1974] 1989, Ben-Amos and Goldstein 1975, Hymes 1981, Mannheim and Tedlock 1995, Paredes and Bauman 1972, Schechner 1988, Scheub 1975, Tedlock 1977, 1983; also more recently Barber and Farias 1989, Bauman 2004, Bauman and Briggs 1990, 2003, Cancel 2004, Drewal 1991, 2004, Foley 2002, Fretz 2004, Hanks 1989, 1996, Harding 2002, Hughes-Freeland 1998, Ochs 2001, Okpewho 1990, Schechner 2002, see also comment and references later in this volume, especially Chapter 11, pp. 189 ff.
[4] I was very directly influenced by Austin's work through attending his 'Words and Deeds' lectures (the basis of his 1962 book) while at Oxford in the mid-1950s.
[5] I have found particularly helpful the overviews and/or contributions in Bauman 2004, Bauman and Briggs 1990, 2003, Clark 1992, Drewal 2004, Duranti 1997a, Duranti and Goodwin 1992, Goodwin 2001, Gumperz and Levinson 1996, Hanks 1996, Hymes 1996, Knoblauch and Kotthoff 2001: Introduction, Ochs et al. 1996: Introduction, Potter 1996. Further aspects are taken up later in the volume.

and traditions from the past or to a canon recognised by elite scholars, but also as to how people are actually acting – performing and entextualising – in the present. This is a perspective with which I think I have always aligned myself, however dimly at times, but which I have seen becoming increasingly visible over the years. Nowadays there is immensely greater appreciation than a generation ago of the significance of context, of audiences and readers, of dialogism and multiple voices, of historical specificities, and of the need to challenge restrictive and self-sustaining ideologies that would hide certain forms and action from consideration. Among the most remarkable developments since the mid-twentieth century has, to me, been this questioning of the narrow focus on text as a spatially defined, self-existent, and atemporal object, and the rise of interest in performance and contextualised action as it takes place in the world.

The final development to note has been the emergence of so-called 'orality studies' and the increasing interest in 'the oral'. Not that this interest either is totally new – I think, for example, of the long continuing work on African oral forms (see Chapter 6, esp. p. 88 n. 6). But from the 1960s and onwards it was decisively shaped and promoted by the profoundly influential work of Walter Ong, Albert Lord and Jack Goody.[6] From the mainly negative definition of 'unwritten' or 'non-literate', the term 'oral' has become a substantive one, endued with its own distinct qualities, the focus of interdisciplinary study, and the foundation for a clutch of specialist terminologies: developments which this volume in part charts. Over the last decades studies of 'oral texts', 'oral literature', 'orature', 'oral performance', 'oral tradition', 'oral culture', 'oral history' and 'orality' have proliferated – and not just for Africa. There are constant volumes and conferences with some permutation of 'oral' or 'orality' in their title.[7] It is a large and prolific body of work with which I have frequently interacted over the years so that this volume in a small way demonstrates and reflects on some of its main developments.

There have clearly been great benefits from this expanding interest in oral forms. Moving from a position where *written* texts seemed to hold the central reality and where the oral forms of both the exotic others and the seemingly uncultivated sections of 'modern' society were routinely ranked below the written productions of the established canon, there is by now a wide appreciation of the existence, the validity and the richness of oral expression as part of the created cultural achievements of humankind. There is now an extensive literature on oral expression and performance, both in its worldwide incidence and more especially for the continent and diaspora of Africa, and a general fascination with the oral has strikingly widened our understanding of what people can do with words, unwritten as well as written. This

[6] For example (among their many publications) Goody 1968, 1977, 1987, 1999, 2000, Lord 1960, 1965, Ong 1967, 1977, 1982.

[7] For a small sample of relatively recent instances see Brown 1999a, Cooper 1995, Draper 2003, Foley 2002, 2003, Fox 2000, Furniss 2004, Honko 2000b, Kaschula 2001, Niles 1999, Ricard and Swanepoel 1997, also references to aspects of 'the oral' etc. in postcolonial studies (e.g. Featherstone 2005: 9, 186ff) and analyses of written literature (see Chapter 11, esp. p. 187 n. 8), and in journals such as *Cahiers de littérature orale* and *Oral Tradition* (see especially the extensive references and discussion in *Oral Tradition* 18, 1–2 (special issue, 2003)); also examples in later chapters.

volume gives a small taste of that work. With the increased appreciation of speech genres, of voice as well as written script, the ear as well as the eye, performance as well as text, the oral arts and voices of Africa are now more extensively heard not only in Africa but on a world scale.

At the same time these developments have sometimes seemed to go to their own extremes, exaggerating the divisions between 'oral' and 'written' or presenting the distinctions in overly evaluative terms, whether demeaning or romanticising. 'Oral' has been used as a surface replacement for currently unfashionable terms like 'primitive', 'simple', or 'tribal' while the widely used concept of 'oral culture' has not seldom attracted to itself some of the generalised character once imputed to 'primitive society': of lack of objective detachment, of old tradition, of communal harmony, close-to-nature authenticity. 'Orality' and 'the oral' remain, at the least, emotive terms, evoking one of the central features by which 'Africa' can be classed as 'other'.

The relations of text, performance, language and entextualisation, the divisions of humankind, and the implications of 'oral' expression within this have thus turned out more problematic and complex but at the same time more interesting than they perhaps once seemed. In this the work of African performers and scholars now takes its influential part, leading us more deeply into the oral performance and sonic style so notable, it seems, for the African continent.

A backward forward look

Let me preface the conventional preview of the ensuing chapters with a short backwards look, for this volume is also an occasion for presenting and reconsidering some of my own words since the 1960s. Here is that additional sense in which this volume treats doing things with words in Africa: by exemplifying and reflecting on the ways that, as one of the scholars who have written and spoken about African forms, I too have used, commented on, processed, and publicised words in and about Africa.

To set this in context let me explain that in my own career I followed the fairly common pattern of starting from a relatively narrow ethnographic focus before gradually moving into more comparative issues, a sequence that the ordering of this book roughly mirrors. Like many anthropologists I was hugely influenced by my first field experience, which for me was on story-telling among the Limba of northern Sierra Leone in the 1960s, and in due course wanted to go on to set this in wider perspective. That led me to attempt a more comparative perspective, both in the context of African oral forms more generally (in *Oral Literature in Africa* 1970), and, later, in a larger international frame (*Oral Poetry* [1977] 1992), as well as various shorter interventions (some represented here) in the on-going debates about orality and performance etc. Later still I tried to widen my understanding further by looking at aspects of musical enactment (especially in *The Hidden Musicians* 1989), by further ethnographic work, this time in England (on musical practices (*The Hidden Musicians* again) and on narrative (*Tales of the City*, 1998)), and most recently by a more multi-modal study (*Communicating. The Multiple Modes of Human*

Interconnection 2002). These various endeavours have given me a rather different perspective on my earlier ethnographic work and its outcomes.

This sequence means that Limba examples are prominent in the earlier chapters so let me hasten to say that this volume is in no way intended as a monograph on the Limba whether of the 1960s or now. As the book advances they gradually recede. I have thus not thought it appropriate to make any gesture towards 'updating' the ethnographic material. The accounts here are to be understood in their historical setting of the early 1960s. I have not in fact visited the area since that time. But in any case the 'them' that I might have found later would no longer have been the 'them' of earlier times, and the language- and locality based demarcations of tribal units current then are possibly now even less a matter of neutral definition than they were half a century ago. Not only have changing national and international networks both reinforced, undermined and extended local allegiances, but the (then) Limba country and its diverse inhabitants have since the 1960s been embroiled in the vicissitudes of political turmoil and horrific civil war. References to Limba ethnography are thus to be understood as relating to one particular period and area to add exemplification to more general discussion rather than a contribution to some in-depth study of 'their' fortunes.[8]

The earlier chapters, then, raise in a culturally specific setting issues that are taken up in a more comparative frame later in the volume. In what ways do people use and link words, and how do they regard them? Can people without writing reflect on language and speech or use abstract concepts to distance themselves from their actions and the world around them? The Limba and others are shown making words work for them at various levels (not that the boundaries between 'levels' are either distinct or neutral): through their reflective practice of speech; through small-scale performative utterances like salutations or apologies; through the artful uses of words in their story-telling performances; and through the interweaving of local narratives and their interpretations with the highly general stories that have been told about 'Africa'.

The chapters in the second main part of the book move into more explicitly comparative vein, while still retaining a predominant emphasis on African cases and occasional illustration from Limba ethnography. They focus principally on the ways words are actively displayed in particular marked performance modes – cultural investments to which people devote special attention and artistry. Can we regard these as forms of 'literature' even though they are oral? If so, what are their qualities? How are they created and in what does their existence lie?

---

[8] In chapters mainly focused on the Limba I have mostly left the ethnographic accounts in the style of their time (though if conducting that research now I would hopefully be more critical over a number of points, not least statements about 'the' Limba or 'Limba practices' etc.). I have however been glad to take the chance to change the original present tenses to past: quite apart from the connotations conveyed by the once-fashionable 'ethnographic present' with its implications of some 'timeless' and homogeneous state in which 'traditional' peoples supposedly lived, the change is a reminder that the events and practices described date to the 1960s, well in the past. Certain later studies provide a longer time dimension (Chapter 2, p. 16 n. 4) but I do not pursue them in this volume.

How scholars have analysed and reflected on the deployment of words in such genres is the starting point of the third set of chapters. 'Oral texts' – to use that commonly applied term[9] – do not have their existence in some unchanging abstract form but are created and formulated for specific purposes by a host of actors and participants of various kinds. Among these actors and participants are researchers and analysts. This part begins with some comment on how as an outside scholar I myself engaged with oral texts a generation ago and formulated their study under the head of 'oral literature'. I look back on the context, motives and assumptions of earlier work and on how far, in the light of more recent scholarship and events, I (and no doubt others) might do some things differently today. I then take up some of the issues that arise when collectors and others construct oral texts – transform performed events into verbalised writing, translate them into other languages, or define them in particular ways. Chapter 11 reflects further on some of the changes in the field over the last generation. Both the concepts of 'oral' and 'orality' and the once apparently clear category of 'scholar' have become less distinct given our widening appreciation of the multiple overlapping ways that people create, participate in and reflect on their oral practices – do things with words.

The final chapter sets the 'oral' in the context of the long-established and powerful narrative which tells of the predominance of language in human culture and of the formative roles consequently played by its oral and written manifestations in the great stages of human destiny. But is this perhaps a limited or an ethnocentric vision of humankind? It raises the question of whether the import of this far-reaching language-based tale is an overly narrow view of the stunning creativity and complexity of human culture whether in Africa or elsewhere – bringing us back to a further consideration of the place of words in Africa.

Running through much of the volume is a continuing engagement with that long-entrenched binary paradigm which has so deeply affected our understanding not only of Africa but of 'the west' that perhaps no writer on Africa can fail to be in some way touched by it. It feeds off the notion of a far-reaching contrast between two great categories of humankind, recurrent polarities variously expressed as the opposition between 'primitive' and 'civilised', 'tribal' and 'developed', 'age-old' and 'modern', 'African' and 'western'. On the one side are pitched the cultures and peoples characterised by modern ways – literate, urban, individualist, creative, scientific, reflective, rational, western. On the other are those steeped in tradition – oral, communal, rural, non-intellectual, primitive, undeveloped, exotic, without history or change, and close to their natural roots, participating in the world

---

[9] The terminology 'oral texts'/'*textes oraux*' has been commonly employed as a handy umbrella way to sum up, broadly, the textualised manifestations of the kinds of oral performances and genres considered in this volume (used, for example, to take cases from a range of dates, starting with the earliest) in Parry and Lord 1954, Whiteley 1964, Andrzejewski 1985, Derive 1985, Barber and Farias 1989, Ngugi wa Thiong'o 1998: 111, Honko 2000a, Traoré 2000, Bauman 2004, Barber forthcoming. It is useful in bypassing some of the fraught controversies now associated with other overarching terms such as 'oral literature', 'oral tradition' and 'folklore' (though ultimately, of course, with its own (textual) implications).

(and in nature) rather than capable of the objective reflective detachment made possible by literacy and western science. Set out in explicit form it looks too far-reached to be convincing – who would now own to believing such an extreme formulation? But whether regarded as an absolute divide within humankind or as poles at either end of some one-track development from the one to the other, this profoundly evocative set of images still, it seems, has a tenacious hold on our imaginations.

It has also long provided an enticing yardstick – a frame of interpretations and conceptualisations – for accounts of the nature of the world and those who act within it, not least, it seems, for the study of Africa. Sometimes one, sometimes another of the key terms has been singled out for attention. But they seldom work alone for so strong are the associations that the conjoined imaginaries willy-nilly seep in; they 'remain below the surface', in Karin Barber's vivid metaphor, 'exerting a kind of gravitational pull' (1995b: 11). At the same time they have been set out and manipulated in multiple ways, and turned to many different ends, coming in differing permutations and historical settings. As with all such binary oppositions they have been notably deployed to divide people and cultures and in doing so given reality and solidarity to those wielding these two-fold categories: definition and clarification to the 'modern' by contrasting it with tradition; to Europe and its mission by opposing it to the primitive and the native, projecting onto those others the properties from which 'modernity' could by contrast define itself. This composite imagery has been handmaid to discrimination, oppression and separation, called on to charter the hierarchical exertion and abuse of power and the (often racist) devaluation of 'the others' – reason enough for challenging it. But equally it has in the past and to some degree the present guided the visionary, if perhaps no less ethnocentric, endeavours of mission-aries, educationalists and administrators to spread 'civilisation', 'develop-ment', 'democracy' and access to the written word. Its predominant message has been the lauding of progress and modernity, formulated in the terms of the enlightened and expansionist west. There has also been the sub-theme of back-to-nature romanticism, prizing the 'world we have lost' and lauding the 'primitive', sometimes in celebration or in challenge to more dominating ideologies, sometimes with a patronising and glamorising glow which can itself tap into processes of suppression or marginalisation. Here 'community', 'tradition', emotion and communion with nature are the prized characteristics, and the move from deep authentic roots into, it seems, the over-rational and secular artificialities and individualities of modern urban life is seen as coming with heavy costs: 'the warm, vibrant ... heart of the mythopoeic nature of the African psyche ... [set against] the cold, barren centre of the (western) mythotechnic realm' (Fox 1980: 212). The earlier derogatory evaluations are turned upside down – but the basic frame of the binary paradigm remains, indeed is all the more reinforced.

This syndrome of assumptions has of course long been contested. It has been the subject of continuing debate over the last generation, one with which, along with others, I have been fairly consistently engaged. As will emerge, these linked binary oppositions are in my view ultimately pernicious in their generalised and loaded imaginaries which conceal so much of the fine

11

detail in which people conduct and elaborate their lives: thus I will be questioning generalised notions about 'participation', 'lack of objectivity', 'tradition', 'unchangingness', 'collectivity' and so on, in particular their blanket application to Africa. Over these recent decades the basic paradigm has in some ways become more explicitly articulated for consideration – and thus the more open to challenge, with gathering doubts about its more extreme and uninformed formulations. But it still retains astonishing force, if in changing metamorphoses, and is a constant if at times latent presence throughout these pages.

The emphasis of the book, finally, is on using words in and about Africa. But the issues it treats and the ways scholars and others have addressed them are not confined to Africa. They revolve around such fundamental questions as the actions of story and story-telling; the concepts of text and textuality and their relation to performance; the ideologies and uses of language; the multi-modalities of performance; the experiences of acting, delighting and displaying in words; the fraught interaction of the notions of 'tradition' and 'modernity' and their entanglements with evocations of 'the primitive', the exotic and the 'other' in our midst; transformations of words, entextualisation, and the dissolving notions of orality, literacy, literature and languge. Using words to consider the imageries by which the apparent orally based 'difference' of Africa is still sometimes projected to define its opposite, helps to illuminate not just 'Africa' but also something of the many harmful and uplifting and delighting and powerful and (an infinitude of) other things that human beings so remarkably and so prolifically do with words.

I

Enacting and Distancing Words in Life and Story

2

The Reflective Practice of Speech and Language

A West African Example[1]

It is not just intellectuals from European traditions and languages that have reflected on the nature and practice of language. This chapter considers a rural West African example of linguistic conceptualisation and action and at the same time gives some background for the example that will be coming into several later chapters.

This particular case is also a route into challenging certain recurrent preconceptions which have long served to conceal the relevance of such local reflections, blotting them out by the assumption that, as Bongasu Tanla Kishani put it in his comments on the interface of philosophy and language in Africa, such reflectiveness is only possible 'in, with, and through written languages' (2001: 27). Even in the late twentieth century, and perhaps more recently too, it has been widely assumed that those living in cultures that made sparse use of writing had little or no explicit awareness of the subtleties and depths of linguistic expression. To this is quite often added the implication that they lacked the power of analysis (or possessed it only embryonically or in small degree), were more dominated by non-verbal forms of expression, and had little or no capacity for abstract thought – emotionally involved in the world around them and incapable of observing or analysing it with detachment. In the great divisions of humankind they were put in the 'primitive' box with all that that implied.[2]

---

[1] First published as 'Attitudes to speech and language among the Limba of Sierra Leone', *Odu. A Journal of West African Studies* NS 2, 1969: 61–77 (also reprinted with minor changes in Finnegan 1988); the introductory paragraphs, conclusion, and some footnotes have been revised, and small stylistic changes made elsewhere, but the main body of the chapter, as a near-contemporary ethnographic report, remains as in the original.

[2] The works referred to in the 1969 original of this chapter might nowadays rightly be regarded as outdated but their claims had widespread currency at the time and still resonate today (they included Abraham 1962: 193–4, Bastide 1968; Bowra 1963: 31–3; Cassirer 1953: 118ff (lack of abstract, analytical or 'philosophical' thought among

This crude picture of non-literate peoples has been queried for many years and by now at the start of the twenty-first century there are of course many less ethnocentric approaches to literacy.[3] Yet it has a persistent hold on the imagination – and in Africa too, not just in Europe. It is still worth re-examining some of these issues in the historico-cultural specifics of one particular case.

'Limba is one, Limba is many': reflecting on language

The case considered here, then, is that of Limba speakers in northern Sierra Leone at one particular period of their history. Let me introduce them briefly as a preliminary to what follows.[4]

In the 1960s, the period to which this discussion refers, the people then classified as 'the Limba' were mostly living in the savannah of northern Sierra Leone, in an irregularly shaped area intermingled with speakers of other languages. They farmed upland rice, their staple food, on the hill slopes, supplementing this by some swamp horticulture and various palm products,

[2] (cont.) 'primitive peoples'); Lévy-Bruhl (1926) on the emotional and intuitive involvement of 'primitive mentality', recycled in the not so dissimilar views among some *négritude* and related writers (e.g. Senghor 1956: 44 ('La raison blanche est analytique par utilisation, la raison nègre, intuitive par participation'; transl. 'White reason is analytical through use. Negro reason is intuitive through participation') and 1961: 99ff, Kaunda 1966: 29ff, Jahn 1961); and the UNESCO view of 'traditional' non-literate peoples as characterised by ignorance and 'darkness' (for example UNESCO 1966: 29, 32–3, 82)). This syndrome of ideas has by no means vanished (see for example in Ong's constantly recycled description of the supposed 'psychodynamics of orality' (1982) or Hallpike's still-cited *The Foundations of Primitive Thought,* 1979, both in its constantly implied image of 'Africa' as the paradigm of 'primitiveness', and in such assertions as 'Verbal analysis of experience, of social behaviour and custom, will be given a low priority ... there is no awareness of "propositions" dissociated from the context of utterance ... Primitive thought is bound up in imagery and the concrete, phenomenal properties and associations of the physical world, permeated by moral values and affective qualities, unco-ordinated, dogmatic and unsubstantiated by argument, static, relying on perceptual configurations and prototypes and the reification of process and realms of experience' (Hallpike 1979: 132, 490)). Jahoda's far-reaching *Images of Savages* rightly notes that 'at the close of the twentieth century ... the images remain remarkably constant ... [and] there can be no doubt that [they] are alive and well, in spite of official condemnations' (1999: xvii, xviii, 245).

[3] For a sample see Barton et al. 2000, Boone and Mignolo 1994, Collins and Blot 2003, Cope and Kalantzis 1999, Street 1993, Wagner et al. 1999.

[4] Unless otherwise specified the statements here refer to the early 1960s, the period when I carried out fieldwork in Sierra Leone (1960/1961 and 1963/4, mainly in the Biriwa, Kasonko and Wara Wara Yagala chiefdoms, based in Kakarima, Kamabai and Kabala respectively). I gratefully acknowledge the support of the Colonial Social Science Research Council and the Emslie Horniman Anthropological Scholarship Fund (1960/1961), and the Alice Horsman Travelling Fellowship, Somerville College Oxford (1963/4). For further ethnographic information about the Limba people at that period see Finnegan 1963, 1965, 1967 and comments in later chapters here; for other periods or areas see Fanthorpe 1998, Ottenberg 1996 and further references there; on more recent developments, largely set in the wider history of Sierra Leone, see Archibald and Richards 2002, Francis and Kamanda 2001, Richards 1998.

not least their favoured palm wine. Some moved away from the area, either to join the growing Limba colony in the capital, Freetown, or going off as young men to seek adventure and resources for bridewealth, often returning after some years to settle once more in their home villages. This region had been among the most remote and, from a western colonial viewpoint, most undeveloped and 'traditional' parts of Sierra Leone where, until very recently, there had been few schools and little or no opportunity for paid employment.

But of course the Limba speakers of this time were far from the untouched, homogeneous or unchanging 'primitives' pictured by either the modernising enthusiasts or the 'Noble Savage' romantics. They had seen Christian missions established in their region, had been under colonial rule for many years, and though mostly not themselves Muslim were well aware of the Islamic cattle-keeping peoples who travelled and settled through the same area and ran their own Koranic schools. And far from living in some state of primaeval harmony and unquestioned 'Tradition', they clearly had a wide range of the familiar human disputes and differences among themselves. It is true however that they were little known to the European world. Northern Sierra Leone had been lightly administered by the colonial authorities and in the 1960s only a very small proportion of children went to either European or Arabic schools, few or no adults in the smaller villages were literate, and northern Sierra Leone continued to be relatively inaccessible as far as modern communications were concerned.

In the 1950s and early 1960s the Limba were commonly looked down on within Sierra Leone. They were dubbed 'stupid' by speakers of other languages and, mostly living in an area remote from the main centres of 'development', were rated by national planners and urban dwellers as among the 'most backward' of what were then identified as the thirteen main tribes of Sierra Leone. One colonial official had influentially pronounced that Limba was 'a very fourth-rate language in which ... it is almost impossible to get any fine shades of meaning expressed' (Sayers 1927: 113) and even by the time I lived in the area the stereotype of the Limba was of typically drunken and uncivilised people, without literature or high culture of any kind.

Their general situation at that time was in fact highly pertinent to the topic of this chapter. Numbering about 183,000 (or at least that was how they were classified and counted in the 1963 national census) they lived in villages located in a roughly wishbone-shaped strip seldom more than twenty miles across that intersected with many other linguistic groups across the northern region of the country. This inevitably brought them into close contact with peoples speaking different languages – Temne and Lokko to the south and west, Kuranko to the east, Yalunka to the north and Susu to the northwest. Those at the margins of Limba areas were often bilingual, or at least able to understand a considerable amount of the neighbouring language(s), and children grew up with a taken-for-granted ability to both understand and interpret between other languages. The Limba men who returned home to visit or to settle down after travelling elsewhere through the many-languaged countries of Sierra Leone and Guinea, brought with them at least some acquaintance with yet other languages, including Krio or the local version of pidgin English.

Within Limba country too there were settlements of 'foreign' peoples, mainly Fula and Mandingo. Itinerant traders or cattle herders speaking these languages were constantly to be seen. In addition, though it is certainly true to say that the Limba themselves were by and large non-literate, they had had some contact with Arabic literacy, and there were a few elementary Koranic schools within Limba country, run and attended by members of the Fula and Mandingo communities. Finally, in the larger towns like Kabala, Kamakwie or Kamabai, Krio was frequently heard and languages other than Limba widely spoken.

In this situation, Limba speakers could not avoid some awareness of the relativity of their own language. It was inescapable that Limba was only one language among many, and that there were many alternatives which to their speakers were equally acceptable – or better – ways of rendering the same sentiments. Limba grew up to an acquaintance with many languages and a sense of perspective about their own.

Nevertheless – or rather because of this – they were quite clear about the distinctiveness of their own language.[5] Limba was in fact variously spoken, in a number of dialects, some of which were barely mutually intelligible. But this did not prevent the Limba themselves, at least in the historical juncture of the 1960s, from seeing it as one in relation to the clearly different languages around them. Their language, indeed, was the main mark by which they at that time seemed to distinguish themselves from the many other peoples in the area.[6] Thus, in spite of their habit of contrasting their own various dialects, they still assumed that one thing that they all shared together as distinct from other peoples was the Limba language. 'The Limba language is one. The Limba are one'; 'We are all Limba – we are all of one language/word (*hutha hunthe*) with each other'; 'There are many Limba languages (dialects), but the Limba language is one'.

The native term was *hulimba ha,*[7] 'the Limba language'. The prefix *hu-* was not only commonly used for terms referring to speech, words or language (as in *hutha ha* and *huluŋ ha* – word; *huthemine ha* – the Temne language) but was the normal prefix used to form an abstract noun (thus *gbaku wo* a chief, *hugbakine ha* chiefship; *thari* run, flee; *huthara ha* flight). *Hulimba ha* can therefore be interpreted to mean not only the Limba language but Limbahood itself. When I did research among the Limba, my statement that I had come to learn about the Limba people was often passed on as 'she has come to learn *hulimba ha*'. Everything that connected directly with language was often

---

[5] Limba is often classified as one of the 'West Atlantic' or 'class' languages within the larger Niger-Congo group; more recently Dalby (1999/2000) has put it in the 'Atlantic' phylozone of the Transafrican phylosector (on the language see also Berry 1958, 1960, Dalby 1965). The orthography here is based on the International African Institute alphabet, and most words and phrases given in the Biriwa form of Limba.

[6] How far this was related to the colonial and missionary practices of defining tribes in terms of the (ostensibly neutral) marker of language is not easy to decide – it must at the least have been reinforced by it and further mediated through the implicit language planning which not only linked language and ethnicity but privileged Krio, Mende and Temne rather than Limba (see Francis and Kamanda 2001: 230ff). At any rate, in the 1960s this perspective seemed to be a thoroughly Limba one.

[7] In some dialectal forms (e.g. Wara Wara and Sela/Tonko) *huyumba* or *huyimba*.

assumed to be distinctively Limba, and I was therefore continuously and spontaneously instructed in new vocabulary, stories, songs, and the requisite greetings in the various dialects. 'Speaking Limba' was even sometimes identified with 'being Limba' in the case of individuals of mixed or foreign birth. I was told several times of people of, say, Temne or Fula parents who were 'now Limba' on the grounds that not only did they live in Limba country (not in itself a sufficient condition) but that they 'spoke Limba'. Conversely, I heard it said that someone who didn't understand and speak Limba was not Limba even if both his mother and his father were Limba; and people 'turned into Krio's' or 'turned into Temnes' when they took over those languages. Living as they did in a small country inhabited by peoples speaking thirteen or so mutually unintelligible languages, the Limba recognised that many of their customs – marriage, for example, or some of the 'secret societies' – were shared by others; but that the Limba language was owned only by the Limba, and was their distinctive attribute.

The Limba, furthermore, were self-conscious about their own language. They liked to discuss linguistic matters, whether in comment on their language as a whole or in comparisons between their different dialects. This was perhaps a natural result of their experience of the many different languages around them, their own distinctive forms of speech, and the fact that so many of them spoke more than one language or were well acquainted with the principle of interpretation from one language to another.

They sometimes commented on their own language in general. 'The Limba language is old', said one, 'the old people tell you stories and tell you what is forbidden and so on; you hear that. The Limba language is not new.' Many Limba expressed pleasure that I had come 'to understand [that is, to 'hear'] Limba' (*ba luya hulimba ha*), and they sometimes contrasted their own language with others, giving imitations of the sounds of various languages; English, for example, was humorously said to sound just like *yɛŋ yɛŋ yɛŋ yɛŋ* or *ŋɛŋ ŋɛŋ ŋɛŋ ŋɛŋ*.

More often the discussion was of the forms of the various dialects, for in other contexts the heterogeneity of Limba was what struck people: *thalimba tha a bɔi* – 'there are many Limba languages.' This was a constant topic of interested conversation. Comparisons were made between the varying dialectal terms: how, for example, some words were quite different in meaning, others had different connotations (like the regular word in the south which implied an obscenity in the north and vice versa), and the greeting terms distinctive of the different areas. They sometimes caused laughter by imitating or parodying speakers of other dialects. Each group liked to claim that its own dialect was the best or purest form of Limba and people sometimes spoke of other dialects as 'bad' (*lethe ta*), 'unintelligible' (*yi sa lu* – 'you won't hear it'), or 'mixed up' (*faŋitande*) with other languages; they also noticed with displeasure when people used a greeting term other than the local one. They were also quite aware of the relativity of their own particular forms – they confessed that they not only laughed at speakers of other dialects who 'can't speak well' but were themselves in turn laughed at by them. In such discussions the characteristics of a language or dialect could be described as, for example, 'deep' (*suŋɔi*, i.e. subtle and not easy to

19

understand), 'fine' (*mɛlɛsɛ,* full of small words, subtle, analytic), 'clean' (*mɛthɛ*), 'broad' (*bukulu,* with longer words), 'straight' (*thumbɛ*), 'good' (*lɔhɔ*), 'sweet' (*thimɔ*); according to one English-speaking Limba, his own dialect, Biriwa, was the one that 'is sweet and nice and straightforward'.

Limba speakers, then, were very aware of these various ways of speaking their own language, and of the possibility of having dialectical differences within one common language. As one old man answered in some surprise when I asked about the reason for the many Limba dialects, 'But why do you ask? Are not English and Krio the same language but with differences? Well, it is the same with Limba.' The existence of dialects, with their basic similarity and detailed differences, was something, they assumed, which everyone could be expected to understand.

Beside such general reflections on the nature of their language and dialects, they also made intentional and conscious use of language for amusement and joking. They took great delight, for example, in words or phrases they considered particularly funny and brought them in to make people laugh. *Thɛŋthɛŋthɛruma,* for example, was a term used to describe humorously the kind of person not able or willing to carry loads on his head; *kutɛŋtɛŋbɛri,* meaning a hollow beneath a bank or wall, was a Biriwa word thought funny in itself and also used as a test word for strangers. Phrases might be introduced for no other reason but amusement, as with the rhythmic words a boy once used to express his hunger in fun, 'Ho ho ha ha nothing in my mouth' (*ho ho ha ha, ntha ka ka hothi*), the amusing name given to an imaginary country in a story, *Katiŋkiritaŋkarakatarina,* or the punning phrase used by mothers to answer a child's continual whines of '*mbɛ?*' ('what?') with 'what, goat?' (*mbɛ bahu?*), mimicking the conventional cry, *mbɛɛ,* of the goat. A form of reduplication in names – like the two fools Dimping and Dampang in a story or the spirits Ningkinangka and Dingkangdingkangthengku – or the repetition of words or phrases were all also used for their effective ring rather than their sense. Nonsense or semi-nonsense words were enjoyed as, for example, in the chant about a spirit, *kɛŋ kɛŋ kɛŋ kɛŋ kɛŋ kɛriŋ kɛŋ,* or the alliterative words sometimes said to be chanted by the fishes, 'thɔ thɔ thɔ the wet season is ending, we are going to be killed' (*thɔ thɔ thɔ thamɔ thɔi ba thɔye / hiri puthɔi miŋ se ba korio*) in which the little fishes were supposed to be stuttering *thɔ thɔ,* trying vainly to speak like their elders. They also took pleasure in representing bird cries in words, like the *kokoro koo koo* of the cock at dawn and the *kutaŋtaŋtaŋtaro* of the francolin. In addition to this, in the various devices of repetition, parallelism, imitation, onomatopoeia, mimicry and exaggeration of tone or length, they had recognised means of using language for calculated effect not just for the communication of information. Their deliberate use of linguistic forms in these various ways revealed a self-conscious awareness of language.

Limba speakers took a certain amount of reflective interest in the analysis of their own speech. Discussion of separate elements and words was made easier by the common Limba word *na* which was used both to introduce reported speech and to put a word or phrase in, as it were, quotation marks. Thus one term, phrase or sentence could be singled out for discussion or elucidation in its own right by prefixing it with *na.* People sometimes came to me spontaneously with the intention of explaining some word or phrase in this way, quoting it for the sole purpose of comment and explication. This habit of considering their own words was also demonstrated in their common use of *hu-* to turn any word into an abstract noun or concept, a device which the Limba employed frequently. The Limba were well aware of the possibility of considering a linguistic formulation in itself detached from its direct social or personal context.

Even what has been said so far should suggest how far the Limba were from conforming to the picture of the primitive as unreflective and unselfconscious, dominated by mythic and symbolic concerns or – the more extreme view – as too emotionally involved with the world to be able to stand back or analyse in any detached or abstract way. This picture was quite untrue of the Limba as I encountered them in the 1960s, at least in the sense that they were well aware of the distinctive nature of their own language as contrasted with others' and were greatly interested in the language they spoke, intentionally using it, among other purposes, for play, comment and meta-analysis.

Language as literature

This reflective Limba use of language also came out in other ways. Among these was the recognition of the artistries of language – language clothed and heightened in what could be termed literary formulations. These, it is true, were expressed in oral rather than written form. But there are indeed senses in which these could nevertheless be regarded as literature (an interpretation elaborated in Chapter 6). What is significant in the context of the present chapter is not the detailed content of this literature but the Limba attitude to it. Contrary to what was once widely assumed of non-literate peoples,[8] their stories and songs were not valued just for functional purposes but also admired and assessed as artistic performances. Certainly there were conventional social contexts for certain specific literary genres – songs, in particular – and performers were fulfilling social as well as artistic roles. It is true too that, just as for written forms, their literature could be used on specific occasions or by specific individuals with a pragmatic intent and in given social situations. But to stress just this side would give a completely unbalanced account of the Limba attitude to their literature. To them, it was something beautiful and wise in its own right, part of *hulimba ha,* handed down to them by 'the old people' and interpreted and re-interpreted through the individual 'heart' (*huthukuma* – another *hu-* word) of the composer/ performer. They were, it was clear, well aware of the aesthetic function of language as manifested in literary display.

In their literature they possessed a medium through which they could – and did – comment in a detached way on the social and natural world around them. Limba story-tellers and singers stood back, as it were, from reality and

---

[8] For more detailed discussion of the once-dominant 'functional' approach to oral literature, see Finnegan 1969, Wauthier 1966: 65ff.

21

used their art to bring out the truth that lay below the surface actions of humans. And here I am not referring just to the 'morals' that closed many African stories, though these did occur from time to time in Limba tales, but to a more generalised and subtle interpretation of how people behave. Some of the examples in later chapters will illustrate how certain conflicts inherent in marriage could be commented on indirectly through some tale on the surface treating of animals; or the ambivalent role of women, at once powerless and powerful, brought out through an individual narrator's portrayal of a girl in one of their stories. Again, the patterns and individualities of character were lightly but vividly portrayed through the dramatic way in which dialogues in stories were performed and presented. Humour and sharp observation came out in such passages as, say, the vivid description of a young girl deliberately decking herself out to make a hit with the men, or a local chief walking forward in his voluminous robes and speaking with pompous dignity. Many of these touches fail to come across in written or translated versions, away from the artistry of the actual narrator and from the situation and characters being depicted, but it was quite clear in the actual situation of story-telling that this kind of detached comment on reality was a central element in Limba literature. The composers/performers in story or song were exploiting their medium whether humorously or tolerantly, maliciously or tenderly, to stand back from the world around them and express their detached reflections on it.

The assumptions that non-written literature arises directly and exclusively from some social occasion and can therefore be explained solely in terms of that; or that it is merely uncreative word for word handing down of 'tradition' with no possibility of change; or that such literature involves mystical participation with the world of nature or consists of childish tales about animals with no depth or subtlety – none of these assumptions were borne out by the actual facts about the Limba. Once these prejudices were removed, the effective way in which Limba literature was used for detached comment became unmistakable to the observer.

A philosophy of language, speech and action

The Limba concept of *gboŋkoli* was another significant and quite explicit strand in their attitudes to language. This term can be roughly translated by the English word 'speaking' but carried connotations of rather greater weight and deliberation than the English equivalent. A thorough analysis of the Limba usage of this word would take us too far afield, but some account of it leads into what could be termed the Limba philosophy of speech and language, throwing further light on the main topic of this chapter.

Gboŋkoli, 'speaking', was one of the key concepts of Limba philosophy and society. It would be impossible to give any picture of their social life and relationships without constant reference to it. A quick look at some of the Limba words built up on this root will give some idea of the range of applications of the basic idea.

Hugboŋkila ha meant 'speaking' (the abstract verbal noun), as well as 'speech' or 'harangue'; it also referred to the act of arbitration performed by the mediating words of chief or elders as they attempted to reconcile two parties by their 'speaking'; hence it could mean a law case, a formal occasion when the old men heard and spoke between the disputants who stated their case with due formality; its plural, *thagboŋkila tha,* referred to cases or disputes. *Bagboŋkoli wo* (pl. *bagboŋkoliŋ be*), 'speaker', referred to one of the several elders who jointly helped the chief to speak successfully between two parties; they spoke in turn endeavouring to make the disputants' hearts 'cool' again, and supported the chief's speaking by their presence, murmurs of agreement and interjections of 'true' (*thia*). *Gboŋkoliɛ,* 'speak for', was what someone in a position of authority did for those for whom he was responsible; groups tended to have one person to 'speak for' and represent them to others, whether the group was that of uncircumcised boys wishing to be initiated, of workers who made up a hoeing 'company', or of adult men going in a group down-country to tap and sell palm wine; a father or elder also 'spoke for' anyone under his control if he was involved in a law case; the elder's speaking and guarantee for him helped the culprit so that he was more easily forgiven or let off lightly 'by grace of' (*thɔkɔ ba*) the one who had spoken on his behalf.

Other forms were found outside the context of formal arbitration. *Magboŋkoli ma,* 'spoken words', could refer to the words of a song, the spoken injunction attributed to someone in authority, 'speech' in the concrete sense (as distinct from the abstract *hugboŋkila*), or forms of speaking, e.g. the different Limba dialects. *Gboŋkilitande,* 'speak together with', was a reciprocal verb referring both to formal discussion and to mere conversation between two or more people; this was a common term and referred to a quality expected of any leading Limba ('if you are sensible you will talk well with people'); a chief in particular should take pains to 'speak well with others', that is, to greet them well, to listen fully to what they said and to reply to them with respect. *Gboŋkilo,* 'to be spoken to', referred to a formal rebuke to some individual, often in the context of a long drawn-out and tactfully expressed series of harangues by the leading old men. *Gboŋkilɔkɔ,* 'speak to oneself', was a less common word; it was used of a man's grumbling and complaining to himself when things were difficult or when he had been wrongfully treated; this was disapproved of, for, ideally, if one had been wronged, the right course was not to fight, abuse or complain but to speak out the complaint explicitly in the setting of a formal 'speaking' before the elders – but sometimes individuals who had failed to gain satisfaction reckoned they had no alternative.

The basic word, *gboŋkoli,* 'speak', was the most common of all. Though it was sometimes used lightly, meaning merely to talk, its root meaning seemed to be to speak formally, responsibly and carefully, most typically in the context of a formal law case or transaction. 'Speaking' was the quality of a chief in his role of reconciling people and thus bringing peace to individuals and to the chiefdom as a whole. It was also a desired attribute and activity of anyone with authority over others – a father 'spoke between' his children, a household head between his dependants, an older boy among his juniors, a respected senior wife among her younger co-wives, a *bondo* (women's society) leader among her followers. Formality of speech applied not only to speaking to reconcile people but also to the whole series of interchanges of formal thanks, requests, offers, or announcements which, as will emerge more fully in the next chapter, occurred in almost every recognised relationship. Formal 'speaking' also included prayer and invocation by the old men as they 'spoke for' (*gbɔŋkoliɛ*) the other members of the community and 'called on' (*yɔŋɔŋ*) the dead, 'recounting their names' (*kɔndi ŋakeŋ ŋa*); and what made it correct to apply the term *saraka*, ritual, to a ceremony or material object was the condition that someone in authority had 'spoken' over it, specifying its purpose in achieving a 'cool spirit' and calling on *Kanu* (God) and the dead. *Gbɔŋkoli* was also used of the formal interchange of speeches at the start of ordeals for witchcraft, of the long rhetorical harangues during memorial ceremonies, and of speaking the words of a story. In all kinds of transactions, whether to do with farm work, dances, political or judicial proceedings, initiations, ceremonies, or negotiations for marriage, formal 'speaking' was an essential part of the proceedings.

There is a further and very relevant point. Not only was 'speaking' a formal activity constantly practised in many different contexts, but the Limba themselves liked to describe their own institutions in those terms. A Limba as well as an outside analyst would say that the main function of a chief was 'to speak' or that men did not expect women to be able to 'speak' properly, only to cry, and people were constantly assessed in terms of their ability to 'speak well'. It was also common to use terms referring to words or speech to describe relationships: two quarrelling co-wives were not in 'one word/ speech' (*huluŋ hunthe*), a wife was given to one chief by another so that they would be in 'one word' (*hutha hunthe*), orders were described as the 'voice' (*thampa*) of the leader, and 'the word (*hutha*) of the chief should hold the whole country'. Again, the country was said to be 'cool' (in harmony) when people were 'in equal words' (*thampa sinthi*); and when 'the words of the chief are heard all through the country', then all was at peace. This kind of phrase was not just extracted from the occasional reference, but could be heard over and over again in daily conversation. If you asked the meaning of *bafunuŋ* (a wise/clever/intelligent person) the explanation was almost always in terms of their capacity to 'speak'. For the Limba, 'speaking' in all its forms was assumed to be one of the most significant and profound activities of social life.

Behind this interest in speaking lay the Limba philosophy of *gbɔŋkoli*. 'Speaking' was an essential constituent of social order and interchange. Certain crucial social moves could only be effected and validated through formally spoken performative acts – the spoken agreements, announcements and other recognitions discussed further in the next chapter. Further, only through good speaking was it possible to keep people's hearts 'cool' (*thɛbɛ*) – a constant Limba term connoting peace, harmony and well-being, whether on an individual or a social level. If a case was decided too quickly, a contract over-hastily consummated, or a quarrel not soothed with lengthy and sympathetic speeches, people's hearts would remain 'hot' and rancorous, and the quarrel was likely to break out again or the contract be infringed. This question of 'cooling' an individual's heart was crucial. The Limba were aware that a dispute might seem to be patched up or a transaction completed

24

without a truly settled intent by the parties to keep to the decision, and the 'heart' that was not fully acceptant of what had happened was bound to break the peace of the community. Even worse, it might turn to witchcraft, the most heinous and most dangerous sin of all, leading to the deaths of individuals and to the disturbance of the harmony of the whole country. Even good 'speaking' could not avail against a settled bad disposition but it was the best resource the Limba had, they felt, to try to ward off such evils. And in cases where wounded feelings or loss of face were involved, they made strikingly effective use of this weapon. They pointed out that in settling a dispute it was of no use to say quickly, 'He is in the wrong' or 'She acted badly.' Rather you should speak at great length, 'going round for long in parables/stories' (*silɔkɔ haŋ ka thabɔrɔ tha*), pointing to the need for good relations within family or village, to the respect due not only to elders but to children or to women, of the respective duties of, say, husband and wife to each other (not least the necessity to speak with honour to the other), and many similar sentiments, platitudinous perhaps and tedious to the observer but extraordinarily effective to the parties involved. Through the various generalisations and analogies (*thabɔrɔ*) uttered by elder after elder, an atmosphere was gradually built up in which it was possible to touch on the faults of the disputants and persuade them to agree. The terminology to describe this process was seldom in terms of 'judging' but of 'speaking well' to each party, 'persuading' them to accept the suggestions, and 'pulling their hearts' so that they would agree unreservedly. Finally they were persuaded to use one of the quasi-contractual phrases explicated in the next chapter and to say 'I accept' (*yaŋ yɛrɔkɔi*) and perhaps to 'beg' the other party with some token gift to restore peace. The underlying philosophy was that unless the two contenders were reconciled with their hearts at peace (*thɛbɛ*) the session had been a failure however 'correct' (from one point of view) the decision might have been.

'Speaking' was, then, central to social action among the Limba, to the making of contracts and cementing of relationships, to their philosophy of society and to their explanation of human psychology. The Limba were not only explicitly aware of the significance of language and of speaking and constantly discussed these topics, but had also developed their own philosophy of speech.

Speech, language and writing

There are, then, three main respects in which I consider the Limba showed their awareness of the significance of language. These were their self-conscious attention to many of their own linguistic formulations; their approach to and use of literature; and their philosophy of 'speaking'. Their reflectiveness was immediately obvious to an observer through the interest they took in their own language and its uses, and their readiness to single out specific terms or phrases for detached comment. The capacity to stand back and comment detachedly on experience through literature was more subtle and elusive, and thus less immediately striking, but was nonetheless unmistakable to anyone with a long familiarity with their life and culture.

The crude stereotypes, whether of the Limba or of non-literate societies generally, turned out to be very far from the truth in the case of Limba thought and action as they emerged in the 1960s. Limba speakers were explicitly aware of the subtleties and depths of linguistic expression; they possessed and exploited abstract terms and forms; they reflected on and about language; and had strategies for standing back from the immediate scene or the immediate verbal utterance through their terminology, their philosophy of language and their literature. Limba thought and practice was infinitely more subtle and complex than many of the popular generalisations about 'non-literate peoples' would still have us assume.

This really is, or should be, too obvious to need saying. Even if dismissive images of non-literate peoples are still surprisingly prevalent, the outdated derogatory ideas about 'primitive mentality' are now rejected by modern scholars and to continue laboriously to repudiate long-rebutted assumptions or recycle yet again the only too familiar debates about 'literacy' should be superfluous. All the same, it is of some interest to note the specific ways in which the Limba case fits so ill with older notions about both the once-assumed 'consequences' of literacy and the lack of detachment and abstraction that non-literacy may seem to entail. In practice the situation seems much more mixed and, in a sense, idiosyncratic.

In some respects the relative lack of reliance on writing in the Limba culture of the 1960s was indeed relevant for the way they conducted their social affairs. As we have seen, they were intensely aware of the relevance of speaking for social relationships and social action – something that should come out even more clearly in the next chapter. It was the 'speaking' which ultimately made valid such transactions as marriage, divorce, transfer of rights over land, or appointment of a headman: here the formal speaking *was* the making of a contract. The functions of written documents in literate cultures were in this sense performed among the Limba by the actual act of speaking – and of this role of speech the Limba were quite explicitly aware.

This social and active aspect of Limba speaking also had implications for the process of education and socialisation – the handing on of the culture from one generation to the next. One common picture of this process in non-literate societies used to be of oral tradition being handed down word-perfectly and unchanging over the generations – a hangover from the out-dated romantic notion of the dominance of 'Tradition' among the 'Folk', the 'Tribe'. It is still worth emphasising that this image did not apply in the case of the Limba. Certainly there were stock phrases and, as elsewhere, a store of cultural traditions – not least linguistic – known and practised more, or less, and with individual variations, by most Limba speakers. The Limba did also talk a great deal about preserving the old forms, of the wisdom of the elders and, even more, of the dead, and of the way in which the 'old people' knew best. But in actual practice, variation, innovation and change came in all along the line (some examples are indicated in Chapters 4 and 5, also further elaborated in Finnegan 1967: 92ff.). One recurrent feature of oral communication, including many forms of oral literature, can be the relative absence of the kind of emphasis on verbal accuracy and the minutiae of exact wordage that is perhaps more often associated with written texts (though that this can be both variable and relative will emerge in Chapter 7 below). One of the striking elements of much Limba oral art was in fact the scope for verbal variation on different occasions and among different exponents, and the creative qualities brought to it by the immediacy of situation-based performance.

The fact, too, that Limba speech was closely intertwined with its performative role and social context, rather than eventuating in some impersonal written page, meant that 'education' was a creative and performative process, involving the interaction of specific individuals and specific occasions, rather than some abstract transfer of formalised knowledge. It may be that contemporary European readers and writers – and especially the teachers and intellectuals among them – too readily over-estimate the part played by book learning in the educational process and everyday practices of their own (literate) traditions and that contexted, performanced and individual processes of learning are everywhere of great significance. But in any case they were of obvious importance among the Limba, an importance which can credibly be connected with their relative lack of interest and experience in written formulations or abstract speculative systems.

On the other hand many of the features of Limba thought and practice ran counter to what might have been expected from some of the dominant stereotypes contrasting literate to non-literate ways. One of the great emphases in analyses of the power of writing has been on its potential for enabling abstraction and detachment: setting out something in an objective fixed state for analysis, something it is presumed must be so much more difficult, if not impossible, with non-written forms. It is an intelligible and in some ways a valid point – but one which makes some of the features of the situation described here all the more striking. One is the Limba detached awareness of the existence, relativity and multiplicity of their own language and its distinctiveness over and against others. In their case the question of writing apparently had little to do with it. The crucial point, rather, seemed to be their constant contact with speakers of other languages and their practice and recognition of the processes of interpreting among them. In this respect indeed we might say that their linguistic awareness was in some ways greater than that of many English speakers who, notoriously, have little direct experience of languages other than their own (and this in spite of an educational system which stresses both literacy and instruction in or about one or more non-English languages). Written formulation certainly can play a part in the explicit awareness of language. But it seems that it is neither a sufficient nor a necessary condition. Perhaps the well-known saying that someone who knows only one language cannot understand even his own is more relevant here than any question of literacy versus non-literacy.

Even more striking was the (perhaps related) Limba capacity for the deliberate contemplation of words and phrases – for setting them out as abstract and, as it were, separated objects for analysis or explanation. In the absence of the objectified detachment of a written page this might be thought not to be possible – but in the Limba case the strategy was through speech. They made good use of certain linguistic features in doing so, both the small marker *na* (which as described above could act to put something into quotation marks) and the 'class' features which formed such a manifest part of their linguistic practice. As mentioned earlier the noun class (*hu-*) which comprised words to do with language was the same as that for abstract nouns. These *hu-* terms were a way of detaching a concept and explicitly setting it apart from the flow of on-going life and talk. Indeed in a kind of metaphor not unlike the English image of 'flow', the abstract concept of (for example) 'speech' – *hugboŋkila ha* – was distinguished from the on-going bits and processes of speaking which were referred to as *magboŋkoli ma* (the actual spoken words, concrete process of speaking at a particular time), part of the *ma-* class which also covered rivers, water, time and flowing things more generally. The possibility of abstract terms and abstract thought was, for the Limba, directly associated with speech – rather than, as in at least some seminal traditions of European thought, with writing or with inner thoughts.

This case then provides one clear example of the problems of the once-assumed clear distinctions between literate and non-literate societies. It illustrates how the specific characteristics of at least one more or less non-literate society were more complex than might have been expected from widely circulated generalisations about literacy. Nor are some such elements likely to be really so unusual. Using language to talk about using language is not after all so extraordinary a human activity, well exemplified in more recent studies such as Hunter and Oumarou's analysis of Hausa 'verbal aesthetic' (1998) or Karin Barber's accounts (1999, 2003) of Yoruba praises being treated as detached and object-like works for local exegesis and quotation.[9] We are also now increasingly, if belatedly, aware that multilingualism and translation between languages are normal rather than unusual features of human experience (see for example Dalby 1999/2000, Feeley-Harnik 1991, James 2003: 141, 143). As Kishani well points out it is time to recognise not just the multiplicity of (putatively separate) languages in Africa but their co-existent plurality and their many translators and polyglots (2001: 42): the Limba are by no means an exceptional case. The reflective practice of language and of exegesis in and through words 'even' in oral settings are among the recurrent themes of later chapters (returned to more particularly in Chapter 11). At any rate with the mid-twentieth-century Limba speakers we see an example of a tradition which could, by and large, be characterised as non-literate but was at the same time marked by an explicit awareness of the existence and significance of language, a capacity to discuss and use language in abstracted and detached ways, a consciousness of its roles in social action and artistry, and a confident philosophy of the social powers of speaking.

[9] For further comment in a comparative framework see e.g. Hanks 1996: 192ff., Lucy 1993, 2001 (and references given there), also works mentioned in Chapter 1, p. 6 n. 5.

3

How to Do Things with Words among the Limba[1]

We can now take up one particular strand in the Limba practice of speech – the deliberate and studied use of certain recurrent verbal phrases to do things. The analysis here draws on the idea of 'performative utterances', a concept that, as is now well-known, was proposed and discussed in the 1950s by the Oxford philosopher J. L. Austin (enunciated especially in his posthumously published lectures, 1962) and has been taken up and extended by many other scholars in later years.[2]

In Austin's original analysis, these are utterances in which using a certain form of words is not to describe or express, nor to make a true or false statement. Rather, their point is to *do* something. If one says 'I do' (i.e. take this woman to be my lawful wedded wife, as said in the course of the marriage ceremony), 'I give and bequeath my watch to my brother' (in a will), 'I name this ship the *Queen Elizabeth*' (at the launching ceremony), or 'I bet you sixpence it will rain tomorrow' these are all instances of words which do not describe or state what is being done – they *do* it. 'To name the ship *is* to say (in the appropriate circumstances) the words "I name etc.". When I say, before the registrar or altar, etc., "I do", I am not reporting on a marriage: I am indulging in it' (Austin 1962: 6). Austin goes on to elaborate and analyse the idea of 'performative utterances', in particular to bring in the wider notion of

[1] First published as 'How to do things with words: performative utterances among the Limba of Sierra Leone', *Man* 4, 1969: 537–52, reprinted here with some minor updates and revisions, and a partly rewritten final section. As in the previous chapter the descriptions of Limba activities apply to the 1960s.

[2] This chapter should be read in the context of the period when it was first written (1969); I have made no attempt to incorporate detailed references to the by now colossal literature on Austin and his aftermath. Some guide to the more recent developments and debates can be found in Duranti 1997a: chapter 7, Hanks 1996: chapter 5, Sbisà 2001, Tsohatzidis 1994, and (in more technical vein) Vanderveken and Kubo 2002; also for some specific points and examples relevant for this chapter in Brown and Levinson 1987, Duranti 1997b, Dlali 2004.

the 'illocutionary force' of such speech acts (a concept to which I will return). But his basic concept of 'performative utterances' is the starting point of his whole exposition of the subject and can, likewise, serve to introduce the present chapter. It proves an illuminating entry point for understanding certain aspects of Limba verbal interchange for although this concept was developed in an English context it is also very directly relevant for understanding certain dimensions of the Limba use and view of speech.

'I agree ... ':
some Limba performative utterances

Let me start with one group of Limba phrases that were quite clearly used with the performative force Austin has described. These are *yaŋ yɛrɔkɔi* (I accept/agree/approve), *yaŋ tɔŋ danthɛkɛ* (I announce/declare/notify/report), and *yaŋ theteke* (I plead/entreat/apologise/pray/acknowledge a fault). These terms were central to Limba day-to-day transactions and in particular to formal negotiations. They were used in making contracts, in the various stages of negotiations and in law cases. A brief discussion of each in turn will serve to give some idea of their force in the context of Limba social action.

The formalised acceptance of a gift, of an item of news, of an offer or move in a formal negotiation, or of a declaration of intention was accomplished by the Limba term *yɛrɔkɔ*, 'accept', agree, or approve. The phrase was not used to describe the facts nor to express a feeling but, as Austin would put it, actually to *do* something – to perform the act of acceptance. As such, it had to be uttered in public, or at any rate before the relevant audience – and, in Austin's words, 'in the appropriate circumstances' (Austin 1962: 6).

Its most clearly formalised application was in the conduct of a law case. The chief or elders trying to reconcile the disputants 'speak well between them', persuading the one to apologise (*theteke*), the other to 'accept' (*yɛrɔkɔ*) this. The aggrieved party might withhold this acceptance for some time, reiterating, for example, 'I will not agree' (*yaŋ sa me*) or 'I don't like that, I don't like that' (*yaŋ thimo ta wuŋ, yaŋ thimo ta wuŋ*). Finally, however, the case was brought to a close by the formal acceptance of 'It pleases me; it is good; I accept' (*wuŋ thime yama; wuŋ alɔhɔ; yaŋ yɛrɔkɔi*) or simply 'I accept' (*yaŋ yɛrɔkɔi*). In this context the words had a legal force: the verbal act formally marked the end of the dispute and the process was described in these terms by the Limba themselves.

An acceptance in words marked the final stage in many other transactions too. In the story of a mother's Faustian pact with a spirit (see Chapter 4, pp. 52ff) the spirit – and the audience – understood well that she was sealing the fatal contract when she uttered the short but weighty phrase 'I accept'. It played a central role in marriage negotiations. After the formal announcements by the suitor, the parents, if they agreed, declared: 'We accept' (*miŋ yɛrɔkɔi*). This committed them, and any going back on this agreement would be regarded as defaulting. Again, a quarrel was often concluded by one party admitting that he or she was in the wrong and making an apology – but the matter was not concluded until the other formally accepted this by *yaŋ/miŋ yɛrɔkɔi*, 'I/we have accepted [it].' Another situation was when an inferior brought a gift to someone considered superior – a child to an elder, a son to his father, a subject to a chief. After long speeches of flattery and explanation by the giver the recipient must reply, and amid thanks and flattery on his side he must at some point or other (probably at several points) perform the verbal act of saying *yaŋ yɛrɔkɔi*, 'I accept'. Otherwise the recipient would be considered not only to have refused the gift and the accompanying speech, but also, just as important, to have refused to accept the obligations involved in an acceptance of the gift. A gift between putative equals could also be treated in this way or even – though in an English context this sounds odd – a gift from superior to inferior. Here, too, the recipient would make a formal acknowledgement of the gift – 'I accept' – and once again recognise not merely the gift itself but the social relationship involved.

Once these words had been publicly uttered in any transaction, they were regarded as a formal, even legal, commitment. As Austin pointed out the commitment or action could still 'go wrong' in a variety of ways; but it was certainly agreed that something had been *done*, not just said. In the act of voicing this agreement in words, the speaker was recognising a relationship and undertaking a certain responsibility.

Next, the phrase *tɔŋ danthɛkɛ*, to 'announce', declare a purpose, or tell important news. This was usually a very formal act. As such it also often involved giving a gift 'to make the words heavy'; but the gift in itself without the accompanying words would not qualify and was not essential for the act to be termed *tɔŋ danthɛkɛ*. The stress was less on the actual content of the communication, which might in fact often have been known to the participants before they were formally 'told', than on its declaration in the required manner and situation.

This act of formal announcement occurred in a wide variety of contexts as an essential part of many aspects of Limba life. It often involved the explicit statement of the official purpose of some visit or ceremony. When visitors came to a funeral celebration, one required stage in the proceedings was the interchange of formal speeches with the relations of the dead; they sat together in one of the verandas and the visitors announced their purpose (*tɔŋ danthɛkɛ*) by saying that they had come in sympathy with their friends, relations or affines, and by giving the gifts they had brought with them. In a memorial ceremony, too, the visitors' formal presentation – 'Here are 4 shillings' or 'Here are kolas' – was also called *tɔŋ danthɛkɛ*. Similarly, marriage negotiations contained several such formal announcements; a man going to declare his wish to marry a girl or to ask for his promised wife to be given to him took a gift as 'notification' (*danthɛkɛ*), and when the girl was brought to her husband, her friends went specially to make a formal announcement of her presence; he too sent back a token gift to declare (*tɔŋ danthɛkɛ*) that he had accepted her. In a law case, the various stages of the procedure were often formally marked by an 'announcement' to the court of what had occurred, often with a gift.

Another example was when the young boys were due to be initiated. Everyone in fact knew that the initiation was to take place that year.

Preparations had been going on for months and the necessary large harvest had already been ensured by sowing extra rice. Yet it was also obligatory for the boys to join in a group to perform the ceremony of carrying in wood for the chief and elders as an 'announcement' of their desire to be circumcised that year. One boy was chosen to express this on their behalf, and he sat with the elders so speeches could be made on each side and he could formally declare their purpose (by *dantheke*) and hear their acceptance.

These formal announcements were also used to recognise someone's authority or ownership. One of the marks of a chief's authority was that he should know everything that happened in his chiefdom in the sense of being formally 'told' – whether or not he in practice knew it already. When a visitor came to the village, he or his host must go to 'announce' this to the local chief. A stranger wishing to settle in the locality had to 'announce' this intention formally to the chief, saying, for example: 'I have come here; I wish to live here, by your grace.' With such words and the offer of a token gift, he declared his intention (*tɔŋ dantheke*) and in so doing accepted the chief's authority. Similarly any other important event in the chiefdom such as a death, the killing of big game, the imposition of a dangerous oath or ordeal, an initiation or an accident – all these had to be formally announced, preferably with a gift, to the paramount or local chief. He in turn accepted and approved by *yaŋ yerɔkɔi*.

The principle of announcing events or purposes also occurred in many other contexts. Sometimes the phrase used was not the highly formalised *tɔŋ dantheke* but the more ordinary 'tell' (*tepe*) or 'ask' (*thɔŋthɔŋɔŋ*). Children should ceremoniously tell their parents of their plans and of their successes or failures, especially when they returned after a long absence; a husband should carefully tell the old women when his wife was pregnant; and an elder be formally told of a dispute when his mediation was requested. A new wife, a new chief, a new chief's drum, or the initiation of a new phase of the farming year should all be shown and notified to those in authority, including those who were the most senior of all, the dead ancestors. To an observer one of the most striking characteristics of Limba life was precisely this constant stress on formal speaking and 'announcing'. Whatever the details, there was always some tinge of formality and of the recognition, through the announcement, of relationships between individuals or groups, relationships both accepted and further reinforced by the formal acceptance by the hearers.

Finally, the interesting and wide-ranging *theteke*. This term meant to plead, entreat, apologise, pray, or acknowledge a fault. Someone would 'plead' by uttering one of the standard phrases which expressed request, entreaty or desire for forgiveness (*yandi, kuloho* or *ilɔhɔ*), usually adding 'I am pleading with you' (*yaŋ theteke yina*). Sometimes this was followed by the pleader clapping, putting a hand on the other's ankle as a sign of humility, or, in extreme cases, lying prone on the ground. A third party might also be begged to intercede on the pleader's behalf and this was usually accompanied by a gift, or, in an important case, by a substantial payment. When someone pronounced the standard words in a prescribed situation, even without a gift, then the action was described as 'pleading'.

Any quarrel should, ideally, be ended by 'pleading' on the one side and

32

'acceptance' on the other. A dispute between two women, for example, or between a husband and wife, might be finished by an agreed apology, usually with the offer of a token gift as the 'plea'. People also formally begged for forgiveness if they had failed to fulfil some obligation to someone in authority over them. Secret society members, for instance, had to 'plead' with their leader if they danced without formal permission; and a sub-chief who was late in bringing the rice due to his paramount chief brought a gift to apologise formally for the delay: it passed from hand to hand among the chief's followers, who each thanked the giver, and finally went to the chief himself to say 'I accept'. Asking friends or neighbours for help with some special task was also referred to as 'pleading'; a man went round begging people to help him to build or thatch his house, or asking his friends to join him in a co-operative hoeing association. A chief's special requests to his people should also, ideally, be described as 'pleading'. Even if there was in practice no question of disobedience, he should always 'speak well to people', thank them for their work and 'plead well with them'.

The Limba term translated as 'praying' was also *theteke,* and the words and actions of prayers were similar to those associated with other begging: people used the same terminology and showed the same signs of humility (in extreme cases, for example, lying prone on a grave to beg a dead father's forgiveness). People pleaded with the ancestors for peace and harmony and a father interceded with the dead for his child in the same kind of way that he would entreat a living chief. In sacrifice, too, the dead ancestors were 'pleaded with' and an animal was killed to give them honour in exactly the same way as a gift accompanied a plea to living people. Even if the audience addressed (the dead) was necessarily somewhat different, in other respects when people prayed to the ancestors they were performing just the same kind of act as when they 'entreated' a chief: they were making a formal acknowledgement of their inferiority and dependence and/or a request for aid or forgiveness. They were similarly expecting that those addressed would recognise *their* side of the relationship, 'accept' the plea and answer it; at the same time they were asserting a continuing relationship between speaker and audience, living and dead. The token gift that accompanied a plea performed the same function whether it was to the dead (the 'sacrifice') or to the living. It helped to 'make the words heavy'; but the act itself consisted in the *words* not in the gift.

'Pleading' was a regular occurrence in Limba village life. Here is an account, as described by one Limba man, about how a husband might need to 'plead' for his wife's return; the various means he was depicted as adopting so as to beg successfully were all standard ones:

> If a husband has acted badly, the wife goes to her parents; the husband comes there for her and pleads for the wife to agree to return. The husband gives kola to the wife's people. Then they go and question her about what it was that made her go away, about why the husband is pleading. Sometimes the husband asks the wife's younger sister to plead for him with their mother. The sister goes to her mother, saying that the husband has confessed to doing evil, he is pleading. The husband must wait humbly. Even if they curse him and say bad words, he must not reply, he is ashamed, he can say

nothing. Sometimes he goes to an old man and gives him kola and pleads, saying that he will not [act wrongly] again. So the old man goes to help the husband to plead with the wife's family. However much they say against him the husband must not reply. The old man may go in private into the room with the wife, and give her wine, and speak well with her to make her agree to return ...

'Pleading' was also common in the related but even more formal context of a law case. Using the phrase in the appropriate circumstances was to make a formal admission of guilt, usually followed up with a gift or payment. An accused witch, for example, must both 'plead' in words as an initial acknowledgement of guilt and also later 'plead' further with material property – money, rice, livestock. Similarly an adulterer had to 'plead' with the husband by first admitting his guilt, often accompanying this by a token payment 'to confess', and later paying a hefty fine. These were extreme cases, for both witchcraft and adultery were serious crimes. In other offences the amount of compensation or fine was usually considerably less and the emphasis primarily on the verbal act constituting the acknowledgement of guilt. If someone 'pleaded well' in words it was considered right and justifiable that they should be let off some of the fine, and the European refusal to be entreated in the Limba way could give rise to misunderstandings on both sides. The main principle in the Limba cases was not so much the amount of compensation paid as the performative utterance of 'pleading', thus acknowledging the culprit's fault and, very important, implicitly promising good intentions for the future. This plea was at the same time to admit the authority of the arbitrating elders and recognise the part the speaker should be playing in village life.

'Pleading', then, was used in personal quarrels, requests for aid or forgiveness and the formal apology or payment of compensation in a law case. When the 'plea' had been made, the matter was then ended and ratified by a formal acceptance of it in the phrase 'I accept' (*yaŋ yɛrɔkɔi*), or 'It is finished' (*wuŋ pati* or *huŋ pɛ*). The culprit or pleader was sometimes also thanked for this 'pleading' and told that they, too, had in that respect done well and shown honour to those they were begging. It was correspondingly considered very wrong not to accede to someone's pleading without a strong cause. As one man put it

> Pleading is a big thing among us Limbas. You will send a friend to the other saying 'Please, please', pleading for you, asking the other to cease [from his anger]. The other will agree when he is entreated – looking to Kanu [God]. It is bad not to accept when you are entreated. Kanu comes to us all. Looking to Kanu – that means listening to the one who pleads.

Even if in practice great amounts were sometimes exacted in compensation, the theory and very often the practice remained that people should 'plead' if they were guilty and they should then be forgiven or let off lightly.

In this Limba practice of 'pleading' – a public acknowledgement of guilt and/or a formal request for aid – something tantamount to a legal act was being performed by those uttering the requisite phrases in the appropriate manner and situation. They set themselves in a certain recognised relationship to those they were addressing. In the case of a formal court action and apology, the utterance was an admission of guilt, withdrawal of the speaker's own claims, and formal acceptance of the elders' assessment and moral position; it was a necessary stage in the settlement of the case. By begging for help, a speaker was also formally acknowledging dependence on another and showing them honour. The theme that ran through all the usages was that speaking the words recognised as 'pleading' was also *doing* something.

'Thanking', 'greeting'
and other spoken acts of commitment

The Limba phrases discussed so far could all be accepted as clear examples of Austin's 'performative' utterances: words which, when publicly used in the appropriate context, were not so much descriptive or expressive but in fact a form of action. The Limba regarded the successful enactment of these quasi-legal utterances as not only accomplishing specific transactions or commitments on a particular occasion but as a formally enacted acknowledgement of wide and often continuing social relationships.

This wider aspect came out even more clearly in a second group of Limba utterances: those used for thanking, greeting and saying goodbye. Though less directly tied to specific transactions like those exemplified in Austin's original cases of marriage, betting, making a will, giving a name, etc. they too can be discussed in the same kind of framework. Making these utterances was essentially to perform an act of commitment – to acknowledge indebtedness or dependence as well as, on occasion, a particular transaction (thanking); to commit oneself to some relationship, either permanent or in relation to some specific contract (greeting); and to announce a particular stage in some undertaking or recognise another's authority (saying goodbye). To the Limba as well as to the outside observer these were unmistakably parallel to the apparently more specific performative utterances discussed above (indeed Austin later widened his original examples to include just such instances, 1962: 150ff).

'Thanking' (*kalaŋaŋ*) was strikingly frequent among the Limba. The most usual terms were *ŋwali* or *wali* (plural *wali bena*), 'thank you', sometimes expanded to the fuller *yaŋ kalaŋaŋ yina*, 'I am thanking you', or *miŋ kalaŋaŋ yina*, 'we thank you'. In spite of the outward differences in form, all these formulations performed the same act. The phrases were usually repeated several times and a full thanking might also be accompanied by clapping (especially by women), by laying a hand on the other's ankle, or by a gift; but here again it was the spoken *words* not the gestures that constituted the act. Sometimes blessings were also included, such as 'May Kanu give you a long life'; 'Through Kanu may you have peace'; or 'By Kanu may you meet with no bad thing.'

Such thanking terms were constantly heard. A gift was formally thanked for as publicly as possible, seconded by the dependants or relations of the recipient. Thanking was the normal reception for those who came home from the farm after a day's work, thanks were due from a husband or guest to the wife who had cooked for them, and a speaker often thanked the audience for being present and listening: 'Thanks to all of you, you who have come' or 'I give thanks to all you who are here.'

Thanking was used in a very formalised way to make an acknowledgement of interdependence between two sides. A husband, for example, must thank the officials who had initiated his future wife, and, later, the old women who helped her in childbirth. He must thank his wife for her contribution to the family farm, her cooking and, above all, her bearing of children. Any friends and relations who visited the new mother always thanked or congratulated her – 'Thank you for parenthood, thank you, thank you, thank you' – but it was the husband in particular who had to speak well to her and bring her rice and palm wine 'to thank her' (*ba niŋ kalaŋina*). In the same way, a person should thank those on whose help he was dependent in performing some work or ceremony. A bereaved son temporarily stopped the women's singing at a funeral in order to thank them with a token gift, and the owner of a farm formally thanked those who came to help him and called out excitedly as they progressed up the rice field: 'Fine (*mbadeŋ*), fine, fine, fine, fine, fine; thanks (*ŋwali*), thanks, thanks, thanks, thanks, thanks'.

Thanks were particularly frequent between chief and people. Someone who had received special help might come to thank him formally, often with a gift; and those who arrived to announce some special event or success were in return thanked for their coming, for their news and for the efforts they had made to achieve the outcome they were now formally reporting. This mutual thanking and honouring points to the reciprocal, even quasi-contractual, nature of authority among the Limba, where the relationship had to be continually acknowledged on both sides, and the mutual responsibilities and interdependence constantly voiced in verbal interchanges.

This stress on the verbal acknowledgement of interdependence is well illustrated in this description – cast in typically Limba terms – of a boy being apprenticed to a master smith:

> When the boy is about seven years old, his father takes him to the smith. He talks to him about the child. He takes a red fowl; his people pound rice; they get oil, they get salt, they get a mat, and bring them. He goes to the smith and says: 'Here is a fowl; here is rice; here is oil; here is the child. We want you to teach him smithcraft.' The smith thanks him well. He says: 'It pleases me, I accept.' He takes the child. The child stays there for a long time, he teaches him ... His relations come and thank the master. They bring rice and a mat and a fowl and oil and money and cloth – everything. They come and thank, saying: 'Here they are. For the child we brought here – you taught him smithcraft; for us now – that pleases us. Here is a token gift to thank you; it pleases us. Here is a gift to thank you.' The master, if it pleases him, says: 'I accept'. They say goodbye, fully.

Here, as so often, the transaction was enacted through the interchange of formalised verbal utterances, in particular of thanking and accepting.

The most formal occasions of thanking were accompanied by a gift, sometimes a substantial one, so a reference to 'thanking' often implied that a gift had also been expected and given. But without the prescribed linguistic action – without, that is, the essential verbal utterance performed on the set occasion between the appropriate people – the gift or payment would not in itself be sufficient to constitute the 'thanks', nor would it be described as 'thanking', whereas a mere verbal act of gratitude, even though in practice less acceptable if given 'with the mouth' only, would still be classed as 'thanking'.

'Thanking', therefore, an institution of such great importance to the Limba, was not ultimately defined as the giving or interchange of gifts. Nor was it to be analysed principally in terms of some inner feeling of gratitude, for that did not need to enter into the situation at all. Though the Limba were clear that thanking was a source of satisfaction to both speaker and receiver, 'making your heart good', this was a result of the thanking not its cause. Rather, Limba thanking was an act of commitment: an institutionalised way of acknowledging – or, by its withholding, denying – some transaction or relationship between people.

'Greeting' may at first sight seem different from the utterances discussed so far. In fact, the Limba 'I greet [you]' (*yaŋ maŋ*) or, the more common form, 'greeting' (*mande, ŋsɛkɛ,* etc.), which performed exactly the same act, were closely analogous to thanking. 'Greeting' was something which the Limba deliberately performed as a formal act. It was regarded as a kind of commitment and acknowledgement in just the same way as 'thanking'.

Greetings were given and expected in many situations.[3] It was taken to be a universal human obligation to exchange salutations with those you encountered in the village, farm or road. People who met on the paths between villages or farms greeted each other (*manande*) and often stopped to enquire about the other's home or affairs. In the village people greeted each other in the morning before leaving for the farm. Husband and wife too should 'greet each other well' and a man must take special care to greet his wife's parents. Children greeted their parents, especially their fathers, morning and evening. Friends and contemporaries were more informal, but even they greeted each other when they met; and when people came home from the farm in the evening they greeted and were greeted by those who had spent the day in the village.

Even these minor everyday greetings were regarded as both an essential social obligation and an act in which a Limba speaker would naturally take pleasure. So during the telling of a story the exchange of greetings between the characters illustrated their common humanity and was much appreciated by the listeners, who sometimes repeated or filled them in spontaneously – and with delight. Someone setting the scene in a narrative might rattle off a long list of the greetings exchanged, with obvious enjoyment to both speaker and listeners in this typically Limba behaviour; or describe with pride and affection the way they themselves had 'greeted someone very well' (*a maŋ wana wulɔhɔi*) or 'were greeted fully' (*mano na feu*). The interchange of

---

[3] Limba greeting terms varied from dialect to dialect and according to time of day, occupation and status of greeter and greeted, and general social situation (they are too numerous to detail here but a summary list from two dialects is given in Finnegan 1963: 325–6). The form was usually 'Greetings' (etc.) rather than 'I greet' and thus may seem not to fit, formally, with the typical performative utterances initially described by Austin ('I name . . .', 'I will', etc.) which are characterised by the first person singular pronoun. However as Austin notes (1962: 70), the same act is being performed whether one says 'I salute you' or 'Salaam'.

greetings was among the delights of life. For one young Limba man, for instance, the most idyllic occasion imaginable was to have a young girl smiling at him with her pointed teeth, bringing him food and greeting him: 'You meet, and say goodbye, and greet again throughout the day.' 'Greeting' was also an essential factor in marriage – if a husband could complain against his wife that 'You haven't greeted me' or that she did not allow his companions 'to come and greet me well' this was treated as a serious charge. Exchanging words of greeting was both an obligation and something to 'make a man's heart good'.

In addition to the regular greetings expected of everyone as a matter of course, there were also situations where greetings had a special meaning or where someone made a special expedition to greet somebody with extra formality. The same word (*maŋ*) was used here referring not only to the interchange of the salutations themselves, but also to the whole act of going to visit someone in order to greet them, the time spent there, and all the talk, and on occasion gifts, that accompanied this. A minor example of this kind of greeting was when someone went out of their way to visit within or beyond the village. A man or woman would go to someone else saying 'I have come to greet you' (*yaŋ se ba na mana*) or 'Your greeter has come' (*bamaŋ wo kɛnda se*). The honour brought by this visit should be answered by a full greeting in reply and, according to the relative status of the visitor, by appreciative attention, gifts, or hospitality. More important were the special efforts a man must make to go and greet his parents-in-law, especially his wife's mother. This was a very formal relationship and one in which it was of great moment to greet very fully and carefully. Even before his wife had been given to him in marriage, the suitor must initiate or recognise the relationship by coming formally to greet his prospective parents-in-law.

Similarly an obligation to come to greet was an understood requirement of a contract or formal relationship. If a man had gained permission to tap wine from a tree on another's land, it was assumed that about once a month he would come to 'greet' the owner; sometimes he brought a hen or some money as part of the 'greeting'; but in any case must come to greet in words saying, for example, 'We thank you, we come to thank you'; the owner should reply 'It pleases us, we thank you, may you not fall from the tree.' In saying this the man acknowledged the other's authority and his own obligations.

This was particularly explicit in the case of chiefship. People's 'greeting' was an inherent part of a chief's authority. When he was first elected people came to see him 'to greet him', i.e. to acknowledge him as chief; a failure to do so would be tantamount to a repudiation of his position. His own dependants and members of his village went regularly to greet him, and sub-chiefs or relations in other villages were expected to come at times for this special purpose; in this way they showed him honour and recognised his authority. Any stranger who came to the village was expected to go to greet the chief and was received and welcomed by him. In addition the chief had many people who were in one way or another especially dependent on him – to whom he had given a daughter in marriage, helped with money or food, or accepted into his household – and these people were especially scrupulous about bringing him full and frequent greetings. A chief or elder was important if he had 'many people'. By this the Limba were not speaking just of the people bound to work for him but of the numbers who could be seen crowding into his veranda to visit and acknowledge him, to 'greet him' (*ba niŋ mana*).

A chief or 'big man' accepted and acknowledged these greetings by 'replying' (*me*) and greeting in turn. This was part of the duty expected of any important personage: to speak well to people. One of the highest compliments that a Limba could pay to anyone was to say 'He knows how to greet you', and this was especially important for a chief. Someone who 'knows how to greet you' was said to be more likely to be elected chief, while an effective accusation against a rival was 'He does not speak well with people; he does not greet them.' A chief should go to the farm to 'greet' and 'thank' people, by this acknowledging the work they were doing and making 'their hearts feel good'. Because of this, one of the reasons why the Limba were sometimes puzzled by the Europeans and Creoles they encountered in positions of authority was that, in Limba terms, they seemed so unwilling to acknowledge their responsibility to the people under them by returning or offering protracted greetings. On the other hand, Limba were correspondingly delighted to follow out their own picture of authority, as involving greeting and kind words as well as dignity, on the occasion of Queen Elizabeth's visit to northern Sierra Leone in 1961; Limba visitors came back overjoyed that she had acted in the way they had hoped of a chief: 'In spite of her fine gown and all the honour she was not proud; she came down to greet the old chiefs who could not walk.' Similarly a well-known Limba of chiefly family who had been to school was praised enthusiastically in another chiefdom many miles away because, although literate, he was not aloof. 'If you met him you would not think he was one who could read – he greets you well and eats with you.' 'Greeting', in the Limba sense of the word, was a necessary part of the relations between an important figure and the rest of the people.

Their custom of greeting, therefore, was one way in which the Limba marked and recognised various relationships. Great stress was laid on the importance of explicitly greeting people, whether superiors, equals or inferiors, and in this greeting the position of the other was accepted. This was particularly evident in the recognised reciprocity of the relationship between chief and people. He was responsible to and for them, just as they were to him, and this was made explicit in the constant series of greetings between them. Running through all these various usages of the Limba term for greeting, whether the quick exchange of a word or the formal visit with gift to greet a superior, was the idea that to greet someone *was* to honour them, to acknowledge a relationship with them and, very often, to commit oneself to accepting their authority. What was exchanged in these greetings was both a recognition of the other's position and, as the Limba continually stressed, 'honour'.

Much the same account could be given of the Limba term for 'saying goodbye'. Like thanking, this was related to greeting in meaning and use, being in some ways merely a special form of salutation. 'Saying goodbye' (*saŋkalaŋ*) was often a required and formal stage in a ceremony or transaction. For several weeks before their seclusion in the bush for their initiation, for example, young boys travelled round all their friends and relatives in their various villages; they came 'to say goodbye' (*ba saŋkalina*). When a girl was told the date when she must finally leave her own home for her husband's, she went round all her relatives to say goodbye: 'I have been given; I am coming to say goodbye to you.' A man intending to leave home to seek his fortune down country should – in theory – say a formal farewell with a token gift to the chief, and the occasion might be further formalised by speeches of thanks and blessings from the chief and elders of the village. Similarly, a man should also say a careful farewell to his father, his father's brother and, if a smith or hunter, to his master in that craft – to all those, in fact, with special authority over him. In saying goodbye, he was formally requesting permission for his new venture and acknowledging that what he was doing was only 'by your grace' (*thɔkɔ ba kɛnda*). The formal act of 'saying goodbye' occurred constantly as a way of formalising the ending of some stage or the movement from one status to another, and commonly made an explicit recognition of the authority of others over the speaker.

The Limba therefore used what at first sight may seem mere idiomatic and trivial phrases – greetings, thanks and farewells – actually to do something, something furthermore which they themselves considered of high value in their social life. The set words were recognised as effective not just as verbal formulae but as actual commitments undertaken in public and in circumstances recognised as appropriate – and at the same time used with conscious deliberation and often with delight. Such utterances not only acknowledged particular commitments (as with the first group considered) but were also understood to have wider implications for the smooth running of social relations generally. They were an explicit way in which individuals acknowledged relationships, undertook social commitments and formally recognised the general social situation. In uttering these forms of words the Limba were doing and not 'merely saying' something, and they themselves were quite clearly aware of the performative force involved.

Speech and action

In many ways the Limba experience and practice was of course unique, the creature of those who utilised exchanges of words to carry out and create their lives in the setting of a distinctive time and place. At that particular juncture the performative force of speaking seemed notably to the fore in Limba practice, and also to be quite explicitly recognised. This can perhaps be linked to a number of other Limba characteristics of the time, like the form of their language, their individual performances and their situation as it was in the 1960s. As explained earlier, Limba speakers were by and large non-literate and made little or no use of written documents or certificates in their trans-actions: the spoken element was thus all the more important. In European cultures with widespread literacy there is a real sense in which the legality of, say, a will, a marriage, a lease, or contracts generally is taken as residing in written words, in a document. In Limba the commitment lay rather in the spoken words and it is scarcely surprising that they were the more explicitly conscious of the legalising and performative force of certain spoken utterances. The absence of written documentation also meant that an audience was important, to act as witnesses, validators and, as it were, recorders, and this, too, brought out the significance of the actual speaking, something delivered to be heard. Again, the Limba did not make much use of expressions referring to inner feelings (though they could speak of these if they wished by referring to the 'heart' (*huthukuma*), and thus there was not the same tendency in Limba as, say, in English to envisage a performative utterance as one essentially describing thoughts or feelings.[4] The emphasis was on the public act of speaking aloud, to be heard by others.

But we can also see the Limba case as both support for, and elucidation of, more general views about the nature and use of speech and language. To start with, the examples here accorded remarkably well with the instances of performative utterances with which Austin opened his account: verbal acts by which some transaction was actually performed, some commitment undertaken or some contract recognised. But the Limba spoken acts often did something more than that. They were also used to ratify some general situation or status (or, contrariwise, to withhold or challenge it), and utilised as a constant tool to create, confirm and maintain social relationships, ones which were – quite deliberately – formulated, continued and, indeed, in part constituted through verbal acts. Like the exchange of gifts which sometimes, but not invariably, accompanied these interchanges of words they were a way of recognising relations and situations. Just as Mauss's famous analysis (1954) sees gifts as having a kind of 'active' force to bind people together, so too, with words. The utterance or interchange of spoken acts in many ways parallels the act of giving or receiving a gift.[5]

This may seem to be stretching the term 'performative utterance' far beyond Austin's original exemplars. Making a specific promise, say, is scarcely the same as the general recognition of a total situation or continuing relationship. But Austin in fact moved on to posit a general 'illocutionary' force in many kinds of utterances: what he calls 'the performance of an act in saying something', 'doing something as opposed to just saying something' (Austin 1962: 99, 133), evident when one takes account of the specific occasion, context and intention. The types of illocutionary utterances he identified overlap with many of the Limba cases discussed here: 'verdictives' (e.g. 'acquit', 'convict', 'diagnose'); 'exercitives' (e.g. 'appoint', 'announce', 'pray'); 'commissives' (e.g. 'promise', 'contract', 'agree'); 'behabitives' (e.g. 'apologise', 'thank', 'greet'); 'expositives' (e.g. 'accept', 'inform', 'affirm') (Austin 1962: 152ff). Though Austin did not specifically say so, this more general theory and the enlargement of his initial list opened the possibility of regarding such utterances not just as specific and isolated acts but as the recognition of wider situations and relationships. Further, it at the same time provided a more realistic perspective on the actual ways that people use words than either the Lockean view of language as essentially for rational statement or the mid-twentieth-century Anglo-American approach in which

[4] Austin in fact points out (1962: 9–11) that it is tempting but misleading to analyse 'I promise' (for instance) as a description of inner intentions rather than a performative utterance.

[5] A similar point is made by Lévi-Strauss when he speaks of the exchange of words as analogous to the exchange of women, goods or services (Lévi-Strauss 1949).

linguistic utterances were essentially divided into two classes, the one descriptive, the other variously labelled as expressive, evaluative or symbolic.[6] Here again Austin's concept of '*doing* things with words' opened an additional perspective.

Two further points need noting, to be taken up further in later chapters. First, just to speak of 'language as action' is not of course the end of the matter and Austin's work points only to certain dimensions. There are manifold ways in which people do things with words, acting as they do within the constraints and opportunities of particular situations and ideologies: not just the ratification of transactions or the creating and confirming of relationships which have been among the themes emphasised here, but also (for example) to play, to challenge, to heighten as literary genre, to comment on human affairs, to expound the meaning of particular verbal or other formulations. 'Words', furthermore, perhaps have particular qualities and susceptibilities for being used to do things which are not so readily found in other tools for action. The more 'literary' enchainings of words which form the main focus of several later chapters, and the ways these are created, formulated and reflected on – all these too are a kind of 'doing'.

Second, and in that connection, it is interesting that these Limba performative utterances were often undertaken with relish and with a kind of explicit care for their form and usage. It was not just 'doing' – but doing pleasurably, beautifully, ceremonially, deliberately. Even the interchange of the small phrases of greetings was among the pleasures and arts of life and represented in story as a kind of mark of humanity (of Limba humanity that is). Such phrases had a special kind of repeated resonance and emotive enactment about them. In a sense they were – at least at times – among the kind of heightened expressions, receiving particular *attention*, that Karin Barber regards as in a sense 'quotable' and detachable from their context, the bedrock of literary textualisation (Barber 2003). For at least some Limba uses of words it seemed not a matter of mere verbal repetition – uttered but not particularly noticed – but of a propensity to both deploy and *attend to* certain linguistic formulations, including the performative utterances discussed here. One could say of course that concepts such as attentiveness, delight or detachability are inevitably relative ones. If so, and if they play some part in our delineation of what it is to do things in, say, a 'literary' or an 'artful' way, then the boundaries of concepts like 'literature', 'textuality', or 'art' must similarly and to that extent be matters of degree.

Limba verbal acts have to be seen within the context of their own cultural practices and ideologies. But at the same time they feed into wider comparative issues and assist our appreciation of that rich, elusive and variegated human resource – language: the locus at once for activated social recognition, for delight and for reflective comment on human life.

---

[6] See, for instance, the English logical positivists (e.g. Ayer 1946: esp. 107ff) and Black's comments on Parsons (Black 1961: 278). The 'symbolic' was at that time commonly taken as typical of so-called primitive or non-western peoples, as in Lévi-Strauss's celebrated emphasis (1962) on the 'poetic' nature of expression among primitives, Cassirer on 'mythical' thinking (1954: 97ff), or Calame-Griaule (1965) on the essentially symbolic nature of speech among the Dogon.

4

The Arts and Action
of Limba Story-telling[1]

The Limba deployment of words also found expression in the more sustained mode of story-telling. Not that there is a clear break between the active and pleasurable uses of words in the performative utterances described in the last chapter – themselves a kind of miniature verbal art – and the deliberately displayed words of narrative performance. Still what we find in story-telling, the focus here, is a more extensively organised and prolonged mode of using words, where narrative imposes a rather different kind of framing.

The general nature of narrative – the subject of many studies over the centuries and of particular interest in recent years – forms one point of departure for approaching any manifestation of story-telling. But this needs to be complemented by the specifics of how stories are organised, created and viewed in particular cultural-historical contexts, and how they fit into the complex of local ideologies and arts. For this we return to the Limba.[2]

The poetry of story-telling

Limba story-telling, like any other, was not some transparent and as it were inevitable manifestation of the human turn to narrative – or at any rate not only that – but organised and conceived within a wider constellation of arts and formulated through specific Limba practices and perspectives. In the mid-

---

[1] An earlier version of part of this chapter was delivered as the Katharine Briggs Memorial Lecture, Folklore Society, London, November 1993, subsequently published as 'The poetic and the everyday: their pursuit in an African village and an English town', *Folklore* 105: 3–11, 1994. The second example in the original lecture and article has been omitted and the remaining discussion extensively revised.

[2] For further information about Limba stories and story-telling see Finnegan 1967, and for Limba transcriptions Finnegan 1963. Extracts in this and later chapters have been in part re-translated for this volume.

twentieth century (the time to which this account again applies) Limba speakers were, as described earlier, despised both by the national planners and by speakers of other languages in the region. They seemed to have little part in the civilised arts as these were then envisaged by the national educational establishment. In their own eyes, however, they had their own rich cultural traditions, well known to all Limba, however unnoticed by outsiders, and perhaps the more resonant for being passed over by others.

Chief among these were music, dance, song, rhetoric, and story – a series of performed arts expressed in unwritten form and context. These arts made up *malimba ma* – 'Limba ways or traditions' – or, more literally and evocatively, 'Limba times' (for the *ma-* prefix brought it within that beautiful class of words to do with time and with flowing water). The term carried connotations of a shared Limba experience of the ways of human beings, part of Limba inheritance from their ancestors. Language, song, music and rhythmic movement in a way formed one complex of artistic expression, and one in which, diffident though they were in what was at the time classed as 'European contexts', the Limba were consciously aware of their own artistry and wisdom – of 'the sense we found from our old people'.

One form this took was the encapsulation of performed words in story-telling. The stories were on varied subjects, most often about animals, about people, or about Kanu ('God') and the beginnings of things. Ambiguous though we now recognise the terms to be, it would be fair to say that in the complex continuum between 'fiction' and 'truth' these tales, at first sight anyhow, fell towards the former end. Even stories about origins seemed not to be told or received as deep or sacred myths or taken any more seriously than other tales. The narrative themes and the skills of story-telling were learned informally. Children started telling stories among themselves as part of peer-group enjoyment, and up to a point everyone was expected to have some ability in the art. Some were admired as better than others but there was no idea of story-telling as a profound mysterious skill or of story-tellers being different from other people. Their audiences were people like themselves, sitting around in groups in the village, or clustered in the evening on the open verandas of their huts. These were informal and enjoyable story-telling sessions, recreation rather than some deep ritual, with the audiences making their own essential contribution to the proceedings through their reactions and exclamations or joining into the choruses of the songs the narrator sometimes scattered through the story. As in any sphere of life, the tellers could no doubt have mixed motives for their narrative activities but essentially story-telling was part of leisure and of mutually shared sociability between teller and audience.

But this story-telling had its own poetics too. However ordinary and in some ways apparently impromptu, it was a performed art-form, not just a conversation. This point needs some amplification.

Story was a recognised Limba genre (*mbɔrɔ*) with its own stylistic conventions. There were set ways to start and end stories. 'Bringing it out' or 'telling it for you' was a kind of offering to the listeners with overtones of the performative utterances noted in the previous chapter, again making use of conventional word patterns to, as it were, set the narrative account into quotation marks: the closing quote mark was signalled by the appropriate signing-off words at the end. There were recognised ways of structuring the stories, and of treating plot, characterisation, diction, rhetoric. Listening to a Limba utterance constructed on these lines you knew unambiguously that it was a *mbɔrɔ*, not any other type of speech, an occasion for the deploying of the Limba story-teller's insight through the artful and appropriate weaving of words. In many ways the structuring and stylistic strategies, though not the detailed ways they were worked out, were the familiar ones of story-telling world-wide. Like other storied genres, written or unwritten, Limba tales depended on the narrative organisation and elaboration of words.

But to focus just on the verbal text would give only a superficial idea of this art form. Performance was crucial. This was a complex and multi-faceted process and involved a wide range of learned skills. Limba story-tellers had skilfully to marshal rhetorical devices like repetition, reduplication, mimicry, gesture, onomatopoeia, and, as so often in African narrative, the deployment of ideophones (mini-images in sound – and more-than-sound). They made artful use of songs, of direct speech (effective in the extreme), and of clever changes in tempo, pitch, and atmosphere. Some of these elements may be dimly detected in the transcribed text. But their full artistic impact can only be appreciated when heard, seen and felt in the actual performance of a skilled narrator. What looks 'simple', trite and literal when read from a text on the page, can be profound, allusive, and full of both sharply observed individuality and universal drama in actual performance.

Characterisation is one example. Orally delivered narratives have some-times been read as 'flat' or 'one-dimensional', lacking in individual personality. And in written transcriptions they may indeed look like merely unreflective routines with no verbalised portrayal of individual character, perhaps little elaboration of inner thoughts or struggles, nothing indicating how unique individuality is worked out against wider patterns. But, in a way that can only be appreciated by experiencing it, *all* these aspects came through in the best performances. As Limba story-tellers knew very well, the verbal text – the prime focus of conventional western definitions of literature and the element captured on the written page – was only one aspect of their art.

The audience played an essential role too – if 'audience' is not too marginalising a term for the active part taken by those other participants in the creative act of narration. Limba story-tellers regularly asked someone to act as their 'replier' (*bame* – from the same word *me* (agree, accept) as in the equivalent performative utterances discussed earlier): it meant that someone took responsibility for not just receiving but actively acknowledging and supporting the narrator's acts. In story-telling the replier enhanced the performance by queries, responses, asides and verbal comments all through the narration. But up to a point *everyone* present had something of that role. They incited and played up to the teller through laughter, exaggerated surprise, shock, sympathy and, in stories with songs, enthusiastic singing or even occasionally dancing to the chorus. Audience engagement was an essential component of Limba narration: an enacted, not a written, form.

There was also a further dimension which it would be easy for readers to miss. In European print traditions of the last few centuries, the distinction between 'prose' and 'verse' seems unproblematic: a straightforward typographic division with 'poetry' quite simply printed differently from 'prose'. But this does not work in an oral context. There the distinction is a matter of degree only – or perhaps of no relevance at all. There are, of course, certain factors in language, performance or local terminology which might incline an external analyst to class particular genres as 'poetry', others as 'prose' – fair enough, so long as we realise that this is merely a relative and problematic judgement.

My initial assumption was that Limba stories – being 'stories' – were self-evidently 'prose'. In my earlier entextualisations I presented them as such, using the standard typographical modes for representing prose forms in European language-texts, and indeed, as in this volume, have continued to do so; it still seems a sensible way to engage with current conventions of written communication.[3] But I now recognise my choice was more problematic than the simple one I assumed at the time and that for oral art the prose/poetry distinction may prove to bring little illumination in itself. It is true that these stories seemed to contrast with classic western genres of 'poetry' in being without metre (at least in the sense I then envisaged it); their vocabulary and syntax were fairly close to everyday talk, which in some respects they were anyway deliberately mimicking; they were not thought to be mysterious or esoteric; and explicitly musical elements were relatively slight. On the other hand, one way in which performance techniques of the kind I have been describing removed story-telling from the conventions of informal conversation – or, at any rate, framed them as a particular story genre – was in their sonic patterning. The cadences leap out when one listens just for sound without being distracted by semantic meanings. As actually delivered, Limba stories were marked, among other conventions, by particular rhythmic, melodic, dynamic, timbred and other aural patterning, and in that way too, for all their everyday secular quality in other respects, they were set apart from everyday life and displayed for special attention. So insofar as a prose/poetry contrast might be applied at all here, I would now place Limba stories further along this multi-faceted and problematic continuum than I had earlier assumed.

Limba stories and story-telling were far from being the products of some undifferentiated 'tribal' or 'communal' Tradition, that once taken-for-granted model for interpreting such forms. They were the performances and productions of individuals. In part this was the corollary of their performed quality. No story could be just some unchanging transmission from the past when so much of its nature lay in its *performance*, for that depended on the individual performer and his or her interaction with an audience on a specific occasion.

---

[3] I suspect one reason for my choice was an implicit assumption that 'prose' was somehow the 'unmarked' 'basic' form, with 'poetry' the unusual and elaborate; so the fact that Limba story-telling seemed more accessible and less 'deep' than their songs made it seem natural to assign it to 'prose' (similar preconceptions were probably not uncommon at that time, thus shaping decisions about the layout and analysis of story texts); on prose/poetry see also Finnegan 1977: 106ff, 1992: 140–41 and for related issues about entextualisation Chapter 10 below.

This was no marginal extra, since a story's import lay in the teller's enactment, characterisation, irony, drama, sense of atmosphere and evocations of inner meaning. The textual transcripts of two narrative performances might look near-identical in plot and protagonists – but be very different as actually performed. There was individual creativity in the verbal constituents too – in the way familiar plots were developed, the conventional structures manipulated, or stylistic conventions deployed for specific purposes. Certainly there were favourite story-lines revolving round, for example, competitions and trickery, the origin of death, winning a wife, the antics of fools, or the results of talking behind someone's back. Stock figures were brought into action, like the powerful chief, deceitful wife, boastful spider, humorous twins, God, Sira and Sara (standard, though not invariable, names for female and male protagonists) and the young hero making his way in the world. Part of the appeal lay in the recognisability of character, plot, build-up, structure, phraseology. But, as in other artistic genres (the high-art forms of the established western literary canon being no exception), individuals worked within and extended these familiar traditions to produce their own individual creations. It was how they marshalled and brought these together into a presentation on an immediate occasion that made it their own: what they performed and created was in this sense a *different* work in each case.

The contribution made by individual story-tellers and their performances was clearly recognised by the Limba. There was little interest in literal verbal correctness for the focus was rather on the artistry of particular performances, and narrators were praised for the verve or drama of their delivery more often than for the plot. It was accepted that good story-tellers heard stories from others but also at times 'thought them out' again for themselves (*simɔkɔ*) before they performed them to an audience. A reflective narrator remarked that he had been thinking to himself about a story for several days while working in the farm before telling it in the evening. He had heard the story in the first place from 'the old people' but had now 'added (put in, enlarged) a little bit' (*ndinti thi wuyeti*), and told it from his own 'heart and intelligence' (*huthukuma iŋ funuŋ*).

But as well as recognising individual creativity, the Limba were also clear that stories were not just the ad hoc result of spontaneous inspiration but also in some way founded in tradition, part of *malimba ma*. When I asked about particular stories, one common response was that 'I heard it from the old people' (*bebɔrɔ be*). This meant both those elders who had told the stories to their children, and the dead ancestors: 'those who lived in the old days'. They were buried in the village, part of 'us' and of village human life, in contrast to the wild things of the bush. It was due to this inheritance that individuals could bring out a story. So it was that a common formula for ending a story was 'since I heard it, I had to tell this story to you'. A Limba narrator did not 'make' (*leheni*) a story in the sense that a smith made a tool, but 'spoke' it (*gb">kɔli*) or 'brought it out' (*funuŋ*). He 'carried it forward' for others to hear. A story was a *mbɔrɔ* (literally an 'old thing'), and the teller spoke it 'by grace of the old people' (*thɔkɔ ba bebɔrɔ be*).

The Limba, therefore, recognised the dual nature of literary art: continual creation and re-creation by individuals while at the same time exploiting conventional styles and themes. They expressed this combination of the new and personal with the old and traditional by attributing the stories on the one hand to the old people from whom they were first heard, on the other to individual narrators who spoke them and thought them out. As one story-teller summed it up, he was taught 'by the dead and by my own heart'.

There was a further point too. The stories were indeed exciting tales, enjoyable fiction to listen to: the clever way a competitor outwitted an antagonist, the suspense of an adventure, the uproarious antics of animals. But even though the events depicted were clearly imaginative rather than 'factual' there was also something true and abiding about them. This sense of the universal in the particular was not so much in any stated 'moral' to the story – there *were* sometimes such morals but these were certainly not obligatory and often just rather casually tacked on as one strategy among others for creating a tidy ending. Rather it lay in the observation of the *kinds* of things people do and say – fundamentally human even in fantastic settings or animal guises – and in the recurrent patterns of human intercourse depicted through the story-tellers' enacted art.

This came through even in the so-called 'simple' animal stories: masks to portray and comment on human beings. The arrogant pushy spider being amusingly – and predictably – outwitted by his weaker wife was one example, strikingly effective when heard in a Limba context where everyone 'knew' that men were of course cleverer and stronger and women must naturally be subservient (in no other context but a story could one say aloud that real life did not always correspond to that conventional wisdom). Or again, there were adventure stories that in their telling brought out the ironies of human life, the relations between men and women, the strengths and weaknesses of political power, or the unambiguous love between mother and son (but might one dare wonder, as in the *Story of Deremu* partially reproduced a little later, if even that might after all sometimes falter?). The commentary came through less in the words and plot than in the small ways that a skilful story-teller conveyed these deeper implications and overtones through the subtlety of the perform-ance, abetted – and this was important too – by the co-creating audience.

Limba performed arts
and the nature of human beings

The complex of Limba performed arts – *malimba ma* – was in one way a united one, not, as in the western high-art theory and practice of recent centuries, a series of relatively distinct specialisms. But it did also have some internal differentiation. Surprising as it may seem in view of the Limba interest in language and speaking detailed in the last two chapters, it was the arts of music, dance, drum and song, not the more verbally constituted forms of narrative, oratory or wit, that seemed to be regarded as the highest forms of artistic expression. This ranking was not verbalised explicitly – it was too deeply assumed as the natural order of things to need stating – but came out in many features of Limba activities and how they spoke about and practised them. There was, for example, a large vocabulary referring to the many genres of song, music and dance, strikingly more elaborate than for story-telling or oratory. Drumming was particularly valued. Everyone could drum a bit, but drumming was also a specialised skill. Specific ceremonies had their particular kinds of drums and styles, and recognised experts (mostly male) who performed at them. Much the same applied to dancing, again both universally practised and with its own experts, both women and men. Some were famous for many miles around and invited well in advance to dance at important ceremonies in and beyond their own chiefdoms. Singing was closely linked to dancing, so when people sang – as they frequently did, for work as well as for play – they also often half-danced. Songs were typically led by a soloist who was usually also the main drummer, dancer or story-teller, and were then taken up in chorus by all of those watching, working, dancing or listening. Singing was in this way similar to dancing and drumming: found both in distinctive forms mastered only by experts, and a medium of artistic expression which could be, and was, participated in by everyone.

The complexity and prestige of these Limba forms is worth stressing. Over the last few centuries of western civilisation we have tended to put 'literature' at the top of our artistic pinnacle – literature, that is, in the sense of a verbal written text. For the Limba it was not so. As we have seen, they most certainly valued and reflected on language and speech. But when it came to organised artistic display music and dance came first. Their poetry, furthermore, came in the form of song: sung and danced as a performance. This makes a marked contrast to that common western image of poetry as something distilled into written words on a page: not *always* the western practice, of course, as William Anderson, among others, so eloquently reminds us in his analysis of Dante's creativity (1983: 7), but over recent centuries a dominant paradigm. The musical, drummed and danced dimensions were the prime Limba focus, with greater prestige for musical, rhythmic and choreographic elaboration than for the verbal.

Despite their broad distribution among all the Limba, these skills were by no means simple or 'natural'. They were learned and conventional arts that had to be mastered gradually by children as they grew up. Acquiring and appreciating these skills was a part of *malimba ma*. It was something all young children were eager to achieve, both in their everyday doings and during the period of seclusion and learning which formed part of both male and female initiation. These initiation ceremonies were among the highlights of the Limba year, and were both preceded and followed by great public displays not of story-telling but of dance, drumming, and song.

The Limba attitude to the experts who had acquired particular skills in these arts was ambiguous. They greatly admired and applauded them – some more than others of course – took pains to organise their presence at large events, and rewarded them not just with honeyed words but also, up to a point and depending on their degree of recognition, with gifts or money. They recognised that such experts had had to learn by watching and listening and practising; they were also realists enough to know that if you were related to an established expert, or lived near one, you had more chance of becoming a successful one yourself. But they also felt that there could be something more to it – a mysterious extra something possessed by these leading exponents.

This linked to the Limba views about the nature of human beings. In Limba philosophy, people were essentially social beings: to be a *wɔ mɛti* – a person of the village or town – was the rightful destiny of ordinary humankind. People lived out their lives as human beings through their family ties in the village, their joint expeditions to the farm, their return at night to the village homestead, the talking and story-telling and law cases in the verandas of their houses, and the tendance and memory of the dead buried behind their huts within the circle of the village. Humankind was not born to venture in the bush, the wild place where spirits and animals roamed, but to run the affairs of the village where humans were in control.

But a few individuals were different. Diviners saw into things hidden from ordinary people. The smiths had communion with sacred and fearsome mysteries. And hunters ventured alone and without fear into the bush at nights. Such individuals had 'four eyes', a special double vision into a sphere beyond where normal humans reach. The highly talented artists were sometimes seen as touched by the same ambiguity. All these beings had special and exceptional powers, beneficial and necessary for society indeed, but at the same time of potential danger to both others and themselves.

These special talents were sometimes portrayed through the image of certain individuals being helped by a 'spirit' (*waali*). How this could happen seemed to be envisaged in a kind of speculative narrative frame. Someone was wandering alone in the bush. He or she was accosted by a spirit – that is, by a wild spirit of the bush, a class of beings distinct from the dead human ancestors who were buried in the village and in a way still dwelled there. These spirits were unhuman and uncontrolled, ruled by caprice and dwelling outside society. The spirit offered the individual a gift: perhaps of becoming a great diviner or dancer or singer, or, maybe, of unusual worldly success in wealth and power. If this was accepted, the spirit would help that individual to become successful far beyond normal people. There were no outward marks to display the relationship, and the possessor went home and said nothing. But it was not the human who was now in control, for one day the spirit might want to be paid. And that payment could only be 'a person', a human life. No one could tell just what happened, but in some mysterious way the dancer or singer or hunter would have to hand someone over to be eaten by the spirit.

When people alluded to this account of the gifted individual, they were scarcely speaking literally (there is no reason to follow those unimaginative arm-chair scholars who suppose that non-literate people are any less capable than those with western education of speaking metaphorically or of imbuing ostensibly 'factual' statements with symbolic or ironic overtones). Nor was it normally organised into a sustained narrative or performed in the way of the publicly enacted stories described earlier. Rather it was a kind of parable about human beings and their nature: a sort of latent narrative occasionally referred to in story (as in the one below) but mostly too deeply known and shared to need overt verbal articulation. This ambivalent view of outstanding talent was not the idiosyncratic fantasy of just one or two individuals, but a recurrent figure through which Limba speakers indicated their vision of artistic and superhuman talent: something to be prized and often enough innocuous – but at the same time with the potential to be dangerous.

The gifted artistic experts, then, were potentially among those with mysterious talent. They carried out the social and essential activities of *malimba ma* – the arts of Limba culture – without which Limba ceremonies, crafts, healing and even material well-being could not be achieved. Indeed their performed arts were not just something to be valued in the large rituals of the year, but ran through Limba everyday affairs too. Rice farming was not an easy way of life. It meant cutting through the rampant growth, hoeing the ground with back-breaking labour, harvesting and threshing the rice, coping with heat and cold, thirst or hunger. But such activities were also experienced through the music, song and dance that so often accompanied or commented on them. In their mundane utilitarian actions the Limba grew up aware of the poetic around them, of ways in which even the hardest task could be imbued with beauty and depth through the medium of art.

Narrative and performance

Set in this context of experiences and enactments and within their wider constellation of arts, Limba speakers and audiences had in their genre of story-telling a wonderful resource through which to mould and express their experience and their view of themselves and of the world, laying them out for recognition and contemplation, as it were, in the frame of fiction. A prime medium for Limba stories was words – but, as I have indicated, it was emphatically not a matter of words alone. Essential to their realisation were also the sonic patternings, visual gestures, facial expressions, interactions with audience and in many cases singing and sometimes dancing or dance-evoking movements by both narrator and other participants. Although story-telling was 'ordinary' compared to the musical and danced genres which were the preserve of experts, nevertheless music and movement also entered into the stories, bringing their own associations and overtones. Stories might be told by unpretentious tellers in everyday rather than formalised ritual occasions, a contrast (relatively speaking) to what could be called the high arts of the great experts in music, song or dance. But they were, nevertheless, a fully deliberate and recognised artistic genre. From one viewpoint there were overlaps between stories and the performative utterances discussed in the last chapter and, even more noticeably, with the shorter verbal formulations in proverbs or riddles (also termed *mbɔrɔ*). But in general, story-telling went unmistakably further in its sustained, multi-modal and deliberate style. Here the verbal acts were even more markedly in quotes, as it were, and on display, demanding attention. The narrative words were deployed and enacted to depict temporally sequenced events through familiar structures, styles and delivery arts, building on images and associations recognised by both narrators and audiences.

Let me take this a little further by extracts from a story told by the talented Limba story-teller Karanke Dema, which I have entitled *The Story of Deremu*.

51

This hinges on a mother taking a spirit to help her and eventually having to pay with her own son, the more evocative for listeners because of the shared Limba vision of the dangers of wild spirits and human fallibility.

The action opens with the hero Deremu going off to the capital city Freetown, as young men often did, to seek his fortune. His mother is left behind in the village, where she is shown engaged in the local pursuit of dyeing cloth and going into the bush to look for indigo. Her search is in vain. It is the dry season and she finds herself surrounded by burnt cane grass, something commonly associated with barrenness, harshness and drought. In the sun's searing heat she is overcome by thirst and can find no water. She comes to a big stream bed

> But there was no water there. She sat down *wɔ hɔŋg!* [a vivid little ideophone conveying the sound and movement of how she flopped exhaustedly down]. She said,
> 'Oh, how I've suffered today since I came into this cane grass to look for indigo. I've not found any, I'm distressed by thirst, I've searched and searched for water but found none. Oh God if only water could come out just here, here where I'm sitting.'
> Then the spirit of the place came out. It said, 'If water comes out, will you pay me?'
> The mother said, 'What will I pay you?'
> The spirit said, 'A man'.
> The woman said, 'I – after the long time I have spent searching round for water, if I find water now, *whatever* you say I'm willing to give you.'
> Then the spirit said again, 'A man'.
> She said, 'I accept'. Thirst was distressing the mother. She accepted there.

The spirit sits her down and brings out great quantities of water.

> 'But I will not let you drink it, unless you pay me what I asked.'
> Then the woman said, 'I have a child; his name is Deremu. But he went to Freetown. When he returns – take him! I give him to you. For you helped me with the water. I would have died but you helped me.'
> The spirit said, 'I accept. All right'.
> The woman drank the water, she bathed, and went away.

The contract is now forged. Both parties have committed themselves through the binding speech act of 'I accept' (*yaŋ yɛrɔkɔi*). So the spirit stays there singing, with a catchy chorus for all to join, to tell his children that wherever or whoever he may be Deremu is his,

> Deremu *yo*
> Deremu *be ye*
> Deremu *yo*
> Deremu is mine
> Deremu is mine
> Deremu, Deremu is mine. *Ye!*

The action switches to Freetown. Deremu gets rich, working under the water as a diver. He becomes a chief with followers, wives, musicians to accompany and praise him, and a horse to ride. He decides to visit his village to see his mother – a stock reason for going home. Your mother above all people is the one who loves you and who shows that love in the food she prepares and keeps for you. But first he goes to a diviner to ask if he will go in peace. The diviner warns him: 'Your mother is keeping war [not food] for you, at the river, in the middle, in a deep place.' So Deremu has many knives made and fastened into his gown, with a special one, worked on by a moriman, set next to his body. Then in his magnificent cavalcade he starts out for home.

> They began to come; musicians and all, wives and all, young men and all. For he was now a chief, riding on a horse. ....
>
> He had sent a message to his mother 'I am coming this month.' She was glad when she got it. But she had not acted well: she had given him to a spirit. She was thinking to herself 'I have not done well.'
>
> When they set out to come, they came to the river. Deremu knew, he had been told, that it was at the river that war was being kept for him – it is here!
>
> He stopped. He got down from his horse. He said to his followers, 'Go across.' They crossed by the bridge.
>
> He was standing on the far side away from them. He put on his gown, the one with the knives. He called out to them, he Deremu, 'You, you who stand on the other side, you whom I brought here – for me it is here, that if I am to find life, it is through God; if I don't find life, so be it.'
>
> His horse was taken over. He stood on the far side. He said, 'When the bridge breaks under me and I am thrown in the water, if you see red blood, weep, my time is finished. If you see black blood, rejoice, I have not died.'
>
> He started out. He reached the middle of the bridge. The bridge split in two. The spirit had broken it. Deremu fell into the water. The spirit seized him. They began to fight there, the spirit struggling to kill him, he struggling to kill the spirit. He drew one knife, and cut at the spirit. The knife broke. He drew another, he cut. It broke. He drew another, he cut. It broke. A hundred knives – they could not kill the spirit! The spirit was all the while struggling to kill Deremu.
>
> He drew the last one, the one kept against his stomach, the one the moriman had worked. He thrust it in here at its throat, he cut through the spirit's throat. He thrust it in here [back of the neck], he cut it through. The spirit could not kill Deremu. Deremu triumphed, he killed the spirit.
>
> Those who were standing on the dry land – when Deremu fell into the water, their hearts were sick. They thought 'Deremu will die today.' They were weeping now. But Deremu had hardened himself. Now they saw the water: it was black!
>
> They started to dance with joy – Deremu had not died! Now they were dancing with joy.

The teller depicts the action not just through his words but by creating the drama and intensity of the events he is enacting. He draws a picture of the hero alone on the far bank of a wide river, watched by his followers from the other side as he stands isolated and in suspense for the fateful moment. The slow, quiet atmosphere in which this is portrayed, as if with breath suspended, is suddenly interrupted by the loud, rapid, violent narration of the struggle between man and spirit in the hidden depths of the water when all is blood and turmoil and Deremu draws knife after knife after knife, the teller vividly demonstrating on his own body the deadly spots where Deremu finally manages to stab and kill the spirit. Then we are brought back to the long hushed suspense of those waiting on the bank, how they begin to weep hopelessly – then their breathless realisation that Deremu is safe, the tense quietness of the description violently broken by the loud and vigorous representation of their noisy relief as – familiar sight to all the audience – they start to dance with joy.

But the story has not yet ended. Deremu drags the dead spirit onto the dry land, and takes out its heart and gall, saying

'My mother bore me; she brought me up, but – but you cannot tell what is in a mother's heart. For my mother intended to kill me. By God's grace I did not die. But for her – where she wanted to send me, I will send her there.'

He resumes his fine clothes, mounts his horse and sets out again, his musicians playing. Meantime his mother awaits him. Karanke portrays her sad anxiety as she waits at home, replaced first by quick excitement and obstreperous happiness when she hears that her son is safe and nearly at the village, then by huge rejoicing and dancing by all the villagers and the followers of Deremu. The vigour of this dance and the excited description of the mother's ecstatic joy are interrupted by the story-teller's sad, reflective aside about what is then seen to underlie the noisy rejoicing, 'she is to die.' Deremu had hardened his heart and got his wife to cook the spirit's heart with the gall. He calls his mother.

'Here is what I've brought you; for it's long since we parted. This is what I've brought you to eat, it is good.' In fact, she is to die. The mother was glad. In fact, she is dying. For she would have killed Deremu ...

When she had finished eating, they came out to dance outside. The musicians played. They danced beautifully. Now the mother was rejoicing.

When she had danced only a little, she fell. When they went near to lift her up, she was dead.

The musicians stopped playing. They all gathered at the place. Deremu got down from his horse. He said, 'Mother, you bore me; I did not act badly. You brought me up. But when I went down to Freetown, you heard I had become well off. I was sending you everything. But you did not take notice of that, you were thinking about killing me. You gave me to a spirit. Now, by God's help, I am still here. I too have a child, but we cannot know what is in his heart. But now the place you wanted to send me to, you have gone there first yourself.'

But she is still his mother and he gives her the finest of burials, not just the usual white cloth but a coffin, gold, and enough gunpowder to fire shots over her grave for seven whole days.

He put her in a chest, so the earth would not touch her body. He took gold and put it on her mouth, more gold in her left hand, more on her right toe. He said goodbye.

Saying goodbye to his mother: 'Mother, you will not say of me that I did not think of you. If I had not hardened myself I would have died. If you bear a child, you too become well off. But you did not think of that with me. But now since you have died, I will bury you well.'

What made the story a profoundly evocative tragedy was not just the moving way it was told – though that was essential – or the deeply entrenched Limba belief that the one person who will *never* betray you is your mother; but also the associations of the world of a-social wilful spirits with what is

54

dark and hidden and uncontrollable in human nature. When Karanke depicted the inner ambivalence of both mother and son – torn between feelings of loyalty and of attack – this was, for Limba listeners, a deep and yet believable commentary on the tragic and unfathomable nature of the human heart.

In one way Limba life was eminently concerned with the here and now – they were not the inhabitants of some myth-laden numinous 'primitive' world. Nor were their stories told in some atmosphere of mythopoeic solemnity. The audiences could be rapt and intimately engaged with the performance, but narrators also sometimes had to struggle for attention and there were almost always other events and noises going on around. These were mostly cheerful light-hearted occasions, not infrequently hilarious (like the example in the next chapter). Nevertheless through their performed stories they had a means to interlace their everyday experiences with an awareness of the poetic, of the deeper hidden elements in human life and of their place in a wider order of things – continuities with the past as well as the present, the far-yet-near, where fantasy, as Scheub puts it, brings 'the joining of fiction and history' (2002: 141). They could deploy the verbal formulations of story to express the tragic, comic, celebratory, ironic, puzzling, continuing elements in human life.

None of this should really cause any surprise. It is not just among the mid-twentieth-century Limba that speech in narrative mode takes this resounding and evocative form and there are many accounts from Africa, as elsewhere, of the extent and depth of stories and story-telling. The Limba use of storied words must be set within its own complex of practices and ideologies certainly, essential for the specificities of the meanings and evocations that they carried. But narrative in its many forms also seems so widespread in human culture that it has been regarded as perhaps one of the truly universal propensities of humankind, creating order out of chaos and giving meaning to what might otherwise be uncontrollable and anarchic. It runs through human speech and action at every level and with many different degrees of formality, through formulations structured by plot and character, set in a temporal and developing framework. It is one of the major forms in which people weave words together to organise, encapsulate and create a vantage point on experience.[4]

In this context too we need to be alive to the *performed* nature of Limba and comparable story-telling. Literary scholars have long reminded us of the mutual influences between art and life, each moulding the other, affecting as they do our interpretation of reality, of ourselves, of our experience. But this

---

[4] For further examples of story-telling in Sierra Leone, see Cosentino 1980, 1982, Jackson 1982, Kilson 1976, Spencer 2002, and for recent more general works on Africa, Scheub 2002, 2004, Yankah 2004 and Chapter 5 below (for a guide to the huge earlier literature on narrative in Africa see bibliographies in Scheub 1977b, Görög-Karady 1981, 1992, also references in Finnegan 1970, chapters 12–13, Okpewho 1983). Amidst the extensive literature on narrative more generally see especially the classic contributions in Bruner 1986, 1987, 1991, Mitchell 1981, Ricoeur 1984, also more recently Alabi 2005, Finnegan 1998, Niles 1999, Ochs and Capps 1996, 2001, Shuman 2005; for issues relating to authority and evidence in oral discourse (including narrative) Du Bois 1986, Hill and Irvine 1992.

has often focused on the verbal, and especially the written, dimensions of texts. The import of Limba stories however — what in a sense they *did* – lay not just in the (writable) words but in the performers' enactment and the audience's experience on the actual occasion. And this was not just a matter of intellectual meaning. It also applied to the overtones, the hints about the nature of power, of marriage, of arrogance, of the strength of weakness, of loyalty, of the hilarities as well as the tragedies of life. The narrators revealed and displayed this nature of human beings and their actions not just through overt words but through embodied enactment: how young girls are liable to cajole you, chiefs to exploit their powers, mothers defend children, wives entrance and perhaps deceive husbands, young men go venturing. To understand Limba narrative as crafted performance brings an additional dimension of atmosphere and evocation, another level of commentary. Beside the cognitive themes of narrative exposition we also need to take into account the resonant acts of multi-sensory performance.

It bears repeating that Limba stories and story-telling were certainly not experienced as some mysterious magic: they were an entertaining part of ordinary recreation. Nevertheless in their story-telling they engaged a form that could weave together the old and the new, the real and the fantastic, the unique and the general – an occasion at once for active co-participation and for the detachment of setting apart in fictional creation. Language was being deployed in the deliberately chosen frame of narrative, in organised, embellished and sustained action that goes further than the shorter linguistic acts described in the previous chapter. In their storying the Limba and others have here developed a crafted way of displaying and using words to actively formulate and comment on the world – one mode of human action.

5

Stories of Africa –
Stories about Africa[1]

The magic moment of performance is indeed one inescapable quality of story-telling. But the narrative themes are of interest too, both embedded in particular situations and stretching in some ways beyond the bounds of particular time or place. Let me plunge straight into another Limba story to introduce this chapter, which is a fairly light-hearted counterpoint between, on the one hand, some Limba (and other) stories in Africa and, on the other, a selection of the larger narratives that have been told *about* Africa.

So – 'A story for you', as a Limba narrator might say:

A spider once lived on earth who was very full of fight.
He went to the elephant and said, 'I want to fight you.' The elephant said 'You're not strong enough to take me on!' But the spider got a rope and said, 'Hold onto this; when you feel it shaking and quivering, *yigbɛ yigbɛ*,[2] it's me; the fight's coming.' He went off.
He went on some way and met a hippopotamus. 'Hippopotamus, I want to fight you.' The hippopotamus said, 'Huh! You're not strong enough to take *me* on!' 'Well, hold onto this rope.' The hippopotamus took it. The spider went off saying 'When you feel it shake and quiver, *yigbɛ yigbɛ*, it's me, me.' (He'd said the same to the elephant you know.)
Well, when the spider had gone off, the elephant moved along not far away from the hippopotamus. When he felt *yigbɛ*, a shake on the rope, he said, 'Aha! look at that! I can feel the spider I'm fighting with.' The hippopotamus tugged too at the end where he was.
They spent all day, the whole of that day, struggling.
But the spider just went and lay down *kɛlɛthɛ*, lightly and easily!

---

[1] This chapter began as an unpublished public lecture at the University of the West Indies, Mona, Jamaica in 2002. Particular thanks to Carolyn Cooper for both her invitation and her most stimulating comments.
[2] The ideophone *yigbɛ yigbɛ* shows the quiver at one end of the rope when it is pulled from the other.

After they'd spent the whole long day there, the hippopotamus let go of the rope: 'I'll go and see if it's really true that all that long time I was tugging away it was really the spider.' Well, the elephant was coming along too.

They met and asked each other: 'Where were you today?' and 'Where were you today?' 'The spider gave me a rope today, saying we would fight.' The hippopotamus answered, 'That's right; it was me he gave the rope to; he said, "Let's fight".'

They stood there greeting each other and saying, 'The spider has tricked us. Look, we were fighting each other not the spider. Brother, wherever we see the spider, let's kill him for that.'

The spider didn't want to be killed. That's why he ran away here to the walls of our houses.

This is a translation of a tale told in 1961, recounted in the veranda of his hut by an old man named Bubu Dema in the hill-top village of Kakarima in the Sierra Leone northern uplands.[3] It can serve as an initial focus for considering some of the frames and characters in Limba narrative before going on to a wider perspective.

More on Limba stories

Among the many topics and characters treated in Limba tales, the spider – the Limba *wosi* – was a hugely popular figure.[4] As soon as a story-teller uttered the word *wosi* the audience would start to smile, ready for hilarity and startlement. Like other trickster-type characters he was not just crafty but also only too liable to overreach himself. Sometimes he was the weak outwitting the strong (though even then, as in that tug-of-war, with a hint of untamed irresponsibility), more often arrogant and a-social, his over-the-top self-aggrandisement often leading to some wonderfully ludicrous downfall.

So here's another tale, this time showing how the greedy scheming spider was typically hoist with his own petard. The audience were keenly involved. They knew from the start that a story with the spider as hero was bound to be funny and exciting and even those who did not know the precise plot were anticipating how it might unfold, adding to the fun. They were well acquainted with the scene being depicted: of people working in turn on each others' farms during the exhausting task of hoeing up the ground ready for sowing; of looking forward to being fed after the long day's work; and, if it was for the chief, of being fed lavishly – not just rice but perhaps the rarer delicacy of cooked meat.

I'm going to tell Yenkeni [my Limba name] a story about the spider. His craftiness is great. His wisdom (ho ho!) is great, ha! very great!

The spider was the herald – announcing things just as it's done in our

---

[3] For the circumstances of its performance and documentation see Chapter 10, pp. 160ff.
[4] Like other translators and transcribers I had to decide whether or not the Limba *wosi* should be transcribed with an initial capital (as proper name), and whether I should translate it into English as 'Spider', 'a spider', 'the spider', 'Mr Spider', 'Bra spider' ... . Taking account of the language and style of the stories and local discussions I chose 'a/the spider' but neither this nor, I conjecture, alternative choices necessarily capture all the ambiguities of the original (see further in Chapter 10 below).

village here. The chief spoke to fix a time for his farm to be cleared. 'Spider, you are to announce the time – Sunday, that is the time for the clearing.' The spider said 'All right.' He announced it twice. He announced it a third time on the evening before. And the chief told all the people that he had brought an ox. 'That's what those who do the clearing will eat.'

Well they set out for the clearing – and you know the spider! He said, 'Today I'll leave the work to the others.' He didn't bring a proper hoe at all but just attached a needle onto the handle instead! 'That's what *I* am going to clear with.' As for the chief, he didn't speak a word. He saw the 'hoe', he didn't speak a word aloud. 'Today, I and the spider . . . because of what he's done, he'll not be eating this day!'

As they went out to clear, the ox was killed. They went and began clearing. The spider took his stance at the end of the row of hoers where there was the least work to do. When he touched the grass with his hoe, *gbuŋ* [this and later ideophones, untranslated, convey directly attributes like the sound, style or movement of some action], when he went *yokore* with the needle, when he went *yokore* with the needle at the grass – it had no effect at all! The chief said, 'All right.' The workers were being congratulated and encouraged, 'Oh men! Oh men! Oh men! Today we are clearing the grass, today we are clearing the grass!' (and all the time the spider was doing nothing towards the clearing).

When he had gone on like that for a long time, the rice was all cooked. The ox was all boiled. The spider was called by the chief, given some tobacco and told, 'Call the people to eat.' He did so and divided out the tobacco. His heart was very happy. 'Today we're going to eat meat, today, meat, much much meat today, today we're going to be filled.' When he had finished calling all the people, they came. They came, all of them, and washed, ready to eat.

Then the chief said, 'Spider, you are now to make this announcement "Listen oh! There's to be a special ritual for the work I'm having done today – that everyone is to eat using the tool he worked with today".' *Haaa!* The spider's heart jumped! *Haa!* that was awful.

The spider looked at the size of the needle he would have to eat his food with – it was narrow, sharp, *sogbeŋ!* He just stood there and thought about it. He was brooding away and muttering to himself apart from the others, his heart was sore.

They all sat down to eat, the spider went and sat down too. They had all washed their hoes – and the spider his needle, his sharp needle. The meat was put on top of the rice and set out. As they sat there to eat, the spider took his needle. But whenever he went *sogbeŋ*, trying to prick the rice with his sharp needle – he would perhaps get just one grain! Then he tried to put it in his mouth. But whenever he went *sogbeŋ* and perhaps pierced a grain – the sauce wouldn't let the grain come off! He was just left with the needle, just licking the needle.

As for those with the hoes, they just went *pɛbɔ* with their hoe, and then another went *pɛbɔ* – and they ate! But the spider tried and tried to pierce the meat – nothing! The meat wouldn't come. The spider brooded away – but he could do nothing.

The chief said 'Help yourselves to the meat from the ox I brought.' Ha! That hurt the spider, that really hurt him. He said, 'All right. Ha! Look at all of us who came to the farm – and no food.'

Later another time was fixed for working on the farm. Again the spider announced it to them all. Do you know what he did this time? He fixed a great heavy hoe-head onto a handle, a *huge* one (like the Fula use to dig potatoes). 'Ha! I went and spent the day hungry that other time. But today, today I'll be eating, today, truly truly today, I'll be filled, today I'll get the biggest share, more than all the others, those ones who ate last time.' (But this time, you know, this time there was no food!)

After he'd fastened on the huge hoe, he set out for the farm. When they went out to hoe, he couldn't see any cooking pots. He couldn't see any smoke rising. He called out as if jokingly, 'Ho ho, ha ha, there's nothing in my mouth. Chief, isn't there any food today then? Ha ha!' Then the chief said, 'Just wait. The food's coming soon.' But all the time, there wasn't any food! All the time he was tricking the spider!

When they'd been hoeing for a long time, the spider yawned – 'Ho ho, ha ha; chief, are we just to spend the day like this then?' 'The food's coming just now.' All the time he was tricking him.

The farm work was finished. The spider got up. 'Ah! I the spider – my craftiness is always getting me into trouble.' It was the result of what he'd done before – clearing with a needle. You see, the chief was crafty too.[5]

The audience found the spider's excitement and disappointment hilarious, specially when he hears he will have to use his needle to eat and the ludicrous way he can scarcely get even one grain of rice to stick to it while everyone else is wolfing down great mouthfuls.

These spider stories were in one way specific to the Limba tellers of their time and place, both in their subtle performances and audience co-creation and through the overtones of their particular events and settings. But the Limba spider partakes too in the kinds of antics and associations of the trickster personae that are found so widely throughout the world. He is not far from many of the African-American and Caribbean Anansi stories too, tales that have by now engendered a large literature on the mingling themes of the irresponsible loutish a-social trickster (the 'badman' who goes beyond the accepted norms), and the justified rebel, the weak against the strong, breaking the unjustifiably imposed rules of dominant society and chiming in with the West Indian motif not of the 'bad' but of the moral 'ba-ad' man with something admirable as well as arrogant about him.[6] Limba tellers and listeners too knew the stories were not just about one clever-silly animal – the spider who was at the same time Spider with his named wife Kayi – but also in a way about human life. These may be tales of animals but they are not 'just' animal tales. As with the masks of classical Greek tragedy, the enduring human issues – even the normally unsayable and ungraspable – can be projected in the guise of animals.

Not all of the Limba stories I heard involved rollicking humour or trickster disasters. There were sad tales too, like the tragic one about why humans die (one version is translated a little later) and the stories, sometimes serious but often light-hearted or deliberately fantastic, in which God features as one character or about how chiefship or rice-farming first began. Other tales were

---

[5] Transcribed (and later translated into English) from my taped recording of Karanke Dema's performance in Limba in Kakarima, northern Sierra Leone, 1964.
[6] For recent overviews of the extensive literature on African and African-American tricksters see Bryant 2003, Owomoyele 2004 and, for earlier discussions, Abrahams 1966, Pelton 1980, Roberts 1989.

overtly about people and their adventures, sometimes just 'a man', 'a girl', 'a child', sometimes stock names like Sira or Sara, sometimes, as in *The Story of Deremu*, with named hero or villain. They revolved round themes of love, of marriage, friendship, competition, chiefship; of the deeds of orphans, of twins, of monsters, of far-fetched and ridiculous fools; or of the dire results of slander or disobedience. As with the animal tales (with which indeed they overlapped), they were shot through with fantasy but also with realism. The scene was often that of village life or of travel between settlements (a familiar experience), but even where the settings were designedly far-fetched and imaginary the characters carried on – the performers *showed* them carrying on – in ways that were familiar and credible. They might be depicted in exaggerated larger-than-life ways but they resonated with the known dilemmas of people's lives and relationships – of marriage, power, love, jealousy. At the same time a kind of enchantment ran through the performed tellings too, moving the narrative into a realm beyond the here and now.

And then there were the many popular tales that culminated in an explicit dilemma: sometimes just a haphazardly tacked-on conclusion to end up a performance neatly, sometimes a setting for soul searching about some (perhaps insoluble) moral and intellectual quandary. Some are little more than exaggerated frolics, like the mini-tale of three men smoking a pipe. One supplied the pipe, a second the tobacco, the third the match, so when a beautiful girl came out of the ashes who should get her? – an occasion for laughter.

Here is a more extended one. It has an engaging plot in its own right but ends with a real question revolving round the familiar Limba theme of the contending children of co-wives. A young man is saved from a series of dangers, even from death, by the love of four women: which child should succeed him?

A chief married a wife. He loved that wife but they had no child. He called a moriman. 'Moriman! I love my wife, but we have no child. I want you to help me, so we can have a child.' The moriman said. 'Well, all right.' He went into his room and stayed there for long time, about a month. Then he came out and said, 'You and your wife will get a child. But that child must be seen by no one, except for you and your wife and the person who cooks for him – just those three people.'

The wife became pregnant, and gave birth. The child was brought into a house, up above, in an attic. There he remained for many years, he grew up there. For many years he was there. He learned to walk on his own. There he was in the house, high up. He became a young man, he grew up tall. He stood up above there on the house, looking at the people below. Over a long long time he looked at the people below.

One day a girl came out in the village. She stood there. The boy came out above. He stood looking. They let their eyes meet, she and the boy. They saw each other. The boy had been told that no other person should see him. But it came that they saw each other – he and the girl.

The girl said, 'I must go and see for myself where that boy lives.' She went and searched for a ladder, she tied it together – a long one. She went and leant it against the house.

The evening came. The girl went there and climbed up. She went in and found the boy there. The boy said, 'E! What have you come here for?' 'I love you. Ever since I saw you yesterday, my heart has not stood still. That's why I've come, I love you.' The boy said, 'But no one else should see me.' They lay down.

As the sun was about to rise, the boy died. The girl – she didn't run away when the boy died. In the morning the woman who cooked for him brought water for the boy to wash. She found the girl sitting there. The child, the boy – he was dead!

She went and called the chief and his mother. 'Come here! come here! I've seen something amazing. The boy has died. But I found a woman there, sitting there.' The chief went with the mother. He went and saw the dead boy, and the girl sitting there. He said, 'E! Have you killed the boy, our son?' 'Yes. It was love that caused it.'

Well then – they called the moriman. 'Ha! that child that you struggled for us to get – he's died.' The moriman said, 'Well then, get me men to go and cut wood and bring it to the village.' The men went to cut the wood and brought it to the village. They put it down. The moriman said, 'Have you a can of kerosene?' 'Yes.' 'Well then, fetch it.' It was fetched. He put the kerosene all over the wood. He struck a light and put it to the wood. The fire caught.

'Aha. Chief, do you love your son?' 'Yes.' 'Well then, go into the fire.' The chief went up, but the fire was hot. [The narrator vividly mimed the searing heat of the fire driving the parents back, much against their will.] He drew back. He went forward again. 'Ah ah, the fire is hot indeed.' He went and sat down. He wept. 'Ah! Chief' said the moriman, 'You do not love your son.'

He called the mother. 'Do you love your son?' 'Yes.' 'Well, go into the fire, so that you can be burnt with your son.' His mother went up too – it was hot. She drew back. She came near again. The fire was hot indeed. She said, 'All right. I will not be burnt too. I will leave it as it is.' 'Well, all right.'

The girl was called, the one who had come and found the boy and caused him to die. 'Girl, do you love the man?' 'Yes.' 'Well then, go into the fire, so you can both be burnt.'

The girl leaped into the fire. They were both burnt, the two of them.

The fire died down. The moriman took the ashes. He went to his room and stayed there for one month. He made a woman and a man, complete. He brought them out as human people. He said, 'Aha, chief. I've completed the task you called me for. Here is the man, and the woman.' The chief said, 'Thank you, thank you, thank you.' He paid the moriman and the moriman went off.

The boy came out with his wife. He said, 'Father, I cannot live here. I will go up country, far away.' 'All right, my son, all right. Go, with your wife.'

They went off travelling. They spent the day travelling – the whole day. But hunger seized the man. He became weak all over, unable to travel. Now there was a woman there who'd ordered out men to clear a swamp garden for her. The men went to clear the swamp. The girl had cooked rice with meat for them – a lot of it – and put the food on her head. Now she was taking it to her workers.

She met the man, the two of them, him and his wife. 'E! that's a fine man, isn't he! I'll follow him in marriage.' The first girl said, 'No! No! No! I won't allow it.' 'E! If you agree to me following him in marriage, I'll take this cooked rice and give it to him, and he can eat it – the rice for my workers. I'll not give it to them.' The other girl said, 'All right.'

She gave him the rice. They sat down and ate. 'All right. Let's go.'

They set out. They went on and met a woman at a riverside, a mother of a young child, washing. She said, 'E! that's a fine man! I'll follow him in marriage.' The second girl said, 'I'll not allow it. No! No! No! I took my rice, the rice for my workers, I gave it to the man, he ate the rice, my workers were left just like that, I didn't give them their rice. Now you come and say just like that that you love the man. I won't allow it.' The other girl said, 'If you'll let me follow him, and let him marry me – you see this water here, this big river? There are many crocodiles here. No one can cross it without throwing someone into the water for the crocodiles to eat. Right then. If you want to cross over quickly in the boat so the crocodiles won't catch you, I'll take my child and throw him to the crocodiles. So – let's cross.' The other said, 'All right. Throw your child in.'

The mother took her child and threw him into the water. They got into the boat quickly, and crossed quickly. The crocodiles didn't catch them. They set off again.

Now, in the village they were going to the chief was by now old. But no stranger was allowed to go in unless he could show where the chief's afterbirth was buried. When they reached the village, the chief's daughter, his first-born, said, 'E! ha! I love the man who's come to our village. I'll go there and marry him.' Then the other one said 'No! No! I won't agree. I took my own child, I threw him to the crocodiles in the river, we got into the boat, we found a chance to cross over. Now we've reached here, this village here, you come and say you're coming to our husband and marrying him. I won't allow it.' The chief's daughter said, 'Oh? If you let me come in marriage to your husband, I'll show you the secret of the village. So then your husband won't be killed. Whenever a stranger comes to this village he has to show where the chief's afterbirth is buried. Well, if you allow me to come to your husband in marriage, I will show him the place tomorrow.' 'All right.' 'Tomorrow when he gets up in the morning and stands on the veranda, and stands and looks, I will be sweeping the compound. And where I beat out the broom – that is the place. I'll do that as many as six times, let him look there.'

Well then, he was tested by the old people of the village. 'Stranger! Well now, a stranger cannot come into the village here unless he can show where the chief's afterbirth is buried. If you don't know the place, we will kill you.' The man said, 'Oh, well, all right. Everything there is, is as God wills.' He went and showed the place: 'Is it not here?' 'It is there.'

The old chief of the village died. After he'd died the stranger who had shown where his afterbirth was was made the next chief. He lived for a long time in that chiefship, and had children by all of his wives. He lived many years.

Then that chief came to die. His wives were left with the children, those the chief had fathered.

Then the wives got up. The one who had gone into the fire with the man said, 'My child owns the inheritance.' Then the next one said, 'It is not your child who owns the inheritance; my child owns it. I took the rice I'd cooked for the workers I'd summoned and gave it to the man, for he was unable to walk for the hunger that oppressed him. My rice saved him. I abandoned my workers.' Another said, 'No. That's not so. My own child – I took him and threw him to the crocodiles in the big river. We found a chance to cross in the boat. If I'd not done that, we would never have crossed the river. The crocodiles would have eaten you.' Then said another, 'E! What about me? I came and showed my father's afterbirth, so the stranger wouldn't be killed. He saw where the afterbirth was buried. My father died. Now, you come and say it is your child who owns the inheritance. No, it is my child who owns the inheritance.'

Well, of all these women, those four wives, whose child owns the inheritance?[7]

Those present debated it light-heartedly but without making much of an issue of it – probably the first wife: without her he wouldn't have survived to marry the others, would he? But the story would have been enjoyable whether or not the narrator had chosen to sign off with an enjoyable intellectual teaser. The deeper import lay less in the verbally posed dilemma than in the story's oblique delineation of the unavoidable tensions of daily life: the position of wives, of women and of children; the forces of individual choices and of love; the contrary pulls of contending obligations and relationships.

Such themes are not confined to Limba story-tellers, nor to the particular era in which I heard them told. Comparable stories among the neighbouring Kuranko speakers have been described as 'allegories' in Michael Jackson's insightful account (1982), a term that perhaps suggests something more systematic and explicit than would be the case for Limba (and perhaps other) tales. But there is indeed a sense in which, as he puts it, narratives can be deployed to 'dramatise uncertainty ... [and] reflect on customs and values which are ordinarily not brought into discussion' (Jackson 1982: 2). It is not so much the specific plots or characters as the social and personal issues formulated through the power of narrative to shape or challenge perceptions and organise experience through the frame of temporally unfolding fiction.

Throughout Africa, and beyond, there are tales of life, death, and struggle, of the birth and heroic careers of miraculous children, of relations between men and women, competition, travel, trickery, failures, successes. Such narratives, written or oral, are not confined to fictional tales with inward-looking local import but also include accounts which directly or riddlingly tell of relations and attitudes between larger powers. Limba historical accounts were oriented towards the Islamic powers and peoples to the north rather than the more west-focused coast, the Nigerian Igbo stories pit their accounts and values against the hegemonic claims of the kingdom of Benin (Okpewho 1998a: 5, 1998b), and narrative after narrative lace their tellings with themes of domination, power, powerlessness, gender, identity, government or resistance. So, too, with the life stories of migrant workers and others in which they organise their experiences and make them real, while in the prolific popular novels people not only steep themselves in vicarious experience but also engage in the meaningful enshaping of their own and others' relationships and of their interpretation of the world.[8] Narrative is not just a matter of ephemeral local performance but has wider ramifications, its

---

[7] Transcribed (then translated) from version told by Fanka Konteh, 1961.
[8] For a recent overview of this flourishing tradition in both European and African languages (often overlooked by generalising scholars) see Newell 2002b, also Furniss 1998 and relevant chapters in Irele and Gikandi 2004.

plots and organisational potential extending beyond particular time and place, a master frame for formulating the understanding of just about every sphere of human endeavour.

Of timeless Africa and modernising west

A narrative frame similarly underlies many of the prevailing approaches to the continent and peoples of Africa, yet a further way in which words are marshalled in the form of story. As with the Limba and other tales, these accounts both shape and express more general understandings and judgements. One of the most compelling of these stories, widely known in both Africa and Europe, is a familiar offshoot of the pervasive binary paradigm. It tells of the timelessness of Africa and its peoples – the tale of a continent that lacks the historical events and actions which characterise the unfolding temporal experience of the west. Africa is age-old, passive, traditional, an earnest of the far-away past when the world was more innocent and closer to nature than now.[9]

This long-told story circulates in continually recycling versions, feeding on that far-reaching mythic division between a world that is traditional, rural, oral, collective and unchanging, set against a newer world of modernity, development, urban-ness, literacy and action. It depicts the colonised and non-westerner as existing somehow outside time – the primitive and non-rational child of nature who must be brought by others into the full historical experience of true humanity. In more romantic versions it carries nostalgic evocations of a time when we – and humankind – were young, in touch with our roots and untrammelled by the impositions of intellectualising rationality. The story pits the artificiality of urban modernity and self-seeking individualism against older harmonious community or, alternatively but with mutually entangled roots, draws two-way contrasts between barbarism and civilisation, Africa and Europe, orality and literacy – opposed stages and types of culture.

The strands combine in the tales about Africa. 'Timelessness' remains one of the 'most common approaches [to African history] ... Africa as a traditional, unchanging or timeless continent, incapable of adapting to modernity' (Chabal and Daloz 1999: 144). The scenario for event and action lies in civilised western societies, we are told, while Africa has remained dormant. Even for the recent 'Commissioners for Africa' Africa is still 'that great giant finally beginning to stir itself from its ... slumber' (Commission for Africa Report 2005: Declaration). This essentially unchanging continent – so goes an intertwined version – is characterised by a series of profoundly ingrained properties. 'African culture', 'the African Mind', 'African Tradition', age-old myths, or the 'real authentic Africa' are the recurrent *dramatis personae* in such tales, enduring not just in Africa itself but in the spreading African diaspora. Used to devalue by some tellers such tales can also be told to identify and celebrate African qualities and pursuits. From *négritude/*

[9] In these sections I have made sparing use of quote marks around such concepts as 'civilised', 'tribalism', 'modernisation' etc. since the stories discussed can be taken as, in a sense, in quotes throughout.

Présence africaine authors like Janheinz Jahn, Father Placide Tempels or Léopold Sédar Senghor and the seminal diaspora writers who in one sense helped to create 'Africa', to more recent 'Afrocentric' approaches by proponents like Molefi Asante (1998) or George Ayittey (2005), influential voices have variously told of the enduring tradition, harmony and communal balance at the heart of true African culture.[10]

In one way these grand narratives seem of a far different order from tales such as those by the Limba tellers presented here, and to work at a different level. But these larger stories can affect our understandings of the local stories – and vice versa. Read within their narrative frame the Limba and comparable local tales might seem best approached as part of a shared African culture, handed down through the ages, dating back, maybe, to something like the start of time.

A Limba story about the origin of death might seem an apt example. This tells how God wanted people to live for ever but his plan was foiled on the way:

> The toad – ah, the toad did not love us. God was squeezing out leaves for a herbal potion. He squeezed out the potion. He wanted people not to see death.
>
> He said, 'But who will carry the potion to the Limba?'
>
> The snake said, 'I will carry it.'
>
> But the toad said, 'No. *I* will carry it to them. We're near each other.' But he – ah! – he did not love us. He wanted to kill us all.
>
> 'Here's the potion' he was told. He put the bowl on his head to carry it, he set out. As soon as he jumped, *tɔliŋ!* [sound and movement of the jump], the potion fell off, *bukute!* [the potion spilling]. He spilt it.
>
> Ah! It had been laid down that whoever carried that potion must not spill it. The toad did not let the snake who loved us bring it to us. The one who hated us, it was he brought it. He went and upset it.
>
> So, if you now see us dying, it is because of the toad. The white people and we the Limba – we would not have died but for the toad.
>
> And now, this is how it is between us and the toad: where we build houses, that's where he loves to be. And that's why we drive him out. But the snake, who loved us in the beginning, is always pursuing the toad – and the toad runs to us for refuge. Well, the one who loved us then, well, when we meet him now, we kill him. We do not kill the toad. Well, God looks at us for that.
>
> Since you said you wanted to hear about it, that is how we are with the toad. That is it. It is finished.[11]

This could indeed be interpreted as springing from a shared African inheritance, for stories on these lines occur widely in Africa (Abrahamsson 1951). The details vary; in another Sierra Leone tale God's chosen messenger was a dog and it was a snake who stole the skin meant to save mankind from death (Carey 1970). But the basic plot is apparently widespread. Here it seems is a perfect example of age-old tradition, of authentic African experience. So too with the manifold animal trickster stories, not just in Africa itself but

---

[10] For some recent reviews of the large and controversial literature around 'Afrocentrism', the diaspora, and the image of 'Africa' (too extensive to cover here) see Baaz and Palmberg 2001, Farias 2003b, Howe 1998, Okpewho et al. 1999, Sweet 2003 (Introduction), Walker 2001.

[11] Transcribed, then translated, from the telling by Sangbang Yeleme, Kakarima, 1961.

strongly surviving through the African diaspora. Such instances seem to exhibit the enduring heart of Africa.

But in other ways the narrative of unchanging homogeneous Africa is less than illuminating. For the Limba 'death' tale, this interpretation turns our gaze away from other significant dimensions. As explained earlier, individual tellers did much to mould their tales and, familiar and evocative as their basic plots often were, their import for those intimately involved in the actual performance went far beyond that narrative skeleton. It was the same here. The version above was from a telling by a young man-boy, Sangbang Yeleme, who had himself experienced his share of tragedy. He had hoped to travel and perhaps go to school but the spirits of the dead had clearly not willed it for crippling stomach pains from which he still suffered had prevented him. Even more crippling, he had been unable to enter the initiation rituals with his peers and was left in the between-state of no longer young boy but not-yet-man. Sangbang told the tale with quiet sadness, evoking the uncontrollable paradoxes and unpredictabilities of life, where the tragedy lay not so much in the bringing of death as in the reversal by which we care for the toad, the one who hated us, and kill the snake who would have helped us. In his telling it was a profoundly tragic tale.

It was not the only version I heard. The basic plot recurred – God sending medicine to stop humans dying, the toad rushing in to replace the messenger and spilling it. But the three individuals I heard telling it each made it something different. Instead of Sangbang's moving and painful drama, a more travelled and light-hearted teller produced a rollicking characterisation of the amusing antics of animals (that is, of people) which had listeners rocking with laughter. A third, the imaginative narrator and smith Karanke Dema, gave a long-drawn-out and ironic account of the different twists in the tale, lengthening it to a fuller conclusion on the emotive Limba theme of the dire results of disobedience. To look only to some arguably 'old' features of the plot in such tellings is to miss an essential dimension of their meaning.

The timeless nostalgic story continues to attract – and indeed for some moods, some viewpoints, some purposes, it can be compelling. Limba elders too, among them the author of the chapter's opening story, often lauded the good old days when children were obedient, elders were listened to and people lived without quarrelling. But as a comprehensive approach to understanding the diverse experiences within Africa, even of people's diverse ways with narrative, it is scarcely convincing. It slurs over the historical shaping of plot or performance within specific regions or periods, of how some are indeed perhaps older (in certain senses) than others, or some but not others defined (and utilised) in particular situations as 'the traditional.' It passes over the multiform events, contests, conquests, struggles, alliances and diversities, that, like anywhere else, are part of Africa's past and present and within which the period of colonialism was only one episode among many. The gathering critiques by African historians and others of the 'timeless', generalising and romanticising mystique of 'Africa' have been making clear that this master story is in many respects positively misleading as an account of the experiences and actions of Africa, of Africans and of their past and present interactions in the world at large.

The theme of 'modernisation' set against tradition gives another twist to the story. The imperial mission and its associated modern developments play their parts in this great narrative, moving Africa onwards in the road to progress. Some versions portray a radical and mutually exclusive disjuncture between the impervious tradition of Africa and the attainments of modernity. Others recount a gradual transition, perhaps with set-backs on the way and survivals of the 'old' Africa of the past. Either way if Africa has a chance of going forward at all, it can only be through following on in the modern ways of the west.

This still popular account resonates powerfully with people's experience both within and outside Africa, partially shaped as this can be by that very story. It is a key theme in many accounts of African history both within and outside the continent, usually going along with the teleological tale of true individuality, creativity and modernity being attained quintessentially through the written word. The 'traditional' stories of Africa, while perhaps valuable in a nostalgic way, are here presented as belonging to an early stage as against literature and culture in their 'full' sense which pertain to written works in European languages accessible to, and valued by, the western scholarly world. Written forms and their alliance with the forces of urbanisation, western education, economic development and 'democratisation' – in short with 'modernisation' – are the road to the future.

This clutch of stories has of course long been questioned, and, alongside other 'grand' narratives, has been forcibly criticised in recent years for, variously, their hidden ideological construction of 'modernity', their ethnocentric self-interest, for mistaking a specific set of historical circumstances for an all-encompassing universal, or for downplaying the diverse pathways of human culture by overestimating the west's modernising impact. But their power has not vanished. We are still, it seems, swayed by the tale of how true communication, development and individual self-fulfilment are brought by the written word and the wonders of modern technology, downplaying the fertile oral modes or suggesting that these, as 'pre-modern', 'pre-literate', 'traditional', or 'backward', are somehow incompatible with the contemporary world of today.

Even just the case of Limba stories back in the 1960s shatters the assumption that without writing, urban development or cash economy there can be no true creativity or change. Limba tales, even those recycling well-known plots, were no passive handing down of 'age-old' traditions. As in any cultural tradition (not excluding, of course, the traditions of western literature and historiography), the repertoire of familiar plots, characters, motifs, metaphors, narrative twists and much more were manipulated and stretched by their individual narrators into personally created and often very different works of art. A talented story-teller like Karanke Dema could indeed speak of himself as learning his stories from earlier tellers and from 'the dead' – but *also* as thinking about his story beforehand and enlarging it from his own heart.

Even a generation ago Limba story-telling was far from focused just on what the 'changeless Africa' proponents would regard as 'traditional' plots and themes. One tale depicted the chief's spoilt daughter refusing to be

68

married without six diamond combs and the hilarious way the chief had to keep going back to the once-poor man who had found diamonds inside a fish; he ended up giving him money, cheques, banks, a house, a car, even a new name, 'you will be called "Millionaire", the money in your hands will never come to an end and everyone who wants anything will have to go and borrow from you' – evocative indeed for an audience well acquainted with the diamond smuggling industry on the Sierra Leonean-Liberian borders. Or we hear a humorous account of how lorries were invented. God handed out gifts to the different animals, with a wheel for the dog and wisdom for the white man (you can see on his bald head where God poured the wisdom-water in). The animals went to bathe – 'their smells were a bit strong where they'd all been rubbing up against each other' – and left their gifts on the riverbank. But what the white man then did was to make off with the wheel. He swam and swam and swam with it across the sea till he got to England and finally worked out what to use it for – a lorry. So now whenever a lorry comes humming along the dog jumps at it to get his wheel back – 'but oh! the power the Europeans had been given! All that happens is that the dog is killed.'[12] All this is basically no different from the case in highly literate contexts where familiar plots and themes are sometimes revered as something 'old', sometimes reshaped into new forms (or both). But this is far from saying that current forms somehow 'belong' to the past or are insulated from the present.

The modernisation story can in fact only with difficulty be brought into accord with the diverse vibrancies of actual practice. Take the case of writing, regularly presented as one of the key factors in the modernising process. It is, certainly, a prolifically used medium and its entanglement with other dominant institutions of the contemporary world means that access to it can carry great social significance. But that is different from giving it automatic (and 'progressive') consequences in itself. The newer literacy studies, rightly critical of the misleading ethnocentric preconceptions built into the one-way civilising (and alphabetising) story, make clear that there are manifold different forms and processes in which writing can be used – or not used.[13] And contrary to the suggestion that oral forms must somehow be part of the past and on the way out in the modern world, in practice they abound in today's towns and villages, among young people as well as old, and in contexts which it would be hard indeed to regard as anything but contemporary. In Africa as elsewhere we see the mingling of oral with other media of expression in so many situations of today, in plays, songs, sermons, life stories … . Spoken and sung genres flourish on radio, television, film and video, on the streets, in the bars, in the homes. Writing, voice, electronic and broadcast media intersect in a host of contexts, vigorous diverse modes of doing things with words that the simplifying stories about Africa would have us neglect.

Many narrators and audiences are still moved by these tales of a timeless Africa with its age-old traditions and lack of history – tales told in Africa as well as Europe or America. There is indeed something uplifting about certain

---

[12] These two stories were told, respectively, by Suriba 'Nevertire' Konteh and Suri Kamara in 1961 (full translations in Finnegan 1967: 206ff, 270ff).

[13] See for example Barton et al. 2000, Cope and Kalantzis 2000, Kress 2003, Street 1993.

of the aspirations which some such stories still project. But as a framework for understanding either the experience of 'Africa' in general or the specifics of African stories and story-telling in particular cases it is too often a denial of the multiplicity of ways that, in Africa and beyond, people creatively do things with storying words.

Of being silenced by outsiders

Another narrative revolves around silence. It imagines an Africa silenced by the successively intruding forces of slavery, imperialism, colonialism, neo-colonialism and globalisation. The narrative is indeed a tragic one. From the horrific fate of the transported slaves, torn by force from their culture, their possessions and their freedom, to the endurers of colonialism and neo-colonialism or the victims of the exploitative economic giants that bestride and exploit the world, this story vividly depicts the external forces acting on Africa and Africans. It has come in varied permutations over the years with many sub-themes and alternative villains, but the basic plot revolves round the sad situation of Africa, cut off by external attackers from the riches of the powerful elsewhere in the world, and outside the mainstream of international culture.

This story has a long background, recounted in many situations and for many purposes. It was told in the struggles for colonial freedom, and again retold where the villain was the neo-colonialism that controlled ostensibly independent states from outside. It brings out not just the overt political and economic forces that silence and imprison the victims but also the cultural and linguistic domination that 'colonises the mind' (after Ngugi wa Thiong'o 1986) and the privileging of alphabetic literacy that not only disvalues but defines into non-existence the oral – and the Muslim – voices of Africa. More recent versions have been powerfully purveyed in the 'colonial discourse' and 'post-colonial' narratives recounted by intellectuals like Bhabha, Said or Spivak to portray the exploited fate of the excluded 'others' of Asia and Africa where even their writings have been colonised.[14] A horde of villains – slavery, colonialism, neo-colonialism, capitalism, Orientalism, 'colonial discourse', 'othering', globalisation – are shown suppressing and de-voicing their victims, quintessentially within Africa but in the African diaspora too and also to an extent in the 'non-western' world at large. The victims are downtrodden into silence by the mighty forces of western expansion and aggrandisement. It is a moving and highly credible tale for its many tellers and hearers both within Africa and elsewhere.

It will scarcely come as news that its more extreme versions have been challenged. The silence and loss was not after all total. African historians have for many years now been revealing the complex actions, factions, politics and viewpoints within the continent of Africa before, during and after the colonial years: to cast these actors as meaningless pawns is both

[14] Stories by now crystallised enough to have been gathered in such collections as Barker et al. 1994, Williams and Chrisman 1993.

patronising and uninformed. Even for the dreadful experiences of slavery that silencing story can be simplistic. African slaves were indeed monstrously deprived of their liberty and their possessions, sometimes defined as excluded from humankind itself – but their voices travelled with them. As vividly demonstrated in such analyses as Betty Kuyk's *African Voices in the African American Heritage* (2003), far from being culture-less, rootless and unspeaking victims, they carried and re-created their stories, oratory, songs, and constructed new forms too. The narratives of colonialism are similarly being reassessed as African perspectives replace or challenge the 'master narrative of colonial domination', as Searing has it (2002: xxiv). The colonised were not mute but active and vocal agents. Ngugi wa Thiong'o recounts the power of orature: 'the resistance aesthetics of the entire anti-colonial struggle ... is best seen in the vast body of oral songs and poems and in the accompanying performances' ([1981] 1997: 23). African voices have long been communicating through written forms too. The vigorous print culture in Africa dates back at least to the early nineteenth century, an active presence in African (not just European) languages. In the colonial Gold Coast people were 'playing the game of life' by turning the tools of literacy to their own ends (Newell 2002a) while flourishing Hausa novellas of the 1930s

> constituted part of a pre-existing and subsequent multi-generic dialogue about the nature of a wide variety of West African societies, and the notion that such a dialogue (in *any* of Nigeria's 400 languages) fell silent in the face of English is, to anyone who knows Nigeria, quite laughable (Furniss 1998: 92).

Leading African historians have long taken issue with the patronising 'victim' story. I think, for example, of Ajayi's well-targeted criticisms of the image of 'the frustrated, paralysed, helpless African' and his challenge to colonial historians to do more than merely regurgitate tales of passively endured exploitation (Ajayi 1968: 200). The tale depicting Africa as controlled by outside powers, where external intruders call the tune leaving local inhabitants inactive and inarticulate, is being countered by scholars both within and outside Africa tracing out the complex actions and influences of the many parties and forces with their local and historical specificities – actions almost totally missing in the generalised tales of sweeping European domination. There has been a comparable reaction against the similarly generalised and often demeaning picture implied in those 'post-colonial' analyses that both underestimate colonial people's agency and build up unsustainably monolithic pictures not just of 'Africa' but of 'colonialism', 'Orientalism', 'imperialism', 'the west', or whoever the current rampaging villain happens to be.[15] The homogenising tales need replacing by more subtle and discriminating accounts of the multiplicities of actors and interested parties, interacting, communicating, contending and changing over the years.

The silencing tales continue to be told and it is perhaps unlikely they will ever themselves be totally silenced. And it is of course true that in Africa, as

---

[15] For relevant discussions see Ajayi 1968, Baaz and Palmberg 2001, Boahen 1987, Chabal and Daloz 1999, Cooper 2002, Searing 2002; in relation to postcolonial theory etc. see variously Ahmad 1992, Barber 1995b, Carrier 1995, Ramamurthy 2003, Thomas 1994.

anywhere, inequalities of access and of power exist – and at local and national levels as well as on a planetary scale. But just because some groups have not been listening (perhaps especially certain circles of intellectuals) it does not follow that no one has been speaking. The stories of Africa tell us otherwise – the actions and human subtleties formulated in the Limba or Kuranko or Igbo tales, the heroic narratives of West African griots, the storied images of Xhosa narrators, Somali and Hausa novels, Onitsha market literature, local newspaper stories, the dramatic productions of Yoruba touring companies, even the self-narratives of famine survivors in the Sudan. Boy soldiers caught up in the horrific civil wars of Sierra Leone told their own stories (Richards 1998) and even under the brutal hand of South African apartheid Basotho migrants recomposed and performed their personal and collective narratives 'because the unauthored life is not worth living' (Coplan 1994: 243). The amazing plenitude of written, oral and dramatised narratives that have circulated in Africa over the years gives the lie to the tales of silence: 'the "subaltern voices" so often assumed to be silent or suppressed can be heard loud and clear if one cares to locate oneself outside Western academies and networks' (Innes 2002). Now as in the past people exploit their ability, in whatever conditions, to use storied words to create and formulate and, in that sense, to control their experiences. They are not silent.

Storying and living

This chapter has juxtaposed some of the many tales told by Limba speakers and others in Africa with more generalising tales told *about* 'Africa.' In some ways these sets of tales are very different. Certainly it would seem naively over-relativistic to put both in the same basket. Limba stories are fictional, light-hearted, orally performed, fleeting, locally based, about particulars. The theoretical tales are serious, non-fictional, of general and para-local reach, often articulated in writing, and on the surface (at least) formulated as truth-seeking and generalised, scholarly analysis not entertainment.

Yet there are similarities. Both deploy heroes, events and outcomes, set in unfolding narrative sequence. There are elements of 'truth' and generality in the first too (in some tellings quite explicitly – an example would be the extended conclusion to Bubu's tug-of-war tale printed below in Chapter 10), while the overtly 'truth-claiming' purposes of the second are often intershot with metaphor, evaluation, sooth-saying and 'just-so' rhetoric. The boundaries of 'truth' and of 'fiction' are notoriously slippery after all, and all narrative genres, whether written or spoken, fiction or realism, have their own poetics. The 'local' seeming tales are not recounted only within the continental borders of Africa, nor are the theorising ones confined to European 'outsiders': they and others like them are told within Africa too. Written versions may seem more permanent and globally transportable perhaps – but are they? Oral narratives too have ways of travel. And they, too, treat of the great as well as the small human issues of life, of change, continuity, assertion of self-interest, dilemmas, agency, drawing them within the frame of narrative.

All these stories in fact – including those I regard as misleading – are examples of the human inclination to do things with storying words in ways that both affect and are shaped by experience. Not just among a few Limba narrators in the 1960s or just in the academic groves of contemporary Britain or America but throughout Africa and throughout the globe people participate in that great human resource of narrative, using stories to create and organise and manipulate their worlds. And this is what is ultimately missed in the generalising stories here – that human propensity for deploying narrative words and in doing so to encapsulate and control and comment on the world they inhabit.

This is not to say that storying can bring all the prizes people might wish for, remove their problems, or transmit some objective and disinterested account of the world. Humans inevitably labour under constraints and limitations – some more directly felt than others – and act within the specificities of their social and historic situations. But, amidst all this, storied words remain an amazing and unending resource. People emplot their actions and their understandings of the world through the narratives they recount and listen to; 'a life as led is inseparable from a life that is told', as Jerome Bruner put it, 'not "how it was" but how it is interpreted and reinterpreted, told and retold' (1987: 31). Whether inside or outside Africa we construct our own and others' identities and aspirations and meanings through stories. Words – the sustained and meaningful unfolding of narrative words – are not 'mere' words but ways of doing and experiencing, of asserting reality.

And there are multiple stories, whether in 'the west' or anywhere else, formulated by tellers and audiences of multifarious backgrounds, interests, situations and times. We surely now no longer assume that we can appropriately speak of 'the' stories of any one time or 'culture'. With all their (relatively) shared perceptions and arts, individual Limba story-tellers varied in their outlook, experience, age, circumstances and preoccupations. Biesele's account of Ju/'hoan (Bushman) narrators similarly reminds us of the dialogues *within* traditions (1999: 162) while Jackson rightly speaks of Kuranko narratives as affording insight 'not into *the* Kuranko world, but into *a* Kuranko world' (1982: 5). Here too the would-be comprehensive narratives fail by leaving little space for creativity and diversity, too often with the implication that it is only some theorising master account constructed by outsiders that can 'really' make sense of African experience – something which could then be 'given' to Africa 'in the manner of overseas assistance' (White et al. 2002: 17).

This significance of storied words, however obvious in some ways, is still worth asserting, not least in face of the tales presenting Africa as somehow different. The images of a 'people with no history', dependent on others for progress or lacking the means of effective expression, still run deep. But the practice contradicts this. Not just in workaday or leisured lives but even amidst the extremest conditions of war or famine people actualise their capacity to story-tell, to chart what Ajayi once called 'the politics of survival' (1968: 199), to organise experience, forge understandings, change perceptions, and somehow reveal meaning through the sequencing of narrative. Plays, novels, self-narratives, stories of empire, tales of tricking and tricked spiders –

all can be used to chart and mould the puzzling, cruel, humorous or precious actualities and dreams of life. In spoken no less than written discourse people deploy that rich resource for creating their lives and those of others – the sustained, organised and co-ordinated narrative sequences of words.

II

Performing Literature

6

Literature as Oral,
the Oral as Literature[1]

It is not just in short performative clusters or in chains of narrative that words are laced together in deliberate and structured displays. They are also marshalled in poetry, song, drama, oratory and much else, complementing and overlapping the forms exemplified so far.

One familiar framework in which words are thus organised and displayed is written literature – not a concept without its own controversies, of course, but nevertheless a reasonably established comparative term for a form of human artistry that is widely celebrated as among the glories of human achievement. This is clearly one significant medium for doing things with words in Africa. It is true that its importance there was for long obscured by the image of Africa as most naturally the home of 'the traditional' and 'the oral'. But by the second half of the twentieth century, when I first became involved in African studies, some of the writing generated in Africa – principally that in European languages – was indeed coming to be recognised and studied as literature.

*Un*written genres however were much less widely known and appreciated. Some oral forms had indeed been massively collected and studied, but what might be considered their literary qualities attracted less interest and there seemed little if any incentive for scholars to treat them seriously *as* literature. Unwritten forms seemed to belong to categories like 'oral tradition' or 'folklore' rather than to literature. They did not fit easily into the familiar categories of literate cultures, were harder to record and present, and, for a superficial observer at least, were easier to sweep aside than written material.

---

[1] Originally published as Chapter 1 ('The "oral" nature of African unwritten literature') of *Oral Literature in Africa,* Oxford: Clarendon Press, 1970: 1–25. Apart from a new introduction, slight verbal amendments, some supplementary footnotes, and the omission of some outdated or over-detailed references, I have left this chapter as it was, a personal statement of its time (present tenses should thus be interpreted in the context of an account written in the late 1960s).

This chapter goes back to the late 1960s to take up these issues as they were emerging then, and in doing so crystallises a perspective which, with all its problems, has in essentials underlain much of my own and similar analyses of African forms over many years. It focuses in particular on the insights – and to some extent the problems – brought through the notion of 'oral literature'. This concept was certainly not new at that time (a point returned to in the next chapter) but had hitherto less often been applied in an African setting. The term 'oral literature' has since then gained wide, if controversial, currency in African and comparative studies and has become an accepted figure in many debates. But it also continues to raise questions, some of which are broached in this chapter and will also be resurfacing, in varying forms, throughout much of this volume.

Literature and performance

To those who have grown up in educational settings which, as in contemporary Europe, lay particular stress on literacy and written traditions, the concept of *oral* literary formulation may appear strange. It seems to evoke on the one hand the idea of crude and artistically undeveloped attempts at the 'real' thing, on the other perhaps of inevitably elusive mystery. Neither of these generalised presuppositions are ultimately justifiable, if only because oral literary forms are as diverse among themselves as are written ones. Nevertheless, there *are* certain characteristics of unwritten verbal art – what I am here terming oral literature – which arise from its oral nature. It is important to give these some attention at the outset as a background for a full appreciation of the status and qualities of many African literary forms.

There is no mystery about the first and most basic characteristic of oral literature – even though it is constantly overlooked in collections and analyses. This is the significance of the actual performance. Oral literature is by definition dependent on a performer who formulates it in words on a specific occasion – there is no other way in which it can be realised as a literary product. In the case of *written* literature a literary work can be said to have an independent and tangible existence in even one copy, so that questions about, say, the format, number, and publicising of other written copies can, though not irrelevant, be treated to some extent as secondary; there is, that is, a distinction between the actual creation of a written literary form and its further transmission. The case of oral literature is different. There the connection between transmission and very existence is a much more intimate one, and questions about the means of actual communication are of the first importance – without its oral realisation and direct rendition by singer or speaker, an unwritten literary piece cannot easily be said to have any continued or independent existence at all. In this respect the parallel is less to written literature than to music and dance, for these, too, are art forms which in the last analysis are actualised in and through their performance and, furthermore, in a sense depend on repeated performances for their continued existence.

The significance of performance in oral literature goes beyond a mere matter of definition for the nature of the performance itself can make an important contribution to the impact of the particular literary form being exhibited. This point is obvious if we consider literary forms designed to be delivered to an audience even in more familiar literate cultures. If we take forms like a play, a sermon, 'jazz poetry', even something as trivial as an after-dinner witty anecdote – in all these cases the actual delivery is a significant aspect of the whole. Even though it is true that these instances may *also* exist in written form, they only attain their true fulfilment when actually performed.

The same clearly applies to African oral literature. In, for example, the brief Akan dirge

Amaago, won't you look?
Won't you look at my face?
When you are absent, we ask of you.
You have been away long: your children are waiting for you (Nketia 1955: 184)

the printed words alone represent only a shadow of the full actualisation of the poem as an aesthetic experience for poet and audience. For, quite apart from the separate question of the overtones and symbolic associations of words and phrases, the actual enactment of the poem also involves the emotional situation of a funeral, the singer's beauty of voice, her sobs, facial expression, vocal expressiveness and movements (all indicating the sincerity of her grief), and, not least, the musical setting of the poem. In fact, all the variegated aspects we think of as contributing to the effectiveness of performance in the case of more familiar literary forms may also play their part in the delivery of unwritten pieces – expressiveness of tone, gesture, facial expression, dramatic use of pause and rhythm, the interplay of passion, dignity, or humour, receptivity to the reactions of the audience, etc., etc. Such devices are not mere embellishments superadded to the already existent literary work – as we think of them in regard to written literature – but an integral as well as flexible part of its full realisation as a work of art.

Unfortunately it is precisely this aspect which is most often overlooked in recording and interpreting instances of oral literature. This is partly due, no doubt, to practical difficulties; but even more to the unconscious reference constantly made by both recorders and readers to more familiar written forms. This model leads us to think of the *written* element as the primary and thus somehow the most fundamental material in every kind of literature – a concentration on the *words* to the exclusion of the vital and essential aspect of performance. It cannot be too often emphasised that this insidious model is a profoundly misleading one in the case of oral literature.

This point comes across the more forcibly when one considers the various resources available to the performers of African literary works to exploit the oral potentialities of their medium. We can note for example the striking consequences of the highly tonal nature of many African languages: tone is sometimes used as a structural element in literary expression and can be exploited by the oral artist in ways somewhat analogous to the use of rhyme or rhythm in written European poetry. Many instances of this can be cited from African poetry, proverbs, and, above all, drum literature. This stylistic aspect is almost completely unrepresented in written versions or studies of oral literature, and yet is clearly one which can be manipulated in a subtle and effective way in the actual process of delivery. The exploitation of musical resources can also play an important part, varying of course according to the artistic conventions of the particular genre in question. Most stories and proverbs tend to be delivered as spoken prose.[2] But the Southern Bantu praise poems, for instance, and the Yoruba hunters' *ijala* poetry are chanted in various kinds of recitative, employing a semi-musical framework. Other forms draw fully on musical resources and make use of singing by soloist or soloists not infrequently accompanied or supplemented by a chorus or in some cases by instruments. Indeed, much of what is normally classed as poetry in African oral literature is designed to be performed in a musical setting, and the musical and verbal elements are thus interdependent. An appreciation, therefore, of these sung forms (and to some extent the chanted ones also) depends on at least some awareness of the musical material on which the artist draws, and we cannot hope fully to understand their impact or subtlety if we consider only the bare words on a printed page.

In addition, performers have a range of resources at their disposal. The artists are typically face to face with their public and can take advantage of this to enhance the impact and even sometimes the content of their words. In many stories, for example, the characterisation of both leading and secondary figures may appear slight; but what in literate cultures must be written, explicitly or implicitly, into the text can in orally delivered forms be conveyed by more visible means – by the speaker's gestures, expression and mimicry. A particular atmosphere – whether of dignity for a king's official poet, light-hearted enjoyment for an evening story-teller, grief for a woman dirge singer – can be conveyed not only by a verbal evocation of mood but also by the dress, accoutrements or observed bearing of the performer. This visual aspect is sometimes taken even further than gesture and dramatic bodily movement and is expressed in the form of a dance, often joined by members of the audience (or chorus). In these cases the verbal content now represents only one element in a complete opera-like performance which combines words, music and dance. Though this extreme type is not characteristic of all forms of oral literature in Africa, it is nevertheless not uncommon; and even in cases where the verbal element seems to predominate (sometimes in co-ordination with music), the actual delivery and movement of the performer may partake of something of the element of dancing in a way which to both performer and audience enhances the aesthetic effectiveness of the occasion.

Much more could be said about the many other means which oral performers can employ to project their literary products – the use, for instance, of vivid ideophones or of dramatised dialogue, or manipulation of the audience's sense of humour or susceptibility (when played on by a skilled performer) to be amazed, or shocked, or moved, or enthralled at appropriate moments. But it should be clear already that oral literature has somewhat different potentialities from written literature, and additional resources which oral artists can develop for their own purposes; and that this aspect is of primary significance for its appreciation as a mode of aesthetic expression.

[2] I would now in the early twenty-first century regard this statement as an over-simplification (see Chapter 4, p. 46).

The detailed ways in which performers enact the literary products of their art naturally vary both from culture to culture and also among the different literary genres of one language. Not all types of performance involve the extremes of dramatisation. Sometimes indeed the artistic conventions demand the exact opposite – a dignified aloof bearing, and emphasis on continuity of delivery rather than on studied and receptive style in the exact choice of words. This was so, for instance, of the professional reciter of historical Rwanda poetry, an official conscious of his intellectual superiority over amateurs and audience alike:

> Contrairement à l'amateur, qui gesticule du corps et de la voix, le récitant professionnel adopte une attitude impassible, un débit rapide et monotone. Si l'auditoire réagit en riant ou en exprimant son admiration pour un passage particulièrement brillant, il suspend la voix avec détachement jusqu'à ce que le silence soit rétabli. (Coupez and Kamanzi 1962: 8)

> (transl. 'In contrast to the amateur who gesticulates with his body and voice, the professional reciter adopts an impassive manner, a rapid and monotonous delivery. If the audience react with laughter or express their admiration of a particularly brilliant passage, he interrupts his flow, indifferent, until there is silence again.')

This might seem the antithesis of a reliance on the arts of performance for the projection of the poem. In fact it was part of this particular performance convention and, for the audience, an essential part. To this kind of austere style of delivery we can contrast the highly emotional atmosphere in which southern Sotho praise poets were expected to pour out their panegyrics. Out of the background of song by soloist and chorus, working up to a pitch of excitement and highly charged emotion,

> the chorus increases in its loudness to be brought to a sudden stop with shrills of whistles and a voice (of the praise poet) is heard: 'Ka-mo-hopola mor'a-Nyeo!' (I remember the son of so-and-so!)
> Behind that sentence lurks all the stored up emotions and without pausing, the name ... is followed by an outburst of uninterrupted praises, save perhaps by a shout from one of the listeners: 'Ke-ne ke-le teng' (I was present) as if to lend authenticity to the narration. The praiser continues his recitation working himself to a pitch, till he jumps this way and that way while his mates cheer him ... and finally when his emotion has subsided he looks at his mates and shouts: 'Ntjeng, Banna' (lit. Eat me, you men). After this he may burst again into another ecstasy to be stopped by a shout from him or from his friends: 'Ha e nye bolokoe kaofela!' or 'Ha e nye lesolanka!' a sign that he should stop. (Mofokeng 1945: 137)

Different again are the styles adopted by many story-tellers where there may be little of this sort of emotional intensity, but where the vividness and, often, humour of the delivery add drama and meaning to the relatively simple and straightforward wording. Lamba narrators in what was then Northern Rhodesia have been particularly well described:

> It would need a combination of phonograph and kinematograph to reproduce a tale as it is told. ... Every muscle of face and body spoke, a swift gesture often supplying the place of a whole sentence. ... The animals spoke each in

81

its own tone: the deep rumbling voice of Momba, the ground hornbill, for example, contrasting vividly with the piping accents of Sulwe, the hare ... (Smith and Dale 1920, Vol. 2: 336).

Even within the same cultural tradition there may be many set styles of performance designed to suit the different literary genres recognised in the culture. Indeed these genres are sometimes primarily distinguished from each other in terms of their media of performance rather than their content or purpose. In Yoruba poetry, for instance, the native classification is not according to subject-matter or structure but by the group to which the reciter belongs and, in particular, by the technique of recitation and voice production. Thus there is *ijala* (chanted by hunters in a high-pitched voice), *rara* (a slow, wailing type of chant), and *ewi* (using a falsetto voice), and even though the content of various types may often be interchangeable, a master in one genre will not feel competent to perform a different type: he may know the words but cannot manage the necessary subtleties of tone and style and the required type of voice production (Gbadamosi and Beier 1959: 9-10; Babalǫla 1966: vi, 23). Many other cases could also be cited where the mode of performance is as significant for the native critic as actual content or structure.

We also need to take some account of the question of improvisation and original composition. In other words, something more may be involved in the delivery of an oral piece than the fact of its actualisation and re-creation in and through the performance, aided by a technique of delivery that heightens its artistic effectiveness. There are also the cases when the performer introduces variations on older pieces or even totally new forms in terms of the detailed wording, the structure, or the content.

The extent of this kind of innovation, of course, varies with both genre and individual performer, and the question of original composition is a difficult one. It is clear that the process is by no means the same in all non-literate cultures or all types of oral literature. There are, for instance, the long-considered and rehearsed compositions of Chopi singers, the more facile improvisation of a leader in a boat- or dance-song, the combination and recombination of known motifs into a single unique performance among Limba story-tellers. There are also cases, like the Rwanda poet just mentioned, where there is interest in the accuracy and authenticity of the wording (at least in outline) and where memorisation rather than creation is the expected role of the performer.

In spite of the importance of these diversities (to be considered further in Chapter 7), one of the striking characteristics of oral as distinct from written literature is often its verbal variability. What might be called the 'same' poem or prose piece may be variable to such an extent that one has to take some account at least of the original contribution of the artist who is actualising it – and not simply in terms of the technique of delivery. Take for instance the case of Ankole praise poems. Since the ideas expressed in these poems are stereotyped and repetitive, the *omwevugi* (poet/reciter) must change the wording to obtain variety:

> [He] has to rely to a great extent upon the manner in which he expresses these ideas in order to give beauty and interest to his poem. Herein lies the art of the

accomplished *omwevugi* who, by the ingenious choice of his vocabulary, can repeat identical themes time and time again, always with a different and startling turn of phrase. (Morris 1964: 25)

Again, there is the production of stories among the Thonga. It is worth quoting Junod's excellent description of this at some length. Having postulated the 'antiquity' of Thonga tales, he goes on:

This antiquity is only relative: that is to say they are constantly transformed by the narrators and their transformations go much further than is generally supposed, further even than the Natives themselves are aware of. After having heard the same stories told by different story-tellers, I must confess that I never met with exactly the same version. First of all *words* differ. Each narrator has his own style, speaks freely and does not feel in any way bound by the expressions used by the person who taught him the tale. It would be a great error to think that, writing a story at the dictation of a Native, we possess the recognized standard form of the tale. There is no standard at all! ...

The same can be said with regard to *the sequence of the episodes;* although these often form definite cycles, it is rare to hear two narrators follow exactly the same order. They arrange their material as they like, sometimes in a very awkward way. ...

I go further: *New elements* are also introduced, owing to the tendency of Native story-tellers always to apply circumstances of their environment to the narration. This is one of the charms of Native tales. They are living, viz., they are not told as if they were past and remote events, in an abstract pattern, but considered as happening amongst the hearers themselves. ... So all the new objects brought by civilisation are, without the slightest difficulty, made use of by the narrator. ...

Lastly, my experience leads me to think that, in certain cases, the *contents of the stories* themselves are changed by oral transmission, this giving birth to numerous versions of a tale, often very different from each other and sometimes hardly recognisable. (Junod 1913, Vol. 2: 198–200)

The scope of the artist to improvise or create may vary, but there is almost always *some* opportunity for 'composition'. It comes out in the exact choice of word and phrase, the stylistic devices like the use of ideophones, asides, or repetitions, the ordering of episodes or verses, new twists to familiar plots or the introduction of completely new ones, improvisation or variation of solo lines even while the chorus remains the same – as well, of course, as all the elaborations and modifications to which the musical aspect is subject. Such additions and changes naturally take place within the current literary and cultural conventions – but what is involved, nevertheless, is some degree of individual creativity. With only a few exceptions, this process is likely to enter into the actualisation of any piece of oral literature, which thus becomes in one sense a unique literary work – the work rendered on one particular occasion.

The variability of oral literary forms has tended to be overlooked by many writers. This is largely because of certain theoretical assumptions held in the past about the verbatim handing down of oral tradition supposedly typical of non-literate societies. The model of written literature has also been misleading in this context, with its concept of exact transmission through manuscripts or printing press. It must therefore be stressed yet again that many of the characteristics we now associate with a written literary tradition do not always apply to oral art. There is not necessarily any concept of an 'authentic version', and when a particular literary piece is being transmitted to an audience the concepts of extemporisation or elaboration are often more likely to be to the fore than that of memorisation. There is likely to be little of the split, familiar from written forms, between composition and performance or between creation and transmission. A failure to realise this has led to many misconceptions – in particular the presentation of one version as *the* correct and authentic one – and to only a partial understanding of the crucial contribution made by the actual performer.[3]

A further essential factor is the audience, which, as is not the case with written forms, is often directly and immediately involved in the actualisation and creation of a piece of oral literature. According to convention, genre and personality, the artist may be more or less receptive to the listeners' reactions – but, with few exceptions (e.g. the solitary working songs, some herding songs, and sometimes individual rehearsals for later performance), an audience of some kind is normally an essential part of the whole literary situation. There is no escape for oral artists from a face-to-face confrontation with an audience, and this is something which they can exploit as well as be influenced by. Sometimes individual performers choose to involve their listeners directly, as in story-telling situations where it is common for the narrator to open with a formula which explicitly arouses the audience's attention, often with the expectation that they will participate actively in the narration and, in particular, join in the choruses of songs which the teller introduces into the narrative. The audience can be exploited in similar ways in the performance of poetry, particularly in sung lyrics where it is common practice for the poet to act as leader, singing and improvising the verse line, while the audience performs as a chorus keeping up the burden of the song, sometimes to the accompaniment of dancing or instrumental music. In such cases the close connection between artist and audience can almost turn into an identity, the chorus directly participating in at least certain parts of the performance.

Even in less formalised relationships the actual literary expression can be greatly affected by the presence and reactions of the audience. For one thing, the type of audience involved can affect the presentation of an oral piece – performers may tend, for instance, to omit obscenities, certain types of jokes, or complex forms in the presence of, say, children or missionaries (or even foreign students) which they would include in other contexts. And direct references to the characteristics, behaviour, or fortunes of particular listeners can also be brought in with great effectiveness in a subtle and flexible way not usually open to written literature. Members of the audience, too, need not confine their participation to silent listening or a mere acceptance of the chief performer's invitation to participate – they may also in some circumstances break into the performance with additions, queries, or even criticisms. This is common not only in the typical and expected case of story-telling but even in such formalised situations as that of the complex Yoruba *ijala* hunters' chants. A performance by one *ijala* artist is critically listened to by other experts

---

[3] The general point here remains important but should also be read in the light of Chapter 7's (later) discussion of prior composition.

present, and someone who thinks the performer has made a mistake may cut in with such words as

I beg to differ; that is not correct.
You have deviated from the path of accuracy ...
Ire was not Ogun's home town.
Ogun only called there to drink palm-wine ...

to which the performer may try to defend himself by pleading his own knowledge or suggesting that others should respect his integrity:

Let not the civet-cat trespass on the cane rat's track.
Let the cane rat avoid trespassing on the civet-cat's path.
Let each animal follow the smooth stretch of its own road. (Babalǫla 1966: 64, 62)

This possibility of both clarification and challenge from members of the audience and their effect on the performance is indeed one of the main distinctions between oral and written literary pieces. As Plato put it long ago: 'It is the same with written words [as with painting]. You would think they were speaking as if they were intelligent, but if you ask them about what they are saying and want to learn [more], they just go on saying one and the same thing for ever' (*Phaedrus, 275 d*).

This leads on to a further important characteristic of oral literature: the significance of the actual occasion, which can directly affect the detailed content and form of the piece being performed. Oral pieces are not composed in the study and later transmitted through the impersonal and detached medium of print, but tend to be directly involved in the occasions of their actual utterance. Some African oral poetry is specifically 'occasional', in that it is designed for and arises from particular situations like funerals, weddings, celebrations of victory, soothing a baby, accompanying work, and so on; again, with certain prose forms (like, for instance, proverbs), appropriateness to the occasion may be more highly valued by local critics than the verbal content itself. But even when there is not this specific connection, a piece of oral literature tends to be affected by such factors as the general purpose and atmosphere of the gathering at which it is rendered, recent episodes in the minds of performer and audience, or even the time of year and propinquity of the harvest. Many oral recitations arise in response to various social obligations which, in turn, are exploited by poet and narrator for their own purposes. In this sense the performer of oral pieces could be said to be more directly faced with actualised social situations and participants than the writer in more familiar literate traditions.

Studying oral forms

These characteristic qualities of oral literary forms have several implications for the study of oral literature. Points which would seem only secondary in the case of written literature become critical – questions about the details of performance, audience and occasion. To ignore these in an oral work is to risk missing much of the subtlety, flexibility and individual originality of its creator and, furthermore, to fail to give consideration to the aesthetic canons of those intimately concerned in the production and the reception of this form of literature.

This is easy enough to state – but such implications are exceedingly difficult to pursue. Not only is there the seductive model of written literature which constantly tempts one to set aside such questions for the more familiar textual analysis; there are also practical difficulties to surmount. The words themselves are relatively easy to record (even though this is often not done with much scholarly rigour): one can use dictation, texts written by assistants, or recordings on tape. But for the all-important aspect of the actual performance – how is one to record this? Even more difficult, how is one to convey it to readers not themselves acquainted with this art form? In the days before the availability of the portable tape-recorder this problem was practically insuperable.[4] The general tendency was thus for the early scholars to rely only on written records of the oral literature they collected. In many cases, furthermore, they were using quite inadequate sources, perhaps second-hand (so that they themselves had no direct experience of the actual performance involved), or in synopsis only with the artistic elaborations or repetitions omitted. This in itself goes a long way to account for the very simplified impression of African oral literature we often receive from these collections (particularly when it is remembered that they emphasised prose narrative rather than the more elaborate and difficult poetic forms). This was all the more unfortunate because the common practice of concentrating on the texts only encouraged others to follow the same pattern even when it became open to them to use new media for recording.

By now there is an increasing, though by no means universal, reliance on the tape-recorder by serious students of African oral literature. This medium has helped immensely in solving some of the problems of recording details of the performance. But the visual effects produced by the artist still often elude record. Furthermore, the problem of communicating the style of performance to a wider audience is a real one; few if any publishers are keen to include recordings with their collections of printed texts.[5] Thus the public is given the impression of African oral literature as a kind of written literature *manqué*, apparently lacking the elaboration of wording and recognisability of associations known from familiar forms, and without the particular stylistic devices peculiar to oral forms being made clear.

Even when the importance of performance is stressed in general terms, more needs to be said to convey the particular style and flavour of any given genre. A full appreciation must depend on an analysis not only of the verbal interplay and overtones in the piece, its stylistic structure and content, but also of the various detailed devices which performers have at their disposal to

[4] There are however some impressive examples of early use of 'the phonograph', for example Torrend 1921 (Northern Rhodesian stories, including songs); Thomas 1910, Vol. 2 (Edo, Nigeria); Lindblom 1928–35, Vol. 3: 41 (Kamba songs, recorded about 1912).
[5] Despite the technological developments since this was written in the late 1960s (in particular the spread of video recording) the situation in the early twenty-first century may not have changed as radically as might have been expected (however, see Chapter 12, pp. 207).

convey their products to the audience, and the varying ways these are used by different individuals. Something also needs to be said of the role and status of the composer/performer who is the one to communicate this oral art directly to his or her public, the variant forms that arise according to audience and occasion, the reactions and participation likely to be forthcoming from listeners and spectators, the respective contributions, if any, of musical or balletic elements, and finally the social contexts in which this creation and re-creation takes place.

All these factors are far more difficult to discover and describe than a mere transcription of the texts themselves, followed by their leisured analysis. It is not surprising that most editions of oral art concentrate on the textual aspect and say little or nothing about the other factors. But, difficult or not, without the inclusion of some consideration of such questions we have scarcely started to understand its aesthetic development as a product of literary artistry.

Various questionable assumptions about the nature of oral tradition and so-called 'folk art' among non-literate people have not made matters any easier. Briefly these include such ideas as that 'oral tradition' (including what I would myself call oral literature) is passed down word for word from genera-tion to generation and thus reproduced verbatim from memory throughout the centuries; or, alternatively, that oral literature is something that arises communally, from the people or the 'folk' as a whole, so that there can be no question of individual authorship or originality. It can be seen how both these assumptions have inevitably discouraged interest in the actual contem-poraneous performance, variations and the role of the individual poet or narrator in the final literary product. A related assumption was that oral literature (often in this context called 'folklore') was relatively undeveloped and primitive; and this derogatory interpretation was applied to oral literature both in completely non-literate societies and when it coexisted with written literary forms in 'civilised' cultures. This opinion received apparent confirmation from the appearance of bare prose texts in translation or synopsis, and people felt no need to enter into more profound analysis about, say, the overtones and artistic conventions underlying these texts, far less the individual contribution of performer and composer. There was thus no need for further elucidation, for it was assumed in advance that little of real interest could emerge from this 'inherently crude' oral medium.

There are also various other special difficulties about the presentation of African oral literature – how, for instance, to delimit literary from everyday speech forms or convey the subtleties or overtones which only emerge fully to one familiar with the cultural and literary traditions of the society. But these do not arise directly from the *oral* nature of African literature and will thus be more suitably discussed later. The main point I want to reiterate here, the more emphatically because of the way it has so often been overlooked in the past, is that in the case of oral literature, far more extremely than with written forms, the bare words can *not* be left to speak for themselves, for the simple reason that in the actual literary work so much else is necessarily and intimately involved. With this type of literature a knowledge of the whole literary and social background, covering these various points of performance, audience and context, is, however difficult, of the first importance. Even if some of the practical problems of recording and presenting these points sometimes appear insoluble, it is at least necessary to be aware of these problems from the outset, rather than, as so commonly happens, substituting for an awareness of the shallowness of our *own* understanding an imaginary picture of the shallowness in literary appreciation and development of the peoples we are attempting to study.

Oral art as literature

So far we have been concentrating on the *oral* aspect of African unwritten literature – the implications of this for the nature of such literature and the difficulties of presentation and analysis to which it gives rise. Little has yet been said about the *literary* status of these oral products, and we have indeed been begging the question of how far these can in fact be regarded as a type of literature at all.

Various positions have been taken up on this question. A number of the scholars who have carried out extensive studies of the oral art of non-literate peoples are quite dogmatic about the suitability of the term 'literature'. N. K. Chadwick, for one, is explicit on this point:

> In 'civilised' countries we are inclined to associate literature with writing; but such an association is accidental. ... Millions of people throughout Asia, Polynesia, Africa and even Europe who practise the art of literature have no knowledge of letters. Writing is unessential to either the composition or the preservation of literature. The two arts are wholly distinct. (Chadwick 1939: 77)

This position is supported, by implication at least, by the many writers who have referred to their collections or descriptions of oral forms by such terms as 'oral literature', 'unwritten literature', or sometimes 'popular' or 'traditional literature'.[6] The opposite viewpoint, however, also seems to carry weight. There is, for one thing, the association, both popular and etymological, between 'literature' and letters or writing. The fact, furthermore, that oral art depends for its creation on the actual (and thus ephemeral) performance of it seems to some to disqualify it from true literary status, so that other terms like 'folk art', 'folklore', or 'verbal art' appear more accurate designations. Added to this is the alleged practicality supposed by some to be the root of 'primitive art forms'. According to this view, even if some primitive formulation, say a story, might seem in outward form, style or content to present a superficial resemblance to a written work of fiction, in essentials, being fundamentally pragmatic rather than aesthetic, it is something wholly different. Finally, individual authorship is often presumed not to be in question in the case of oral forms, being replaced, according to current fashions, by such supposed entities as 'the group mind', 'the folk', 'social

---

[6] Notable early examples include Koelle 1854, Bleek 1864, Chatelain 1894, Seidel 1896, see also references in Finnegan 1970: 29ff and a number of *Présence africaine* writers and critics from the 1940s on (more recent examples are discussed in later chapters).

structure', or simply 'tradition', all of which equally result in a finished product with a totally different basis and orientation from that of written literature. This kind of view, then, would draw a basic distinction between, on the one hand, the products of a written literary tradition and, on the other, most if not all of the instances of verbal art included in this and similar volumes.

In this controversy, my own position will probably be clear from the discussion so far. It is that, despite difficulties of exact delimitation and presentation, the vast body of African oral tales, poems, songs, recitations and declamations fall within the domain of literature (the class of literature I call 'oral literature'); and that it is misleading as well as unfruitful to attempt to draw a strict line between the verbal art of literate and of non-literate cultural traditions.

In part this approach is an arbitrary one. It is, after all, open to anyone to produce a wide enough definition of 'literature' for all the examples mentioned here to fit within its limits – or a narrower one to exclude them. But it is also adopted because it has been found that to approach instances of oral art as *literary* forms and thus proceed to ask about them the same kind of questions we might raise in the case of written literature, has in fact been a productive approach leading to both further appreciation of the oral forms and a deeper understanding of their social role. Such an approach is in principle its own justification – how justifiable it in fact turns out to be in leading to greater insight can be left to the readers of this and comparable books to judge (or, better, of such original and detailed studies as, for example, Babalǫla 1966, Kagame 1951, Nketia 1955).

But there is also more to this view than whether or not it is a fruitful one. It seems to me to bear more relation to the empirical facts than its opposite in that many of the apparent reasons for the supposed cleavage between oral and written forms have in fact rested on mistaken assumptions. So, even though I am not attempting to put forward any new definition or theory of literature – an attempt likely to raise as many difficulties as it solves – some of these misleading points should be clarified at this stage.

The first point can be easily disposed of. The etymological connections between literature and writing may seem at first a clear validation for limiting the term to written forms. But even if we are prepared to be coerced by etymologies (and why should we be, unless to rationalise already held assumptions?), we must admit that this association by no means exists in all languages – we need only mention the German *Wortkunst* or Russian *slovesnost* (pointed out in Wellek and Warren 1949: 11) – so it can hardly be said to have universal validity.

The fact of a positive and strongly held popular association between writing and literature is more difficult to deal with. Current prejudices may be false, but they go deep. And this is especially so when they are securely rooted in particular historical and cultural experiences, so that the familiar and traditional forms of a given culture come to be regarded as the natural and universal ones, expected to hold good for all times and places. This kind of ethnocentric preconception has had to be revised by scholars in other spheres such as, for instance, the study of modes of political organisation or religious practices, as they are viewed in the light of wider research and thus greater comparative perspective. This, it seems now, may also be the case with the study of literature. In spite of the natural reluctance to regard very different verbal forms as of ultimately the same nature as our own familiar types, we have at least to consider the possibility that the literary models of (in effect) a few centuries in the western world, which happen to be based on writing and more especially on printing, may not in fact exhaust all the possibilities of literature.

This is rendered more intelligible by considering further the relationship between oral and written literature. This is a difference of degree and not of kind: there are many different gradations between what one could take as the oral and the printed ideal types of literature. It is perhaps enough to allude to the literature of the classical world which, as is well known, laid far more stress on the oral aspect than does more recent literature. Even laying aside the famous and controversial question of the possible oral composition of Homer's great epics (universally passed as 'literature'), we can see that the presence of writing can coexist with an emphasis on the significance of performance as one of the main means of the effective transmission of a literary work. For the Greeks there was a close association between words, music and dance – one which seems much less obvious to a modern European – and Aristotle, still accepted as one of the great literary critics, can give as his first reason for considering tragedy superior to epic the fact that it makes an additional impact through music and visual effects (*Poetics,* 1462a). Throughout much of antiquity even written works were normally read aloud rather than silently, and one means of transmitting and, as it were, 'publishing' a literary composition was to deliver it aloud to a group of friends. In such cases the relationship of the performance and transmission of literary works to the content is not totally dissimilar from that in African oral literature.[7]

What was true of classical and mediaeval literature is also true of many cultures in which writing is practised as a specialist rather than a universal art and, in particular, in societies without the printing-press to make the multiplication of copies feasible. Those socialised in the western educational tradition are so accustomed to associate the written word with print that we tend to forget that the mere fact of *writing* does not necessarily involve the type of detachment and relatively impersonal mode of transmission that we often (perhaps wrongly) connect with printing. Transmission by reading aloud or by performing from memory, sometimes accompanied by improvisation, is not at all incompatible with some reliance on writing – a situation we find not only in earlier European societies but also in Africa. Here again the contrast between fully oral forms on the one hand and the impersonal medium of print

---

[7] Chaytor comments pertinently of mediaeval vernacular literature: 'In short, the history of the progress from script to print is a history of the gradual substitution of visual for auditory methods of communicating and receiving ideas. ... To disregard the matter and to criticise medieval literature as though it had just been issued by the nearest circulating library is a sure and certain road to a misconception of the medieval spirit' (Chaytor 1945: 4); on 'oral' elements in manuscript culture see also McLuhan 1962 (also additional references in Chapter 7, p. 104 n. 4).

on the other is clearly only a relative one: we would hardly suggest that works written and, in part, orally transmitted before the advent of printing were therefore not literature, any more than we would be prepared to state dogmatically that the Homeric epics – or an African poem – only became literature on the day they were first written down.

Even in a society apparently dominated by the printed word the oral aspect is not entirely lost. Perhaps because of the common idea that written literature is somehow the highest form of the arts, the current significance of oral elements often tends to be played down, if not overlooked completely. But we can point to the importance of performance and production in a play, the idea held by some at least that much poetry can only attain its full flavour when spoken aloud, or the increasing but often underestimated significance of the oral reproduction and dissemination of classic literary forms (as well as wholly new compositions) through radio and television. Add to this the interplay between the oral and the written – the constant interaction in any tradition between the written word and, at the least, the common diction of everyday speech (an interaction which may well be heightened by the spreading reliance on radio and television channels of transmission), as well as the largely oral forms like speeches, sermons, children's rhymes, satires depending in part on improvisation, or many current pop songs, all of which have both literary and oral elements – in view of all this it becomes clear that even in a fully literate culture oral formulations can play a real part, however unrecognised, in the literary scene as a whole.

Even so brief an account suggests that our current preoccupation with written, particularly printed, media may give only a limited view and that the distinction between oral and written forms may not be so rigid and so profound as is often implied. It is already widely accepted that these two media can each draw on the products of the other, for orally transmitted forms have frequently been adopted or adapted in written literature, and oral literature too is prepared to draw on any source, including the written word. To this interplay we can now add the fact that when looked at comparatively, the two forms, oral and written, are not so mutually exclusive as is sometimes imagined. Even if we picture them as two independent extremes we can see that in practice there are many possibilities and many different stages between the two poles and that the facile assumption of a profound and unbridgeable chasm between oral and written forms is a misleading one.

Some further misconceptions about the nature of oral forms – some of them touched on briefly earlier – need be reiterated in this context. First, the idea that all primitive (and thus also all oral) art is severely functional, and thus basically different from art in 'civilised' cultures. To this it must be replied that this whole argument partly arises from a particular and temporary fashion in the interpretation of art (the rather unclear idea of 'art for art's sake'); that since there is little detailed empirical evidence on the various purposes of particular genres of oral literature – it is much easier to write down texts and presume functions than to make detailed inquiries about the local canons of literary criticism – this assertion rests as much on presupposition as on observed fact; and, finally, that the whole argument is partly just a matter of words. How far and in what sense and for whom a given

91

piece of literature is 'functional' and just how one assesses this is as difficult a question in non-literate as in literate cultures. Certainly we can say that even when we can find a clear social purpose (and the 'occasional' aspect in oral literature varies according to genre, composer and situation just as it does in written literature), this by no means necessarily excludes an interest in aesthetic as well as functional considerations.

The question of authorship in oral literature has already been mentioned in the context of performance and of the composition that arises from this. By now, few people probably take very seriously the concept of the 'group mind' or the 'folk mind' as an empirical entity to which the authorship of particular literary pieces could be assigned. But in the case of the oral literature of basically unfamiliar cultures this idea acquires an apparent validity mainly from ignorance of the actual circumstances involved. Again, this is a large question that cannot be pursued in detail here. But it can be said categorically that while oral literature – like all literature – in a sense arises from society and, being oral, has the extra facet of often involving more direct interplay between composer and audience, nevertheless it is totally misleading to suggest that individual originality and imagination play no part. The exact form this takes and the exact degree of the familiar balance between tradition and creativity naturally vary with the culture, the genre and the personalities involved. But it is clear from the detailed studies of multiple forms of African literary genres that the myth attributing all oral literature either to the 'community' alone or, alternatively, to one particular portion of it ('the folk') is not true to the facts; and that the whole picture is much more complex than such simplified and speculative assumptions would suggest.

A final point which has, I think, wrongly deterred people from the recognition of oral forms as a type of literature has been the idea that they have only resulted in trivial formulations without any depth of meaning or association. This impression has, it is true, been given by the selection and presentation of much of the African verbal art that reaches the public – the emphasis on animal tales and other light-hearted stories (relatively easy to record) rather than the more elaborate creations of the specialist poets; and the common publication of unannotated texts which give the reader no idea whatsoever of the social and literary background which lies behind them, let alone the arts of the performer. Quite apart from mere problems of translation, the difficulties of appreciating the art forms of unfamiliar cultures without help are well known. We need only consider – to take just one example – how much our appreciation of Shakespeare's

> Like as the waves make towards the pebbled shore,
> So do our minutes hasten to their end ...

depends, among other things, on our knowledge of the particular art form (sonnet), its whole literary setting, the rhythm, phrasing and music of the lines, and, not least, on the emotive overtones of such familiar words as 'waves', 'minutes', 'end' which bring us a whole realm of associations, sounds and pictures, all of which can be said to form an essential part of the meaning. This is obvious – but it is often forgotten that exactly the same thing applies in oral literature:

92

Grandsire Gyima with a slim but generous arm
(*Nana Gyima abasateaa a adɔeɛ wɔ mu*) (Nketia 1955: 195, 245)

is the first line of an Akan dirge, and seems of itself to have little poetic force
or meaning. But its significance appears very different when we know the
overtones of the concept of generosity, metaphorically expressed here through
the familiar concept of the dead man's 'arm'; the particular style and
structure, so pleasing and acceptable to the audience; the rhythm and quasi-
musical setting of the line; the familiarity and associations of the phrasing;
the known fact that this is a mother singing for her dead son whom she is
calling her 'grandsire' in the verse; and the grief-laden and emotional atmosphere in which these dirges are performed and received – all this makes such
a line, and the poem that follows and builds on it, something far from trivial
to its Akan listeners. Similar analyses of other genres would also reveal ample
evidence that the charge of triviality in oral literature as a whole rests far
more on ignorance and unfamiliarity than on any close acquaintance with the
facts.

There is one further problem that should be mentioned here. This is the
difficult question of how to distinguish in wholly oral communication
between what is to count as literature and what is not. Are we to include, say,
speeches by court elders summing up cases, an impromptu prayer, non-
innovatory genres like some formulaic hunting-songs, formal words of
welcome, or the dramatic reporting of an item of news?

This is a real problem to which there is no easy solution. However, it has to
be said at once that despite first impressions there is no difference *in
principle* here between written and unwritten literature. In written forms, too,
there are problems in delimiting 'literature'. It is largely a matter of opinion,
for example, as to whether to include science fiction, certain newspaper
articles, or the words of popular songs. Opinions differ, furthermore, not only
between different individuals and different age and social groups, but at
different periods of history. The problem, clearly, is not unique to oral
literature.

In considering this question of the possible distinction between 'literary'
and 'non-literary', the issues in relation to oral literature are really much the
same as in the case of written literature. First, some cases are clear-cut. These
are instances where many of the conventionally accepted characteristics of
'literature' mentioned in the next paragraph are clearly applicable, or where
the African examples seem directly comparable with literary genres
recognised in familiar European cultures. In other words, once the concept of
an oral literature is allowed, there will be little or no dispute over cases like
panegyric poetry, lyrics for songs, fictional narratives, or funeral elegies.
Other cases are not so clear. Here, one criterion must surely be the evaluation
of the particular societies involved – we cannot assume *a priori* that their
definitions of 'literary' will necessarily coincide with those of English culture.
Since the evaluation of some form as literature is, as we have seen, a matter of
opinion, it seems reasonable at least to take seriously the *local* opinions on
this. Thus when we are told that among the Ibo 'oratory ... calls for an original
and individual talent and ... belongs to a higher order [than folk-tales or

proverbs]' (Achebe 1964: vii), this ought to incline us to consider including at least some rhetorical speeches as a part of Ibo oral literature (although among other societies with less interest in oratory this may not be the case). Again, proverbs are sometimes locally thought to be as serious and 'literary' as more lengthy forms – and in some cases are even expanded into long proverb-poems, as with the 'drum proverbs' of the Akan. Finally we have verbal forms that are clearly marginal: obviously not 'literature' in their own right, and yet not irrelevant to literary formulation and composition. We could instance metaphorical names, elaborate greeting forms, the serious art of conversation, and, in some cases, proverbs or rhetoric. These may exhibit an appreciation of the artistic aspect of language and a rich background from which more explicitly literary forms arise – a relationship perhaps particularly obvious in the case of oral literature, but not unknown to literate cultures.[8] There is no distinct or single point at which one can draw a definite dividing line, even though one extreme might seem clearly 'literature', the other not.

Earlier I made the negative point that many of the assumptions that seem to set oral forms totally apart from written literature are in fact questionable or false. The same point can be put more positively. Oral literary forms fall within most conventional definitions of 'literature' in the traditional western high art canon (save only for the point about writing as a medium, not always included in such definitions), and the problems arising from such definitions mostly apply to oral as well as to written literary forms. In other words, though I am not putting forward any one particular definition of 'literature', it seems clear that the elements out of which such definitions tend, variously, to be constructed are also recognisable in oral forms, often with exactly the same range of ambiguities. The basic medium is words – though in both cases this verbal element may be supplemented by visual or musical elements. Beyond this, literature, we are often told, is expressive rather than instrumental, is aesthetic and characterised by a lack of practical purpose – a description equally applicable to much oral art. The exploitation of form, heightening of style, and interest in the medium for its own sake as well as for its descriptive function can clearly be found in oral literary forms. So, too, can the idea of accepted literary conventions of style, structure and genre laid down by tradition, which are followed by the second-rate and exploited by the original author. The sense in which literature is set at one remove from reality is another familiar element: this too is recognisable in oral literature, not merely in such obvious ways as in the use of fiction, satire, or parable, but also through the very conventionality of the literary forms allied to the imaginative formulation in actual words. The same applies to the diversities relating to different genres, periods, participants or local evaluations – these are to be found with oral as well as with written forms. If we prefer to rely on an ostensive type of definition and list the kind of genres we would include under the heading of 'literature', this procedure gives us many analogies in oral literature (though we may find that we have to add a few not familiar in

---

[8] The strategy of my 1970 survey was to proceed from more obviously 'literary' genres like praise poetry, elegies, religious poetry, lyric and extended prose narratives through more questionable cases like proverbs or riddles to marginal forms like names or word-play.

recent European literature). Among African oral genres, for instance, we can find forms analogous to European elegies, panegyric poetry, lyric, religious poetry, fictional prose, rhetoric, topical epigram, and perhaps drama.

Whichever approach we adopt we shall run into some difficulties and unclear cases (in the case of *oral* literature the problem of delimiting literary from everyday spoken forms is perhaps a peculiarly difficult one). But the point I want to stress is that these difficulties are fundamentally the same as those that arise in the study of any kind of literature.[9]

All in all there is no good reason to deny the title of 'literature' to African forms just because they happen to be oral. If we do treat them as *fundamentally* of a different kind, we deny ourselves both a fruitful analytic approach and, furthermore, a wider perspective on the general subject of comparative literature. We need, of course, to remember that oral literature is only one type of literature, a type characterised by particular features to do with performance, transmission and social context, with the various implications these have for its study. But for all these differences, the general conclusion must surely be that there is no essential chasm between this type of literature and the (perhaps more familiar) written forms.

[9] For discussions of the question of African oral forms as 'literature' in the 1960s and earlier see Whiteley 1964: 4ff and references there.

7

Is Oral Literature
Composed in Performance?[1]

A great impetus was given to the concept and study of 'oral literature' – and of 'the oral' more generally – by what became known as the 'oral-formulaic theory' developed by Milman Parry and Albert Lord. The publication of Lord's hugely influential *The Singer of Tales* in 1960 led to an explosion of comparative studies of oral literature. Initially rooted in research among South Slavic heroic singers, the approach and findings came to be widely applied not only to Homeric epic and Old English poetry but to oral forms as a whole.

This theory was concerned in particular with the question of how lengthy oral poems (and, subsequently, other unwritten literary forms) could come into being without the use of writing. To answer this, oral-formulaic scholars turned to the evidence so eloquently presented in *The Singer of Tales* to demonstrate from live field examples how oral literature was actually composed. It was created, they concluded, *during* performance by composer-performers drawing on a store of formulae – of traditional formulaic expressions – which enabled them, without writing or word-for-word memorisation, to pour forth their long oral songs in uninterrupted flow.

This promised to lay the foundation for an abiding definition and characterisation of all oral literature and for a time the oral-formulaic theory seemed to sweep all before it. The present chapter offers some comment on

[1] A more extended version appeared as 'What is oral literature anyway? Comments in the light of some African and other comparative material', in B. A. Stolz and R. S. Shannon (eds), *Oral Literature and the Formula,* Center for the Coordination of Ancient and Modern Studies, University of Michigan, 1976: 127–66 (reprinted in John Miles Foley (ed.), *Oral-Formulaic Theory. A Folklore Casebook*, New York: Garland, 1990; a few passages and quotations also appeared in Finnegan 1977). Apart from some compression and abridgement (in particular the excision of more lengthy texts and most non-African examples) and the addition of some minimal updating footnotes, this has again been left much as it was, as a statement of how things stood in the mid-1970s (see also p. 97 n. 2 below).

this fertile approach – by now less dominant but still with some influence and relevance – and brings it into conjunction with some of the evidence from Africa. The conclusion must be that, despite the insights brought by this tradition of analysis, it treats only one among several different ways in which composition and performance can be related. As will emerge in the examples indicated here the ways that people put together literary words in oral performance are in fact vastly more diverse than suggested in the generalising oral-formulaic school.[2]

The Parry-Lord model and African literary forms

Half a century or so ago, this formulation of the oral-formulaic theory marked a highly significant step in the comparative study of oral literature. Though I must eventually query certain assumptions in Lord's classic *The Singer of Tales* (1960) and the work it inspired, let me first comment on the illumination it brought for considering African forms. Two points above all stood out: first, the variability of oral literature and absence of *the* single correct version; and second, the uniqueness of *each* performance as delivered by the composer-performer on one particular occasion. Going along with that was the elucidation of how conventional themes and formulae are used and re-used in differing combinations and contexts by poets as a basis for their own original compositions: creativity through tradition. None of these points were totally new. As those acquainted with earlier Russian work or with the Chadwicks' great *Growth of Literature* (1932–40) will already know, most had been stated in one form or another before. But their argued and explicit synthesis supported by detailed field-based evidence was particularly effective in its timely challenge to the still influential romantic folklore school with its stress on memorised transmission over the generations.

The rejection of memorisation, to be replaced by an emphasis on variability and unique performance, had important implications for the understanding of African oral literature, prose as well as poetry. Many writers on Africa had previously assumed that stories and songs were memorised word-perfectly, authoritatively asserting this or conveying it in the way they collected and presented their texts (the implicit model seemingly being that of a definitive printed or manuscript work). Others, however, had pointed to the changeability and performance features of oral forms. A good example is H. A. Junod's description of Thonga story-telling, quoted earlier (p. 83 above). He had published this in 1913 (long before Parry and Lord), based on observations over many years as a missionary. It is worth recalling its main lines which will ring true to anyone familiar with oral-formulaic studies. Thonga stories, in his account, were characterised by both 'antiquity' and variability:

[2] Some oral-formulaic scholars have more recently been developing this approach in highly sophisticated and evidence-based directions, including due attention to diversity (see for example Amodio 2005 and, in particular, Foley 2002, 2003 and references there). The earlier generalising positions are still recycled elsewhere, however, and I believe the critique here is still worth asserting.

> They are constantly transformed by the narrators and their transformations go much further than is generally supposed, further even than the Natives themselves are aware of. ... I never met with exactly the same version. ... First of all *words* differ. Each narrator has his own style, speaks freely and does not feel in any way bound by the expressions used by the person who taught him the tale. ... [In] *the sequence of the episodes*, although these often form definite cycles, it is rare to hear two narrators follow exactly the same order. ... [The same applies to] *new elements* ... [and], in certain cases, the *contents of the stories* themselves ... this giving birth to numerous versions of a tale. (Junod 1913, Vol. 2: 198ff; for a fuller extract see above p. 83)

Here can be seen the kinds of processes later so well elucidated in the oral-formulaic theory, the combination of unique performance with traditionally known plots and themes.

Much the same processes were at work in Limba story-telling. Narrators quite often said they were telling the same story as one previously told by someone else (or by themselves). On the face of it there seemed no reason to disbelieve this. But probing further revealed much the same pattern as with the Slavic heroic singers: that despite the narrators' assertions, in practice their versions *did* differ. Similar episodes appeared in different stories, certainly, but with varying protagonists (sometimes humans, sometimes animals or supernatural beings, for instance) and in differing combinations and orders. There was a store of possible stock endings which were selected (or not) according to the wishes of the narrator and nature of the audience. The 'same' story might end in one telling with a moral, in another with a joke or dilemma, in another again with some aetiological explanation. As mentioned earlier (Chapters 4, 5) the same basic plot could be developed very differently by two different narrators, not just in wording but in the overall action, detailed episodes, names of characters, general atmosphere, characterisation and conclusion. Even versions by the same narrator were not identical in different performances. A comparable balance to that described by Parry and Lord between 'tradition' (the stock in trade on which the Limba narrator could draw) and 'originality' (the creative contribution of the individual narrator) can be detected in the corpus of Limba stories and the observed activities of story-tellers.

This analysis of Limba story-telling obviously draws much from the insights of Lord and Parry (supplemented by Propp's analysis (1958) of 'functions' in Russian fairy tales). The points so well stated in *The Singer of Tales* come up again and again: variability, the uniqueness of separate performances and the interplay of known themes and expressions. The theoretical backing given by oral-formulaic scholars has been of the greatest assistance to students of African oral narratives in questioning earlier presuppositions about exact memorisation and reproduction.

Similar points have been made about poetry too, with many parallels to the simultaneous composition/performance that Lord describes for Yugoslav poets. In the *nyatiti* 'lyre' songs of the Luo of East Africa described by Anyumba (1964) composer-performers built on known themes to create a new and unique composition. The most common context was the delivery of the laments expected at a funeral. The performer appeared on the occasion and sat there, singing at the top of his voice, sweating profusely and drinking plenty of beer; before him was the plate into which his admirers dropped their pennies. There were set conventions within which he must compose. These were partly musical but included stock themes and word-groups like 'sealed in dust', 'asleep on its arm', 'sleep seated', and a series of praise names which could be introduced into the verse, commonly those of the deceased's maternal and paternal uncles, his family, clan, country and loves. The song was elaborated further by introducing particular circumstances and incidents, popular ones being the adventures and conversations of the deceased, conventionally used to epitomise the sorrow and shock of the bereaved. Building on these conventions, the poet put together his song, aided by a great deal of repetition. It was based in one sense on his traditional and ready-made repertoire, but he fitted it to the occasion by adding in 'an uncle here and a grandfather there together with any knowledge he may have of the attributes of the deceased' (Anyumba 1964: 189). The Luo poet thus produced a unique and appropriate lament on a specific occasion, one in which his powers of composition and performance were greatly admired: 'The skill and beauty with which the musician is able to improvise at such moments is a measure of his musical and poetic stature' judged both by his skill on the instrument and by his ability to weave a story or meditate on human experience (Anyumba 1964: 190, 188).

A broadly oral-formulaic approach would also seem to apply well to some of the praise poetry recorded from Africa. Though not set in the narrative frame of the Slavic songs, this was nevertheless a developed, highly regarded and specialist genre in many of the traditional states of Africa, providing an illuminating parallel to the heroic poetry studied by Parry and Lord. This is evident for example in M. G. Smith's vivid account of composition-performance in one type of Hausa praise-singing in Northern Nigeria (1957, also Scharfe and Aliyu 1967). Smith describes the strategies of solo praise-singers who operated on a freelance basis, roving round the various villages of the countryside. The poet would arrive in a village and start by finding out from the local praise poets who the wealthy and important individuals in the area were. With this vital information, he took up his stand in some public spot and called out the name of the man he was intending to eulogise: his 'praisee'. He proceeded to his praise poem proper, building in the conventional themes of his praisee's ancestry, nobility, prosperity and influence, his many dependants and his political connections – interspersed with frequent demands for gifts. If sufficient recompense was paid over he sang his thanks and announced the amount. If not, the tone changed. The song continued with the same themes, but this time all in an unfavourable light: it recounted the praisee's meanness, poor reputation, menial occupation, poor treatment of dependants, and disloyalty to political allies. If there was still nothing paid over, the innuendo became sharper, the delivery more staccato, until at last the final insult was reached: imputation of servile ancestry. Since an experienced singer knew how to choose a time when all the local people were likely to hear – in the evening or the early morning when people were still at home from the farm, or on a market day – the unhappy victim was usually only too thankful to surrender and pay up.

99

Such cases fit well with the findings of Parry and Lord in Yugoslavia. There is the fluidity of the detailed wording, dependent on the circumstances and personnel involved; the inevitable lack of any concept of a correct version for a given praise song; and the combination and recombination of conventional themes by the poet. The older model of exact memorisation and a single authentic text would clearly have been less than illuminating here.

Even in the case of group singing – on the face of it the least likely place for anything but memorisation – there can be adaptation and innovation in a way not wholly unlike the model presented by Lord. This is through the leader/chorus pattern commonly found in African singing. The soloist introduces new words or variations while the chorus either repeats the soloist's lines or follows on with a known and repeated refrain (or some combination of those principles). With certain Shona songs in the then Southern Rhodesia (now Zimbabwe) described by Hugh Tracey (1929) for instance, the chorus part remained the same but the soloist (*mushairi*) was allowed scope for originality of phrasing. He had stock ways of coping with this. If he was unable to compose the next verse quickly enough, he would repeat the last one several times or yodel the tune to give himself time to think. If he was completely stuck he ended up by signing to a neighbour to replace him in the lead.

Such points might perhaps seem too obvious to be worth lingering over. But there was a period (and it is not finally past everywhere) when, with a few magnificent exceptions, this sort of account would not have seemed plausible at all. The earlier concentration tended to be either, on the one hand, on the concept of inert tradition from the far-distant past or, on the other, on the spontaneous improvisation to be expected from the 'primitive' as the unself-conscious 'child of nature', unfettered (and unhelped) by recognised artistic conventions. Both emphases were, in their different ways, inheritances from the romantic movement and its attitude to 'the folk'. Added to this was the stress by many earlier functional anthropologists on stability, lack of change and the 'traditional' institutions of 'the tribe' and 'the society' as a whole – with, therefore, little interest in the processes of creativity, far less the personalities of individual poets or the balance between originality and tradition.

There is much, then, in the interpretations of the oral-formulaic school that turns out to be of great significance when applied in general terms to oral literature in Africa. Others had of course made some of these points earlier but their exposition in *The Singer of Tales* provided a classic reference point to which workers in the field could respond and appeal.

But – and this is the point I have been working up to – this approach is perhaps *too* good. Precisely because the general insights of *The Singer of Tales* are, as I have suggested, so useful in the study of some forms of oral literature in Africa (and elsewhere), it is tempting to swallow the theory whole, and to go overboard for all the detailed analysis and implicit assumptions in the Parry-Lord thesis and its adherents. This would be a mistake, the more important to recognise because of the unquestionable attraction and applicability of many aspects of the theory.

100

What is 'oral literature' anyway?

The points I need to tackle here are first, the basic concept and differentiation of 'oral literature' and then, arising from that, of 'oral composition'. This will eventually bring me round to the topic of the 'formula'.

Reading through many of the oral-formulaic analyses, one gains certain impressions (not always stated explicitly) which I will initially lay out baldly here: first, that there is a single and identifiable phenomenon called 'oral literature' (or more specifically 'oral poetry') about which it is possible to generalise; second, that this 'oral literature/poetry' is radically different from and opposed to written literature/poetry; and third, that the term 'oral composition' likewise refers to some clear-cut and identifiable process, so that if one has deduced 'oral composition' from the evidence (e.g. from a study of formulae) one has discovered something definite and meaningful. All three assumptions can do with some critical analysis.

Take, first, the differentiation of 'oral' from 'written' literature, and the idea that this is a single phenomenon about which one can generalise. It is stated quite explicitly in Parry's own description of his aim in turning to Slav oral poetry:

> The purpose of the present collection of oral texts has ... been made not with the thought of adding to the already vast collections of [South Slavic] poetry, but of obtaining evidence on the basis of which could be drawn a series of generalities applicable to all oral poetries; which would allow me, in the case of a poetry for which there was not enough evidence outside the poems themselves of the way in which they were made, to say whether that poetry was oral or not, and *how* it should be understood if it was oral. ... A method is here involved, that which consists in *defining the characteristics of oral style.* (Parry and Lord 1954: 4, italics in original)

This interest in generalising about 'oral literature', 'oral poetry', 'the oral style' and so on has been very much part of much of the work inspired by Parry and Lord. There is constant use of such phrases as 'the oral method', 'the oral technique' (Buchan 1972: 55, 58), 'the oral poet', 'the oral technique of verse making', 'oral texture' (Notopoulos 1964: 21, 24, 52 etc.), 'the clearly oral characteristics' of the *Song of Roland* (Nichols 1961: 9n), 'the irrefutable statistical facts that distinguish the texts of Homer from those of poets known to have composed by writing' (Nagler 1967: 274), or 'the method of oral poetry' (Curschmann 1967: 42). Paralleling Lord's claim that 'with oral poetry we are dealing with a particular and distinctive process in which oral learning, oral composition, and oral transmission almost merge' (1960: 5) are many equally confident generalisations. Magoun's much-quoted 'Oral poetry, it may safely be said, is composed entirely of formulas, large and small, while lettered poetry is never formulaic' (1953: 447) is followed by Notopoulos' similarly bold description of the 'facts of life about oral poetry' where 'the society which gives birth to oral poetry is characterised by traditional fixed ways in all aspects of its life' (1964: 50, 51).

In keeping with this is the second assumption: that of a fundamental distinction between written and oral poetry. *The Singer of Tales* tells us that

> The two techniques [oral and written] are ... contradictory and mutually exclusive. Once the oral technique is lost, it is never regained. The written technique ... is not compatible with the oral technique, and the two could not possibly combine to form another, a third, a 'transitional' technique. ... It is not possible that [a man] be *both* an oral and a written poet at any given time in his career. The two by their very nature are mutually exclusive. (Lord 1960: 129)

Similarly, 'as literacy spreads throughout the world at a now rapid pace, oral poetry seems destined in time to disappear' (Lord 1965: 591). This became the standard line among oral-formulaic scholars: 'One important lesson of the field experience of Parry and Lord is that literacy destroys the virtue of an oral singer' (Kirk 1965: 22). 'The literary and oral techniques of composition do not mix in a true oral poet' (Notopoulos 1964: 19) or, in Nichols' words, 'the existence and propagation of an oral tradition, as the now classic studies of Milman Parry and Albert B. Lord have shown, depend on conditions of composition and recitation which are quite distinct from those found in a literary tradition' (1961: 9).

These two assumptions – the identity of 'oral literature' and its radical difference from written literature – need to be examined carefully.

There are, of course, ways in which what can be termed oral literature does broadly differ from written forms, chiefly in the matter of its being *performed*. But to assume a definitive break between them is an exaggeration, and a misleading one. The two terms, I would argue, are relative ones, and to assign any given piece unequivocally to either one or the other – as if they were self-contained and mutually exclusive boxes – is to distort the evidence.

Oral and written literature in Africa are in practice often relative and overlapping rather than mutually exclusive categories. In Africa, the influence of literacy through Christian missionary activity has deeper roots than often recognised and there have also been many centuries of Islam and Islamic literacy, especially in the great Sudanic and east coast areas, which it would be highly misleading to treat as some superficial and intrusive phenomenon. In West Africa, for instance, the long Hausa 'Song of Bagauda' appears in both written and unwritten form (Hiskett 1964–5). In Swahili verse there has long been constant interchange and influence between orally composed and written verses (Harries 1962: 3–5; Werner 1918; Whiteley 1958), while Somali oral poets not only make use of radio as well as face to face delivery, but have also 'used writing ... as a visual aid to their oral memory' (Mumin 1974: 3). In fact what some might label 'mixed forms' have had a long history in the continent of Africa – forms which are at some point written but reach their fullest actualisation and circulation by being performed orally. This includes, for instance, twentieth-century political songs and hymns in many areas (exemplified in Finnegan 1970: 284ff, 185ff), Swahili religious poems publicly intoned for the enlightenment of the masses, Fulani poems declaimed aloud, or Hausa compositions memorised as oral poems and sung by beggars, chanted on the streets at night or performed over the radio.[3]

---

[3] Examples are from the pre-1976 literature; many parallel cases could be drawn from more recent work (see Chapter 11, pp. 182ff, also p. 104, n. 4 below).

As for the oral composers/performers themselves there seems ample evidence that neither literacy nor an acquaintance with written literature necessarily interfere with oral composition and performance. I will give just a few instances of what I consider is in practice a widespread phenomenon in Africa (as elsewhere).

Let me return my own experience of Limba story-telling. One of the best narrators I encountered was totally illiterate: Karanke Dema, gifted as both musician and story-teller and, as a smith, in close touch with the traditional mysteries of the men's secret society. In his blend of creativity and tradition as well as his brilliant and personal use of the local conventions, he might seem a clear example of the kind of traditional oral artist depicted in *The Singer of Tales*. But I have to admit that he was run very close – and possibly, in local eyes, excelled – by Kelfa Konteh, whom I met on one of his periodic visits to a larger village on the main road north where I stayed for a time: a young man undertaking a teacher's training course and well acquainted with the written word. He utilised the typically Limba interplay of recognised themes (including some episodes pretty clearly drawn from his school background) as well as all the accepted tricks of delivery, deployed to great dramatic effect. He was not the only literate narrator I encountered, and in terms of performance and composition I would find it hard to differentiate between those oral narrators who were non-literate, on the one hand, and those with varying degrees of literacy on the other. I based my analysis of style and composition in Limba story-telling on the productions of both.

This situation is far from unparalleled. I have heard a magnificent oral narrative performed by a highly educated Yoruba pastor in western Nigeria, for instance (the sermon is of course widely practised as an oral art by notably literate preachers). Many accounts of twentieth-century oral poetry in Africa include school songs among the other categories of verbal art. These are not just crude rhymes or derivative aping of foreign teachers. In Dinka 'school songs' from the southern Sudan, for example, the schoolboys' position is likened to that of traditional age sets:

> The moon of December has appeared
> Our age-set in white [lit. 'the White Bull'] sees it from all flanks
> The age-set which obeys orders. ...

> I am building my home
> The home of the children of learning
> The home where words of children flow even at night.
> To the age-set in white, jealousy is unknown. (Deng 1973: 250–51)

Francis Deng, their native collector and editor, considers poems by literate composers as basically no different from other more 'traditional' types of poetry in terms of their structure and composition.

It is, after all, hardly surprising to find this kind of interplay between oral and literate modes, for the two have interacted and overlapped for centuries in vast areas of our planet. It is not only in Africa that such instances are documented. From the many cases of written notes for oral delivery used, for example, by Chinese mediaeval ballad singers 'to jog their memory before and during the performance' complemented by printed versions for literate readers (Doleželová-Veleringerová and Crump 1971: 2), or the interdependent oral and written versions of the great epic cycle of Gesar in Tibet and Mongolia (Stein 1959: esp. Chapter 3), to the well-known oral-written interplay of English and American ballads (Laws 1957, Rollins 1919), such interaction between oral performance and written text is nothing new or strange. Nor can such instances be unequivocally assigned to a clear-cut and separate category of 'oral' as opposed to 'written', for elements of both may enter in. The same would apply to modern so-called 'songs of protest', to work songs – of miners, lumberers, road-workers, prisoners (Greenway 1953, Jackson 1972) – as to Irish 'rebel songs': all in some senses composed and performed orally, yet produced in a context of widespread literacy to which it is hard to believe the poets are impervious. One can also mention forms such as 'jazz poetry' – specifically intended for oral performance – or the so-called 'underground' English poets with public performance as their preferred mode of publication, and the preparedness of a leading poet like Adrian Mitchell to improvise when delivering his own poetry: 'I change poems when I read them aloud' (quoted in Horovitz 1969: 358). This again recalls the overlap between oral and written media in classical antiquity, where oral performance coexisted and mingled with a literate tradition and public recitation was the regular form of publication, or the kind of blend of oral and written elements in the oral delivery of mediaeval Europe that the rigid distinctions envisaged by Lord and Parry simply cannot account for.[4]

Such examples may seem to be merely repeating what is already well-known or, alternatively, setting up so wide a definition of 'oral literature' that the term ceases to have any meaning. But this latter point is precisely what I am driving at. When one looks hard at the detailed circumstances and nature of literary phenomena in a comparative context, historically as well as geographically, the concept of 'oral literature' *does* cease to be a clear one. There are varying ways in which a literary piece can be oral (or written): 'orality' is a relative thing.

It is, of course, possible to set up a narrower definition of oral – in the way Lord in effect does – confining it, say, *solely* to pieces composed during oral delivery on the model of Slavic singers. There is nothing in principle impossible about such an attempt. But this kind of restrictive definition seems to me to do no justice to the realities of the many different and overlapping forms which literary formulations have taken throughout space and time.

A convinced disciple of Parry and Lord might claim that much of this is beside the point, for what is involved is not the medium itself nor the outward circumstances of composition or (still less) performance, but the oral 'mentality' of the poet. After all a number of Parry and Lord's 'oral poets' were in fact literate, and Lord himself admits that literate poets are possible. But what he *is* interested in is whether they have an 'oral' or a 'written' 'mentality' (Lord 1960: 138). This line has been followed by many other writers, focusing on the 'psychology' of oral composition, 'the mental processes in oral poetry'

---

[4] Original [1976] references cited included Crosby 1936, Curschmann 1967: 50ff, Hadas 1954: 50, Shippey 1972: 97–8; more recent studies include (among many others) Coleman 1996, Thomas 1989, 2003, also the useful overview in Foley 2002. For more contemporary cases see Chapters 11 and 12.

(Notopoulos 1964: 59), the 'mental template' (Nagler 1967: 269) or 'the oral mind' (Buchan 1972: 57).

This, however, is equally unilluminating, for two reasons. First, the general impression in *The Singer of Tales* is that there is solid evidence for the claimed 'incompatibility' between 'oral' and 'written' methods – yet this ultimately comes down to what must be, in effect, a psychological speculation which it would be hard to prove and which anyway comes close to a tautology. Second, the tone in which this argument is put forward smacks very much of the concept of 'primitive mentality' that was once – but is no longer – prevalent in anthropology. Some writings in the oral-formulaic school remind me of this supposedly distinctive mentality of 'primitive' peoples with their reliance on 'tradition' and unchanging norms, and their involvement with magic and religion (e.g. Lord 1960: 66–7, 155, Notopoulos 1964: 51). These speculative and elusive generalisations are in themselves questionable and provide little support for the apparent conclusions being drawn. The assumption of this kind of divide had received apparent backing from the popular writings of Marshall McLuhan with his stress on the 'auditory and magical domain ... of primeval man' (1969: 79) and the movement from an oral to a visual mode of knowing with the development of writing and print (he made explicit in his *Gutenberg Galaxy* (1962: Prologue) that this analysis had direct links with *The Singer of Tales*). His conclusions can, similarly, be criticised as not only emotive and somewhat opaque but as exaggerating both the 'orality' of non-industrial cultures (and individuals) and the 'literacy' of more recent western civilisation. To ignore the complicated and mixed ways in which human beings, now and in the past, have made use of a whole range of different media makes for an elegant model but does scant justice to the complexity of the real world. A similar point could be made of the 'torn between two [ostensibly incompatible] worlds' image in some African novels. As the leading Nigerian historian Ade Ajayi put it, 'These dramatic presentations of culture conflict may be good literature, but are seldom good history or psychology' (1974: 15).

The binary opposition of 'oral' and 'written' may seem initially plausible – but only until one looks hard at the facts. So it is worth repeating once again that 'orality' and 'literacy' are complex and relative notions, and manifest themselves in the real world in a number of overlapping ways. 'Oral literature' (or 'oral poetry') is similarly not a strictly separable and clearly defined category.

This point – obvious though it must seem in many ways – is significant for many of the findings of the oral-formulaic school. We are told that that a given piece is an instance of 'oral literature' or 'oral poetry' as if this statement in itself provides solid new information about the piece: as if assigning it to the category of 'oral literature' tells us something specific and meaningful that fits in with 'the oral mind' or the 'natural' context for oral poetry. I would suggest, on the contrary, that saying something is 'oral' could only be the beginning. One also wants to know 'oral' in what sense? how far? in what circumstances? for whom and when? and so on. Since 'oral literature' turns out to be so *relative* a phenomenon, to take many differing forms, and to relate in varying ways to writing, it seems sensible to regard it as setting the parameters within which further questions can be asked rather than accepting it, as such, as the end result of research. I suggest that we can no longer be as certain as Lord and his followers when they assume that we now know what 'oral poetry' and its characteristics must be like. The reality is more complex and less predictable.

We need furthermore to resist the temptation I think we have all felt: to exaggerate the 'orality' of non-literate cultures and individuals. There are traces of this in the Lord-Parry research.[5] In fact many oral-formulaic studies treat the literary piece under consideration in a kind of vacuum, divorced from the written media that in almost all cases certainly lurked, nearer or further, in the poet's background.

'Oral composition'

This leads on to the question of 'oral composition' which has similarly sometimes been presented as a single and specific thing. Thus, if one can conclude from an analysis of the evidence ('formulaic' or whatever) that, say, *The Odyssey* or *The Song of Roland* originated from 'oral composition', the implication is that one has discovered something definite and precise (see Duggan 1973, Nichols 1961).

This impression is clearly given in *The Singer of Tales*. 'For the oral poet', writes Lord, 'the moment of composition is the performance ... singing, performing, composing are facets of the same act', and 'we now know exactly what is meant by these terms [oral poet and oral poems], at least insofar as manner of composition is concerned' (Lord 1960: 13, 141). Lord's encyclo-paedia article on 'oral poetry' confidently opens 'Oral poetry is poetry composed *in* oral performance by people who cannot read or write' (Lord 1965: 591). This claim has been accepted with alacrity by adherents of the oral-formulaic school. Lord is credited with 'demonstrating how a traditional poetry is composed', and thus clarifying 'our understanding of oral poetry's characteristics of style' and the 'principles' of 'oral composition [which] are basic and hold good for all oral traditions' (Buchan 1972: 55, 58). There are frequent references to the process of 'oral composition'; as if this is one single and identifiable process: 'the manner in which oral poetry is composed' (Curschmann 1967: 40), 'the technique of oral composition' (Alexander 1966: 21), 'the oral method of composition' (Kirk 1965: 17). A theory which began as applicable just to heroic narrative poetry gets extended – sometimes by the original theorists themselves – to encompass every kind of 'oral poetry', its characteristic apparently being 'oral composition'.

I would query this impression on two main grounds. The first is really just an extension of my previous argument. If there is no one simple category called 'oral literature' (or 'oral poetry') but only a complex and relative series of possibilities, the same is likely to be true for 'oral composition'. It cannot be assumed without detailed comparative investigation beyond just the Slavic

---

[5] Several of the singers recorded were in fact literate (Parry and Lord 1954: 54) but this is little explored. Parry refused singers he considered not to be 'the inheritors of a genuine tradition' on the grounds that he was only concerned with 'the poetry as it exists naturally' (1954: 13).

case that 'oral composition' is of one predictable kind for there are likely to be varied ways of composing orally, linked to different social circumstances or to the varying ways literary production and distribution are organised in different cultures and periods.

The second reason is more specific – it is just not true empirically that oral literary forms are always composed-in-performance. There are a number of known cases of composition *before* performance and of instances where, contrary to all the expectations so many of us had built up from our oral-formulaic reading, memorisation rather than improvisation is in fact involved. In these cases, composition and performance, conjoined so inseparably in the Parry-Lord analysis, can be split apart.

Somali poetry provides one illuminating case. In Somalia, in the Horn of Africa, oral poetry is a highly developed art. It has been extensively studied, both in its modern phase where radio and tapes as well as face-to-face delivery are employed, and in its earlier development. It includes many different genres, from lengthy *gabay* poems, sometimes of several hundred lines, to the miniature one- or two-line *balwo* lyrics (see Andrzejewski and Lewis 1964). Poetic composition is a highly prized and much-discussed art among the Somali – 'a nation of bards' as they have been described by some observers – and an admired poet can become acclaimed throughout the country. A Somali poem is always the subject of interest and discussion, drawing criticism if it is considered mediocre. Because they are aware of this 'Somali poets rarely perform their work until composition is completely finished in private' (Johnson 1971: 28) and 'spend many hours, sometimes even days, composing their works' before they perform them (Andrzejewski and Lewis 1964: 45). A poet's compositions, furthermore, become his own property, under his own name, and any other poet reciting them must acknowledge from whom he has learnt them. A good poet has an entourage of admirers some of whom learn his poems by heart and recite them. Then others, too, hear these recitations and they in turn memorise them if they consider them sufficiently beautiful and important. As is made clear in Andrzejewski and Lewis's analysis, it is indeed a matter of memorisation rather than simultaneous composition/performance. They emphasise the

> feats of memory on the part of the poetry reciters, some of whom are poets themselves. Unaided by writing they learn long poems by heart and some have repertoires which are too great to be exhausted even by several evenings of continuous recitation. Moreover, some of them are endowed with such powers of memory that they can learn a poem by heart after hearing it only once, which is quite astonishing, even allowing for the fact that poems are chanted very slowly, and important lines are sometimes repeated. The reciters are not only capable of acquiring a wide repertoire but can store it in their memories for many years, sometimes for their lifetime. We have met poets who at a ripe age could still remember many poems which they learnt in their youth.
>
> In the nomadic interior whole villages move from place to place and there is constant traffic between villages, grazing camps, and towns. Poems spread very quickly over wide areas and in recent times motor transport and the radio have further accelerated the speed with which they are disseminated.
>
> A poem passes from mouth to mouth. Between a young Somali who listens today to a poem composed fifty years ago, five hundred miles away, and its

first audience there is a long chain of reciters who passed it one to another. It is only natural that in this process of transmission some distortion occurs, but comparison of different versions of the same poem usually shows a surprisingly high degree of fidelity to the original. This is due to a large extent to the formal rigidity of Somali poetry: if one word is substituted for another, for instance, it must still keep to the rules of alliteration, thus limiting very considerably the number of possible changes. The general trend of the poem, on the other hand, inhibits the omission or transposition of lines.

Another factor also plays an important role: the audience who listen to the poem would soon detect any gross departure from the style of the particular poet; moreover among the audience there are often people who already know by heart the particular poem, having learnt it from another source. Heated disputes sometimes arise between a reciter and his audience concerning the purity of his version. It may even happen that the authorship of a poem is questioned by the audience, who carefully listen to the introductory phrases in which the reciter gives the name of the poet, and, if he is dead, says a prayer formula for his soul. (Andrzejewski and Lewis 1964: 45–6)[6]

The practice of Somali poetic composition brings home the point that there are other modes of composition in oral poetry beyond the oral-formulaic Slavic model.

The case of Mandinka griots' narrations is also instructive. As Gordon Innes reveals in his detailed analysis (1973) these have a fascinating blend of stability and change, involving both memorisation and fluidity. At first sight the various versions of this 'Sunjata epic', known throughout the Manding area of West Africa, seem to offer an exact instance of the composition-performance familiar from Lord's writings. It concerns the exploits of the great hero Sunjata as he established himself as king of Manding and Susu. Multiple versions exist. As Innes writes of the many versions found both in the Gambia (where his research concentrated) and elsewhere in the Manding area

> one almost has the impression that the Sunjata legend consists of a repertoire of various motifs, incidents, themes (call them what you will), and that each griot makes a selection which he strings together into a coherent narrative. (Innes 1973: 105)

He goes on however to show that this initial impression is at best over-simplified. He conducted detailed comparisons across a number of versions. One set were recorded by two brothers, Banna and Dembo Kanute, both widely regarded as outstanding performers. They had learnt their craft from their father, assisted (in the case of Banna) by the elder of the two brothers. Innes notes the differences in their versions. Starting presumably from the same repertoire, their performances differed both in the ground covered in two major incidents and in a number of details. So far then, there was the sort of fluidity one would expect from the comparative Yugoslav material. Furthermore there were indications that each brother adapted his version to the situation in which he performed, for example if leading members of the audience traced their descent from figures in the Sunjata story.

But when Innes came to a detailed examination of two versions by one and

---

[6] This account is supported by more recent work on Somali poetry, see for example Orwin 2003 and references there.

the same griot – Bamba Suso – another dimension emerged. Two of his performances of the Sunjata story were recorded, one for Radio Gambia, another to an audience which included Innes himself. The most striking point was their close similarity, in places extending to word-for-word repetition.[7] Though there was certainly not verbal *identity* throughout there was nevertheless a greater amount of exact repetition than one might expect from pressing the Yugoslav analogy. A degree of memorisation was clearly involved. The model of simultaneous composition-performance has to be modified here to include the point that much of the 'composing' must in some sense have *preceded* the performance – to a much greater extent than, say, in the composition-performance of the Yugoslav Avdo Međedović or the Kirghiz bards described by Radlov (1885). As Innes sums up his findings:

> At first sight the two pieces of evidence presented here seem to contradict each other. The evidence from the Kanute brothers shows that in the course of his professional career a griot's version of the Sunjata legend may undergo considerable change. The evidence from Bamba, on the other hand, shows that a griot's version may remain remarkably stable, both in content and language, over a period of time. Different interpretations of this evidence are no doubt possible, but, taken along with other evidence, it suggests to me a pattern of life in which a griot in his younger days travels extensively, listens to other griots and borrows selectively from them, repeatedly modifying his own version until eventually he arrives at a version which seems to him the most satisfying. With repetition, this version will become more or less fixed, and even the words will tend to become fixed to some extent. But even this version will of course vary from performance to performance, depending upon such factors as who happens to be present and in whose honour the performance is being given. (Innes 1973: 118)

In other words, a single model of the relation of composition to performance will not cover all cases. Lord's dictum that what is important in oral poetry is 'the composition *during* oral performance' or that 'oral narrative is not, *cannot* be, memorized' (Lord 1965: 592) can blind one to the interesting ways that elements of composition, memorisation and performance may variously be in play. in or before the delivery of a specific oral poem, perhaps even changing at different phases of a poet's life.

Similar points about the division between composition and performance come out in other African examples. The long panegyric poems in Rwanda and South Africa, for instance, are often quoted as outstanding examples of specialist oral art. Yet in Rwanda there was often memorisation of received versions of the praise poems, with minimal variation in performance, and the original composers were remembered by name (Kagame 1951). For Zulu praise poetry Cope concludes categorically that the specialist praise singers attached to the courts were concerned more with 'performance' than 'composition': the singer 'has to memorize [the praises of the chief and ancestors] so perfectly that on occasions of tribal importance they pour forth in a continuous stream or torrent. Although he may vary the order of the sections or stanzas of the praise-poem, he may not vary the praises themselves. He commits them to memory as he hears them, even if they are meaningless to him' (Cope 1968: 27–8).

[7] For the detailed examples see Innes 1973: 115–16.

Prior composition followed by careful rehearsal before public performance is quite frequently mentioned as the accepted practice for certain genres of African oral literature. Among the Sudanese Dinka, for instance, people sometimes called on an expert to compose a song to their requirements.

> While an expert composes for others, people must be near him to memorize the song as it develops. The composer mumbles to himself, constructs a few lines, tells the people to 'hold this' and sings the lines. As he proceeds, they follow him. When a song is completed, the expert is likely to have forgotten it, while they remember it in full. (Deng 1973: 85)

A comparable process was used for some songs among the Zambian Ila and Tonga, notably the women's song known as *impango*, which was always composed prior to performance. The woman whose special song it was to be first had to think out the rather lengthy words, then called in friends to help her. Together they went to a maker of *impango* songs who listened to the 'owner's' ideas, and then worked on it over several days. The women were called together for a rehearsal for several evenings until they had thoroughly mastered the song. Then the owner continued to 'sing the song in her heart' and practise it on her own and if she forgot anything asked one of her practice party for help. By now she could feel fully mistress of her *impango* and when invited to a festival was prepared to stand up and sing it in public (Jones 1943: 11–12).

Deliberate and protracted composition divorced from the act of performance, though certainly not universal, is in fact quite widely found in the practice of oral poetry. In some poetic traditions furthermore a distinction is sometimes made between poets (responsible for composition) and reciters (responsible for performance). The difference between the mediaeval European *trobador* (composer) and *joglar* (performer), for instance, is not unlike that between the Somali poet and reciter, or the composers as opposed to the performing bards of Rwanda. Here indeed, as in other examples discussed above, it does after all make sense to entertain the notion of an abiding and recognised text separated from performance. The situation is very different from the Yugoslav case where 'singing, performing, composing are facets of the same act' (Lord 1960: 13).[8]

In short, it becomes clear that 'oral composition' is not a single unique process at all but takes different forms in different cultures and circumstances. Even if one leaves out of account any contexts in which writing plays a part – unrealistic though such an omission would be – it emerges that even in the narrow sense of totally unwritten composition and performance, the relationship between these two processes varies: sometimes they are closely fused into one single activity (as with Slavic or Kirghiz epic), sometimes the performance is preceded by composition as a separate and distinct activity – with varying degrees and overlaps between these two extremes.

The relationship between composition and performance in oral literature is more open than the definite sounding term 'oral composition' might seem to imply. The theory that oral composition and performance are always fused

---

[8] For other cases of prior composition, together with the (common) complication of oral-written interaction, see Finnegan 1977: 79–87 and 1988: 86–109, also Chapter 11 below.

and that there is basically just one kind of 'oral composition' turns out not to be supported by the comparative evidence and certainly not to be true of all African forms.

The place of the formula

This brings us finally to the question of the 'formula', one of the basic planks in the oral-formulaic theory. This concept has been subject to a range of varied critiques which there is no need to follow in detail here.[9] I would however suggest that one reason for the continuing popularity of the concept despite the attacks on it has been the feeling that here at last we have pinned down some real characteristic of that special mode termed 'oral poetry' (and, by extension, 'oral literature'). In that context, 'the formula', I would venture to suggest, has become a matter of faith rather than something definite and precise. Once one removes the assumption that there is a special and separate category of 'oral poetry', that motive for identifying 'formulae' and 'formulaic phrases' disappears with it. There is no longer the need to search for the special stylistic feature of 'oral poetry' – for there is no such specific and identifiable category.

In any case, what really is 'formulaic' about the poetry that has been analysed by 'oral-formulaic' scholarship? Is it really something precise and separate? If one takes a narrow definition, in terms say of identically repeated word patterns, then, as has often been pointed out, this does not always easily apply to literatures other than those in which it was first 'discovered' by Lord and Parry. While if one takes a wider definition – one in effect implied not only in later extensions of the theory but also in statements like Lord's 'every line and every part of a line in oral poetry is "formulaic"' (1965: 592) – then the specificity of the concept evaporates and we are left with nothing solid despite the impressive-looking statistics. Are we not then dealing with something much vaguer and harder to pin down, something that in fact tends to be common to *all* verse (written as well as oral): the patterned repetitiveness of poetry altogether, building on accepted patterns recognised within the particular poetic culture involved? As has been pointed out by Nagler (1967: 291) this is perhaps little different from the structured repetitiveness of language itself – the combination and recombination of known elements in new but old patterns. In this sense poetic language whether 'oral' or written is merely one kind of language, and the occurrence of repeated patterns in oral poetry need not in principle any longer be regarded as some special and puzzling case to be explained in quasi-mystical terms like 'dependence on formulae' which seem to set it apart from other poetry.

Thus to spend too long trying to pick out some satisfying definition of 'formula' on the assumption that here at last is something specific to oral artists – its necessary or its sufficient condition – seems to erect oral art into a special mysterious domain characterised by an apparently precise but in

[9] Earlier discussions include Benson 1966, Rogers 1966: 102, Watts 1969; for an overview of more recent work see Foley 2002.

practice wholly elusive type of unit: 'the formula'. Any poet – whether Anglo-Saxon *scop* or modern jazz poet – has to 'work within the restrictions of his medium' (Cassidy 1965: 83) and within a specific social and cultural context; this surely applies to both 'oral' *and* 'written' poetry. Why therefore look primarily to repeated word patterns (as in the narrower definition) which form only part of the poet's conventional art, and not to all the other accepted patterns like music, parallelism, figurative language, use of soliloquy or address, themes known to be specially evocative for specific audiences, and so on? These may equally shape (and aid) the poet's diction, written or oral, and form part of accepted convention – and yet are seldom included in discussions of 'formulaic style'. The reason for this relative neglect, I can only conclude, is that these more complex points, so obviously shared with much written poetry, could only cloud the apparently simple yardstick, achievable in essence by word counts, which seemed to have emerged as the differentiating element between the category of 'oral literature' on the one hand and 'written literature' on the other.

'Orality' as multiform

This chapter has focused on a series of somewhat negative points. 'Oral literature', I have argued, is not after all a single clear-cut category, nor is it opposed in any absolute way to written literature. 'Oral composition' similarly is not just one kind of process, predictable from some detectable kind of style called 'formulaic' but on the contrary – and despite the assertions of Lord and others – takes a number of different forms. From one point of view this has been a critical rather than a constructive discussion.

However I would also claim that something positive has emerged too. The main point to emphasise is how very varied oral literature/oral poetry can be, both within and beyond Africa. It is found in many more manifestations than just the Slavic heroic poetry on which so much analysis has been founded. So even if one knows that a piece is in some sense oral, it is still an open – and a fascinating – question just what form that 'orality' actually takes. There are many other aspects worth exploring to try to answer that question: how was the piece delivered and performed? how widely known? how circulated and why? performed for whom (a very significant point often)? and in what circumstances? Questions like these can sometimes no longer be answered – hence perhaps the great attraction of the oral-formulaic approach in Homeric studies where answers could apparently be deduced from the text itself, possibly all we now have to go on. But in other cases, I suspect, more information could be found on these aspects than has hitherto, due to the concentration on 'oral composition by means of formulae', been actively sought.

Given the great variety of oral literary forms and the differing ways that 'oral composition' can take place, there is no short cut to discovering the exact process of composition and performance involved. In each case one has to ask further detailed questions about the circumstances and conventions of the particular piece itself and of its social and poetic background, as well as the personality (and in some cases age) of the individual poet. It is entirely appropriate too, I suggest, to ask about its relation to the written word. To rule out a possible relationship with writing on the grounds of some supposed absolute quality called 'orality' seems totally unjustified, and I would certainly go along with considering the kinds of questions raised by say, Adam Parry (1966) about the possible relation of the Homeric epics to writing, even at the same time as accepting that they are in some senses 'oral'.

It has been asked, 'Do we need a looser definition of "oral"?' (Russo 1974). To this, in the light of the arguments here, I would answer most definitely yes. And if we answer 'yes' to this then, as Russo goes on, 'hope for scientific precision must be left behind'. Here again I would agree if by this is meant precise generalisations that could be applied to some single category as a whole (whether 'oral literature', 'oral poetry' or even the more specific 'oral narrative poetry') or could locate 'oral composition' as one identifiable process across space and time irrespective of cultural and personal differences. The variations are too wide and too important for such generalisations to be either true or useful.

8

Time, Performance and Literature[1]

By the late 1970s and 1980s the term 'oral literature', though never uncontroversial, had become increasingly familiar in Africa and elsewhere.[2] In many circles it was now accepted that oral arts of the past or present could be treated as comparable to written literature – in their verbal constitution, literary qualities, generic conventions and, to some extent at least, the kind of analyses to which they could be subjected.

The interest was usually primarily in the 'literature' side of the equation, in particular its textual dimension. This had of course underpinned the huge and continuing research endeavour devoted to the collection and analysis of texts – taken to be *the* constant form in which literature is existent and through which it can receive wider circulation. Even in the oral-formulaic school, for all its interest in performance, the key process of formulaic analysis depended on textualised realisation – on having visible texts to work with. Indeed the whole idea of 'literature' seemed naturally to be intertwined with that of some abiding textual presence.

In this chapter, however, I want to turn the spotlight on a different aspect –

---

[1] An earlier version of parts of this chapter appeared in *Short Time to Stay: Comments on Time, Literature and Oral Performance* (12th Hans Wolff Memorial Lecture, 1981), African Studies Program, Indiana University, Bloomington, 1982. Though it has been substantially abridged and compressed, it is again mostly left as a statement of its time. Apart from the occasional added footnote it must therefore be read as relying on evidence that was available (some unpublished) by the early 1980s.

[2] The earlier interest in oral literature (see Chapter 6, p. 88, n. 6) had by the early 1980s been reinforced not only by oral-formulaic studies (Chapter 7) but by a spate of both African and comparative work by anthropologists, folklorists and linguists (see for example Andrzejewski and Innes 1975, Bauman 1977, Belinga 1977, Bright 1981, Finnegan 1977, Görög-Karady 1981, 1982, Lindfors 1977, Okpewho 1979, Paulme 1976, Scheub 1977b, Tedlock 1972, 1977, 1980, the established series *Classiques africains* (1963–) and 'Oxford Library of African Literature' (1964–), and journals or series such as *Cahiers de littérature orale* (1976–) and *Research in African Literatures* (1970–) and *African Literature Today* (1968–); for subsequent developments see following chapters.

the temporal dimension. One characteristic of oral literature is that, being oral, its existence depends on performance, that is, on a specific occasion or occasions, in a way that a permanent written text does not. This performance is necessarily an event *in time*. It both itself takes up time and depends on co-ordinating a number of activities within time.

This sounds a simple point, scarcely worth the stating. But the active organisation needed to put on an oral performance has often been overlooked. In the case of African oral genres, this neglect has perhaps been encouraged by the unexamined belief that such forms, being 'African' and 'oral', somehow bubble up of themselves in some natural and primaeval way and that the planning of time is of little moment in some close-to-nature unfolding of rural life. To take temporal aspects seriously also presents something of a contrast to the way literature is so often pictured as something which exists in space rather than in time. The image has been of something outside time, with some kind of permanent existence in its own right above and apart from the immediate pressure of the moment, somehow transcending the detailed occasions of everyday and conveying its message and its beauty across differing groups and historical eras. Even in the study of oral literature there is still sometimes an implicit model of 'literature' as something permanent and timeless which can be abstracted for study as 'text' set out in space.

Is this misleading with oral literature? Performance-oriented and 'ethnography-of-speaking' scholars have drawn attention to the 'event'-based nature of oral art – not so much spatial text as 'story-telling event' or 'communicative event'.[3] I follow a similar outlook here, linking this with questions about the organisation of time and of people's timed activities.

Organising and timing poetic performances

So how are performances of African oral literature organised in time? Does this involve planning? How are people's activities co-ordinated and scheduled? Behind such questions we have constantly to remember the oral nature of this literature. Like Herrick's daffodils,[4] oral forms, unlike written texts, have 'short time to stay' – indeed no time to stay without some organised and recognised event in time: they depend on this actual event – the performance – for their existence.

Co-ordinating people's activities so they come together at the same time and broadly for the same purpose is basic to the ordering of time in any society and, in particular, to the organisation of oral literary performance. For though there are occasional instances of solitary songs, the typical context for literary realisation is that people must be present together at one time and

[3] In the original lecture (1981) I particularly mentioned Dell Hymes, Robert Georges, Dan Ben-Amos, Roger Abrahams, Richard Bauman and Dennis Tedlock: their still-seminal contributions are now supplemented and extended by more recent work (see Chapter 1, p. 6 n. 3 and further discussion in Chapter 11).

[4] The allusion here and later is to Robert Herrick's beautiful poem 'To Daffadills' ('Faire daffadills, we weep to see / You haste away so soone ... We have short time to stay, as you / We have as short a spring ...' (1869: 132–3).

place – performer(s), participants, audience. Unlike written literature which arguably can in some sense 'exist' alone, oral literature depends essentially on people's co-activities.

Let me give some examples. One evening in September during my stay in northern Sierra Leone in 1961, I saw a crowd of people in one of the compounds outside the chief's hut in the village where I was then staying. They danced, sang and drummed for several hours, producing songs of the kind that could be recorded and published as texts of Limba oral poetry.

How did this apparently unpremeditated happening come about? In fact it formed part of a series of events involving careful preparation over several months, leading up to the boys' initiation ceremonies in the following April dry season. This initiation did not take place every year and its enactment depended on the interlinked actions of a large number of people. The boys themselves had to have been working hard all year, and the previous season too, to ensure a plentiful harvest for the rice needed for the ceremonies: otherwise they could not take place. Each had to formally petition his father according to the due forms to allow him to enter the ceremony, and in turn each father had to visit the chief to make a ceremonial request for his son, guaranteeing that there would indeed be enough rice for the occasion and accompanying his visit with the expected gifts and appropriate oratory. So time had already had to be found, and co-ordinated with others – for the visits, organising the gifts, and arranging through many months' labour that the due harvest would be forthcoming.

This initial sequence was followed by the boys undertaking formal visits as a group, setting the time in advance so they were free at the same time. One was to the local chief, making formal speeches and bringing gifts of palm wine and huge loads of heavy firewood (procuring both again took time). It was on that occasion that the evening of dancing and singing that I witnessed took place. This was an expected phase in the sequence but did not invariably happen in any given village and itself depended on prior planning. The group of boys had to clear their intention with the local chiefs, with the elders and with the recently initiated youths. In each case this involved a lengthy interchange on the lines of 'we want to dance ...', with formal speaking by both sides. The women, too, had to be ceremoniously requested and agree beforehand to act as chorus; so too with the lead singers and the expert drummers. When suitable local experts were not available, they were sought from other villages and had to make their way through the bush paths to be ready at the set time. Whether or not local, their participation had to be ensured beforehand with due interchange of gifts and words. One of the performers that evening told me that he had spent a long time earlier in the year making himself a new drum in readiness for this and similar occasions.

This single event then, which in textual terms could be abstracted into a few pages of poetry, in practice involved the co-ordination of a large number of people – not just the eighty or so direct participants in the performance, but also all those whose authority was sought or whose activities, often over the months, were necessary for providing rice, palm wine, or the standard gifts of kola nuts. An organised series of activities and decisions lay behind what on the surface might have looked a spontaneous event taking place in some kind of 'natural' way among a crowd of undifferentiated people. Yet the performance would not have been realised – the particular example of that genre of sung poetry would not have come into existence (and been collectable) in its particular formulation at all – without that specific event in time having been arranged through all those co-ordinated activities.

The same pattern was true of other Limba songs. In each case, their actualisation was through performance at a specific time and place and behind this was a series of organised activities, sometimes on a greater sometimes a lesser scale, depending on the genre and expected context. The singing and drumming that took place throughout the whole night preceding the final initiation ceremony in the dry season involved even larger scale co-ordination and numbers. Hundreds of people came together, many having travelled miles through the bush with their gifts, and lengthy preparations had to have been made by their local hosts for their entertainment. On a smaller scale were such occasions as the performance of special hunting poetry in a celebration known as *madonsia* following a hunter's killing of a bush cow. The date was settled and after the due preparations had been completed the hunter came out in the village at night with his followers (who, again, had to organise their time and commitments to be present), watched by spectators and participants from the village who had arranged their time to participate in the event.

This applied even to Limba work songs – a form which, of all others, might seem to spring up spontaneously and has, indeed, been taken as representing the biological roots from which rhythm and poetry perhaps ultimately grew (as in Jousse 1925). But these, too, sometimes needed some prior organisation. When the rice had to be hoed into the hillside, working parties were formed beforehand with plans for a particular day – and part of the planning was engaging a lead singer and drummer to take up position at the front as the hoers progressed up the steep hillside and answered in chorus to the leader's verses. He was not usually paid, but expected careful words of invitation in advance, and thanks and perhaps a token gift later. In their varying ways all performances of Limba sung poetry depended on similar co-ordinated activities leading up to and making possible the realisation of the literary event on a specific occasion – organising the necessary musical instruments and instrumentalists, the preparation of food and gifts for performers and audience, the presence and participation of both leader(s) and chorus, the interchange of formal speeches and permissions, and the coming together (sometimes after miles of travelling) of a number of people at the same time.

Every example of oral literature is dependent on some such background of co-ordination and planning for its performance in time – that is, for its actualisation as a piece of literature at all. Or, at any rate, this is one way in which such literary events can be looked at, whether or not they are also 'collected' and abstracted on a page as a 'text'. It is not such a strange perspective after all, for as Howard Becker rightly puts it for artistic action more generally, it is common for an artist to work among 'a large network of co-operating people all of whose work is essential to the final outcome' (Becker 1974: 769). Oral performances necessarily involve a number of people who are acting with full deliberation and knowledge in their appropriate roles with the definite and effective intention of bringing about a specific temporal event, the literary performance.

I suspect that every collector of oral forms who has taken any interest in the background to performance could expand on similar patterns of co-operation. In his account of Iwi Egungun chants among the Yoruba, for instance, Qlajubu (1974) explains how these were performed at the yearly festival of the Egungun society – a large occasion which demanded long advance organisation, involving not only the singers (who had undertaken special training and, for some chants, exact memorising) but also preparing the instruments, costumes, food and so on. The spectators could well number hundreds or thousands and the chanting extend for hours, sometimes the whole night through. Again, the Ijaw *Ozidi* saga, published as a lengthy text of several hundred pages (Clark 1977), depended on a long and complex series of activities – procession, sacrifice, a succession of dances, and spectators gathering at the due time (Clark 1977: xxxii ff). Even more protracted organisation lay behind the Bagre myths of the LoDagaa people of Ghana studied by Jack Goody (1972). One can look at these primarily as texts (and substantial ones, too, over 5,000 'lines' each) but also as performances organised in time – the outcome of a sequence of activities which far from just bubbling up from some deep 'mythic consciousness' involved hard-headed choices and co-ordination over many months during which extensive and time-consuming preparatory activities and ceremonies had to be undertaken. The culmination was the Bagre society initiation ceremony to which people travelled for many miles from settlements all around. Special arrangements had to be made for the 'Bagre Speakers' to be present. These were experts who had learned the recitation (another lengthy task) and had to repeat and teach it to the initiates. On each of the required occasions (there were several) the recitation had to be repeated three times – again, no light task: LoDagaa sometimes got around this by arranging for two people to recite at once as a 'way of saving time' (Goody 1972: 58, 69). This series of activities was not carried out just for the sake of reciting a particular piece of oral literature, but as part of a whole complex of ceremonies of which the myth-recital formed one part. Nevertheless it is striking that the actual realisation of what could, from one viewpoint, be abstracted as a piece of text on the printed page, or, in another prevalent (if misleading) model, as some natural expression of mythopoeic imagination, in practice depended for its enactment on a protracted series of carefully planned actions by a range of different people, each with their own part to play.

Prior organising of literary performance is not just a feature of large-scale annual ceremonies but also applies to those of more select groups. In Akan communities in West Africa members of particular associations such as the military and hunting 'companies' attended regular gatherings at which songs and drum poems were performed. A series of named officers and specialists were responsible for such events, among them the master drummer, various other expert drummers, lead singers and chorus. Company members were also called together for special occasions like a member's funeral or, as Nketia describes below, for notable success in the hunt:

A few weeks prior to the celebration ... the hunter (who must have previously sent presents of meat to both the head hunter and the chief of the town) now comes in person or sends a messenger with some drinks to the head hunter and informs him of his intention to celebrate his recent successes. The head hunter then accompanies the messenger to the chief and he and his elders are informed. The news is then passed on to all master hunters in the district, most of whom like to be present on such occasions to 'help' their fellow hunter, but more so to enjoy the fun of the celebration. Drummers and singers are invited.

When the day fixed for celebration approaches, the song dialogues already described are performed anew. The hunter with his attendants (boys in training) announces himself at the outskirts of the town by firing a gun. He bursts into song:

Amoafo, offspring of the father of mother Amoafo,
Amoafo, brother of Kwabena Ampadu,
Amoafo, run and meet me with open arms,
For I have killed a powerful game.
Amoafo, Amoafo,
Please run and meet me.

He is met by a gang of people. There are exchanges of songs: recitations of praises, declamations, congratulations, etc. as before. He is carried shoulder high through the town, to a background of much singing, to the place of celebration where the chief and elders, master hunters, men, women and children are gathered. He goes round shaking hands while drummers and singers call to him with his own strong names and praise appelations. ...

The hunter is of course very busy, joining in the singing, alluding to his experiences in the lead to the chorus refrains, and dancing with a gun in his hand, making symbolic gestures, impersonating animals, and so on. (Nketia 1963: 86–7)

The amount of organising or communication necessary to set up this event beforehand is striking, together with the number of people in different roles who had to interact on the day itself.

Even performances which seem more spur-of-the-moment depend on co-ordinated activities and prior organisation. Take the Yoruba *rárà* chants studied by Hans Wolff (among others). These were performed during a festive gathering in the houses of some wealthy or influential notable.

At any time during the course of the party the singer may begin chanting. There is no theoretical length limit to a chant, and the same *rárà* may be repeated, with variations, a good many times. When several performers are present, they often alternate in performing so that there may be chanting for the full duration of the festivities. (Wolff 1962: 50)

But specific events in time had to take place to make this apparently informal series of performances possible at all. The singers had either to be invited or to hear of the occasion through their communication networks so as to ensure being present. They had to make sure they had the necessary knowledge of the history of the family they were visiting, including the names of numerous family members both dead and alive, detailed information which took time to acquire. Furthermore, such singers were experts who had had to learn their craft over many years either through apprenticeship (for men) or frequent practice and experiment (for women) (Babalọla 1973: 80). Top singers tried to arrange for drum accompaniment (yet more co-ordination needed) and in return the hosts were expected to organise gifts of food, drinks and sometimes money (Babalọla 1973: 81, Wolff 1962: 49). Many actions had to come together for the *rárà* texts recorded by Wolff and others to come to fruition as events in time, that is, to come into existence at all in any real sense. It was not just anyone who could initiate an oral literary event or at any time – it had to be someone with the appropriate background, and the accepted temporal conventions had to be observed and the other people involved broadly act within their accepted roles. It might all look immediate and carefree, but once again depended on co-ordinating the activities of numerous people.

Prior planning of a more direct kind sometimes takes place even with relatively individual or small-scale performances. As illustrated in the previous chapter, not all oral literature arises through composition-in-performance and prior composition can sometimes be a lengthy and pain-staking process. There was the protracted composition of Chopi *ngodi* songs (Tracey 1948: 2ff) or the 'patient and diligent' process of composing certain forms of Bedouin ceremonial poetry prior to its being 'scrupulously memorized word for word' (Meeker 1979: 113). Or again, to recall one of the examples from Chapter 7, many of the Dinka oral poems collected and published by Francis Deng (Deng 1973) were not in any sense composed on the spot. Someone who needed a song for a particular purpose went to an expert who did the composing. Those present were charged with the task of memorising it for the individual client, who then owned it and could sing it on a later (probably already planned) occasion. The composing itself might involve considerable time, for it could sometimes only be completed after special investigation into the family's history (Deng 1973: 78, 85). Here again as in the many comparable cases of prior composition in both Africa and elsewhere we see the careful expenditure and planning of time.

We can also ask just how long such oral literary performances last. A simple-sounding question – but often enough we do not know the answer. Many of the big annual events at which oral performances were staged extended over many hours, commonly all night (for example chants at Iwi Egungun festivals (Ọlajubu 1974: 36) or songs at Limba initiation ceremonies), though in such cases the oral poetry might be broken up into a number of shorter pieces. Sustained poetic performance of what could arguably be regarded as 'one' piece could also be quite lengthy, though perhaps seldom extending over very many hours. Southern African panegyrics sometimes ran to some hundreds of lines, but at least in the case of the Xhosa as documented by Opland, the actual performances lasted a matter of minutes (the longest Xhosa oral poem he heard took half an hour, Opland 1980: 6, 31). Some West African performances were longer. The Malian Sunjata narratives analysed by John Johnson took two and four hours each in performance, the Mande hunters' *Kambili* song was presented in four performances lasting for over five hours in all, Bambara performances took two to three hours, while the Fulani recitations recorded by Seydou (1972) seem to have taken a little under three quarters of an hour. At the other extreme Fang sessions could apparently last for ten hours, twenty-four hours or even all night, and the Ijaw *Ozidi* saga was recorded in 'an actual performance ... told and acted in seven nights to dance, music, mime and ritual'.[5]

Often, however, collectors and enscribers have given little or no information about the background in time or even of whether the text was performed and/or recorded in one session. 'The text is the thing' and so long as that was sufficiently captured it might seem enough just to concentrate on that. But it is at least clear from such examples that, though the absolute number of hours of the performance itself may sometimes be uncertain and perhaps not always that large, it still does take up finite amounts of time and draws on the time of several people (sometimes large numbers) both in advance preparations and on the specific occasion – 'art' as Becker has it, 'as collective action' (1974).

Story-telling as events in time

So far I have been speaking about what could be termed oral *poetry*, which one might perhaps expect to be more elaborately planned than the forms conventionally classified as story-telling. But it is also worth asking about the stories which have been so extensively documented – documented that is in the sense that hundreds of volumes of entextualised African narratives have been published (see, for example, Scheub's extensive bibliography, 1977b). Might these tales, too, involve comparable time planning and co-ordination?

We can return to the Limba for an example. Here, certainly, story-telling was on the relatively spontaneous end of the spectrum in contrast to the more formalised ceremonies for which the date was fixed well in advance. Rather than deciding beforehand to have a 'story-telling session' people often just slid into exchanging stories, often stimulated by young boys asking each other riddles. Yet even here there were still temporal conventions to be observed. Many activities had to be co-ordinated to make it possible for people to gather together at the same time – story-telling did not just 'happen' of itself.

The evening was the usual time for stories. This meant that people had to have come home to the village from working on their farms, often some miles away, and be in the relaxed mood for enjoying story-telling. They had to have had their main meal of the day (normally the early evening) and this in its turn depended on a whole series of actions by a number of people: cooking, eating with the due forms (the father being served first and so on), clearing away; and behind this yet again lay all the organisation necessary for acquiring the food and the means for cooking and preparing it: getting the firewood, rice, leaves for the sauce, pounding the rice, fetching the water (a

---

[5] For these examples see Johnson 1978, Vol. 2: 21, 19, Bird 1972: 280, Kesteloot and Dumestre 1975: 22, Dumestre 1974: 66 (the longest text published took just under one hour), Seydou 1972, Clark 1977: ix, Pepper and de Wolf 1972: 7, Ndong Ndoutoume 1970: 18, Belinga 1977: 11. Later work, especially that on epic (see Chapter 9, p. 153 n. 9), provides additional figures: in their authoritative overview Kesteloot and Dieng report (1997: 30) that each of the examples of epic in their collection lasted at least one hour.

time-consuming task for the women and children), making the fire, boiling the water. Furthermore people were not really relaxed without palm wine in circulation and that depended on the daily evening visit of individual owners to their palm trees outside the village for the gourd left hanging there to collect the wine during the day. These activities had to be completed before there was even an opportunity for the telling of stories.

As well as all this, people had to be present in sufficient numbers to make telling and hearing stories a rewarding experience. Preferably this involved not just a narrator but someone to formally 'reply', and a circle of participants who not only reacted to the narration but also joined in the chorus of the songs, perhaps twenty to thirty people. Such groups often gathered on the veranda of one of the houses in the village (the largest group usually at the chief's house, but this was not the only place), so people who wanted to take part had to discover where their companions were and where stories were going on (if they were). Despite the public nature of many Limba activities, their villages were not so small that any one person automatically saw or heard everything that was going on or that all events were essentially 'communal' ones.

A further requirement was that there was nothing else taking up people's time on that particular evening. This may seem obvious, but it can be forgotten that in rural contexts, too, time is not unlimited (it can be too readily assumed that urban dwellers or industrial employees are the only people who are ever short of time). There might be a law case on the chief's veranda occupying leading elders and numerous onlookers, a formal welcome or interchange of greetings for a visitor, a village ceremony, a dance. Individuals could have other activities which on that particular evening they preferred to pursue – gossiping with friends, arranging to consult a diviner, playing with their children, weaving, basket-making, preparing tools for the farm or smithy, dancing, bush hunting (for the gifted experts), leather-work, sewing, spinning, hair-dressing, playing a musical instrument, making bead aprons, or, a common recreation, sleeping. Such activities had their time conventions and constraints too (some depended, for example, on access to a lamp) but they were all potentially alternative ways of spending time to that of telling stories.

Relatively spontaneous though they were, Limba story-telling sessions did not just happen naturally but depended on a series of co-ordinated actions and decisions. Broadly similar patterns seem to occur widely in African story-telling (insofar as this aspect is described that is – most publications concentrate primarily on texts). Wala story-telling sessions in Ghana, for instance, took place when people had returned from their farms in the evening and after they had 'had dinner' with all that that implied (Fikry-Atallah 1972: 398). Similarly, Bini family story-telling was in the early evening after the completion of work (including women's work, for the wives, too, were present, Ben-Amos 1975: 24). Among the Haya of Tanzania, stories were told within the household while the evening meal was actually cooking (Seitel 1980: 26), while Xhosa story-telling was 'essentially a private matter' carried out among people who knew each other well so as to ensure greater rapport (Scheub 1975: 12) – a situation involving less need for contact among a wider group but still demanding co-ordination of individuals with differing commitments and roles.

Time constraints about when stories must *not* be told are another common feature of African (and other) story-telling. Among the sanctions said to uphold the common prohibitions against telling stories in the day time are such penalties as going bald, livestock disappearing, general disaster, or horns growing on the narrator's or listener's head (Evans-Pritchard 1967: 18, Finnegan 1970: 373, Gecau 1970: 6–7, Hunter 1961: 534, Scheub 1975: 9–11; also Ben-Amos 1977: 27–8). I have always assumed that such prohibitions were not taken literally nor considered very seriously. Certainly, they are broken at times. However, the idea behind them is perhaps significant. It involves a recognition of the temporal dimension of story-telling in the sense that this both takes up time (which during the daytime should be spent on other activities) and is dependent on people being at leisure at the same time, free for story-telling. It also marks such performances as (temporally) separated off from the communications of everyday living and for leisure rather than work. Such separation is perhaps of particular moment in oral literature. With written forms, the physical mark of publication in a particular format on the written/printed page is what in a sense defines it as literary art; once that primary demarcation has been settled it matters little *when* we actually read it. With oral art such differentiation is (in part) indicated through conventions about the appropriate *time* for its enactment.

There are also questions about how long such performances took. African tales are often quite short (as delineated in the published collections at any rate) though the sessions in which they are told can be lengthy. Limba story-telling could extend to three to four hours, even though individual stories mostly lasted only a few minutes (half an hour at most among those I recorded) and a similar pattern seems evident elsewhere too (e.g. Wala in Fikry-Atallah 1972: 398). Other stories took longer. Ben-Amos (1975: 22, 51) speaks of Edo story-telling sessions in Benin going on all night 'till daybreak', in some cases consisting of just one story. He also encountered one narrator who told narratives lasting twelve and eighteen hours in two sessions and others who told the same stories taking two to three hours (Ben-Amos 1975: 51). In Sierra Leone Cosentino attended a three-night stand by a leading Mende story-teller in which he told what was essentially one story (with digressions) to an audience of six hundred people (Cosentino 1980). Among the Kalabari in the Rivers area of Nigeria, the pattern was different again – the same story carried on night after night, often stopped at an exciting point to lead on to the next night's session (Horton 1969).

Most accounts of African narratives emphasise the *content* of the stories and say little about its temporal context. Indeed it is tempting – I am as guilty here as anyone – to feel that having recorded the text one has then 'got it': the specimen has been collected and can be taken away for further analysis. I did not find it difficult to collect texts of Limba stories, but confess I am less clear how long individuals spent on story-telling when I wasn't there, how they chose that rather than something else, what compromises they had to make to co-ordinate such sessions. I surmise other researchers, too, may be a little unclear on such points. Possibly because of this gap, together with the still prevailing romantic view of 'natural' and untrammelled rural life, the impression has somehow got around that the African countryside was every evening filled with story-telling peasants gathered under palm trees in night-long sessions to pour out tales about the exploits of the tortoise or the ancestors. This may sometimes happen – but it can't just be assumed on the evidence of the story collections. There are still questions about when and how often and for how long such time events take place – how they are organised and co-ordinated, how much planning is involved, how people choose when (and when not) to tell stories.

When we consider these various poetic and narrative examples it certainly appears that the organisation of time – and of verbal art – in Africa is not confined to large-scale patterns dominated by seasonal and annual cycles, nor is it a matter of something passively accepted as part of some natural order. It scarcely accords for example with Pierre Bourdieu's famous comments on Kabyle peasants' 'attitude toward time':

> Submission to nature was inseparable from submission to the passage of time in the rhythms of nature. The profound feelings of dependence and solidarity toward that nature whose vagaries and rigours he suffers, together with the rhythms and constraints to which he feels the more subject since his techniques are particularly precarious, foster in the Kabyle peasant an attitude of submission and of nonchalant indifference to the passage of time which no one dreams of mastering, using up, or saving ... Free from the concern for schedules, and ignoring the tyranny of the clock ... 'the devil's mill', the peasant works without haste, leaving to tomorrow that which cannot be done today. (1977: 57, 58)

Rather there are a number of specific events – some necessitating lengthy planning, others more spontaneous but still dependent on short-term temporal co-ordination – which have to be actively organised and brought to realisation at some specific time. Each of these events makes a recognised point in time. In Africa as elsewhere time is not 'seamless' but divided up – created – by the events defined through social activities and in the social interaction of participants: one significant case among them being the co-ordinated actions enabling the enactment of literary performance.

Internal temporal features, sustainability and the 'unity' of texts

So far I have been mainly dealing with the external temporal ordering of oral literary performances. Let me now shift the focus to the temporal dimension of what could be called the more 'internal' properties of some African literary forms.

I have already touched obliquely on this in speaking of the temporal characteristics which help to define certain narrations as 'stories' – they must be actually told at one time (the evening) not another (the day). This kind of differentiation, both between ordinary and special events and among different genres, not infrequently turns (at least in part) on the temporal sequence of acts immediately leading up to and during the performance. There are many parallels to the Limba practice of introducing a story with a series of formulae – one way of setting the following narration in inverted commas, as it were, the equivalent of the printed page in written literary traditions. This kind of sequence may still be detectable in the enscribed text (though often not reproduced in full). Other defining procedures before or during the performance are sometimes not represented in the collected 'text' at all however and yet may play a significant part in the actual event. The audience was put in the right mood for Mandinka historical narrations for example, and the event defined as a literary one of a certain type, by a special musical introduction (Innes 1976: 26). Fulani-Hausa oral singers' performances at installation ceremonies were introduced by a conventional and expected sequence of actions: first the apprentices and praise shouters appeared, led by senior apprentices who performed for a half to one and a half hours before the master singer came on to be introduced by the praise shouter, and only then did his performance start (Abdulkadir 1975: 148). Musical themes and interludes are often important. In the Fulani heroic narration recorded by Christiane Seydou 'chaque moment de l'épopée se trouve, de la sorte, annoncé, préfiguré par la phrase musicale correspondant à sa dominante affective ou dramatique' (transl. 'each moment of the epic was in a way announced or foreshadowed by the musical phrase corresponding to its dominant emotional or dramatic theme') (Seydou 1972: 49). Similar scene setting was effected by the opening glee or curtain raiser in Yoruba opera/drama (Adedeji 1977), in this case with the extra purpose of gathering in the audience. Ricard's analysis of Lomé concert parties and plays describes the role of the initial music in defining the start of the performance and marking its appropriate time divisions:

> Sunset was invariably accompanied by the first twangs of the head guitar. Music was responsible for the temporal division of the performance. In the monotonous progression of the day, the real beginning of the show occurs when the orchestra starts to play. A unique moment beginning at a precise time – day must end before the music begins. From 7 to 9:15 pm the musical prologue serves to attract passers-by into the bar and helps warm up both actors and public. The musical prologue resolves one of the essential problems of all theater: how to begin? (Ricard 1974: 166)

The actual enactment in time is not always represented in the spatial sequence of the text on a page. By this I mean that it is often not clear how to answer such questions as: whether the piece as re-presented in the text was actually presented in a single performance or in bits (perhaps put together by the collector later); and, if the latter, whether the different performances were in some sense regarded as serials, to be performed as soon after each other as circumstances permitted (like the Ozidi seven-night performance (Clark 1977) or the Mende narrator's three-night stand (Cosentino 1980)); or ones that could equally be separated in time. Did the performances represented in the single-line format of a written text in fact include *several* lead-performers and/or participants (involving yet further elements for investigation about the co-ordination of their joint performances) or are the words on the page those of just a single narrator/poet? What was the balance for the participants between 'active involvement' and 'vicarious identification' (to follow Abrahams' useful terms, 1976: 207)? Was the narration 'fluent' and sustained (the way it looks after publication) and were there also repetitions, asides and interludes?

And finally – another aspect which it is hard to represent on the printed page – how did performers manipulate time in their actual performances?

These questions are often not easy to answer; indeed some authoritative publications give little or no clue at all as to such aspects. But they inevitably follow from taking the temporal dimensions of oral literary forms seriously – as ultimately realisations in time. Unlike written texts they have 'short time to stay' and an understanding of their nature, including their generic character-isations, is intertwined with such questions. Let me touch very lightly on a few of them.

First, the question of the direct flow or otherwise of the oral presentation in time. Because of the influential model of a text as something which runs on evenly over the page in a linear and single-line mode, it has seemed natural to focus on one dominant performer and ignore other contributions as 'interruptions' to the 'real' literary piece – 'real' being defined as what is abstractable as linear written text. But it seems that in African story-telling a number of people often contribute and that this is not necessarily conceived as disrupting the on-going presentation. Certain kinds of interpolation *are* sometimes classed as interruptions, as when Xhosa or Kamba novice story-tellers fail to hold the audience's attention or to present the story to their satisfaction (Scheub 1975: 13, Mbiti 1966: 25). But in other cases an element of dialogue was expected, as with the Limba story-tellers' practice of singling out a 'replier' to interject exclamations, questions, prompts and formal replies throughout the narration. In a printed text this would look like a secondary diversion or interruption, thus rightly ignored, but was very much part of the performance as actually realised and experienced as an event in time. In other cases again, a narrator draws in those present to participate, leading them in as a chorus in the songs he initiates or eliciting responses from the audience. Thus in a Gbaya narration:

Narrator:	Young men, listen to a tale!
Audience:	A tale for laughter, for laughter,
	Listen to a tale, a tale for laughter.
Narrator:	Young men, listen to a tale;
Audience:	A tale for laughter, for laughter,
	Listen to a tale, a tale for laughter.
Narrator:	Great men, listen to a tale;
Audience:	A tale for laughter, for laughter,
	Listen to a tale, a tale for laughter. (Noss 1970: 42)

Cosentino explains how a story-teller's response to the ritualised challenges – 'Don't tell lies' – in Mende story-telling could lead to a long secondary narration. In one case this took up most of one whole night, followed by yet another response to a further taunt before the full narration was concluded (Cosentino 1980: 55, 75).

This kind of interchange – 'interruption' only in terms of a textually based definition – does not occur just with stories. Ọlajubu describes how a Yoruba Iwi artist at Egungun festivals coped with audience interpositions within the framework of his chant: 'he devises ready poetic expressions with which he answers questions, checks noise makers and wards off other interruptions without having to stop his chant' (Ọlajubu 1974: 39). Interpolation was a

126

common feature of Yoruba *ijala* hunters' chants (and doubtless many other oral forms). Babalǫla illustrates the chanter's reply to a challenge which was itself uttered in *ijala*-chanting form, i.e. part of the *ijala* performance:

> It all happened in the presence of people of my age.
> I was an eyewitness of the incident;
> Although I was not an elder then,
> I was past the age of childhood. (Babalǫla 1966: 61)

In other genres, the convention was for audience members not to make interpolations during the presentation, and this understanding again forms part of the conventions of the event and genre. Thus interjections are expected and appreciated in Mandinka narrations regarded as 'fictional', but *not* in the performances of the more seriously regarded performances about Sunjata – apart, that is, from the presentation of money: 'friends and relatives of the griot's host are expected to step forward with their contributions, and they give these to the griot without any interruption of his performance' (Innes 1974: 10).

Such features form part of the distinctive internal structuring of a specific literary genre, as do the occurrence or otherwise of musical prologues or interludes, or the repetition or sharing of particular segments by several performers. It has been only too easy, however, simply to edit them out as interruptions or 'redundant' to the real underlying flow. But this reliance on the limiting spatial model of the text can cut off a full appreciation of the oral literary genre as it was actually performed in time – and that, to repeat, is the manner in which oral literature is realised and has its existence.

A second complex of questions revolves round how far the texts we have represent single performances in time, or how far composites whose unity may be in part brought about by the collector and collecting process itself.

Take the many collections and analyses of African 'myths' for example. Are these always based on actual narrations at a particular time? Or are these 'myths' sometimes in fact potential rather than actual sequences, in the sense of representing generally held beliefs but not necessarily enacted in a verbalised or narrative form? These are perfectly recognisable and valid alternatives of course – but they are not the same thing. Thus some publications may be misleading when they refer confidently to 'myths' with the implication that these necessarily took the form of explicit narrations as events in time. This expectation is easy for both collectors and readers to step into, perhaps partly due to the intellectualising tradition among many western scholars, with their inclination to subsume other people's beliefs under the models of western classical and scriptural literatures. Hard questions about the time factor (when were these myths actually narrated?) would do much to clarify the differing forms which people's beliefs can take – sometimes, certainly, expressed in sustained narrative form, but sometimes not.

Published poems and narratives often give the impression, through being presented as a single linear text, that they are from one performance in time – an impression that may or may not be factually correct. Some collectors are helpfully open about the standing of their texts. Thus Driberg's collection of

Lango and Didinga poems was sometimes, he explains, based on direct translation, while other poems 'are synthetic, composed of snatches heard on different occasions, each accurate in itself and homogeneous in content, but not originally one song. I am responsible for combining the different fragments in an appropriate unity' (Driberg 1932: 1). Again, Boelaert's publication of *Lianja* – 'l'épopée nationale des Nkundo ... authentiquement indigène' ('the national epic of the Nkundo ... authentically indigenous') (1949: 1) – was explicitly a synthesis of several versions.

Often however collectors say little if anything about whether or how far a collected text was actually (or indeed characteristically) performed as one event. In the past this was so of many of the published editions of 'epics' (with the increasing use of tape recorders, the provision of this kind of information is becoming more usual). Certainly it does now seem clear that, as mentioned earlier, lengthy performances do take place – lengthy that is, in the sense of lasting two, three or four hours, which when transcribed can run to several thousands of lines of text. Some examples are the Mande two to four-hour historical narrations amounting to around 1,000–4,000 lines in print, the Bulu *mvet* 'épopée camerounaise' (Cameroonian epic) of about 1,600 or in another case 5,000 lines, or the Fulani *récit épique* (epic recital), 'Silamaka et Poullori', which extends to about fifty pages of text.[6] But even in these cases unclarities sometimes remain about whether these were normally delivered in one session, and some collections divide up the text into a number of 'songs' or '*chants*'.[7] Some published texts represent a composite version, as Christiane Seydou for one makes clear in her lucidly argued explanation distinguishing the differing versions of the Fulani epic she presents (1972: 62ff). In general however the existence in parts of West Africa of lengthy performances as actual events in time is by now well-attested.

Some Congolese cases, however, raise more questions. The Nkundo *Lianja* synthesis has already been mentioned. There is also the famous Nyanga *Mwindo* epic. A text extending to about one hundred pages in translation has been published (Biebuyck and Mateene 1969), followed by a later volume of other epic texts of forty to fifty pages each (Biebuyck 1978b) – on the face of it clear evidence of a substantial epic tradition among the Banyanga.

But how far do such texts represent actualised performances of epics among the Banyanga? It may come as a surprise to learn that the evidence is far from straightforward. Biebuyck had for some time been looking for an epic in the area but had hitherto, he says, always been unsuccessful because every potential narrator was 'too old and too confused or ... did not remember the complete text', or was 'simply uncooperative'. Until he found Mr Rureke, the narrator of the published *Mwindo* text, he had been unable to get a 'complete and coherent text' (Biebuyck and Mateene 1969: vi). Nor had Mr Rureke ever before delivered it as a whole (despite being the single great performer in Nyanga country at that period according to Biebuyck and Mateene 1969: 17).

[6] For these conclusions see among others Dumestre 1974: 20, Innes 1974, 1976, 1978, Johnson 1978 (esp. Vol. 1: 219–20), 1980, Kesteloot and Dumestre 1975, Belinga 1978, 1977: 11, Seydou 1972 (also references on p. 121 n. 5).

[7] Belinga 1978 has fifty-five *chants*, Pepper and de Wolf 1972 has twelve *chants*.

The narrator would never recite the entire story in immediate sequence, but would intermittently perform various select passages of it. Mr. Rureke, whose epic was presented here, repeatedly asserted that never before had he performed the whole story within a continuous span of days. (Biebuyck and Mateene 1969: 14)

He was persuaded to give a performance for collection; but even then, this had to be spun out over twelve days, during which time Mr Rureke – although the greatest contemporary performer – became extremely tired and hoarse and had to be treated 'regularly with some European ointments and mouth-washes'. Biebuyck subsequently collected several other texts; some 'fragmentary' only and all shorter than Mr Rureke's. One (at least) came from an assistant who had worked closely with Biebuyck and knew well what was sought; some were provided in written form (1978b: 10–12).

If one shares Biebuyck's assumption that despite its lack of current actualisation a whole epic in textualisable form must somehow lurk somewhere (possibly, he speculates, with 'Ur-Pygmy' connections) then it might seem reasonable to suggest, as he repeatedly does, that the shorter narratives 'really' represent 'fragments of epics' (Biebuyck 1972: 258, 1978a: 337) and conclude that the 'promise of an even bigger harvest [of epic texts] is overwhelming' (Biebuyck 1978b: ix). If, however, one considers that performance in time is a condition of existence for *oral* literary forms, then the case looks different. One might question in what sense something can really be claimed to 'exist' as a single work when it can be said, as of the '*Mwindo* epic', that 'the whole work was seldom performed at a single session. It would take up too much time' (Harries 1970: 98).

The model behind such statements is that of a written work. Just as short extracts or separate chapters can be quoted from an existing written text in the full confidence that the whole work remains behind in some established written form, so with oral literature it has been tempting to assume that short episodes which could in principle be combined together must 'really' be fragments of some continually existing whole which lies behind these. The result, I suggest, is an assumption – and a potentially misleading one – that some underlying text must somehow always be really 'there' in some abstract and enduring sense irrespective of its actual realisation as an event in time.[8]

Issues relating to the temporal circumstances of performance seem of little significance within the spatial patterning of a text-on-a-page. But they force themselves on our attention once we start taking the *time* element of African oral literature seriously, and accept the implications of the idea that, unlike written forms, the existence of oral forms lies not in spatially defined text but in their realisation as actions in time, in temporal performance events.

Timing and text

A final question concerns the internal timing of an oral piece as it was actually performed. The topic has been brilliantly treated by others, above all by Dennis Tedlock (see below), so I will be brief.

[8] For different slants on this see Chapters 10 (on the multiple hands involved in enscription) and 11 (on such concepts as 'mental text'). Further controversies to do with 'epic' are taken up in the next chapter.

Oral texts on a printed page give almost no indication of the timing used in performance. I say 'almost' because the spatial conventions of paragraph indentation, chapter or section separations, and lineation can convey some hint of what in oral performance may be represented largely (though not necessarily solely) by temporal divisions. Thus the typographical markers which, in a written tradition, can conventionally define something as 'poetry' by printing it as separated lines, can also be used by translators of oral texts to convey something of the timing – the *pauses* above all – in the performance. Beyond this, however, representations as text mostly give absolutely minimal information about the performer's use of time. And yet, as I found from my observation of Limba story-telling, manipulation of tempo can convey drama, characterisation, structure and depth of meaning in a narration which as bare verbal text looks bald and unimaginative. By omitting such aspects, we misjudge the narrative's literary qualities. For the very effects which, in *written* narrative, would be conveyed by a greater elaboration of the words, are in *oral* narrative represented (in part) through the artistry of timing. As Dennis Tedlock (1985 [1980]: 349) suggests, we would surely regard as inadequate a notation for music which retained the notes but gave no indication of the timing, of the lengths of notes, rests, ties, time signature, sustained or changing tempo. And yet that is precisely the way texts from oral performances are normally published.

Some experimental notations have attempted to convey such points of timing on the written page, notably by Tedlock for Zuni narrations (1980) and, on similar lines, by Peter Seitel for Tanzanian Haya tales (1980, see also El Shamy 1980, Tracey 1967). An example will show the sort of text that can result from using conventional typographical devices (indenting, separation and special signs) to represent pauses of various kinds and changes in tempo such as long-drawn-out words (a full explanation is given in Seitel 1980: 36ff):

Now when she has come to the water . . .

  o

she speaks.
She says, 'Bojo, child-of-my-mother,' she s-a-y-s,
                                'My sister-
    in-law,'
        she says, 'Woman-of-people-forbidden-horn,'
She says, 'better to return and let me make amends, Woman-of-
    people-forbidden-horn.'
                    She says,
'Nine cows and nine maidservants, Woman-of-people-
    forbidden-horn.'

  o

She begins there,
        'Listen to my sister-in-law speaking.'
        She says, "Woman-of-people-forbidden-horn."
        She says, "Eight cows, Woman-of-people-
           forbidden-horn."
        She says, "Nine maidservants, Woman-of-people-
           forbidden-horn."

> Little tree, shake yourself. Let us from
> the spirits now return.
> Little tree, shake yourself. Let us from
> the spirits now return.'
>
> (Seitel 1980: 145)

Such experiments drew attention dramatically to the extensive information omitted in most written representations and went some way to unsettling the complacent acceptance of linear texts as the 'normal' way to present and analyse verbal art.[9]

Such features of timing can be significant for questions of genre differentiation and for the distinction often drawn between 'prose' and 'poetry'. Prosodic qualities like rhythm and metre are closely related to (if not wholly dependent on) timing but analysis of the linear text alone, especially when apparent 'redundancies' or 'unnecessary' repetitions have, as often, been edited out, may not yield the information necessary for a full understanding of inner structure. Taking timing seriously has sometimes meant reassessing the nature of certain oral pieces. Thus it has been argued for example that many Native American narrations currently printed as prose texts should be more appropriately represented as verse. As Dell Hymes summed up in a much-quoted statement

> All the collections that are now in print must be redone. They do not show the structure of the texts they present. ... Hidden within the margin-to-margin printed lines are poems, waiting to be seen for the first time. With all these collections we are at a stage corresponding to that at which the Exeter book was known to contain an Old English text called 'Beowulf', but at which it was not yet known that the text concealed an organization into alliterative verse. (Hymes 1979: 35)

Controversies remain about how widely such reassessment can be applied but this has certainly led to a major rethinking about the nature of printed (and ostensibly 'prose') Native American narratives and, as indicated in Chapter 4 above, has stimulated similar questions for some African oral literature. Can ostensibly 'prose' narratives sometimes be reanalysed as 'verse' if we take the time dimensions of performance into account?[10] Might this lead rather to a greater awareness of (for example) 'rhythmic prose' in African tales? Or should we question whether in the case of oral literature the distinction between prose and verse is really as solid or relevant as it seems in typographically bound settings? Exploration of the different 'speech modes' in Mandinka *Sunjata* performances (e.g. in Innes 1974) certainly suggests that more subtle differentiations than the blanket prose/verse distinction are needed and that attending to questions of inner timing (and other performance factors) undermines the assumption that typographically displayed prose is the 'natural' form with others to be seen as special deviations. Hans Wolff made a similar point in his study of Yoruba *rárà* chants when he indicated three main 'discourse' varieties in Yoruba, insisting, in opposition

---

[9] Additional possibilities are now available through multi-media representations, computerised text processing and the web (see further in Chapter 12, pp. 207ff).
[10] On the relevance for terminological controversies over African epic, see Chapter 9.

to the model of prose as the standard form for study, that all three equally demanded linguistic description (Wolff 1962).

Questions about timing can thus illuminate features of oral works which may be crucial for a full understanding of their qualities as forms of literary expression. Further they help to problematise a paradigm so deeply rooted over recent centuries of western literary formulation that it is hard to recognise, let alone query: that the natural and 'normal' representation of literary expression is in spatially displayed linear text. It can be helpful to offset this by a model in which, as for oral literature, its realisation can be understood as being in time, its performance as a *time* event and its inner timing as one central facet of its artistic development. Such a model replaces the common association between 'literature' and the concept of a permanent text somehow existing 'out of time', by a focus on the potentialities and subtleties of the temporal ordering of performance. McLuhan's famous generalisations (1964) about 'auditory' as against 'visual' man are surely too sweeping. But they help to draw attention to the spatial connotation of one dominant view of literature and the need for this to be complemented by a fuller appreciation of the crucial temporal dimensions in African and other oral literatures.

Literature and time

Might all this lead to some overall conclusion about the distinctive characteristics of African oral literature? that these perhaps lie in its rich sensitivity to timing (witness, too, the rhythms of Afro-American music), a contrast to the visual perceptions of cultures dominated by the written word?

Perhaps – but it might ultimately be more productive to extend the lessons from considering the temporal dimensions of oral forms to look again at written literatures. In analysing printed texts, too, could it be argued that we may have taken the spatial too seriously and overlooked the temporal? Do (written) literary practices not have more oral – and thus temporal – dimensions than we usually care to confess? Think of the sonic experience of reading poetry, of drama, of reading aloud, of the ubiquitous lyrics of popular music? Here, too, internal timing surely plays its part in defining the artistic structure.

Or recall the temporal aspects of setting up and realising oral performances – these also, if in different detail, have their relevance for the creation and experience of written literature (in Africa as well as elsewhere). It might seem nonsensical to ask how *written* literary forms are in fact actualised in time – surely literature exists just through having been written down: it is palpably there, permanently, in the text? But there is also a sense in which its full existence is *not* realised just through bound volumes being in catalogues or on library shelves, but through being actually read – realised in and through an event in time. Parallel issues could be pursued as for some of the oral forms considered here – do people in practice read books in bits or at a sitting? consume them in serial form or as single units? in sequence by numerical page order, skipping round, starting at the back? These are surely the active processes by which literature is actually realised in time, in its way 'performed'.[11]

Exploring the temporal settings and qualities of African oral performances can provide a foundation for going beyond the paradigm of literature as timeless spatial text. I am not arguing that taking this kind of temporal perspective is the *only* way to approach African – or any – literature. But adding in the temporal dimension and looking at literary production and consumption as performances in time can, I suggest, open up a wider and more truly comparative appreciation of the actualisation of literature.

[11] Since 1981 (the date of the earlier version of this chapter) such topics have of course been receiving much more attention (see also Chapter 12, p. 210 n. 6.

III

Working with Oral Texts

9

Constructing
'Oral Literature in Africa'
Hindsights a Generation Later[1]

The 'oral texts' that scholars take as their units for analysis do not have some autonomous or self-evidently demarcated existence nor do they persist in some unchanging abstract abode – though that is often the impression given by the easy way we use terms like 'oral tradition', 'story', 'poem' and so on. This is not to deny the reality of the verbally entextualised elements of human action and experience. But these take various forms and rather than being solid abiding entities they are created – and manipulated – in diverse, over-lapping and changing ways, shaped among other things by the actions of those who capture certain dimensions into writing and assign them particular labels. This is a much more multi-sided process than often realised – certainly more complex than implied in the familiar models of some formulated text out there waiting to be analysed by the scholar or of a clear separation between the creator of the text on the one hand and its reader and analyst on the other. Such paradigms, questionable perhaps for all literature, are particularly unhelpful for considering oral genres. Many overlapping hands are often at work and it is not a simple matter to disentangle their various contributions. There are not always clear boundaries between composer, performer and audience, between analyst and artist, between the local exponent, the enscriber and the interpreter of texts – all may play some part in forming and interpreting what eventually comes to be enshrined as an 'oral text' of some particular kind.

In this and the following chapters the emphasis is tilted towards the more 'outsider' facets of this complex spectrum: that is, on issues that arise when

---

[1] An earlier version of this chapter appeared as 'Reflecting back on "Oral Literature in Africa": some reconsiderations after 21 years', *South African Journal of African Languages* 12, 2, 1992: 39–47 (based on a paper for the 6th African Languages Association of Southern Africa (ALASA) Conference, University of Port Elizabeth, South Africa, 1991); though the basic lines of the published article remain it has been revised throughout, some sections omitted or compressed, others substantially extended.

scholars and collectors capture performed events into written texts, translate them into other languages, or define and analyse them in particular ways. We will need to return to this apparent division between insider-exponent and outsider-scholar, but for the moment this part starts by turning the spotlight more directly on some of the things that analysts and collectors do with the words that they are working with and perhaps at the same time moulding.

This was a process that I was certainly involved in not just in working with Limba stories and story-telling but when I tried in the mid- to late 1960s to construct some overview of what was then 'known' – recognised by European scholars that is – about the verbal arts in Africa. The book I eventually produced in 1970 and chose to entitle *Oral Literature in Africa* (its first chapter reproduced as Chapter 6 above) has to my surprise stayed in print for well over thirty years and been turned to some use as textbook and/or reference work. To that extent it has perhaps affected people's interpretations, both in apparently uncontentious matters and through a measure of (often illuminating) controversy.

So it may be of some interest if I say a little to put that volume into the perspective of the period when it was written, and reflect on some of the factors that shaped its coverage and presentation, not least why I gave it the title I did and why I used the label 'oral literature'. I will go on to comment on problems it tried to address and the general outlook with which I approached it, also on how far, looking back, I might now want to tackle some things differently. I will not attempt any account of the substantive work that has appeared since that publication but rather focus on issues of theory and methodology which shaped how I presented certain of these ways with words in Africa, and relate them to some perspectives of today. The aim is less to dwell on my own individual motivations (though they undoubtedly enter in) than to exemplify from the case of one particular work how the specificities of personal and historical circumstances can combine with more general perspectives of the time to represent oral productions (whether of Africa or anywhere else) in a particular light.

Some academic and personal background

First, then, some comments on how I came to write *Oral Literature in Africa*. This starts from personal and subjective considerations, but also touches on issues which, I believe, still deserve attention.

As with many others in my generation I began university studies with the then widely studied subject of classical Greek and Latin. Reading those wonderful texts – prose and poetry, drama and history, oratory and epic – was to me a magical and enthralling experience and one reason for an abiding interest in literature. Reading them through the eye and with careful attention to the plenteous critical commentary that accompanied them gave me great respect for the care needed to present and analyse texts with the utmost rigour. Reading them aloud, as I often did too, gave me some incipient awareness of their sonic qualities as well. I then switched to postgraduate studies in social anthropology, wishing to extend my knowledge beyond just the cultures of Greece and Rome (much though I loved them) and learn something about African cultures. This led to my first experience of fieldwork in Sierra Leone in the early 1960s where as will already be evident I became enthralled by Limba story-telling (in the process having to revise my classically based ideas about the solidity of texts), and took this as the topic for the doctoral thesis I completed in 1963.

One task in any thesis is of course 'the literature survey'. I was keen to undertake this in any case as I wanted to set Limba story-telling in a comparative scholarly context and publicise it further among scholars. But I found the task extremely difficult. The sources were scattered and diverse and the field not a recognised or coherent one in British scholarship. I was thus delighted to find a reference to an apparently forthcoming book on 'African prose' which I felt would surely pull together the threads of this disparate subject and give some overview of what had or had not been done – exactly what I needed. As it turned out the book was an anthology of African traditional prose texts to be edited by Wilfred Whiteley (1964): still important as the first volume of the influential Oxford Library of African Literature series but not the analytic survey I had envisaged. Those earlier hopes influenced my subsequent realisation that some book of this kind might provide the kind of help to others that I had earlier wanted for myself.

That was one motivation for the work. The other was that when in the early 1960s I started reading about oral forms in Africa I found the subject had little visibility in scholarly circles. Having, as I have said, become a great admirer of the artistry and insights in Limba story-telling – and following this of other genres in Africa – I had expected African prose and poetry to figure among established academic interests, parallel to those of past or present European traditions. It was amazing to find that this was not so, in English-speaking circles at least. There were a few magnificent exceptions, of course, among them B.W. Andrzejewski, Jack Berry and Wilfred Whiteley at the School of Oriental and African Studies in London, C. M. Doke in Southern Africa, J. H. K. Nketia in Ghana, and, among the influential American folklorists and anthropologists, W. R. Bascom and Melville Herskovits. But in general there was little systematic interest within British or even African universities; and even the two monograph series, *Classiques africains* (1963–) and the Oxford Library of African Literature (1964–), were only just getting off the ground.

It is interesting now to look back and consider the study of African oral literature in the early 1960s. In one way of course the conceptualisation of oral texts as 'literature' and their acceptance (under various labels) as worthy of serious study was not in itself new (see for example Chapter 6, pp. 88ff above). This did not just begin in the mid- to late twentieth century, as sometimes supposed, and the term 'literature' had long been applied to certain texts from the classical and mediaeval European literary canon that might now be termed in some sense 'oral'. And though we can now deplore the relative lack of appreciation for African forms and the sometimes derogatory or romanticising attitude of many scholars, there had been immense efforts over many decades in the collection of texts in Africa and elsewhere, often under such headings as 'folk' or 'tradition' but sometimes, too, using concepts like 'oral literature/popular literature'.

Nevertheless, in university literature departments, even in Africa, the main focus was on literature in European languages; and when works by African authors *were* considered it was principally the written forms (novels in particular). With few exceptions linguists concentrated on language rather than literature, while at that period most anthropologists, at least those with a British background, were limited by their particular focus on social functions, 'traditional' institutions and social stability, and showed little interest in artistry or individual creativity – hence the need I felt at that time to make a point of countering that prevailing mind-set. Folklorists, particularly those based in America, did indeed take some account of African oral forms, usually under the terminology of 'folktales', 'folklore', 'oral tradition' or, less often, 'verbal art', but for the most part were more interested in material from western cultures. 'African studies' centres were beginning to develop in African universities, but even they seemed more something to be indulged on the periphery rather than part of the university's central interests. It is true that there were important individual exceptions, but in general the study of oral literature in Africa was seen as marginal – if indeed it was thought of at all – rather than an established subject for teaching and research. Not only in uninformed popular views but even in some scholarly circles the model of Africa as a continent without literature or culture was still a powerful one. As I discovered time and time again from my own experiences, those interested in pursuing research on African oral forms were widely assumed to be preoccupied with primitive folktales, 'tradition' and outdated tribal lore from the past rather than a living literary culture. Oral literature had indeed little visibility.

And yet – the paradoxical thing was that so much was already known about the subject. The practitioners themselves of course – the story-tellers, the praise singers, the orators – already knew well what they were doing, even if their views had little sway in the world of western scholarship. A huge amount had been collected and published by earlier missionaries, administrators and academics, and there was an abundance of material in specialist journals and in newspapers, as well as weighty book-length collections. Nor were these just translated texts and summaries, extensive though these were; there were also comments, analyses and linguistic or ethnographic reports, and massive compilations in the scholarly traditions of French and German philology. But from the viewpoint of those embarking on the study of oral literature in the early 1960s, this rich material was near-impossible to get to grips with. It was scattered among many different sources (certainly not together on library shelves) and difficult to find. It was only too easy for scholars, not just beginners, to assume that little or nothing was known which could make it reasonable to speak of a tradition of African oral literature or its scholarly investigation.

Part of the rationale for *Oral Literature in Africa,* therefore, was to make the topic of 'oral literature' (as I conceived it) more visible as a scholarly subject and more accessible to potential researchers and enthusiasts. I needed to work through much of this earlier material for my own purposes – but I also increasingly wanted to establish the subject as worthy of being incorporated into university courses and as an area on which valuable research should and could be carried out. I hoped I might provide some foundation for this development by clarifying what was already known or not known, stimulating further questions, providing guidance to other published work, and (in the tradition I had inherited from my classical studies) identifying points of controversy to which scholars could address themselves.

My aims were thus intellectual rather than political. I began from the needs of my own doctoral research, was obliged to set this in a wider academic context, and then went on to build on this by tapping the resources of the African universities where I was teaching during the 1960s (especially the valuable Doke collection in the library of the then University College of Rhodesia and Nyasaland, and the magnificent 'Africana' library at the University of Ibadan in Nigeria). This was all fairly conventional academic research, if on a not so usual subject. But looking back I have to admit that my own values and aesthetic judgements did also play a part, even if not altogether consciously. Brought up in Ireland, convinced of the importance of looking to cultural achievements too often brushed aside by currently dominant cultures, entranced by the beauties and depths of, first, classical literature, then Limba story-telling and later of so many other literary forms in Africa – from all this I had conceived a passion to try to convey some of these insights to others too. I was also, I suppose, imbued from my own family, school and political background with a view of the value of every human being and of the importance of recognising their achievements and insights as worthy of serious consideration, however differently they might be formulated in different cultures.

So what I cared about was not just political or economic equity – important though this had to be – but also parity of esteem, of dignity. This was what seemed to be missing in many scholars' approach to African cultures. So, if I may be forgiven some personal sentiment before returning to a proper academic tone, it has been a source of joy to me to see the high-profile development of so much vigorous research and teaching on oral literature at African colleges and universities (happily rendering my own book increasingly out of date) and to feel that – partly by good luck in its timing, partly because of the efforts of so many teachers and students and local well-wishers over the years – my own book, with all its controversies and its faults, played some part in facilitating this development. For this reason, too, I greatly value the welcome I have had from fellow-students of the subject within Africa. One of the more moving experiences of my life, I confess, was hearing Professor Marivate of the University of South Africa's Department of African Languages commending the role of my book in raising and maintaining the 'dignity' of African oral literature (Marivate 1991) – something I so thoroughly wanted to achieve.

Those recurrent problems of terminology

These personal and intellectual preconceptions doubtless influenced both what I found and the way I presented and defined it. But let me turn away from more individual preoccupations to some questions of terminology which were at issue a generation ago and remain of some current relevance too. Insofar as the book's title and discussion in the book have played some part in focusing research and further debate since its publication it may be worth unwrapping some of the hidden preconceptions from which – not always knowingly – I was working at the time.

Looking back, I can see that each word of that innocent-sounding title – 'Oral literature in Africa' – was more problem-laden than I fully recognised when I was working out the book so many years ago. Even the apparently unavoidable 'Africa' and 'in' conceal important issues. Whether writing in the 1960s or now, how justifiable is it to produce any book under the generalised label of 'Africa' given the cultural, linguistic and political diversities within Africa, the different peoples and groups, or the contrasting periods of African history? Does such terminology imply particular stances in the earlier positions about *négritude* or in current debates about 'Afrocentricity' or about some special and generalisable qualities perhaps distinctive to 'African culture'? Or can using the terminology of oral literature 'in' Africa rather than 'African oral literature' do something to side-step such arguments? These issues do not go away, and may if anything be of even greater potency now than in the past, politically as well as intellectually. Finally, the 'in' hints at one of the assumptions in my treatment, namely, that oral literature needs to be looked at not only in literary terms but also in its social context: a perspective still up for debate.

Then there is that knotty term 'literature'. It remains an elusive and controversial concept, both on its own and when set together with 'oral'. I was up to a point aware of some of these issues in the 1960s and did try to pay them some explicit attention early in the book (1970: 15ff, reproduced above pp. 88ff). I still think, now as then, that questions about 'the' definition of literature are interesting but ultimately not particularly up to me to solve, if indeed solvable at all, while the etymological problems that some scholars have had with putting together 'oral' with 'literature' seemed to me rather obscurantist and silly – as if we worry about original Greek derivations when we use words like 'political' or 'economy' in modern settings – and in any case often narrowly ethnocentric. I did briefly tackle the problem of how to differentiate between 'literary' and 'ordinary' speech forms (1970: 22ff, see above pp. 93ff) but recognise it would now call for more extended discussion in view of recent work by sociolinguists, anthropologists and others on 'framing', different speech codes and spoken genres. By the later chapters I suspect I was probably treating the term 'oral literature' as relatively unproblematic. Many of my main sources were texts which, whatever their earlier provenance, were by then written down and seemed in principle analysable by the same kinds of processes I and others were accustomed to using for European literary texts. I was not then aware that newer terms such as 'orature' would be coming along, but in any case was at that time committed to 'literature' as one way of sweeping away many then-prevalent demeaning terms and assumptions. 'Oral literature' had already been used in comparative writings by some writers on Africa and, in more comparative vein, by such earlier authors as H. M. and N. K. Chadwick (1932–40, 1939) and more recently by Albert Lord (1960) and his followers; it was also very much in accord with my own interest in literature from my earlier classical studies. So essentially, despite its problems, it seemed to me the obvious term to use. But looking back I realise others might not have agreed and the title – and the book – could have been constructed otherwise.

I don't have any major regrets about this, and by now 'oral literature' has certainly become a widely used – if still contested – term in the study of African forms.[2] Numerous works have appeared in many languages and areas of the world under the title 'oral literature', including many specifically devoted to Africa, and it has also made some inroads into university and (notably in East Africa) school curricula, with textbooks to match. There is by now a large profusion of specialist monographs and collections related in one way or another to oral literature, oral narrative, oral poetry, linking African genres into the wider comparative work and vice versa. African oral genres, among others, have become increasingly visible as something of literary significance.

That 'oral literature' terminology which I chose to use might thus by now seem too well established to need discussion. But it has also become evident that both the concept itself and the idea of applying the term 'literature' to oral forms does still raise a number of issues. Some have been touched on in earlier chapters but it may be illuminating to bring certain of them together here (others are taken up in later chapters).

One of the most important single developments since the 1960s has been, in my view, the increasing interest in issues of performance. Anyone who has had first-hand experience of live performance will already have some appreciation of this, and indeed it is an aspect I have always considered of crucial relevance for the study of oral forms (e.g. 1967, 1970, 1977). But our understanding has been hugely sharpened by the contributions of performance-oriented scholars, starting especially in the late 1960s and now developing in new directions.[3] Such work has particularly highlighted the actual performance-event and process, the delivery skills of performers and how they are used, the significance of occasion and the interactions with the audience: elements which, far from being merely contingent and marginal – as in the traditional textual model of literature – are not only necessary for the realisation of oral literary forms, but of its essence. It has become clear that to understand fully these forms, we have to ask questions not just about the text of 'the story' or 'the song' but also about the dynamics of the actual occasion, the role of audiences, the perhaps-multiple performers, and the various verbal and non-verbal media used. The rewards of pursuing such issues and found-ing them in detailed ethnographic investigation have been increasingly demonstrated in some notable African studies over the last years.[4]

At the same time they also raise questions not just about 'mere' termi-nology but, more radically, over *what* it· is that we are dealing with. The term

[2] For further discussion and examples of alternative terminologies see Chapter 11, pp. 190ff.
[3] In particular the influential wave of folklorists and anthropologists cited in Chapter 1, p. 6 n. 3, also Chapter 11 below.
[4] For example, to mention just a very few, Barber 1991, 2000, Brown 1999, Chimombo 1988, Coplan 1994, Kaschula 2002, Kromberg 1991, Moyo 1986, Okpewho 1990, Yankah 1985, 1995.

'literature' does still carry connotations of a one-line single-author product, something crystallised and final, and centred on the verbal. This draws attention away from precisely the kinds of questions about process to which the performance-oriented approach has directed our interest. If we want to pursue such questions – and many would say they represent some of the most fruitful perspectives on oral expression in Africa as elsewhere – then should we be more critical of the term 'literature', even perhaps reject it for 'oral performance', 'oral/aural art', 'orature' or even the vaguer 'communicative event'?

The unease about the 'literature' paradigm is reinforced by the critiques of the once unquestioned concept of 'text'. The last chapter considered the limitations of a spatial model of text. That image is still a powerful one. But its problems are coming to be more recognised, at least as regards the long-held sense of a hard-edged work, a finalised and self-existent product which could be taken for granted as *the* defining basis of literary forms. From one direction studies of the significance of performance in relation to oral texts have raised questions about the 'performancing', and thus in some sense contingency, of written (not just oral) texts. From others, moves in critical theory have demoted the once unchallenged position of the text, and unstable electronic versions have brought direct experience of the less-than-hard nature of text. Furthermore we are now increasingly aware of the problematics of transferring multi-channel oral genres into the single channel of writing and of the arguably ethnocentric assumptions implied in defining multi-media performances primarily in terms of verbalised texts (see Chapters 10 and 12 below). It starts to be a question rather than a conclusion how far and in what senses a particular phenomenon, written *or* oral, is in practice 'textual' or 'texted' and in what its 'entextualisation' or its 'textuality' consists. The answers may be complex and relative – but they can certainly no longer just be taken for granted.

Keeping unquestioningly to the term 'literature' risks obscuring such issues. Once we say 'literature' it is easy (though not of course inevitable) to presuppose some durable text which somehow has its own absolute existence, independent of and superior to its contingent performances. It is also easy to go on to assume traditional textual models for the circulation and analysis of such literary texts – as textualised works – or to confine interpretation to the conventional textual analyses developed over many generations of western scholarship. Such analyses still have their rewards, certainly. But what the term 'literature' sometimes conceals are the additional questions now coming to the fore, and the controversial nature of the textual model it so often evokes.

Other potential problems are less radical, but still worth noting. They include the unconscious temptation, engendered by the term 'literature', of too quickly equating African forms with the literary genres of the traditional western literary canon. The use of comparative terms is a stock problem in any attempt at cross-cultural work, of course, and in some ways unavoidable (a point to return to). But it is particularly insidious in the field of literary typology, where what is imposed may be outsiders' definitions – often, indeed, value-laden classifications linked to politically or culturally dominant

144

traditions rather than local experience or perceptions. Once something has been identified as 'literature', furthermore, this may then get treated as a given, even as somehow independently existent irrespective of its social or political context or the historical specificity of its formulation.

Along the same lines, the term also insidiously conveys that the definitive dimension is the verbal – embellished perhaps by other media but the prime core which is of interest and which makes something literature. But again, as suggested several times in this volume, we cannot take this for granted in any given case. Further, this model can only too easily tempt us to brush aside those other genres that are today sometimes grouped together under the broader head of 'popular culture': not itself a wholly limpid category either but certainly one that brings us into touch with vibrant dimensions of African performance arts. Also the term 'literature' can – though it need not – suggest an unhelpful separation between (overtly) verbally based 'literary' genres on the one hand and, on the other, the films, plays, songs, popular novels, vehicle slogans, broadcasts or dances of contemporary (or indeed earlier) Africa. Similarly, it can suggest some kind of hidden hierarchy between the implicitly 'schooled' and established image of 'literature' and the arguably more multi-media and emergent qualities of 'popular' genres. This was already something of an issue when I was writing in the 1960s (and in fairness let me say that I did include some examples which nowadays might be labelled as 'popular culture'). But as illustrated in Chapter 11 below, the study and (perhaps) the extent of such genres has proliferated since then with consequences for the once comprehensive-looking concept of 'literature'. In this respect its potential limitations now look more obvious.

There are many issues then underlying that innocent-sounding second word in my title. The term 'literature' can indeed blind us to questions and approaches which have been opening up over the last decades. Should we then give it up?

Everyone will have their own views here, not least because the choice of terminology of course has to vary with aim and context and, as illustrated in the previous chapter, there are *some* purposes for which other terms provide a better way in. But for me the advantages of 'literature' mostly seem to out-weigh the costs. It focuses on features to which I do indeed wish to pay attention. It highlights creative, aesthetic qualities, and the significance of heightened and formalised linguistic activities in a culturally recognised setting – all terms with their own controversies but indicating features to which it is good to draw attention. It also draws the study of Africa into the terminology and debates of international comparative scholarship, with mutual benefit for scholars both within and outside Africa, and provides a basis for the visibility and worth of African literary forms on equal terms with those from anywhere else. And African texts, like those elsewhere, must equally be open to problematisation, susceptible to the same kinds of analyses as written literature, and with comparable controversies linked into the rise (and sometimes fall) of contending theoretical approaches, whether structuralist, psychological, narratological, Marxist, feminist, post-modern, post-colonial – or whatever. Here, too, the contribution of studies of African forms and their contrast and comparisons with others can build mutually

145

illuminating contributions to wider international scholarship than might be possible if they were ghettoised under some special label.

Even the problems of the term can be illuminating. It is true that 'literature' is not only an abstraction but arguably, like 'language', carries a series of culture-specific connotations (an aspect further explored in Chapter 12) and that to refer to the forms and actions that can be embraced by the blanket English word 'literature' brings us into contact not just with one standard formulation but with a host of diversities and fluidities. But I can only say that any kind of comparative study involves *some* general concepts, and focusing down on features around the concept of 'literary' happened to be the key interest of my 1970 book. Provided we bear in mind the too-often buried implications of the term, whether in Africa or elsewhere, it can indeed contribute critically to the comparative study of human artistry and action.

In short, for many purposes I myself would still support the term, while recognising that it is not the only possible one and that for some contexts others may be preferable. Most important of all, I would argue, is the realisation that we have an obligation to think carefully about its implications, consider both its benefits and its costs for particular purposes, and try to confront the issues explicitly. The term is indeed illuminating – and will also rightly remain controversial.

So far I have skated around the first word of my title – a term I thought relatively uncontentious, if slightly unusual, when I was constructing *Oral Literature in Africa*. But as will have become increasingly obvious throughout this volume 'oral' too has its problems. So let me here just refer briefly to certain considerations that have been emerging since the late '60s (to be returned to later, especially in Chapter 12).

'Oral' had already often been used to suggest a general contrast with what is written, but that opposition has since become more explicit. It has been crystallised in particular in what has become known as 'the orality/literacy debate'. The controversies usually turn on the questions touched on in Chapters 1 and 2 above (and to an extent underlying this volume as a whole) concerning whether literacy and orality represent different and opposed modes, how far literacy has generalisable consequences, and whether there is some distinctive type of culture, form or way of thought which can be classified as 'oral' and/or characterised by 'orality'. This is not the occasion to go over these issues yet again, merely to say that any user of the term 'oral' needs to be sensitive to their existence.[5] Given the controversies it has now probably become even harder than it was in the 1960s to apply the adjective 'oral' in an unloaded sense which by-passes the debates and carries no connotation of the various features that have been attached – controversially – to the generalised concept of 'orality'.

A further issue lies in the common assumption – partly originating in the debates just mentioned, but also existing independently – that oral and written media represent separate and mutually independent modes of

---

[5] For various viewpoints on the debates see Biakolo 1999, Finnegan 1988, 2001, Goody 1968, 1999, 2000 (among other works), Hofmeyr 2004a, Ong 1982, Ranger 2003, Schousboe and Larsen 1989, Vail and White 1991: chapter 1; also references in Chapter 1, pp. 7–8 and Chapter 2, pp. 15–16, and further comment in Chapter 12 below.

communication or expression. As will already be clear, I have long held the view that there is nothing strange or unusual in the interaction of oral and written forms, and that plentiful examples of this are found in Africa, as elsewhere, both now and in the past. Some were already illustrated in *Oral Literature in Africa*. I would go even further now, for the evidence has been amassing over the years, and argue that not only have such interactions been a regular part of human communication and expression for many centuries and in most parts of the world, but that it is time to move decisively away from the idea that such interactions are 'transitional', as if some half-way position between two separate stages. Even the terminology of 'interaction' now needs revision. For it may not be a question of the relation between two separate things, as 'interaction' implies, rather that – up to a point and within the constraints of convention and practicability – people are prepared to use whatever combination of media is available to them, whether these happen to be print, song, graphics, manuscript, visual display, audio recordings, live performance, or whatever – and do so undeterred by scholars' abstractions prohibiting such mingling as mutually incompatible. Africa offers many examples of these combinations, sometimes as prominent in supposedly 'traditional' oral forms as in those now sometimes classified as 'popular culture'.

This leads into a second dimension of the term 'oral': its implied contrast with the non-spoken or non-verbal. Using the adjective 'oral' to qualify 'literature' focuses attention primarily on its *verbal* constituents. But as the many studies of performance now make clear, oral delivery involves more than just words. There are also non-verbal sonic components (including music), kinesic and proxemic elements, the role of the audience – co-creators of performance but not necessarily in verbalised ways – and material and visual accoutrements: all features which may be essential for the recognised conventions of performance in any given genre, but neglected by focusing on the verbal constituents suggested by this sense of 'oral' (something to which I again return in Chapter 12).

It is still a convenient term to signal certain dimensions and phenomena, and, more important, debates. But it is liable to carry many potentially misleading connotations, hopefully now more appreciated than in the past, in particular the way it has somehow seemed to acquire a (highly controversial) kind of capitalised technical solidity in such phrases as 'oral culture', 'oral style', 'Orality'. Though I do not regret using it in my 1970 volume, if writing now I would certainly want to include more explicit and critical discussion of the term.

That joint phrase of 'oral literature', then, concealed many issues, far more indeed than I recognised a generation ago. Few may perhaps accept Walter Ong's etymologically based condemnation of it as a 'monstrous concept ... [a] strictly preposterous term' (1982: 11). But perhaps one of the benefits of the term, with its feel of oxymoron, is precisely that it *has* something slightly provocative about it, the flavour of making a point against the usual conventions which can startle us into paying attention. It rightly continues to form the focus of argument – debates which are significant for our understanding of the communicative and aesthetic processes in Africa (and not just Africa), today as in the past.

Topics to revisit

The study of oral literature and of Africa have of course moved on since I was compiling my survey in the late 1960s. Any proper report of the diverse and extensive work over the intervening years would be impossible – the reason indeed that I have never essayed a 'revised' edition of my book. But let me comment here on a handful of issues (others are taken up in later chapters) where, with hindsight, I might now pursue things rather differently from my 1970 attempt.

First, the question of oral composition. Writing in the aftermath of Albert Lord's *The Singer of Tales* (1960), I was much influenced by his analysis of composition-in-performance: the way in which oral poets produced variable but equally authentic performances drawing on a store of formulaic phrases and themes. To me this was a wonderfully illuminating way of looking at oral composition and performance.

However in time I became doubtful about the universalising tendencies among many oral-formulaic scholars and aware of counter-examples which did not fit the theory. Some are already mentioned in passing in *Oral Literature in Africa*. But from the perspective of today I recognise that some more explicit critical analysis of the topic would have been useful, together with further counter-examples. Some of these issues and examples are discussed in Chapter 7 above (in its first version written some six or so years after I completed *Oral Literature in Africa* and involving some shift of emphasis). To recapitulate briefly, contrary to what was suggested by the founding oral-formulaic scholars prior composition of oral forms *does* sometimes occur; so too does memorisation and the concept of a 'correct' version. The once heated debates over these issues have now settled down into some mutual convergence between once-antagonistic views, and most serious comparative scholars of oral forms recognise diversities as well as similarities, stress the importance of detailed field studies of living traditions and are cautious about arguing from specific instances to would-be universally applicable generalisations (see e.g. Foley 1988: 108ff, 2002). That set of controversies may have somewhat receded (though not quite disappeared) but the complex relations of composition and performance remain a fascinating topic in Africa as elsewhere, still raising issues that any contemporary analysis would need to address explicitly.

A second group of topics relates to narrative. One of the few explicitly theoretical chapters in *Oral Literature in Africa* was devoted to differing approaches to narrative, to provide some critical summary of the then influential contending approaches. The subject has emphatically moved on since. There have been many new collections, important analyses such as Okpewho's survey (1983) and the very substantial work of French scholars such as Denise Paulme and Veronika Görög-Karady on the morphology and themes of African stories, as well as extensive comparative work under the head of narratology. Africanist scholars have been making their own distinguished contribution to narrative studies more generally and approaching the issues from a variety of perspectives, a trend which renders my meagre approaches in 1970 increasingly out of date.[6]

Third, approaches to the study of genres have also been changing, something I need to comment on at greater length. Earlier perspectives had been much influenced by the emphasis in both folklore and literary study on universally valid genres or types, almost with a permanent and 'correct' existence in their own right, not to be subverted or mingled with others. It was easy to assume that African oral art, too, must naturally be formulated within such genres – genres which were drawn from the traditions of western literary culture. Up to a point this was perhaps inevitable. Cross-cultural comparisons always involve translation, and translation can never be perfect (or, indeed, neutral). But such attributions can also be imposed with little thought about their appropriateness or potentially political connotations, on the assumption that they stand for absolute and unchanging things – and once so labelled these attributions tend to become unchallengeable.

How to refer to the diverse generic conventions of African oral forms if writing in English – still often the language of scholarly discourse – remains a problem. Indeed once the question is raised, rather than just assumed, it becomes clear that even the processes and basic criteria for classifying literary genres at all are a matter of disagreement (see examples in Finnegan 1992: 142ff). This was a question I was already struggling with in *Oral Literature in Africa*. Insofar as I was interested in presenting it as *literature*, to be considered on an equal basis to other literatures, it seemed at the time natural to start from the broad categories with which I and my likely readers were familiar, largely rooted in European literature and, in particular, in the classical Greek and Latin literatures which at that time held such sway. Thus I drew on – though did not confine myself to – widely accepted and, as it were, 'dignified' categories like panegyric, elegiac, epic, lyric, drama, myth and (if somewhat differently based) the apparently contrasting forms of prose and poetry. I felt that these categories were not always the right ones to capture the specificities and richness of African forms, and in some cases said so. But I had to start somewhere and it seemed at the point a sensible and practical way to lay African literary forms before the readers (in fact I'm not sure that, given the material as it was known at that time, there were better alternatives). The problem, of course, was that by following this (rough) categorisation to group the material into separate parts and chapters the volume perhaps seemed to imply certain fixed divisions (poetry and prose in different parts, and separate chapters for panegyric, for elegiac and religious poetry, for lyric, and for children's songs etc.). In justice I might add that these categories were described as provisional and relative, used for convenience of presentation rather than the basis of any abiding typology; and that the importance of taking account of local typologies and terminologies was also stressed both explicitly (1970: 78–80) and in many of the subsequent substantive discussions. But still the organisation of the book probably gave

[6] See (among many others) Ben-Amos 1975, Cancel 1989, Cosentino 1982, Görög-Karady 1980, 1984, 1990, 1994, 1997, Görög-Karady and Seydou 2001, Jackson 1982, Okpewho 1983, 1998a,b, Paulme 1972, 1976, Scheub 1975, 2002, 2004, Seitel 1980 (also Finnegan 1992: 39ff, 171ff and further discussion and references in Chapters 4 and 5 above).

the impression of a more solid and generalisable basis for classifying than was really justified, and I mostly limited the direct problematising of such labels to just a handful of terms.

I did, as I say, express some doubts about the too-ready application of certain English-language terms to local genres, commenting in particular on 'myth', 'folk-tale', 'drama' and 'epic' (1970: 326ff, 319, 500ff, 108ff). Not that such terms are necessarily always inappropriate and looking back I think I was perhaps sometimes over-sceptical and certainly ignorant of material which has now become better known (I think in particular of recent work on African theatrical performances[7]). But I remain convinced that we do well to take a critical approach to the way western-derived genre terms have some-times been invoked under the unthinking assumption that such types have some kind of absolute existence and that African forms need to be presented under such terms if they are to receive proper international recognition.

The example of 'epic' is a much-discussed instance in this context, so let me treat it more directly here, thus amplifying the passing comments in earlier chapters. In western literature and history the term has had a particularly emotive ring. It has regularly evoked the model of the early Greek epics of Homer – crucial to the classical Greek experience that is so often envisaged as *the* cradle and paradigm of western civilisation. This Eurocentric vision of 'epic' was later further extended during the period of nineteenth-century nationalist movements by romantic assumptions that any nation worthy of the name had to have an epic to match.

> There was a feeling abroad that every European nation should have its epic, a feeling so strong that where there was none an epic was, if not invented, nevertheless somehow got together and produced. (Hatto 1980: 18)

There was also the assumption, rooted especially in the influential work of the Chadwicks on 'the heroic age' (1932–40), that the 'natural' evolution was for 'early' societies to move through a stage of heroic epic before progressing to other forms of literature. Together these formed an emotive background to a parallel assumption that seemed to be around in the context of twentieth-century colonial and post-colonial Africa, often linked to implicit evolu-tionary preconceptions, that 'an epic' was the natural form through which incipient nations could express and formulate their identity and make their mark.

Against this background, it should have been no surprise that many European-trained scholars at the time started from the unquestioned belief that there *must* be epics in Africa and moved rapidly to put that European-derived label on the forms they recorded (or sometimes went looking for). But when I examined the evidence as it existed in the 1960s, it seemed to me that many of these ostensible examples resulted from the unspoken assumption that African cultures, being at an 'early' stage of development, somehow *must* be characterised by having heroic epics in the same way as these were found in the course of European development from the Greeks. There was also the more generous-minded, but in the end perhaps equally patronising, view that

---

[7] For example, Barber 2000, Barber et al. 1997, Conteh-Morgan and Olaniyan 1999, Olaniyan 2004.

incipient nations of the twentieth, as of the nineteenth, century *should* have their epic poetry and that identifying and documenting this – perhaps helping to draw it out – was part of according due status to African cultures. The unspoken model relied on by the scholars, publishers and readers of the time was commonly that of epic in something of the same sense as the Greek models – that is, as normally then defined, a long narrative poem. Looking closely at the cases of African oral forms dubbed 'epic' in the 1960s I could not avoid noticing that many did not accord with that expectation, in terms of length, narrative character and/or of being 'poetry'; nor were such issues discussed by most collectors. How long is 'long' is a moot point of course. But some were short by any standards, or, as in the Congolese examples cited in Chapter 8, seemed less single works than a series of performances cobbled together by (mainly) European scholars with their own agendas or, perhaps, even written in (implicit) accord with their expectations by their local assistants. Others again seemed panegyric rather than narrative, or predominantly in prose rather than poetry. A few potential examples looked as if they would repay further study but by and large most of the African forms to which the title of epic had at that time been applied were either closely related to written forms in the Arabic script (some Swahili *utenzi,* for instance, were apparently direct translations from Arabic originals) or in practice, like the famous *Lianja* example from the Congo, mainly in prose with occasional verse insets.

Searching for particular Eurocentric genres and paths of development and then imposing them on the local material without some critical analysis and explanation of their appropriateness still seems to me poor scholarship. It is true that this stricture can apply, as I have said earlier, to any kind of genre attribution, within as well as across cultures. But the case of epic seemed especially flagrant and emotion-driven. My conclusion had to be that, contrary to the commonly held Eurocentric developmental model of the time, and with some possible exceptions that had still to be explored, the evidence in the late 1960s suggested that (I quote from the conclusion to my discussion in Finnegan 1970: 108–10)

> Epic poetry does not seem to be a typical African form. Some exceptions can of course be found ... nearly all of which need further published elucidation ... [But] the *a priori* assumption that epic is the natural form for many non-literate peoples turns out here to have little support. (1970: 110)

This in time became a highly controversial statement (sometimes, incidentally, rather inaccurately quoted) and resulted in a vast amount of further debate and analysis.[8] So let me say first that in some respects I would still hold to the general position that underlay it. I still think scholars should be suspicious of potentially ethnocentric generic terms and of collectors who rush to apply such labels without careful investigation of the specifics or of the issues raised by imposing foreign classifications, above all those carrying a heavy baggage of political and evaluative connotations – a matter perhaps,

---

[8] Among the early contributions to the debate see for example Ben-Amos 1983, Biebuyck 1972, 1978a, Johnson 1980, Okpewho 1977, 1979, Opland 1980, Seydou 1982, for more recent work see below, pp. 152–3.

as David Coplan put it, of 'cultural politics' more than of literature (1987: 12). After all when you come down to it what is actually so special about 'epic' that it should have stirred such passions? And must every culture fit into the particular view of human history based on the 'development-as-from-the-Greeks' model when there are so many other variegated riches to explore in African verbal artistries?

But in other ways I recognise my conclusion as a statement of the times, not only constrained by the material then available but also as engaging with theoretical and comparative debates then being played out but perhaps now of less force. I was at the time particularly concerned with the west-centred evolutionary presuppositions that so often seemed to blight the presentation and interpretation of African texts. By now both the arguments and the field of study have, fortunately, moved on. On the empirical front there is abundant evidence compared to the 1960s (my 1970 publication only covered work up to the end of 1967). There are perhaps still occasional traces around of earlier evolutionary preconceptions, but, more important, new theoretical ideas and methodologies have been brought into the discussion. Simplified questions like 'Is "the epic" an African form or not?' can be replaced by sophisticated analyses of both newly recorded and older texts and by well-argued analyses of what might or might not be termed an 'epic' (or 'epic elements') in an African context. I much welcome these developments. Indeed I admit that one of my hopes was precisely that my deliberately challenging 1970 note on epic would stimulate further research and analysis. And if the debate has occasionally been more passionate than academic, and my own position at times misrepresented, that is perhaps understandable in view of the (still?) emotive background I have mentioned.

This new work is too extensive to cover even in summary here but let me just draw brief attention to some of the developments. There are new viewpoints on what might be meant by 'epic' or 'epic-type' compositions in terms, for example, of 'cyclic' rather than 'unitary' forms (Johnson 1980: 311) and of the role arguably played by writing in the recognition or consolidation of epic forms (e.g. Opland 1983: 212ff). The critiques of the once-accepted distinction between prose and verse are also relevant – perhaps certain African forms originally transcribed as 'prose' (and thus on one definition not poems) should not have been so classified? and in any case perhaps the prose/poetry distinction needs to be replaced by more subtle and multi-faceted analyses (see specially Okpewho 1977, 1979)? Further the important concept of a performer's 'mental text' initiated by Lauri Honko, notably in his edited *Textualization of Oral Epics* (2000), may throw new light on the practices of both performers and collectors, and lead to a more evidence-based re-evaluation of what may have previously appeared to be merely fragmented and 'artificially' glued oral texts. In one way the controversies remain: cross-cultural and cross-chronological generic attributions continue to be elusive, a matter of convenience and judgement rather than with some ultimate verity. One still needs to balance the disadvantages at any given time of using particular genre terms, with their potential for giving a misleading impression of certain features of the form in question (especially if the chosen term carries strong moral or political overtones), against such advantages as facilitating comparative work or – as has happened with 'epic' (or, indeed, 'literature') – pushing at narrower earlier boundaries to open a wider and more informed view of the ways people may use words in sustained, decorated and in some sense poetic narrative.

But by now the whole debate seems somewhat misconceived insofar as its implicit focus was primarily on the 'traditional genres' of Africa – as if more recent constructions or enscriptions, or such cases as the Arabic-influenced Swahili poems, did not 'really' count. I would not quite own to such a presupposition in my analysis, pointing to the emphasis even in my 1970 account on the need to consider 'new' and emergent genres and include interactions between oral and written forms; but I wonder whether my note on epic perhaps unconsciously carried some hints of that? By now at any rate the term 'epic', perhaps in a more flexible and open sense than was current some decades ago, has come to stay in many collections and translations of African verbal art. The flood of publications of and on texts described as epics by now bids fair to rival the earlier prime focus on narratives (stories, myths, folktales, legends and the like): it is an extremely popular subject. And if I am sometimes doubtful whether in all cases their roots always go as far back in sustained and activated local performances as some editors imply, then at the same time I recognise that all texts have been constructed at one time or another (a search for some 'natural' and non-contrived setting would be fruitless) and that these texts are now an established part of the corpus.[9]

In any case we are hopefully no longer concerned with generalised battles about the 'existence' or otherwise of 'the epic' in Africa but can engage rather with the diverse and changing specificities of generic conventions and their activation in the many different forms of oral (and written) literature to be found in the continent both in the past and now. Some do in certain respects overlap with conventions once taken to be typical of 'epic' either in the once-established western high art canon or in Eurasian tradition more generally; others are more analogous to panegyric or lyric; others perhaps to none of the traditional genres of European literatures – but in all cases deserving study in their own right. The once-unquestioned concept of the universal applicability and permanence of literary genres which underlay some of the conceptualisations of African art in the past has given way to an interest in instabilities and emergence, to the detailed analysis of specifics rather than generalities, to more sophisticated treatments of the problems of cross-cultural translation and to the study of the new and (in some eyes) 'hybrid' genres that are a feature of modern Africa.[10]

---

[9] On epic and *épopée* see further the particularly useful collections, overviews and/or bibliographies in Belcher 1999, Ben-Amos 1983, Johnson, Hale and Belcher 1997, Kesteloot and Dieng 1997, Okpewho 2004b, Seydou 2004; also – to cite only a small fraction of the burgeoning and varied work – Austen 1999, Belcher 2004, Conrad and Condé 2004, Diabate 1995, Diop 2004, Gayibor and Ligier 1983, Hale 1998: 131ff, Jansen 2001a,b, Johnson 2003, 2004, Kesteloot 1989, 1993b, Ly 1991, Meyer 1991, Mulokozi 2002, Okpewho 2003, Stone 1988, Thoyer 1995, Traoré 2000, also earlier examples cited in Chapter 8, p. 121 n. 5.

[10] See Swanepoel's perceptive discussion (1983) of Sotho *dithoko tsa marena*; also, for 'mixed' genres, Chapter 11, p. 182.

What theoretical perspectives?

In a way everything I have said so far has related to theoretical issues, so this final section is scarcely moving on to a new topic. Nor am I intending to embark on some deep theoretical exposition which might provide The Truth about African cultures: I think that endeavouring to investigate the rich complexities of human cultural expression is more interesting than striving for some overall 'theoretical framework'. Nevertheless let me end with a few remarks about the implicit approach that shaped my 1970 book and its relation to other theoretical trends both then and now.

Oral Literature in Africa was never meant as a contribution to theory. With the exception of parts of the Introduction and of Chapter 12 (on 'prose narratives') it was rather intended as an evidence-based review of what was known to that date, and a foundation for others' subsequent first-hand work. I hope it did indeed serve something of that purpose. But I now realise that, as with all intentions of that kind, there were also latent theoretical assumptions, worth reflecting back on.

The book was partly a critical one in that it took up a stance broadly opposed to two powerful approaches of the time. It was anti-evolutionist and anti-functionalist. That is, it questioned the unilinear view of human development as an upwards progress, defined in Eurocentric terms, a ladder on which supposedly 'traditional' African cultures had to be classified as still at a relatively early stage – a popular approach in the nineteenth century and still influential in many circles in the 1960s (sometimes now, too, within loaded terms like 'development', 'modernisation', 'democratisation'). The anti-functionalist position did not mean rejecting the interest of investigating functions – indeed one of my concerns was to enlarge more 'literary' analyses by attention to social context – but rather a critique of the then focus in structural-functionalist anthropology on just *one* kind of function: upholding the social structure and maintaining the status quo (see further Finnegan 1969). This I considered a reductionist and limiting vision, which ignored the many other possible roles of oral art.

As against these positions, I suppose I instead wished to highlight the creative, individual and aesthetic aspect of human culture. I also wanted to replace the prevailing vision of Africa as the arena of 'the old' and 'unchanging', and of passive blind 'Tradition', and instead highlight the way people used oral literary forms actively and creatively, and for 'new' as well as 'old' purposes. To me there seemed nothing inappropriate about change or about combinations of older or newer media: I did not see why people in Africa should be presumed to be less able in principle to manipulate new challenges than their European counterparts or act less creatively (they might have had different constraints on their choices perhaps – but that is another story).

I was also putting forward a view of literature and of human culture in which looking just to the analysis of literary form and meaning on the one hand, or just to social functions and contexts on the other was not sufficient. I believed that insights from *both* literary and social scientific methodologies were needed: an approach that by now may seem unexceptionable but even many years later still sometimes needed arguing. While important for the study of *any* form of artistic activity, including written literature, for oral literature it is crucial. Here, to look to 'the text' on its own, separated from the analysis of its social context and its activated realisation, provides a peculiarly limiting perspective.

The book also assumed the importance of combining a comparative approach with detailed ethnographic research. I was not thinking here of some search for general laws or cross-culturally valid uniformities but rather of a sensitivity, gained from comparative study, to possibly recurring questions and patterns (differently though they might be realised in detail in different situations); caution about over-hastily accepting dogmatic statements about 'the facts', whether of one's own or another's culture; and that deeper appreciation of the special features of one's own culture and research topic that can only be gained from seeing it in comparative perspective. With this also went the belief (a typical one for an anthropologist) that this comparative perspective had to be combined with attention to the detailed ethnographic evidence – no doubt with different results in each culture and historical period – rather than just taking the scholarly generalisations on trust and assuming they applied whatever the local situation. Indeed one of the rationales for making scholarly theories explicit is precisely that a critical awareness of their content can prevent one from implicitly assuming that they 'must' hold good in every case, and therefore ignoring the need to investigate the ethnographic detail.

I might not have enunciated these assumptions in such explicit terms earlier, but they did indeed lie behind my approach to researching and writing *Oral Literature in Africa*. They thus no doubt shaped how I tried to search out and understand the material then available, and the way I formulated its presentation in the book.

I hope I will not appear too dated if I say that I would still in essence take the same basic approach today. There have been many changes and developments since 1970, however, and if I was constructing the book again today there would be not only, of course, a vast amount of new research to consider, but also new emphases and insights. These are too many to treat here (some are discussed in the following chapters), but for the purposes of looking back at my 1970 analysis in particular let me just briefly add three particular slants on the material to which I wish I had paid further attention at the time. None run counter to my original approach – indeed in some cases form extensions of it – but they do give further viewpoints on the older issues.

First, looking back now I think my original analysis was sometimes too bland, perhaps giving the impression that the oral literary forms were always and necessarily equally accepted by or open to everyone. That was not untypical of the period when the book was written. We are now more sensitised to the political and differentiated nature of oral forms (indeed of all forms of human action and expression). Not only is oral literature produced in specific historical and social contexts but its formulation and communication may well be constrained not just by 'free' artistic choices but also by the exercise of power or the manipulation of particular interest groups. Up to a point of course I was aware of this; and was also to an extent dependent on sources which were often themselves somewhat uncritical on such points. But nowadays I would certainly want to look more probingly for differential meanings and control, for whose views were being represented, and who controlled the processing and circulation of the texts and for what purposes (I return to this in the following chapters, especially in regard to the enscripting of 'texts', Chapter 10).

Linked with this is a second point: our increasing appreciation of the multi-layered nature of human action and expression, something that we need to take account of at every level. The varying forms of oral literature we study may well not have any given and single function or meaning. Each is likely to be multivocal, to involve more than just a single 'front' performer, to evoke multiple meanings in different situations and for different parties even in the same audience, and to have a multiplicity of functions. There was something of that in my 1970 volume, but nowadays, as I explore a little further in Chapter 11 below, most scholars would probably want to make much more of it.

Finally we are now more aware of issues of intellectual property than a generation ago, and rightly so. Despite my wish to insist on the importance of individual creativity rather than communal tradition, and my concern to document the names of narrators in my own field research, I do not think I did enough to highlight this aspect in my more comparative writing. It was partly that I was, again, to a large extent in the hands of my sources, many of which dated from a period when tribal rather than individual responsibility was often taken for granted and if any name appeared it was that of the (usually European) collector. Admittedly, questions of responsibility and of ownership present complex issues. But all the same, looking back, I wish I had grappled more explicitly with this and made more effort to extricate names or, at least, some further details (gender? age? background? ...) about specific individual performers in the few cases (for there were some) where such information was given.

Let me conclude this chapter with one last point. *Oral Literature in Africa* presented what I believe was a reasonably fair and straightforward account of the evidence available to me in the 1960s and a reasonably balanced analysis of how, at that time, one might approach it. But that is many years ago now. And even at that date it could not be the last word on the subject. A large proportion was unavoidably based on others' accounts rather than first-hand observation, and though by good fortune I was able to have access to an extensive and varied range of source material in both Africa and Britain this was clearly by no means comprehensive and was circumscribed furthermore by my own geographical, disciplinary and linguistic limitations. It would be counter-productive indeed if the review as it stood in 1970 was treated as some authoritative and permanent picture of oral literature in Africa or some perfect terminology through which to capture the complexities of oral forms, whether we call them 'texts', 'literature', 'performance' or whatever. Since 1970 there have been a multiplicity of new forms, new processes, new approaches and new research, including re-analyses of older forms. Attending to these new developments – both substantive and theoretical – and not only to the older established traditions, interesting as these are, must be one of the important challenges for the future. This may not be a simple or even an innocuous undertaking, but I am still convinced that it remains of the greatest significance. And it is more too than a narrowly academic topic – important as it is for scholars to bear their part – for it also touches on those great riches of our joint human experience, expression through language and through literature.

10

Creating Texts
Transformation and Enscription[1]

One of the many things human beings do with and to words is manipulate
them at one remove, in some way detached from the present moment and its
action. They study them, translate them, recontextualise them, reflect on
them. Creating and manipulating written texts is one major form in which this
is done – in the last analysis perhaps not really 'at a remove' at all, but certainly one notable and prolific way in which words are worked on.

It is scarcely surprising then that written textual representations have – for
centuries – been a medium through which verbalised acts performed in Africa
have been captured and in some guise transported to wider audiences. Texts
have been printed in innumerable volumes of 'folk-tales', 'stories', 'epics',
'poems', 'songs', 'proverbs' and so on. They are written down in manuscript
and unpublished notes and more recently as transcriptions of audio recordings. The processing into text has often been under the control of non-native
collectors, usually with the additional step of African-language expression
being transferred into a written European language. The arts of Africa have
become known in many ways; but a central mechanism has long been through
their representation and circulation as written text, the main basis for their
designation under such terms as oral literature, oral texts or the various
generic terms by which they have become cross-culturally designated.

This chapter explores some of the processes and actions through which
such texts have been constructed. The once-conventional if unspoken wisdom
was that in the published African stories, myths and the like we come face to

---

[1] An earlier version of the first, second and fourth sections appeared in E. Sienaert, N.
Bell and M. Lewis (eds) *Tradition and Innovation: New Wine in Old Bottles?* Durban:
University of Natal, 1991, pp. 1–23 and of the third in Peter France (ed.) *Oxford Guide
to Literature in English Translation*, Oxford University Press, 2000, pp. 112–15; but the
present chapter has been so extensively reworked that, like the 'texts' discussed here, it
has been transformed in the process.

face with authentic and quintessentially 'African' forms, independent of intrusive foreign actors or contingent social and historical specificities. We are now more circumspect. We cannot avoid the awareness that complex and often highly political processes commonly play a part in creating ostensibly 'above the battle' cultural products and traditions, and that the 'myths', 'proverbs', 'oral traditions', or 'oral histories' contemplated by scholars and others were not picked up pebble-like as finalised natural objects. Over and above the input of performers and their co-participants are massed a congeries of other interested parties – researchers, collectors, translators, publishers, educationalists, politicians, readers. The 'African tale' or 'oral poem' in a published collection was constructed not just by some original speaker or singer but by other hands too.

Over recent years there has been increasing attention to the complexities of what initially seemed the straightforward and finite task of capturing an oral form into writing (again something I would want to consider more seriously if rewriting *Oral Literature in Africa* today). We have been well reminded by, among others, Richard Bauman and Charles Briggs' recent *Voices of Modernity* (2003) that far-reaching ideologies and practices of linguistic representation play a part in shaping linguistic artefacts, all the more powerfully when these can be projected as 'oral', 'traditional' or exotic (and often, by the same token, as unequal). The actions and preconceptions of the multiple collectors and enscribers who worked on capturing into writing the oral productions of Africa may be as important for understanding the final written product as the apparently solid evidence of 'the texts themselves'.

Amidst these many actors I want now to concentrate mainly on the role of researchers and collectors: a convenient (if ultimately elusive) shorthand for those engaged in the active identifying, enscribing, translating, publishing or studying of oral forms, especially in their transformations in some sense or other into written text. The formative role of such researchers in shaping the texts – and thus in representing and publicising the oral arts of Africa – has received too little attention.

This chapter surveys the main procedures by which 'oral performances' have been re-presented as 'oral texts': that is, as texts which in some sense have (or are deemed to have) their origin in some performed oral event but are now documented and disseminated in writing. Representing such forms through the written word is a centuries-old mechanism for getting a handle on them, with written text long accepted as an (apparently) uncontentious and transparent medium for making visible the units that scholars scrutinise, as well as the proper outcome for their own analyses. But writing is actually a somewhat awkward medium for representing multimodal performance, and a series of steps are needed for spoken performance to become trans-formed into written display. Not that there is anything surprising or unusual about such transformations. The problem rather lies in the fact that we are so often ignorant of what processes and parties were actually in play and that even when we know or could perhaps find out, it is only too easy to ignore them and treat the resultant texts as if innocent and natural products.

159

The initial capture

Researchers have long wished to make some record of the oral form(s) they are studying. There might be several ways of doing so but perhaps the commonest strategy is to somehow catch it in a moment of performance. Even this apparently obvious step is not a simple one however. For what is being recorded is itself shaped by the encapturing act and by a range of choices, primarily though not wholly controlled by the collector, like the medium used, the selections made, or the setting for the capture, all of which can have far-reaching implications.

Dictation is one prime method for capturing text, particularly common of course in the period prior to the widespread accessibility of audio-recording devices and even now still utilised. It takes various forms, along a continuum from planned occasions where dictation is the explicit aim to snatched attempts to 'take down' what a collector hears during the flow, perhaps in note form for later amplification. The procedure affects the resultant text. The rather sketchy-looking texts of some earlier publications of African stories can be connected to the way they were 'collected', their repetitions and circum-locations constrained – or missed – in the process of dictation. Printed texts which confine themselves primarily to the basic plots or, going to the other extreme, are elaborated in florid and somewhat imaginative retellings may well have eventuated from hastily penned notes or general discussion rather than any kind of word-for-word transcription of performance. But since the processes by which the 'story' reached the page are usually not described the eventual reader is likely to be left in ignorance of many aspects of the original.

The resultant text is also affected by the parties involved – who speaks the dictated material, who enscripts it into writing, their respective agendas, their relationships to each other, and who, so to speak, calls the tune. The simple-sounding procedure of 'dictation' is intertwined with the specific setting and constraints within which it is enacted, moulded among other things by individual personalities and by culture-specific expectations which may or may not be shared by all parties in the procedure.

To illustrate how local conventions can affect the outcome let me take the example of how we created a text for the Limba tale quoted in Chapter 5 about a spider tricking an elephant and hippopotamus into a tug of war. It was told by an old man named Bubu Dema and in this case (unlike many others) I captured it from his dictation rather than on tape. The disadvantages were obvious. It meant missing out on the 'full' performance situation, audience participation and sonic artistry for which audio recording had proved so much richer a medium. And yet it was practical at the time. He felt like telling it when I happened to be chatting with him outside his hut – that very moment, too, no chance of going back for my tape recorder. In this particular context furthermore dictation was in some ways not totally inappropriate. As explained earlier, the Limba were well aware of both their own language and of linguistic diversity and had devised effective strategies for interpreting between languages. Whenever a respected non-Limba-speaking visitor was present, and certainly at most large rituals, formal 'speaking' meant enunciating utterances in short chunks, pausing for someone to transform this into the other language, then resuming with another chunk. Such situations were not some mechanical chore or time-consuming interruption but, as not uncommon in West Africa, an honour to the leading personalities engaged, giving their words weight and attention. Indeed the same process was used not just for inter-language interpreting but for reinforcing the voice of authority and making it more weighty. This was another context then in which the Limba awareness of the externalisable dimensions of language was manifested – of setting blocks of speech before the listeners, objects for interpreting and special attention. It was further marked by the way the speech as a whole was somehow objectivated – set in quotes, as it were, through the opening and, in particular, closing formulae that enclosed the full utterance.

Bubu was well acquainted with these practices both in general and because as an elder he had had long experience of playing leading roles in such interchanges. To tell his story in chunks interspersed by pauses was nothing strange but a process in which he could rightly take the lead and receive honour through my attention to and transformation of his words. In this case it was into my notebook rather than re-spoken in a different language, and for a story rather than public oratory. But he recognised the basic procedure, was content to co-operate with it and, as we shall see, to exploit it to his own purposes.

Such cases remind us of the potential diversities behind the ostensibly transparent technique of dictation. It can vary with genre too. It would have been out of the question to take down *songs* in this way, or, if not impossible, then extremely alien to accepted Limba practice. To understand fully the reality of any dictated text, Limba or other, thus demands more than just reading the written outcome, but also some grasp of the range of features likely to have affected the dictation process and what it meant to the participants – questions on which published collections seldom expatiate.

The eventual texts are also of course shaped by whose versions have been selected for dictation in the first place (a topic taken up further below), by how full a version is expected from the speaker and how extensively the transcriber tries to represent what is said. The same Limba story again provides an example. My presence as an attentive dictatee in fact gave Bubu a fine opportunity to move into a protracted moralising conclusion about how dreadful it is for someone to cause a quarrel between other people (especially his betters!) and how that evil habit first began from the spider's antics here. The text reproduced in Chapter 5 recounted the spider deceiving the elephant and hippopotamus and then when discovered fleeing from their wrath. Here is Bubu's continuation:

> The spider didn't want to be killed. That is why he ran away here to the walls of our houses.
>
> It's the same with two people. You go into a house and make a quarrel. You have nothing yourself, but you go and make a quarrel between better people. You make the better ones fight because of you, you who have nothing. You made them fight without seeing each other. So you see, someone who's good at trouble-making

injures people. Because he hadn't great strength himself, he set a fight between those who were great.

So too with a Limba man who has nothing in the village himself – he makes two people fight. 'If we'd known about it at the time, we wouldn't have fought; it was the spider made us fight, we hadn't seen each other. That's why we said that wherever we saw the spider we would kill him' [This is Bubu quoting the elephant's and hippopotamus' pronouncements]. It was because the spider heard them saying that in the bush, that he ran away to us humans. If you see us Limba making two people fight when we have nothing ourselves we are not good. They didn't fight each other unseen for no reason [they fought only because the spider misled them]. You see then – long ago people were afraid to make trouble against each other, and that is why; that is why people were always afraid to make trouble against each other. It began with the spider.

Since I had heard that story, I told it to Yenkeni [my Limba name]. That is it. It is finished.

This style of conclusion was far from unknown in Limba story-telling but Bubu was someone who liked to draw it out to extra sententious lengths. Both as an elder and as a personality with a talent for endless moralising he relished a captive audience for his words of wisdom. If he had been addressing only the children present they might have curbed his style by becoming inattentive and unresponsive but he knew I was hooked. But I, too, was making decisions – if not altogether conscious ones – about which parts of the 'story' I would attend to and write down. Maybe I was inadvertently showing by my body language at what point I was expecting his final words of closure? At any rate he did finally, as above, draw it to an end. Not just Bubu's actions but also my own (conveying perhaps that the story 'proper' as I envisaged it had reached its end) created both constraints and options which directly affected in what form the later-printed text was formulated and captured.

The relation between spoken words, dictation and textual encapsulation has sometimes been tortuous indeed. Take the justly famed collection of Dahomean stories published by M. J. and F. S. Herskovits in the 1950s. The medium was again dictation, but this time via successive translations. The collectors are admirably open about the process:

> Our method of recording was to take the text directly on the typewriter as our interpreters translated [into French] the narrator's flow of the story, given in Fon, the language of Dahomey. Except for native terms, or some locution phrased in Negro-French, which was set down as given in order not to interrupt the flow of translation, we wrote in English. ...
>
> The use of the typewriter brought out interesting reactions. At first, both teller and translator, watching the play of the machine with fascination, spoke on and on; some of the fullest tales were recorded under the influence of the novelty of having what was said taken on the typewriter. Later, when they were accustomed to the sound of the keys, they would on occasion attempt to confound the *yovo*, the whites – that is, ourselves – by talking rapidly and by including the elaborations of the actual story-telling session to test our typing skill. ...
>
> We recorded the songs to the stories after the whole tale had been told, for no electronic apparatus was available at that time, and singing had to be done into the horn of a small machine that recorded the songs on cylinders. To have attempted to record songs in their proper places would have meant a serious interruption of

narrative continuity. Instead, we noted the initial phrases of each song, and the full Fon text was taken down with word for word interlinear translations when the song itself was recorded at the end of a session. (Herskovits and Herskovits 1958: 6–7)

Texts formed through dictation do not usually build on such multiple overlapping layers (though perhaps more often than we know?). But whatever the details or specificities, the act of creating text from dictation is always a matter of transformation – more, or less, radical – rather than of mechanical transfer. The enscriber makes choices about which elements to catch in writing: opening and closing formulae? indications of volume or speed? repetition? elements judged to be 'digressions'? songs? different modes (singing or intoning as opposed to speaking for example)? The nature of the resultant texts depends on such decisions.

Selectivity is in fact a crucial factor in all stages of creating text, and indubitably so during its initial capture. This maybe appeared innocuous enough when researchers saw 'oral tradition' as passive and repetitive – having 'got' one version, that was then it: *the* tale, myth, tradition, life story, historical narrative or whatever. Nowadays it is seen as more of an issue, one that cannot really be avoided. Which versions are captured and whose? the 'best', the most extended, the most popular (if so in whose assessment?)? how many versions of 'the same story'? Even with products by the same author/performer, there may be an issue about which is given pride of place. It is true that some oral performances – and some genres, some traditions, some individual poets – are characterised by a degree of textual stability. But others vary, more, or less, extensively, on different occasions even by the same performer. The version chosen often privileges one particular event – fair enough, except that it is often implicitly presented as if a generically authoritative and, as it were, standard text. Collectors also select what they consider integral (to be recorded), what secondary, and (as I did with Bubu's story) where a potential text starts and finishes. This may sometimes fit reasonably with a document-based expectation that texts are finalised and solid products with defined edges. But for some oral forms – and some written ones too? – this leaves uneasy questions about just what has and has not been captured and presented as 'the work'.

Another thing that can get left out are the personal names of performers, composers, or co-participants. These seldom figured in early collections of African texts which were largely formulated in terms of their origin lying with the tribe, community or 'tradition' rather than individuals. More recently it has become commoner (though not invariable) to provide information that, quite apart from any ethical issues, may be directly relevant for a full understanding of the texts that eventuate. At any rate if names are not noted at the start they have little chance of re-appearing later – yet another of the many factors during this initial stage which influences the eventuating text and its future interpretation.

The *setting* for the initial stage of text-creation can also crucially affect the final products. The folklorist Wilgus famously remarked that the standard charge that some text had been recorded 'out of context' was always too simple: 'in truth, material is always collected "in context" – it is just that the context is usually that of an interview' (Wilgus 1983: 373). Over the years we have become more aware of the complexities of that simple-sounding word 'interview', with its social dynamics, expectations and politics (see for example Briggs 1986, Giles-Vernic 2001, Ibrahim 2001). And if 'interview' is not always quite the term, still Wilgus's basic point is surely right – there is always *some* specific context and this helps to shape the outcome.

Such contexts have commonly been classified under the threefold categories once delineated by Kenneth Goldstein (1964: 80ff) as 'natural', 'artificial' and 'induced natural' – ultimately unsatisfactory perhaps but helpful both in alerting to the range of possibilities and in making explicit the models that, under varying terminologies, often lie behind collectors' assumptions. Many earlier collectors implicitly claimed some kind of 'natural' or 'spontaneous' setting for their collecting – they were capturing the 'primary' materials unaffected by outsiders – and neither they nor their readers felt much need to elaborate on the details. In practice few if any oral texts could have been documented in that literal sense of 'natural'. In just about all endeavours to capture oral texts – and certainly those recorded through dictation, by purpose-designed writing or by audio recording at least in its more obtrusive forms – there must have been at least some element of setting up the action for the collector.

Little though the resultant publications usually convey this, some of the earlier documenting probably tended more towards Goldstein's second category of 'artificial settings'. Specially arranged sessions had a rationale within the antiquarian tradition: just as natural objects could be classified and studied irrespective of their habitat, so texts could be gathered equally well anywhere, whether *in situ* or with an overseas informant in one's study at home. Similarly, earlier emphases on salvaging 'old' or 'traditional' forms justified setting up collecting sessions with any informant that could be enlisted before everything got 'lost'.

Such performances are particularly open to being affected by the collector's expectations (or perceived expectations), encouraging, say, shorter – or longer – performances, or resulting in more – or less – carefully studied delivery. This does not necessarily make the resulting texts valueless (as I once tended to feel in the case of the *Mwindo* epic): such cases have their own reality, and can also be fertile occasions for innovation and emergent new forms. But it does suggest that in interpreting such texts we do well to take some account of how and in what settings they were created.

Something like Goldstein's third category – 'induced natural' settings (1964: 87ff) – gives possibly the most common contexts for the initial capture of African texts. Goldstein pictures a collector getting someone to set up a performance occasion; the collector attends as part of the audience and unobtrusively make some kind of record. Researchers can in fact often draw on local convention by, for example, inviting a praise singer to perform at a party, contributing towards a memorial ceremony, or acting as host for a session of riddling and story-telling whilst at the same time arranging for a tape recorder etc. in the background (recording devices are often in practice ignored, sometimes even an expected part of the proceedings). Such 'inducing' may of course affect the performance more than the collector realises. But since after all performances commonly depend on instigation by groups and individuals, it may scarcely seem unusual if researchers take an overt role (and in any case, where do you draw the line between intrusive researcher and local participant? – a point to come back to).

The categories shade into each other. Where my writing down of Bubu's story would come, for example, is perhaps a matter of opinion; here, as in other cases, much depends on local practices. And while Goldstein's categories helpfully highlight certain often neglected dimensions of the recording/documenting process, they can also lend themselves to the questionable assumption that research objects are already there, uncontaminated by interventions from outside – we just need to get the best setting for capturing them. Is there really any such thing as a truly 'natural' or truly 'artificial' situation? Some settings may indeed be contrived more by 'outsiders' than 'insiders' and the power relations more complex than acknowledged in the eventuating texts. But what matters is probably less the generalised categories than the specifics in the setting, not least the key actors in the situation, and who took what role in setting it up, what powers they exerted, and the constraints and inducements they were acting under. The researcher/collector is one, but only one, of these many different participants whose actions and viewpoints contributed to the occasion.

It is also only too easy, when we see the smooth textual result, to forget that the setting might have varied from a familiar and recurrent situation in which performers were delivering relatively crystallised text, to one in which they had perhaps *never* strung together the words in this particular frame before; or, further, the way that it will have in some degree or other been affected by the expectations of collector, performer and/or sponsor. The innocent-looking text that results tempts us to ignore its moulding by that initial recording setting and its participants, factors about which we are usually left in ignorance.

Finally it is worth mention that text has also quite commonly been created not from the situation of performance but through being specially written by someone acquainted with the local language and culture. Such writers build, or are thought to build, on their own experiences and recollections of performances – in one way a kind of inner dictation, it might be said, perhaps from a recalled re-created performance. This once perhaps seemed to give direct access to the 'original' forms, free of external intrusion. But such writing, too, is shaped by current arrangements and conventions. Missionaries, researchers, administrators, or educationalists have sought or welcomed written texts of particular kinds. Their scribes and collaborators were often, like Biebuyck's assistant in his quest for the Nyanga *Mwindo* epic (above, p. 128), themselves well aware of – and persuaded by – their employers' or teachers' expectations. The writers' own backgrounds had their effect too. Sometimes they may have been well versed in, even noted exponents of, the genres being sought – but not always. Schoolboys were commonly set to produce texts, whether or not they had much, or any, expertise in the genres they were expected to transfer into a written medium (and often, further, into a European language). Some writers were steeped in a European educational and religious tradition, not without its own influence in shaping the outcome, and many must have had their own agendas as members of particular interest groups. Nor is this just a matter of history. Now, as in the past, texts are being produced by writers who naturally have their own expectations, purposes, stereotypes and target audiences.

It would be over-simple just to complain that such written texts give 'inauthentic' representations of the 'original'. They, too, are in their way originals and the enscribers their authors – doing things, as ever, with words. Their productions may start off new literary genres or extend established ones. The danger is of taking them for what they are not: they are written forms, more, or sometimes less, related to memories and experiences of performed oral genres and moulded by many other experiences and pressures as well, rather than direct and neutral transfers, culture- and interest-free, of some prior oral performance. And the same general point could be applied to the initial formulation of all texts envisaged as somehow capturing oral performances. As with other forms of doing things with words the 'oral texts' we encounter need to be considered with some understanding of, among other things, the situations and processes through which, right from the start, they have been selectively and complexly constructed.

Snaring into writing

This brings us inevitably into the topic of transcription. Nowadays that term is most commonly used of transforming audio recordings into written words, but it can equally be applied to textual capture direct (in some sense) from live performance, as in the examples of dictation referred to earlier. Sometimes taken to be a relatively mechanical task not requiring much expertise or judgement, the processes of transcribing are in fact far from simple and the choices made in relation to it can have radical effects on the creation of text.[2]

The first factor, perhaps surprisingly, is the script used to transcribe into. For most readers of this volume some form of alphabetic script might seem the natural and inevitable choice. But it is not the only possibility. Take the example of Mende stories from Sierra Leone. The standard collections (such as Cosentino 1982, Kilson 1976) are based on alphabetic transcripts. A fair enough format – but there could have been others. Arabic script has a long history throughout West Africa, including Sierra Leone, used not just for works in Arabic but also for writing and transcribing in local languages. Other writing systems had also been invented and put into use in parts of Sierra Leone during the nineteenth and early twentieth centuries (Dalby 1967–9). One example was the syllabary devised specifically for Mende by the tailor Kisimi Kamara in 1921 which in the 1920s and 1930s was attaining some popularity in Mende country, eventually to be ousted by the European 'Africa' alphabet promoted by the colonial administration.[3] By the mid-twentieth

---

[2] The particular challenges raised by video are not pursued here, nor are detailed practical or technical points (already well covered in the standard folklore and oral history manuals). For perceptive treatments of general transcription issues see Bauman and Briggs 2003 chapters 6–7, Bendix 1997 chapter 7, Graham 1995: 152ff, Haring 1994: Introduction, Honko 2000, Ochs 1979, Woodley 2004.

[3] On the Mende script and its treatment see Dalby 1967: 18–25, 44–5, Francis and Kamanda 2001: 232, Tuchscherer 1995, also Bledsoe and Robey 1993.

century alphabetic transcription certainly seemed the natural form, above all for a British or American researcher (as it did to me). But in assessing how the texts we deal with have been formulated we do well to remember that the Latin alphabet is not a universal medium for enscripting oral utterances, just one culturally and historically specific variant which in turn affects the outcome.

Other transcription choices – about spelling for example – at first sight seem trivial but the orthographies or dialect chosen can have political as well as technical results for the eventual texts, sometimes with further repercussions if, for example, systematic forms have not been established or there are loaded sectional conflicts. And even the use or otherwise of capitalisation may have consequences. I was surely not the only one to hesitate over such points as whether to write down *wosi* or *Wosi* (the Limba spider). My choice of the former had knock-on effects for the translated and printed texts and got built into the eventual analysis; as mentioned earlier, 'a/the spider' gives a rather different impression of the nature and action of the stories from the alternative (and also widely accepted) choices of 'Spider', 'Mr Spider' or 'Bra Spider'.

Even punctuation and layout affect the outcome for, contrary to the impression often given by the resultant text, it is not always obvious just how divisions should be signalled in writing, for example by marking paragraphs, sentences, lines, stanzas. Transcribers also construct the text through the ways they deploy (written) conventions such as quote marks, direct/indirect speech, question marks, exclamations, or whether they transcribe something 'as verse' or 'as prose' (and if as verse, how demarcated into lines or verses). Indications in the delivery, both verbal and non-verbal, may indeed feed into such decisions. In Shona performances for example 'gestures and other bodily movements are distributed in such a way that an observer can often sense the shape of sentences, paragraphs, and the rising action of a story simply by observing these movements' (Klassen 2004: 150). But assessments like this, which ultimately help to shape the text, are seldom unchallengeable. By the end the text looks smooth and trouble-free and by then the transcriber may well have forgotten the initial problems (in my own case it was quite an effort to recall the decisions I grappled with at the time: they had just become part of the completed transcript). But each was one step in the creation of text.

There is also the question of which portions are transcribed at all. It is during the transcription process, whether from existent tape or live dictation, that it is decided – though seldom reported – which portions are 'central' enough to deserve the laborious task of writing them down. Performances do not always have clear-cut edges. To return to Bubu's tug-of-war tale: in one way its start and end *were* clear both from his bodily demeanour and from the opening and closing formulae, a common feature of Limba story-telling, and I carried on writing down from his dictation until he reached that point. But if I had been faced with an audio recording and/or interested only in capturing the 'story text', I might well have transcribed only the first portion and omitted the lengthy moralising at the end – arguably a distraction from the 'story proper' even though Bubu, enjoying himself, held back on his closing formula until he had had his say. It might have seemed quite reasonable to take only the first part – indeed that is exactly the portion I selected for Chapter 5. Decisions of this kind, usually unflagged and often perhaps not even conscious, are probably the rule rather than the exception in transcribing texts.

Which *elements* of performance are transcribed – or ignored – also very directly affect the final text. Are repetitions – of particular words, of new narrative moves, of lengthy dialogue exchanges, of song choruses – transcribed over and over again? and if not, is this suppression noted? So, too, with asides, 'interludes' or 'digressions'? And then there are sobs, shouts, yodels or sung and/or instrumental music which are essential in some genres but sometimes not represented at all in the transcribed text. Jan Knappert for example takes a strong line on recordings of Swahili epics:

> The epic itself ... has to be washed clean of all these additional beautifications [of singing, music etc.]. Let the musicologists have the disks with mainly music on them. The epeologist wants only the parts when there was nothing but reciting of the epic. ... Remember that epic, from Greek epos, means 'word', 'speech', and so, it is words we want. (Knappert 2000: 252)

It is often assumed that these non-linguistic performance features are not part of the 'text proper' and hence of its transcription. There may indeed be arguments for censoring them for certain purposes. But it is unquestionable that in these – not unusual – cases the final text owes much to the transcriber's editorial hand.

Printed books typically present sequences of single lines, a long-familiar and compelling model for transcribers. But it poses a difficulty for capturing the many oral performances where simultaneous or overlapping speakers are taking part. Here, it could be argued, play scripts or, better, musical scores might provide more appropriate models than the one-line typographies into which most oral texts are poured. There is no transparent way to capture the multidimensionality of oral performance into writing: to transcribe the vivid characterisation and inner feelings that can be represented in delivery, or the unverbalised intimations of atmosphere, emotion, tension, irony, dialogue and detached 'meta' reflection that oral performers can signal through speed, pitch, volume, pace, facial expression, gesture, emphasis, nuance, dramatisation, repetition and/or direct interactions between performer and audience. Some transcribers aspire to capture such performance qualities through stage directions, annotations or special typographies. Others preface their texts by some general comment on the problems and the strategy adopted. One example is Egudu and Nwoga's admirably honest and revealing introduction to their collection of Igbo verse, worth quoting at some length:

> Because the performer is in contact with his audience he is capable of interjecting references to individuals without confusing the audience as to the trend of the main material. He is able to shift from one situation of thought to another, indicating that he is doing so by a mere change of facial expression or gesture of the hand or body. Moreover, and this is significant, except for narration, the oral situation calls for succinct statements rather than for long logical discussion. The performer is therefore expected to show expertise, not in the building up of a complicated sequence of thought, but in the variety of expressions with which he can state, expand and deepen a single statement. When this fails the result is uninteresting

tautology. When it succeeds it is a marvellous exposition of imaginative wealth.

In writing these verses down, therefore, there has been the need to cut out from the transcriptions those interjected passages which were the outcome of interplay between the performer and individuals in the audience and keep to the main line of thought. (1973: 3–4)

An extreme position is to avoid written representation altogether on the grounds that trying to transfer a multi-channel source medium with aural, visual, kinesic, artefactual, proxemic and perhaps tactile elements, into a receptor medium (writing) with more limited channels is to distort it so seriously, while purporting to represent it, that it is best not attempted at all. Lurking behind all this is the recurrent problem of the incommensurability of single-line print with the dynamic and often multi-modal flow of perform-ance, its repetitions, histrionics and combinations of several voices. Much is inevitably left out in transcription and what is trapped into writing may be only a short synopsis, passed off as representing some full performance but in fact privileging content – or at any rate verbally writable content – over form. The look of the resultant texts is at least in part a consequence of how those in control have coped with the practical difficulties of enscribing performance.

Many researchers have quietly side-stepped such questions. But ignoring them is also a decision which, again, has effects on the nature of the resultant texts.

The hidden hand of the transcriber thus contributes mightily to the end result. Texts circulated as arising in some sense from oral performance are regularly presented as if authoritative, especially if sanctioned by having been transcribed direct from audio recordings. But without knowing the strategies adopted by the transcriber(s) it is inadvisable to accept this at face value. Clearly there is *some* relation, more, or less, close, between text and perform-ance. But oral texts are not simple 'primary' or 'authentic' data.

Text-making through translation

Inter-language translation has no doubt been one mode of organising and re-organising words throughout human history. It is yet a further way in which people commonly do things with and to words, and one which is also now attracting increasing interest as an interdisciplinary topic in itself.[4] It is also another far-from-neutral phase in the creation and manipulation of oral texts.

Though my focus here is primarily on translating 'oral' texts, let me also note that their 'oral-ness' does not exempt them from general translation issues such as arguably contending pulls of content or form, diverse meanings for differing audiences or historical contexts, figurative and poetic expression, intertextuality, potentially unequal power relations between 'source' and 'target' cultures, or the politics of publication and selection. Such issues, mostly not pursued here, do still need flagging given the still-common

---

[4] Notably in the now recognised field of 'translation studies', see for example Bassnett 1997, 2002, Bassnett and Trivedi 1999, France 2000: part 1, Hermans 2003, Munday 2001, Venuti 2004.

stereotype of oral forms as somehow outside time or impervious to social or political pressures. Since oral performances, too, are characterised by artfulness, originality and historical situatedness, translating them is as complex and controversial as with written texts.

Many oral texts have originated in cultures with colonial/ex-colonial backgrounds and/or from groups pictured as in some way marginal or exotic (the stereotypical setting for 'oral' practices). Unsurprisingly their translators have thus often reflected and reinforced contemporaneous stereotypes of 'the primitive', 'The African', and so on. Sometimes this is through a linguistic style designed to somehow convey childish, crude or uneducated expression, sometimes through framing the translations so as to slot into genres perceived to be 'simple', 'primordial', 'early' etc., sometimes by versions conveying romanticising evocations of the mystical, mysterious or archaic. Attempts to represent the linguistic structures of some African language by un-English word-for-word equivalences have also sometimes seemed acceptable even where this would be unthinkable if translating from European or Asian languages. In an incisive critique of this manner of translating Andrzejewski instances

> The young woman threw the pestle on the ground; she took a stone; she chased the bird, saying: 'It is making me noise'. The little bird went. She has pounded. The *mbombo* is finished. She takes up; enters into the house. (Andrzejewski 1965: 99)

Such translations, as he comments, bear no relation to any linguistic reality – the structural characteristics of the sentence cannot be meaningfully transposed from one language to another.

> It is no more sensible to attempt to do this with an African language than it would be to introduce the concept of grammatical gender into a translation from French. What could be the purpose of producing this kind of anti-English? Why did the writer not turn the conventions of narrative style in this African language into its equivalent in English, as he would surely have tried to do if he were working with French or Classical Greek. (1965: 99–100)

The 'word-for-word' cribs, useful for linguists understandably concerned with previously undocumented languages, were for long a standard procedure. The result was sometimes precisely as pinpointed by Andrzejewski – readers were simply confirmed in their expectation that 'African oral literature is very inferior stuff' (1965: 100).[5]

Translators' aims and expectations play a part. Some were shaped by the impressive history of biblical translation into local languages in Africa sustained by 'the belief', as Isabel Hofmeyr puts it, 'that texts could cross languages and cultures so as to bring the "same" form of belief and consciousness into being' (2004b: 20). Implicit assumptions about the likely audience can affect the result, interacting with translators' and readers' (historically and socially situated) expectations about what kind of linguistic style is appropriate (my decision to re-translate some of the Limba stories in this volume into a slightly more contemporary English idiom would be one example).

---

[5] On translations into the language of dominant cultures see also Bassnett and Trivedi 1999 (on 'post-colonial translation'), Niranjana 1992, Tedlock 1972.

Sometimes the aim has been to adopt the idiom of genres familiar in the target culture, Elizabethan lyric for example – pleasing to some but from another viewpoint 'straining after archaic idioms and techniques that have an all too foreign flavor' and giving the impression that without such tinkering the original 'has no place in the European poetic sensibility' (Okpewho 1992: 294). Or the idea may be to convey something of the 'ring' of the original – not necessarily in a demeaning or 'othering' way but simply because the translator wanted to somehow communicate an impression of how the original sounded. Another aspiration has been to draw on the African originals to 'enrich other tongues' (Ngugi wa Thiong'o 1986: 8). But whatever the motives and practices, the process of translating inescapably alters and re-forms the text – not mechanical transfer but textual transformation.

Translators naturally formulate their products following the written conventions familiar to themselves and their target readers. Thus it is often translators who have given the text a title (a common pattern in western writing but not necessarily in oral performances) or attributed an author (again a common written expectation but in the case of oral forms sometimes more complex and multiple – or perhaps already suppressed by the collector or transcriber). They may decide on how far to recognise and display internal structure, dialogue or repetition, and on the format as prose or poetry (conclusively signalled typographically but, as already mentioned, not always clear-cut in the original). The translator carries forward and further influences the shaping processes of enscription.

Translators face similar problems to transcribers about how to represent performance qualities which in oral realisations may be intrinsic to the meaning, form and artistry of the original. In effect a double translation process is involved, not just from one language to another, but also from an oral to a written mode. Scheub brings this out well for translating Xhosa story-telling:

> How does one effectively translate the verbal and non-verbal elements of such a tradition to the written word? ... It is impossible to consider the verbal elements of the performance in isolation from the non-verbal, yet there is no useful way of transferring the non-verbal elements to paper. The superficial plot seems the easiest of tasks for the translator, yet a dynamic translation of the plot might obscure the underlying structures which give logic and meaning to the work ... [The Xhosa narrator] will leave gaps in the plot from time to time, which are filled in by the audience. To find an artistically pleasing means of filling in those gaps for an alien reader without interfering with the subtle balance being created by the artist in other regards is another special translation problem. (Scheub 1971: 31)

Translators, like transcribers, sometimes tackle this through additional notes, inserted adverbs, or 'stage directions'. One example comes in my translation of the Limba 'Spider and needle' story (Chapter 5): 'He called out as if jokingly "Ho ho, ha ha, there's nothing in my mouth"' (p.60). 'As if jokingly' is not there in the Limba *words* in the narrow sense, but was clear in the context of delivery, important enough, I reckoned, to need conveying in translation – but it *was* in one sense an addition. Other translators have tried special typographical devices to convey something of the performance dimension, or at least make some acknowledgement of the problem. Many however slide over such issues, giving the tacit impression that the translated text re-presents a comparably 'texted' original.

Features regularly screened out in written translations are on similar lines to those commonly suppressed in transcription, but even elements that survive the transcription phase can cause translation problems later. Ideophones[6] are common in African story-telling but not easily translated, like the Zulu *khwi* representing turning round suddenly or the Thonga *peswa-peswa* of a lady walking with high-heeled shoes. In Bubu Dema's tug-of-war story the heavy struggle of the two huge animals contrasts vividly with the light-hearted way the spider went and lay down *kɛlɛthɛ*, his tiny body almost soundless. And while translators can scarcely be expected to reproduce every detail of performance, they may have to deal with genres where there are layers of meaning, differentially understood perhaps by the audience, or where *several* performers play significant roles. Such features may look merely 'secondary', to be brushed aside when the translator gets down to the 'text proper'. But in the oral performance that the translator is in some sense trying to convey they may be of the essence, and ignoring them is indeed to transform the original.

The standard model of (written) translation assumes a stable original text or, put more strongly, 'it is up to the writer to fix words in an ideal, unchangeable form and it is the task of the translator to liberate those words from the confines of their source language' (Bassnett 2002: 5 citing Octavio Paz). But translators come to texts that have *already* been moulded and to that extent changed through the decisions made during both initial capture and transcription. The transfer from an oral to written form has already been one kind of translation – far from a transparent or automatic representation – so this second translation between languages is already at a double remove from the original.

Translated oral texts thus need to be read with an awareness of the assumptions which underlie translators' renderings. This is not just something of past centuries or confined to 'coloniser'/'colonised' relationships. Now as in the past, and in Africa as elsewhere, translators may (or may not) convey denigrating, simplifying, glamorising or other impressions of the original through the terminologies, content, interpretations or stylistics of the texts they create.

Recent approaches to translation are now increasingly recognising the creative, mediating and non-mechanical nature of translating and that the choices inevitably made by translators may themselves be shaped by current interests and preconceptions (see for example Bassnett 2002, especially 1–10). In this context translators, too, are creative artists whose formulations exist in the world and have their own impacts. There is now an interest not so much in questions about the 'faithful' representation of some original as in such processes as 'transcreation', re-writing by local authors, and general issues about transformations between different modes of realisation. Such issues can be raised equally, if not even more markedly, in the case of translating oral texts where the creative role of translators has clearly been of crucial

---

[6] On African ideophones see (for example) Childs 1994, Okpewho 1992: 92ff, also more comparative accounts in Besnier 1990: 423ff, Kawada 1996.

importance in bringing the oral performances of Africa in textual form to a wider public throughout the world.[7]

The fate of the finalised text

The products of all this transcribing and (often) translating are then usually stored, distributed or published in what gets to be accepted as their final definitive forms. But even then the making has not ended. Here, too, collectors and researchers are regularly influenced by the conventions and genres of their own backgrounds, which in turn mould how they conceptualise and present their texts. Print – that taken-for-granted medium – often carries messages through (for example) its layout, typographies, bindings, choice of paper, headings, divisions, visual and tactile impressions. It can, for example, explicitly or implicitly signal that a text falls within particular categories and genres familiar from written literature, such as 'poem', 'prose', 'children's literature', 'epic'. We may no longer automatically picture genres as fixed and would accept that earlier labels – even those as apparently clear as 'poem', 'narrative', 'song cycle', 'folk-tale', 'saga', 'history', 'tradition', 'school text' – may have owed as much to the publishers' or collectors' formulations as to the material itself. But once published in a particular format texts easily become fixed within that category, making it hard to question later. It is true that, both for publishers' marketing and for international communication, some cross-cultural labelling is probably unavoidable. But we also need to remember that such attributions highlight some dimensions more than others and certainly do not represent some direct transfer of an unmediated original. Such labelling, whether stated overtly or through the hidden messages conveyed by binding, layout or typographic handling, are another tacit but powerful influence on text construction – and hence on the 'evidence' used in further analysis or classification.

Multi-modal performance qualities raise further difficulties for storing and/or publication, for at this stage, too, features like music, gesture or dance are poorly captured in print-based texts. One line is just to ignore them on the grounds that the verbal text is the key. Jan Knappert perhaps expresses an extreme position on this but its broad outline would probably have been implicitly accepted by many in the past (perhaps now too): he writes of Swahili epic that

> The transformation of a sung text into a written text is a difficult but necessary process without which the epic can never be offered to the scholarly community as a meaningful work of art. We can listen to tapes and even watch videos of performances ... but they will not be more than meaningless song. (Knappert 2000: 255–6)

Others have made some attempt to pin down the non-verbal dimensions. Sometimes musical dimensions are captured in musical transcriptions or indicated through musicological commentary (though more often they are

[7] On translation from oral performances see also Brown 1999: 5ff, Okpewho 1992: 294ff, Sammons and Sherzer 2000, Scheub 1971, Swann 1992.

quietly ignored). Gesture and movement are occasionally – and partially – indicated through dance-transcription systems. Illustrations may also appear with the finalised text. Line drawings can communicate some pictorial dimension and are relatively plentiful in texts designed for school or popular reading – produced by artists who may or (perhaps more often) may not have some acquaintance with the genre as performed. Other illustrations are directed to conveying something of the original performance, like the wonderfully illuminating photographs of Xhosa and of Tuareg story-telling (Scheub 1977a, Calame-Griaule 1985) that accompany and amplify the printed text and give such a vivid impression of the gestures and sequential dynamics of performance.

As mentioned earlier special typographies have also been utilised to indicate some of the performance qualities, in particular by writers associated in the 1970s with the journal *Alcheringa/Ethnopoetics*. Their aim was to present 'performable scripts (meant to be read aloud rather than silently), experiments in typography, diagrams, and insert disc recordings' (Editorial, *Alcheringa* new series 2.1, 1975). Peter Seitel's representation (1980) of a Haya tale (above, pp. 130–31) gives some indication of how such texts built on existing linguistic or musical conventions to indicate features like timing (pauses, lengthening syllables, etc.); volume, intensity or stress in speaking; tonal contours; other actions such as gestures and audience reactions.[8] Though such representations are not universally favoured or, indeed, practicable, nor are they themselves, any more than other formulations, free of their creators' enscribing hands, they do nevertheless often vividly convey aspects of personal creativity, innovation and subtlety lost in more conventional layouts. These imaginative projects for formulating and presenting oral texts have now been further extended through the electronic opportunities offered by new typographies, desktop publishing and (as indicated later) web display.

A further input into moulding the eventual form comes once again from print's bias towards the single performer. The finalised text is commonly in one-line bounded format, something which can give little impression of simultaneous or overlapping voices or of the complex tensions between performers and audiences (illustrated, for example, in Yankah 1985). Sometimes the linear single-voice text *does* indeed represent crucial aspects of the original. But in most publications this is just assumed and we end up with one-line textual simplicity with little explication of how far this matches features of some original oral performance which it purports to reflect.

The constraints of publishing, with its established technologies and markets, still greatly affect the form in which texts are publicised (or not … much remains concealed in textual or recorded form in archives, theses, museum stores or private cupboards). This may be changing with the increasing viability of audio and video. These are perhaps not as prevalent as some enthusiasts suggest and often enough the eventual publication target may still be written text; nor are such products necessarily less shaped than written text by earlier choices, a process likely to be taken even further at this

---

[8] For further examples and discussion see Briggs 1985, Fine 1984 esp. chapter 7, Tedlock 1980, 1983.

final stage (film- and record-makers are well accustomed to drastic editing). Still they do obviously offer an evocative, dynamic and multiplex mode for representing oral performance and disseminating it to wider audiences in ways that may well expand in the future. This is added to by the opportunities for self-publishing, electronic text processing and, even more strikingly, web dissemination which not only give new options but have to an extent altered power relations, bringing new parties into the frame. Small-scale and local publications have of course long appeared, in Africa as elsewhere, but they are now easier to produce. And what once might have been purely written 'oral texts' are being accompanied or replaced by more multi-dimensional formulations (see further in Chapter 12) – these are, of course, also creatively processed and mediated, but arguably supplement the one-line print textualisation by more overtly multi-modal and/or locally controlled publications, globally accessible.

All in all we have to face the fact that the 'oral texts' which in some sense purport to represent oral performances have not arrived through some neutral process of transference. Nor can we assume that in the written texts of African forms circulating as the standard versions we have somehow captured the authentic original and unmediated performance. As Jan Jansen concluded his detailed account of performances of the famous *Sunjata* epic, 'the epic as we know it from the text editions may to a great extent be the product of our own fascination for the written word and the tape recorder' (2001b: 36). The products we deal with – whether printed in neat lines, elaborated in new typographies, held on audio-cassette, broadcast on local radio, shaped into a widely distributed film or displayed through the web – have been constructed through a series of (often hidden) choices by people engaged in one or more of the manifold stages of text-making.

Enscripting: an uneasy process – or not?

Looking back from the present it is easy to condemn many of the text-creation processes of earlier collectors. Their frequent status as powerful outsiders and the demeaning and/or romanticised images and ideologies which often shaped their interpretations and, hence, their text-making may now seem shocking. Somewhat shocking, too, must be the impression that the oral texts we work over and contemplate are after all far from direct representations of African (or other) oral forms but rather the artificial products of (often) external creators – even something akin to fabrications?

But that is to over-simplify and I want now to consider another perspective on the matter. We need to recall that all texts are after all creatures of their time and age, sometimes of a series of times and ages as they are interacted with and moulded differentially by a variety of actors – we cannot expect 'oral texts' to be any different. Further, even among the earliest enscribing of African texts members of local interest groups of one kind or another – not just the 'outsiders' – have been engaged in the documenting, transcribing and translating of local forms. We have presumably by now abandoned the model of 'untouched', 'natural' or 'traditional' forms. In any case there have long been intellectuals in Africa well acquainted with writing and with inter-language translation, especially (though not only) through the rendering of Arabic-inspired originals in local languages and the long-established missionary translations of the Christian Bible which relied so heavily on local expertise. The importance of 'African intellectual brokerage' (as it is well described in Hofmeyr 2004b: 14) has too often been ignored in the past but is certainly part of the mix. It is true that we cannot blink the power relations and literary fashions that have sometimes influenced the formation of texts. But we must also accept that all of those involved – not just the 'outsiders' – had their own complex mixed agendas and expectations. Someone involved in the processing of texts could – and can – be simultaneously researcher, outsider, insider and reflective participant in what they are creating. The contributions and positions of *all* the multiple participants in the enactment and creation of text ultimately need to be considered rather than (selectively) to be dismissed as in some way unreal or invalid. And such participants must therefore include performers and their audiences, local 'research assistants' and enscribers, African scholars and intellectuals, short-term visiting academics, teachers, schoolchildren, tourists, publicists, politicians, writers – indeed everyone who takes part.

Rather than simply condemning the procedures of earlier collectors it can be more productive to explore the specificities of how particular texts came to be created – and perhaps continued to be reinforced or challenged – through the actions and ideologies of inevitably interested parties; and how both these social and historic specifics and the eventuating texts themselves affected expectations for future productions, whether as school lessons, presentations to strangers, vocabulary for discussing texts, tourist shows, political oratory or future performances. Even what might from one perspective be justifiably claimed as *mis*understandings can from another be seen not just as consolidating what is (perhaps controversially) defined as 'old', but also as developing and propagating new versions of those 'traditional' forms: one kind of innovation.

Is this not the kind of human processing and negotiating that has always been going on everywhere, by no means unique to Africa? Far from a matter of some natural bedrock being forcibly displaced by the imposition of the artificial new medium of enscription, people's ways of doing things with words have regularly been founded in the interaction of many participants, using and negotiating and adapting them in multifarious transformations to a whole variety of purposes.

These historical processes are illuminating to study rather than just to dismiss. They are all real ways that people do things with and to words inside and outside Africa. The processes can, certainly, be selective, carving out certain elements rather than others – but by that very fact they are also ways of creating and enclothing reality. Enscription can indeed, as we have seen, be problematic and is, like most of human activity, entangled with power relations and socially sanctioned arrangements as well as with individual interests and creation. But the resultant texts are real verbalisations, created and utilised by real people.

A recurrent theme of this chapter, perhaps of the volume as a whole, has been an unease with attempts to 'reduce' to a fixed spatial and portable artefact the multi-modal temporalities of performance. And we should indeed be more conscious of the creative manipulations of text-making processes, of the often-hidden agendas or inequalities of the several parties involved, and of the problematics of 'oral texts' being tacitly passed off as either some primary and enduring representation of African verbal art or as some comprehensive mirror of original performance. But it would be equally simplistic to deny *any* relation between the two or sweepingly to dismiss the whole enscription process as merely the misguided creations of outsiders coming in to mangle performance by (mis)confining it for the first time into spatially exhibited and artificial text – as if verbal genres were ever somehow quintessentially pure and un-worked on, removed from human manipulation or the specificities of historically situated power relations; or as if there would never have been any idea of textual crystallisation, exact repetition or multilingual translation in Africa without the influx of colonising ideologies and practices. Nor should we exaggerate the opposition of text and performance (an issue to be taken up again later) or be tempted into falling back into some simplified image of Africa as the primaeval home of multimodal 'performance', Europe of unilinear 'text'. Apart from the obvious points that Africa is no stranger either to writing or to the complex interplay of human relations, with all that implies, this would also be to brush aside the variegated ways in which 'oral' genres whether in Africa or elsewhere may be more, or less, characterised by a degree of textual stability – which in turn means that the relation between (writable) text and unique performance needs to be investigated in specific instances rather than castigated in general terms. Enscription is not always, or in all respects, experienced as uneasy.

Transforming between languages is nothing strange either. It is a long-practised way in which people do things with words and is well known throughout Africa. The same goes for mutual interchanging between media. We only have to recall drumming used to (in some sense) represent human speech, visual images to tell stories, musical enactment of narrative, dance dramas, puppet theatre – 'trans-forming' from and across media is a common part of human action. Certainly there are diverse conventions about what 'corresponds' to what, diversities which may indeed be at odds between different groups, viewpoints, temporal periods and cultural traditions. But that only makes them the more interesting. Nor are the transformations and portabilities sketched in this chapter anything to be surprised about. The process of recontextualising, whether in similar or differing media (or languages), is nothing unusual either; and exploiting it for newly developing genres is hardly idiosyncratic to Africa. Rather than either condemning or praising, we should look more deeply into the processes of text creation and the interesting to-ing and fro-ing among and between different media within agreed – or differing or contested or newly emerging – conventions about what counts as 'equivalent' to what.

Let me at the same time end by reiterating the point that in approaching 'oral texts' we need to be aware of the layers of interpretation and human action that have brought them into the form in which they are now circulated. Just because they and their backgrounds are somehow 'oral' or have become classified under authoritative-sounding terms like 'orature', 'oral literature', 'oral texts', they do not for that reason stand outside the normal historical processes nor has their transformation into text been a neutral and transparent transfer. They are no more primary, timeless or 'natural' than the written texts of European cultural traditions with which they intersect and the qualities we impute to them may sometimes lie with the collectors and publishers as much as with their imagined originators. To understand their status it is essential to take account of the actions, agendas, ideologies and socio-historical specificities of *all* the parties who have worked in their processing, transforming and enscribing – in their creation.

11

Conceptualising Oral Texts and Beyond[1]

So, having enscripted oral performance – or at any rate something – into written texts, what then have scholars taken these texts to be? This chapter briefly outlines certain of the changes which I have seen taking place over the last generation, to complement and expand the developments touched on earlier.

From oral tradition to contemporary dynamics and popular culture

When I first encountered African oral texts just after the mid-twentieth century they were basically envisaged as something *old*, to be explained in terms of 'tradition' and the heritage from the past. This was part of the backward-looking approach that has cast so long a shadow on the conceptualisation and study of African forms. It was interwoven with that enduring image of Africa as early in the stage of human development, characterised by collective communal institutions and dominated by tradition – the antithesis of modernity. It seemed incontrovertible that to study the native products one had to look to the traditional. This emphasis on the past was further encouraged by the then preoccupation with 'traditional' institutions in British functionalist anthropology, by the core assumptions of folklore studies, and by the influential philological interest in the texts of antiquity. Even the emerging oral-formulaic studies, for all their openness to performance, insistently delineated the texts and poets they dealt with as 'traditional'.

[1] This chapter had its genesis in an unpublished paper 'Reflections on oral literature and the academy in Britain' for the 2nd International Conference on Oral Literature in Africa ('Oral Literature and the Academy') hosted so superlatively in 1995 by the University of Ghana, Legon. It has been extensively updated and recast, however, and little if any of the original remains.

Oral texts were thus conceptualised as in some sense existent in, and dating from, the past. They could suitably be summed up and analysed through such terms as 'folktales', 'tribal inheritance', 'oral tradition(s)', and age-old 'myths' from 'time immemorial' – all common phrases in the 1950s. The truly authentic texts, it was commonly assumed, originated in an oral setting, produced by non-literate native speakers within a traditional mind-frame, uncontaminated by foreign intrusions.

There were of course exceptions to this focus on the past. Even in the 1960s there was some interest in, for example, topical urban songs, political propaganda and radio broadcasts, and as time went on more scholars were starting to regard contemporary and innovative forms as, after all, pertinent to the analysis of oral texts.[2] But the main weight lay elsewhere. My 1970 book on 'oral literature' was constantly described as being about oral 'traditions', and I vividly recall being chided both orally and in writing by the influential American folklorist Richard Dorson for allowing it to stray beyond its apparently proper field of 'folk traditions' (Dorson 1972: 10).

> Composed topical songs, connected, say, with internal politics, as in the examples she gives of the bickering in Guinea between the French adminis-tration party of Barry Diawadou and the R.D.A. ... party of Sekou Touré, hinge on passing personalities and do not sink into tradition. ... [The folklorist should focus on the] tribal inheritance ... traditional cultures hidden under and penetrating into modern ways. (Dorson 1972: 17, 67)

Today there are still traces of this perspective. But overall the field looks very different. Oral texts are no longer automatically assumed to belong to the past with deep roots in traditional culture, fit objects to be scripturalised into written text. Scholars now look for their examples to young people as well as the old, to the educated not just the non-literate, to towns as well as country-side, to industrial workers and broadcast performers, and to disruptive or innovative forms not just the old guard. Change and contemporaneity are now part of the picture.

Insofar as 'tradition' is now a topic it is more often taken as a malleable concept or practice that people play on and manipulate. The idea of some fixed and agreed corpus belonging to the past has been decisively broken up by greater awareness of the actively managed construction of 'traditions' and of the way they occur in all societies: 'not frozen in time' as Makang rightly puts it, nor opposed to 'modernity and progress' but 'in continual develop-ment' (1997: 325). What is defined as (in some sense or other) traditional varies in different periods, groups and situations. It can be an idiom for achieving a diversity of ends – political, aesthetic, identifying, asserting a place in the present, and much else. Notions of 'tradition' or 'the traditional' can be part of local categorisations in ways that are highly pertinent to contemporary issues but might have surprised the earlier generations to which they are sometimes attributed. South African women migrants' *kiba* songs, classed as 'traditional' music (part of *wa sesotho*), are developed in

---

[2] For references to this earlier work see Finnegan 1970 (esp. Chapter 10), also, from a little later, such works as Andrzejewski and Innes 1975, Coplan 1978, Finnegan 1977, Johnson 1974, Lindfors 1977.

vibrant and changing forms which both evoke the notion of 'home' and 'origin' and formulate their identity as migrants in town (James 1999: 16, and *passim*). Or again Dan Ge masked performers in contemporary Côte d'Ivoire are presented as playing with what they at any given time define as 'traditional', exploited in subtle and multifaceted ways as part of their modern lives (Reed 2003). Such studies illuminate processes that are as salient for the present as for the past and for Europe no less than for Africa.

All this has contributed to an altered vision of oral texts, no longer automatically assigned to some uniform 'Tradition' of the past but also regarded as creatures of the present. Recent studies take in their stride such examples as a child praise-singer on South African television, poetry on video or the web, pop groups in urban settings, Hausa market-place burlesque, life stories, love songs, community theatre, a rap band, trade union songs, praises for the Namibian Otjiherero radio service, for Nelson Mandela or for the South African football team, and the intersection of writing, voice and broadcast media in a plethora of contexts.[3] Poetry, song and story turned to political purposes or ideological struggle now come unquestionably within the scholarly purview. There are studies of Ethiopian peasants using poems to comment on the 1975 land reforms or 1990s regime change, of the poetry of civil war or independence struggle, of 'electric griots', of oral performances relating to AIDS, of praises for graduation ceremonies, and of 'performing the nation' through song, music and dance in contemporary Tanzania.[4]

And it is no longer 'collective' tradition but the ways that individuals – now often named – manipulate the repertoire. Thus another study documents how the poet-singer Micah Ichegbeh builds on an Igede tradition called *adiyah* which incorporates 'proverbs, masquerades, dialogue, riddle, mimicry, spectacle and song ... drawing its great resonance from its direct response to Igede experience' (Ogede 1993: 53). He is shown turning his talents on the 1979 elections when Shagari of the NPN became the first elected civilian President of Nigeria, defeating the UPN leader Awolowo. His electrifying performance celebrated political victory and mocked political defeat:

> Awolowo did dare to touch Shagari
> A duel is in the making
> A duel is in the making, surely!
> A duel is in the making
> Just like Omakwu did dare to touch Ogo Okpabi
> A duel is in the making
> A duel is in the making, surely!
> A duel is in the making
> (Between) NPN, UPN
> A duel is in the making
> A duel is in the making, surely!
> A duel is in the making. (Ogede 1993: 54)

The performance by Ichegbeh's ensemble on 27 July 1981 held its audience

---

[3] For a few examples among many see Brown 2003, Furniss 1996, Gunner 1986, 2004, Kaschula 2001, 2003, Kavari 2002.
[4] See Gelaye 2001, Ezeigbo and Gunner 1991, Pongweni 1997, Hale 1998: 274ff, Bourgault 2003, Dauphin-Tinturier 2001, Mutembei 2001, Neethling 2003, Askew 2002.

rapt by its captivating melody and his group was victorious: 'the audience yelled in jubilation and rose in unison to roar out a thunder of applause so loud that it was heard many kilometres from the site' (Ogede 1993: 54). Far from conceptualising oral texts as something of the past, such studies now increasingly present them as part of the on-going concerns, great and small, of modern life.

This has promoted a new look at activities in the past too, no longer automatically assigning them to some supposedly unchanging 'oral tradition' of earlier times or by-passing cases held to be 'non-indigenous'. There is thus a renewed interest in historical accounts of earlier genres or events such as the 'concert parties' that flourished in the Gold Coast from the early twentieth century (Cole 2001, Ricard 1974), Islamic literary forms (see among many others Orwin and Topan 2001 and Gérard's well titled *Afrique plurielle* 1996), the Xhosa poet using his panegyric craft to praise the Christian God rather than his chief in 1827 (Kaschula 2004: 431), or the annual *Snow White* show produced since 1935 in a Zaire mission school run by Bavarian sisters with its mix of 'Lomongo songs, tunes from German folklore, Tyrolian costumes, and the young Zairean girls' sense of acting' (Colleyn 2004: 127). So, too, with other documented forms which might once have been bypassed as 'imported' or 'foreign' – the kinds of examples to which many of us paid too little attention in past years.

Newly emergent genres or forms drawing on a mix of languages or media are no longer automatically brushed aside as somehow hybrid or un-African, an untoward departure from the pure and authentic genres of the past. They are now recognised as part of the whole picture, consonant with the more recent approaches which bring out both the 'normality' and the rhetorical effectiveness of what would once have been dismissed as 'mixed' genres.[5] This goes with the (belated) recognition that adaptive and changing genres are nothing new in Africa – or anywhere presumably. They have been part of Hausa culture for generations (see Furniss 1996), and there are notable studies, too, of newly developing genres such as the Somali *heello* (Johnson 1974) or the hymns of the Zulu Nazarite church (see also examples in Andrzejweski et al. 1985, Kaschula 2001). Or take the rap hip-hop Sierra Leonean Funky Freddy and his band, or the *bandiri* form in Sokoto where solo male-voice performances accompanied by drums and chorus draw together standard Islamic vocabulary with a delivery style reminiscent of both praise singers and Indian film song (Bubu and Furniss 1999: 30); a successful female pop singer in Mali, at once local and transnational (Schultz 2001); film representations of Sunjata and other narratives (Hale 2003, Jorholt 2001); Zulu radio drama (Gunner 2000); or the 1998 release of a CD by the Xhosa praise poet Zolani Mkiva set to contemporary hip-hop music in a mixture of Xhosa and English (Kaschula 1999: 62, 2003) – all these nowadays seem as appropriate for study as the poetry and stories documented by the nineteenth and early twentieth century scholars.

The study of African forms now interacts with that of contemporary popular culture. Oral texts are set in the context of modern politics, youth cultures and – in some cases – commercial exploitation and mass media

[5] On 'mixed/hybrid genres' see for example Briggs 1993, Gunner 1991, Muana 1998: 47ff.

productions in a global arena. The precise scope of the phrase 'popular culture' may remain controversial;[6] but drawing African genres within the ambit – and debates – of that term has given a new impetus and, equally important, drawn them within the same framework as those studied elsewhere, another step in the de-marginalising of African forms. In Africa as in Europe or America or India people elaborate their arts, verbal and other, in the settings of modern urban life, among the show-off young not just the old-established experts, among factory employees, trade unionists and migrant workers as well as rural farmers, celebrity-led as well as grassroots, amidst exploitative commerce no less than in (supposedly) rural harmony. It is no longer just a matter of 'verbal texts', furthermore, but of music, film, dance, drama or electronic media in which, no less than in western settings, the verbal entextualisation may be merely one dimension of the whole. There are accounts of popular theatre in Nigeria and elsewhere (Barber 2000, Barber et al. 1997), of worker poetry and plays in Natal (Gunner 1994), of Hausa popular culture (Furniss 1996), of Swazi poems created in both oral and written forms (Sithebe 1997), of a Xhosa poet crafting versions to a range of settings (Kaschula 1997), popular songs in Zimbabwe (Vambe 2000), and a host of forms spilling over into each other as 'styles of cultural production and consumption overlap and interpenetrate' (Barber et al. 1997: xviii). By now such processes no longer seem strange or odd:

> Modern popular culture is a scene of metamorphoses and mutations, in which written texts are performed, performed texts can be given a written recension, and a network of allusions and cross-references enables audiences in whatever state of literacy to access texts in one way or another. (Barber 1995b: 12)

The study of broadcast and recorded media has similarly taken on new vitality. Fardon and Furniss's (2000) study of African broadcast cultures ranges from local radio stations in African languages in Benin or advertising on Hausa radio to the multiple voices of Sudanese airspace and much more. Admittedly scholars still sometimes patronise or marginalise commercial or broadcast media, or forms popular among urban workers or youth fans; but they are certainly now more often taken as serious subjects for study, challenging the earlier backward-looking perspective on oral texts. The rapid spread and establishment of this wide field has been one of the striking developments over recent years.[7]

And then, from another perspective, there is the interest in the complex interweaving of oral with written forms which brings oral texts into conjunction with the study of written literatures, including them within 'post-colonial' studies. It is true that (as discussed later) the terms of such analyses can be controversial. The point here, however, is that what was once envisaged as a distinctive and separate field – the products of 'traditional Africa' – now comes squarely within what many would regard as the 'mainstream', relevant for debates about contemporary written literatures.

---

[6] For comment in the context of Africa see especially Karin Barber's groundbreaking overview (1987), also Barber 1997c: Introduction, Barber et al. 1997: xviii–xix, Coplan 2001, Faber 2004, Fabian 1998.

[7] By now established enough to have its own *Readings in African Popular Culture* (Barber 1997c); see also references in n. 6 above.

Oral texts are in consequence no longer automatically conceived as something rooted in one language, linguistic unit or 'tribal' culture but as potential players in a cosmopolitan arena. This should actually be nothing new. After all there have been global connections for centuries in and beyond Africa – international trade in goods and people, movements and settlements, missionary proselytising in Christianity or Islam, colonial encounters, cultural and political links. But there now seems a clearer acknowledgement of such interactions, as well as some appreciation of the long and continuing incidence of multilingualism, of the fluidities between languages both globally and across Africa (cf. Dalby 1999/2000 vol. 2: 25, 28), and, as in several examples noted above, of the creative exploitation of what might once have been seen as mutually exclusive languages. A study of Islamic poetry in Africa now considers the interface between local expression and the wider world of Islamic learning (Orwin and Topan 2001), an account of an underground popular singer in South Africa describes the mix of Afrikaans with contrived Jamaican-accent overlay (Jury 1996: 105), and the transnational connections of African music, film and dance are by now well recognised. Diasporic practitioners and commentators have entered the picture too, together with the inter-continental distribution of African-related popular forms like rap music, hip-hop or dub poetry. Certain genres and performances will of course continue to have local flavour or, like the singer Funky Freddy pictured on the front cover, to play creatively with themes that resonate among specific groups. But scholars now also accept the existence of far-flung forms and trends, especially in music and film, which interact within and across Africa, interwoven into the complex spectrum of multi-media arts and activities across the globe.

This widening of vision has been crucial for current approaches to what was once commonly ring-fenced as 'oral tradition'. Oral texts, insofar as they can be envisaged as having some kind of distinctive status at all, are now conceived not as essentially belonging to some old and somehow autochthonous shared tradition but as created and changed and manipulated for many purposes and through many media by active participants in the world, present no less than past.

From unilinearity
to historical specificity and multiple voices

These changes in outlook have been complemented by a growing interest in the social and historical situatedness of oral texts (as of much else). They may once have been envisaged as products of some uniform 'oral culture' or of a 'tribal culture' where 'all the members share the values, participate in the rituals, and belong fully to the culture', as Richard Dorson had it in his *African Folklore* (1972: 4). But now the spotlight is turned rather on the *specific* parties, contexts and power relations through which particular texts are formulated at specific times. It is neither the grand-scale progress from orality to literacy nor 'culture' in general that draws attention but the named individuals, agents or backers who in their various capacities have brought things about, and the historical settings and ideologies in which they and others act.

A concern with ethnographic specifics had of course entered into some earlier studies of oral texts (one factor indeed in my own long-lasting doubts over generalised conclusions about oral forms). But what is notable now is the widespread attention to historical contexts and dynamics, and to the multiplicities of diverse viewpoints, genres, cultures, situations, gender, age, locality, power, local conceptualisations, and historical specificities. It is no longer just generalised concepts like 'literacy' or 'orality' but diverse literacies and oralities. A text – or action – can be 'oral', or have 'oral' aspects, in different ways depending on the situation and the dimension being considered. It can be a case, for example, of oral composition (in some sense or other) but written transmission; of a text that is at some point written but mostly projected in live performance; of notes or scores for or from performance; of audio-recordings, broadcasts, videos. All of these and a host of other permutations are common in Africa as elsewhere, diversifying the essentialising notion of 'oral'. Similarly, rather than striving for some generalised conclusion about say, oral composition or expression, the impetus is now more often to consider perceptions and experiences in specific cases – locally formulated viewpoints on composition among Xhosa singers or Somali poets and audiences for example, or the detailed meta-language of Hausa verbal aesthetics (Kaschula 2002, Orwin 2003, Hunter and Oumarou 1998). Oral texts are now likely to be attributed not to some generalised oral heritage or process but to specific individuals. What may at the outset have seemed conceptualisable as some single phenomenon has become a series of multifarious specificities, not to be predicted in advance.

This goes along with a greater attention to how so-called 'local' or 'traditional' experiences take various forms according to people's specific situations. Just as anthropologists are now rightly sceptical about the homogeneity once implied by the pervasive notion of 'culture', so, too, across many disciplines there is now less talk about 'the' story, 'the' poetic tradition, 'the' genre, and more about people's specific actions and conceptualisations linked to, for example, their gender, age, religion, political affiliation, education, place, craft, livelihood, social hierarchy, and more. We hear of interactions between power, marginality and the politics of language in specific settings or of how certain genres can be privileged (Furniss and Gunner 1995). There are accounts of the struggles individuals engage in, whether for space to construct and define meaningful popular forms in face of powerful elite ideologies in Southern Africa (Gunner 1994) or by named blind singers in northern Sierra Leone working to attract and retain their audiences and integrate their songs with their personal life experiences (Ottenberg 1996). And it is not just the immediate circumstances in which the players of the moment find themselves, but also the lights and shadows cast by their histories, their performances perhaps entangled with the heritage of the past – real and imagined – as well as the constraints and opportunities of the present. Beyond this, too, are the ideologies and translocal institutions through which the participants' interpretations are filtered or struggled over. Scholars are now more likely to look not only to the acts and products of those directly

185

engaged but also to the influential perceptions that move them – perhaps themselves linked into wider world-wide mythologies – and the educational, publication and social arrangements with which they are interwoven.

Such perspectives also intersect with current transdisciplinary interests in the interactive and co-created nature both of linguistic acts and of communication more generally. Participation has become a focus of interest. Researchers now take note of the multiple participants so often actively engaged in performance – not just lead soloists but duos and trios and choruses, not just front performers but backing groups too, leading into questions about their mutual roles and relationships that could not arise while text was basically imagined as univocal. Daniel Avorgbedoe's 'psycho-musical' approach, for example, speaks of how the Ewe singing group 'essentially constitutes one *voice*, communicating one text with the help of a melody ... a type of *hypnotic* effect whereby all the individual participants are submerged in an unconscious explicit act through the conscious manipulation of a crafted medium' (1990: 217–18). How far all those involved in these or comparable events would share that view might attract differing interpretations. But the point is that such questions have now become matters for explicit exploration rather than ruled out by a single-voiced ideal model of text.

Audiences are becoming more visible too. As Steve Chimombo aptly expresses it for Chichewa oral literature in Malawi

> Oral narrative is not only a matter of presenting the plot to the audience or collector. It is a two-way process involving the narrator and the audience so intimately that the narrative's very existence depends on this relationship being established from the outset. (Chimombo 1988: 83)

In Ichegbeh's performance (see above) the audience's participation and their 'thunder of applause' were central to his art: it is hard 'to recreate a live sense of Ichegbeh's *Adiyah* performance in cold print because Ichegbeh is a volatile performer whose voice, stage body movement, gestures and rapport with the audience are better heard than seen' (Ogede 1993: 53). Altogether audiences and publics are now taken more seriously (see esp. Barber 1997a, b), studied among other things as historical products formulated through varying arrangements and controls and with some appreciation of the range of ways that, as Karin Barber puts it, 'performances constitute audiences and vice versa' (Barber 1997a: 347ff, 353ff). And besides the diverse relations between performer and audiences there is now further interest in the potentially changing dynamics during performance, and the spectrum of roles, more, or less, sustained in differing situations, which can extend well beyond the immediate moment into the complexities of publics, counter-publics and pathways of circulation.

This has reinforced the recognition that multiple actors can be involved in any given performance and hence in at least some senses in (various stages of) the 'oral text' that may eventuate. Scholars are now looking not just to performers, audiences and fans, but also to organisers and publishers, transcribers and translators (creative roles too, as we saw in the previous chapter). And this can also mean going beyond the participants' overt actions as performers or audiences to consider that they, too, are interpreters and analysts – interpretive voices that in the past regularly went unheard given the long presumption that outsiders were the knowledgeable analysts. Once again the apparently simple object of the oral text has become re-conceived into something more complex and multi-layered.

Alongside this also goes a sharper appreciation of the creative processes of enscription (such as those considered in the previous chapter) and their implications for approaching the resultant texts. The polyphony of multiple voices is suppressed when they are caught into one-line univocal print; so too are dimensions of performance which exploit more than just words. The assumption that such textual forms are sufficient has now been affected by the possibilities of audio recordings, of various forms of video, and, still more, of CD-ROM and web representations, all of which help scholars to catch – and thus explicitly notice and build into their conceptualisations – the potential multiplicity and diversity of participants and modalities in any given 'text'. These complicating features in what used to be envisaged as straight verbal text are now more clearly recognised and built into the analysis, thus in turn changing how we conceive the existence of an oral text.

Such complexities once again bring into question that long opposition between 'oral' and 'literate'. By now this is more widely seen as simply inadequate for understanding how people manipulate words in Africa today (or in the past or anywhere else, it could be added). The presupposition that writing inevitably and in the nature of things ousts oral expression has mostly been replaced by the view that insofar as 'oral' and 'written' can indeed be distinguished the interesting point is not to elevate either the one or the other but to look at their mutual interweavings. This approach is now espoused (up to a point) in postcolonial scholarship, where 'oral forms in African societies ... have a continuing and *equal* relationship with the written' (Ashcroft et al. 1998: 166–7). Many scholars would now accept Abiola Irele's position that orality comes through in African written literature too, 'a literature whose distinctive mark is the striving to attain the conditions of oral expression even within the boundaries established by Western literary conventions' (Irele 2001: 19). As Liz Gunner sums up a current perspective:

> The book itself, in terms of written literature from the continent, has been profoundly influenced by orality. It could be argued that the directions taken by contemporary written African literature have largely been shaped by the presence of a substantial and established body of rhetoric holding deep knowledge with which writers have often felt compelled to engage, even when moving from the African language/s in which the poetry or narrative is expressed, to writing in English, French, or Portuguese. (Gunner 2004: 3)

The once apparently separate states of 'orality' and 'literacy' have been brought together in the many studies about how 'written' productions such as novels or poetry in European languages built on, developed out of, or retained traces of, prior oral formulations or styles, the resultant works thus having in this sense dimensions of both oral and written.[8]

---

[8] See (among many other examples) Adu-Gyamfi 2002, Bourgault 1995, Brown 1999b, Ezenwa-Ohaeta 1994, Fraser 1986, Jones et al. 1992, Kane 1974, Makward et al. 1998 especially Part 1, Okpewho 1988a, Ricard and Swanepoel 1997, and relevant chapters in Irele and Gikandi 2004; also the cogently argued critique of the evolutionary 'from

Such analyses can be illuminating indeed when related to specific works or genres set into specific historical context. At times, however, they have been formulated in highly generalised terms or invoked an image of teleological progression 'onwards' to the written which not only ignores the long history of written genres in the continent but also casts the 'oral' – as if quintessentially 'African' – as something essentially of and from the past; a kind of survival interacting with, or perhaps still shining through, the colonising written modes from outside. Here, as Eileen Julien perceptively remarks, '"orality" has become a metonymy for "African"' (1992: 10).

That perspective is now complemented, however, by a greater emphasis on the creative ways that artists choose to exploit a mix of the resources open to them amidst which none is *in itself* necessarily more 'old' or more 'African' than any other. Thus Graham Furniss makes clear that a written/oral distinction cannot take us far in the analysis of Hausa genres, and in common with other recent scholars challenges the older historical framework in which 'modern', written, and 'European-type' genres are pictured as developing out of earlier 'traditional', 'oral', and indigenous ones.

> Rejecting an evolutionist perspective produces a concomitant shift of attitude towards one of the major divides in the discussion of African literature. Rather than see texts/performances as manifestly separated into two exclusive categories, the 'oral' and the 'written', by which the 'oral' is repeatedly raided for influences upon the 'written', such a view entails an attentiveness to the migration and overlap of textual material between the media of communication (speech, writing, recited reading, written recension of oral improvisation and electronic media) in the process of working and reworking theme after theme. (Furniss 1996: 1)

'Oral' and 'written' are here envisaged not as counterpoised but rather as merely among the range of media (themselves complex and variable) which people deploy to do things. Certain genres may deliberately employ both written and unwritten features – and sometimes other media – or move in and out of alternative formulations or exploit them in overlapping and interwoven ways. South African praise poets for example have long used writing as well as oral production, mingling the two as suits their purposes (Kaschula 2002, Opland 1998, 2005). So, too, with hymns, political songs and slogans, dramatic scripts, stories and much else – they move in and out and across the complex and permeable oral-written boundary. Karin Barber graphically depicts the 'writing-saturated orality' of the Yoruba popular theatre (1995a: 7), while in another context Martin Orwin has shown how for certain forms of Somali poetry the process of writing is not essentially different from editing and revising oral versions (Orwin 2003: 345). Both 'oral' elements and those represented as 'traditional' can be played with and manipulated in highly

---

[8] (cont.) orality to writing' model of some (certainly not all) of such analyses in Julien 1992, Barber 1995b, Chabal 1996: Introduction, Ricard and Veit-Wild (2005), also (above) Chapter 1, p. 2 n. 1. 'African literature' and its history is still sometimes equated with writing in English, French or Portuguese, neglecting the prolific work in African languages ('European languages' have also of course themselves in some contexts and for some people become as familiarly used as some reputedly more 'indigenous' languages).

sophisticated and effective ways. In Jamaican dub poetry resonances of 'the oral' are introduced to both political and poetic effect through the spellings of their printed forms – less phonetic transcription than deliberate assertion of the oral Creole voice in the midst of a print culture once restricted to the written 'standard' language of European English. The growing impact of close-grained studies shows up as obtuse the generalised dichotomies of oral-African-traditional-old on the one side as against written-European-modern-new on the other.

So it is no longer so much a matter of linear single-voiced texts, far less of membership of exclusive uniform categories like 'the written' or 'the oral', but of the varying play and intersection of diverse voices, multiple media, serial transformations. As illustrated earlier, the processes of enscription are not simple one-to-one transfers but a maze of decisions and interventions. The practices of reading and writing, too, have their complexities, with multiple actors and co-creators, plural layers and associations. The trend has emphatically been towards an enhanced recognition of the complications of varying situations, multiple participants and historically situated action, rather than the singleness of univocal written text or uniformly conceived and teleological historical sweep.

The picture of reality as essentially captured in the one-line-text or the single modality is giving way to a greater sensitivity to what I would sum up as multiplexity – a term that points to the possibilities of overlapping multi-plicities, running through a range of multiple media, modalities, partici-pants, voices, situations or historical specificities. From this perspective the instances of single-voiced texts – and in certain senses there are indeed some – become just one of many possible transformations, no longer the unexamined norm but themselves no less needful of situating and explaining than any other. Performers and their audiences no doubt often knew this already. By now many scholars have also moved on from a simplex view of oral texts to conceptualisations which take greater account of their potentially multi-voiced, multi-dimensioned and multi-situated qualities.

Performance, orature and text

Scholars trying to engage with the nature of texts which are in some sense 'oral' have long been tussling with the interaction of 'text' and 'performance' – a recurrent theme over recent decades (and so, too, of this volume). This has sometimes become a battle, some acclaiming the priority of 'performance', others that 'the text is the thing'. Evocations of the enduring mythic dichotomy are also drawn in when, as often, 'performance' comes to be equated with the 'oral' (and African), and 'text' with the 'written' (and European). In the study of African oral forms there have indeed been attempts to bring 'performed' and 'textual' together, but even so the balance has often seemed to tilt to one or the other – 'text' pulling towards the model of the western literary (written) canon, with, as Weate points out, the connotation of something to be *read* (2003: 27); 'performance' towards the ephemeral and emergent. I have certainly not escaped that tension. I tried to give each due weight in my approach to African oral literature (as in Chapter 6 above), but am aware of the differing emphases of the relatively textual perspective of Chapter 7 (not everything arises in emergent performance for there are also prior composed and memorised texts) as against Chapter 8's argument that text-based models obscure a proper appreciation of the performed reality. The dilemma to some extent continues, further exacerbated by the split between evanescent performance and enduring text presupposed in the ideologies and institutional practices associated with western hard print.

Over the years, however, there have been significant attempts to tackle their interaction in new ways. One notable strategy for confronting the issues head on has been the development of special terms to bring out the textual-*and*-performance qualities of African forms. They include concepts such as 'orature', 'auriture', 'oraliture', 'oralcy' or 'oraurality', terms which largely avoid the connotations of writing or of print.[9] These complement or replace the 'literature' terminology by conceptualisations that are not only arguably less ethnocentric and less script-based but might also, at least to a degree, bypass the performance/text opposition. This development has largely been led by African and Caribbean scholars and writers. Many, it is true, do use the term 'literature' (the International Society for Oral Literature in Africa for example has numerous African members) but others have additionally or alternatively turned to new frames of reference, getting right away from the traditional scriptist model with its implicit conceptualisations in terms of western literary genres.

Of these terms 'orature' has been the most influential. Coined in the 1960s by the Ugandan critic Pio Zirimu and soon invoked in East African debates on the politics of culture and the literary canon, it was brought into wider circulation by the Kenyan writer Ngugi wa Thiong'o (1986, see also 1997: 23, 133ff, 1998: chapter 4, and Brathwaite 1984: 23). It was partly a way of tackling 'the difficulties of containing the world of the oral text within that of the literary' (Ngugi wa Thiong'o 1998: 111). But it was also seen as a positive concept as against the perceived negative connotations of 'oral literature' as not quite attaining the norm of full (i.e. written) literature. 'Orature' stands in its own right. 'Oral' takes precedence but the word also carries an echo, set in its own terms, from 'liter-ature'. Oral realisation lies at its heart, a perspective reinforced in the emphasis on the centrality of the vocal in African and Caribbean tradition so powerfully formulated in the Caribbean author Edward Brathwaite's *The History of the Voice* (1984).

The term 'auriture' similarly evokes the voice but amplifies it by bringing in hearing too. As David Coplan comments in his stunning treatment of migrant workers' songs in southern Africa (1994)

> 'auriture' places the emphasis on the ears of the hearers, who include both performer and audience, and hence, properly, on the intended and experienced aesthetic transaction between all participants in a performance event. (Coplan 1994: 8–9)

[9] See for example Drewal 1991: 6, Farias 2003a: xxvii, lxxxv ff, Kishani 2001, and discussion below. Additional terms include 'verbal art(s)' (a long-established term), 'literary orature' (Swanepoel 1997: 121), 'lit/orature' (Fox 1999: 376), '*vocalité*' (Paul Zumthor in Calame-Griaule 1989: 13), and 'oralature' (Rosenberg 1987: 75).

'Aural' and 'aurality' draw our attention not just to the speaking mouth (oral) but also to the hearing ear and the auditory ambience. A similar sensitivity to both dimensions of sound – produced *and* heard – comes in Peek's 'auditory arts' (Peek 1994), Kishani's 'oraurality', 'oraural', 'orauralise' etc. (Kishani 2001) and more recently Kaschula's 'technauriture' or 'technologised auriture' where he illuminatingly brings us up to date by considering rap, dub poetry, slam and contemporary Xhosa praises on radio, television, musically backed audio discs, CD-ROM and the web (Kaschula 2003).

Each term alerts to slightly different viewpoints but what all have in common is a move away from more verbally texted dimensions into an appreciation of voiced and sonic qualities, the auditory – sometimes multisensory – relations between participants, and the active dialogues of performance. It is true that the prime focus is often on the acoustic facets rather than a full range of modalities (a point to return to in the next chapter). Nevertheless by their challenge to more scriptist models, such terms have decisively widened recent approaches to conceptualising oral forms. At the same time – though perhaps not yet to their full extent – they have mutually interacted with parallel analyses of forms outside Africa. There are accounts for example of the 'aural' features of public reading in late mediaeval England and France (Coleman 1996) and comparative studies of oral poetry across the world, from South African praise poetry and Slavic heroic singers to contemporary slam singers in North American towns (Foley 2002). Oral texts exist not in verbal transcript, or at any rate not just in that, but in the voiced performance.

This is complemented by the critical unpacking of the notion and practice of 'text'. Concepts of 'textuality', 'entextualisation', 'recontextualisation' and 'intertextuality' have brought out processual and relativistic dimensions and unsettled the picture of 'text' as a decontextualised and solidly enscripted entity with its own autonomy, hard edges and stability. Text and textualisation, too, are recognised as historical and cultural constructs, realised in contingent situations and by no means above the battles of social life as it is lived. On the same lines scholars are becoming more sensitive to the kinds of processes touched on in the previous chapter. As Lauri Honko sums it up in his magisterial discussion of text as process and practice

> The concept of oral text has experienced a revolutionary development in recent years. What used to be an innocent object of research, a verbal transcript of an orally performed traditional song (with or, more commonly, without musical notation), has been problematized from a variety of angles by questioning its boundaries, apparent fixity, performative representativity, situation and cultural contextuality, co-textual and intertextual environment, discursive function and ideological bias. The modest transcript has undergone acute source-criticism: its textual origin and linguistic accuracy, its methods of documentation, transcription, translation, editing and publication have been subjected to scrutiny, not forgetting the singer's 'voice' (always in danger of suppression), the collector's purposive role in the making of the text and the editor's impact on the final form. (Honko 2000a: 3)[10]

---

[10] On aspects of textualisation see in particular Barber 2003, Bauman 2004, Bauman and Briggs 1990, 2003, Hanks 1989, Honko 2000a,b, Silverstein and Urban 1996.

The impact of terms such as 'orature' has been further buttressed by the growing interest in 'performance' and the emergence of 'performance studies' as a recognised academic field. In some circles the paramount paradigm for approaching oral forms has now become performance – its process, con-texting, dynamics, co-creation or multi-modal presence. Here oral texts are to be conceived as existent primarily, perhaps solely, in the embodied temporal occasion of performance. 'Oral literature exists only in the here and now' is how Graham Furniss has it (2004: 47), or, in Robert Cancel's words, 'There is no verbal art outside of performance' (2004: 315). The primary form, the original, is the oral performance: *that* is the reality in which oral texts live.

From this viewpoint oral text exists in the unique situated moment. It is realised in active and embodied participation, in public theatrical display or, less tangibly, in the en-performancing of a written text, the 'now' when the reader personally experiences and re-creates it – 'performs' it and makes it their own. This indeed has been the great insight of the various 'performance approaches', reacting against ideologies and practices chained into the model of written words. So rather than its existence residing in enduring 'text', each performance is actualised – and to be analysed – in its own mix of com-municative channels: its particular place and timing; its participants and their potentially diverse perspectives and struggles among themselves; its activated arrangements of music, words, singing, colour, somatic involvement, dance, material display or whatever – all the elements realised in one immediate event. Performance is evanescent, experiential, actualised, emergent in the participants' creation of the moment: 'performance's only life is in the present' (Phelan 1993: 146).

The importance of performance is now recognised across a wide range of disciplines (certainly not confined to studies of Africa) and explored in a variety of ways too extensive to elaborate further here.[11] But there is also a further twist in the long dialectic of 'text' and 'performance', for the focus on performance is now being balanced by a revival of interest in 'text' – or at any rate in the 'something' by virtue of which performance itself is more than just the performing moment. To quote Lauri Honko again,

> 'The performance is king' paradigm relativized text, the next paradigm will probably relativize performance. Any performance is a compromise, an intelli-gent adaptation of tradition within unique situations structured by a con-fluence of several factors. It can be understood only against a broader spectrum of performances of the same integer in similar and different contexts. (Honko 2000a: 13)

Taken together with the concept of 'entextualising' as process, this has meant a new look at the relations between textuality and performing, seeing them not as counterposed but as essentially co-dependent and co-present. From this perspective *all* literary forms are in a way double-sided. They are indeed created in the magic moment of experienced performance, but also enlarged

---

[11] Works from this huge (and varied) literature that I have found especially illuminating include Barber 1991, 2000, 2003, Brown 1998, 1999a, Cancel 2004, Coplan 1994, Drewal 1991, 2004, Foley 2002, Fretz 2004, Harding 2002, Honko 2000a, Hughes-Freeland 1998, Okpewho 1990, Schechner 2002, Scheub 2002, Schieffelin 1998, Yankah 1995, also others referred to in the text here and earlier works above, p. 6 n. 3.

into or rooted in or reverberating with something more abstracted, detachable from the flow, imbued with memories and connotations for its participants which go *beyond* the immediate moment.

The continuing focus on performance is thus now being complemented by a renewed interest in the ways that performance does *not* after all exist solely in the vanishing moment. It is not just a single event, a situated outburst of sound and movement, but a performance *of* something. There is a sense in which it exists as an object for reference and exegesis.

Karin Barber formulates an illuminating perspective on this in her seminal discussion of text and performance in Africa, worth quoting at some length:

> What happens in most oral performances is not pure instantaneity, pure evanescence, pure emergence and disappearance into the vanishing moment. The exact contrary is usually the case. There is a performance – but it is a performance *of* something. Something identifiable is understood to have pre-existed the moment of utterance. Or, alternatively, something is understood to be constituted in utterance which can be abstracted or detached from the immediate context and re-embodied in a future performance. Even if the only place this 'something' can be held to exist is in people's minds or memories, still it is surely distinguishable from immediate, and immediately-disappearing, actual utterance. It can be referred to. People may speak of 'the story of Sunjata' or 'the praises of Dingaan' rather than speaking of a particular narrator's or praise-singer's performance on a particular occasion. And this capacity to be abstracted, to transcend the moment, and to be identified independently of particular instantiations, is the whole point of oral traditions. They are 'traditions' because they are known to be shared and to have been handed down; they can be shared and handed down because they have been constituted precisely in order to be detachable from the immediate context, and capable of being transmitted in time and disseminated in space. ...
>
> This would have been heresy fifteen years ago. The study of oral performance had been so impoverished by earlier attempts to convert oral genres into the equivalent of written literary texts that performance theory had had to fight hard to liberate it. The exhilarating discovery of the importance of 'composition *in* performance', of improvization, of interaction with the audience, of gesture, tempo, rhythm, and bodily expression, of the emergent and the processual, meant that performance theory, at least in its early stages, was adamantly opposed to anything resembling the concept of 'text' in literary criticism ... held to distort and reify the fluid, emergent, improvizatory, dialogic and embodied nature of performance. But things have changed. On the one hand, a more flexible and inclusive definition of 'text' has been proposed that is not tethered to written or even to verbal discourse (Hanks 1989: 95). ... On the other hand, anthropologists working with oral traditions have begun to try to get at how the evanescent, momentary performance can none the less be regarded as something abstracted or detached from the flow of everyday discourse. We have begun to try to see how work goes into constituting oral genres as something capable of repetition, evaluation and exegesis – that is, something that can be treated as the *object* of commentary – by the communities that produce them, and not just by the collector or ethnographer. (Barber 2003: 325)

This directs us to the something existing *beyond* the immediate moment, realised in a more or less externalisable mode. It is of course partly a matter of degree and takes diverse forms. It can be more, or less, explicitly crystallised, abstractible and portable. It may take relatively intangible form, a potentiality for realisation rather than a text in some invariant form. In a memorable phrase now being taken up by a number of scholars Lauri Honko conceives of a 'mental text' lying behind a performer's ability to deliver lengthy epics: 'the element uniting the different performances of a particular epic by a particular singer' (Honko 2000b: viii, also Honko 2000a: 22ff). On (perhaps) somewhat similar lines we hear of the 'word-hoard of the storyteller' which enabled the 1963 performance of the Ijaw *Ozidi* saga in Ibadan (Okpewho 2003: 1), or the 'imagined script' in a Yoruba travelling theatre company which 'occupies a conceptual space somewhere between text and improvisation' (Barber 1995a, Brown 1995: 2).

This also recalls the examples of oral texts such as those mentioned in Chapter 7 which are composed prior to performance or enacted by other than the composer – clear cases of somehow externalised texts. The famous case of Somali prior composition has been further pursued in recent analysis of the 'definitive' and repeatable nature of Somali poem-texts, subject to edition and revision before public performance; Orwin reports the Somali perception that 'a poem may have a "life" away from the immediate context of its composition' (2003: 341). Karin Barber goes on to consider the inseparability of the performative and entextualising dimensions in Yoruba and other praise poetry. On the one hand discourse is rendered 'object-like', making exegesis and quotation possible, with the perception that these words pre-existed their present utterance and could continue to exist after it. On the other the entextualisation is not fixed as an unchanging monument for Yoruba praises are notably fluid and dynamic in their realisation, re-activated in new contexts of utterance.

> Entextualization ... is not the opposite of emergent performance, but rather its alter ego; they proceed hand in glove with each other and are the condition of each other's possibility. For text must be treated as the object of attention – by exegesis and by being quoted in new contexts of utterances – in order to attain meaning, while a performance that was truly ephemeral would be a performance of nothing. (Barber 2003: 332)

The literary exegeses of active practitioners received relatively little attention in the past, perhaps in part because a capacity for objective reflection and detachment was long denied to those involved in the once-supposed 'participation' of oral and non-western experience. That simplified ethnocentric paradigm is (hopefully) now on the way out, and it is clear that it is not just the Limba who (as illustrated in Chapter 2) can take a detached and externalising approach to linguistic acts alongside their 'lack of literacy'. An interest in local interpretations is now a growing point in approaches to oral texts, whether linked to local theories of literature or aesthetics more generally (e.g. Chimombo 1988, Derive 1989) or to local conceptualisations of the nature or aim of particular forms. Thus some genres, such as Hausa religious poetry, are expected to be didactic, others to be obscure (Furniss 2001, Barber 1999) while in Yoruba *oríkì* poetry praises like that being chanted by Sangowemi on our book's cover are interpreted as the key to a subject's essential nature so that uttering someone's *oríkì* meant calling upon or unlocking hidden powers (Barber 1984: 503). Sometimes the exegesis is highly explicit. Classical Somali poems were re-recited over many years accompanied by explicit commentaries and discussion, and as B. W. Andrzejewski explains (characteristically anticipating more recent trends)

> Since poems frequently dealt with matters which were topical at the time of composition, the reciters added ... explanations in prose which gave an account of the original circumstances. ... I have witnessed on many occasions ... discussions among Somali connoisseurs of poetry, during which either the merits of a particular poem or the correct interpretation of a difficult passage were the subject of debate. (Andrzejewski 1981: 1–3)

This is not to say that people's explications are necessarily unanimous. Czekelius gives the example of Berba tales (north-west Benin) as audience members discuss them and come to different conclusions.

> In the literary criticism of the Berba ... it is the *variability of interpretations*, the inherent potential of a tale to evoke again and again different thoughts and associations, its capacity to stimulate public debates on current issues, which lend quality and significance to Berba oral literature. (Czekelius 1993: 132)

This occasion for varying exegesis is what is conveyed, she suggests, when Berba say 'the story is very rich!' (Czekelius 1993: 132). It can also be the very ambiguity of a story – a 'crafted sought-after opaqueness' – that 'invites listeners to create significance' (Fretz 1994: 241, 232, cf. Jackson 1982). People construct the meanings of oral texts not just through the direct productions of their voices and their heard reception on a given occasion but also through their interpretations and debates.

Performance goes beyond the immediate moment in another way too. Enactments from past and present meet, the intersection of permanence with evanescence. Elin Diamond captures this well in her proposition that 'Performance, even in its dazzling physical immediacy, drifts between present and past, presence and absence, consciousness and memory ... [and] embeds features of previous performances' (1996: 1). To one degree or another partici-pants in performance are implicated in memories and resonances that both exist in, and go further than, the here and now, evocations *beyond* the immediate moment. Scheub comments of Xhosa stories

> The full performance of the story is ritualistic in the sense that the audience has been there before, has had those adventures before, and regularly revisits the stories to recover those experiences. Storytelling always involves echoes, a shadowing of the past. (Scheub 2002: 121)

Memories and imaginations of other performances may pervade the experience, whether it is the sonic, kinesic and thematic reverberations of a Xhosa praise poem; the multiple associations – postural, acoustic, visual, identifying – of a simple interchange of greetings (token of humanity) in a Limba story; the sung, costumed, theatrical, drummed resonances of a popular Yoruba play; or 'merely' the awareness and expectations of the con-ventions of the genre. Those who have engaged in related performances and experiences can scarcely expel those ramifying associations and inter-textualities from the uniquenesses of a single performance. Even an apparently unfamiliar performance or the en-performancing of an unknown written text can evoke personal or shared resonances from a multiplicity of situations and imaginings that exist alongside the immediate moment.

All this throws yet another light on oral text, here conceptualised as realised not just in immediate temporal performing but also in the enduring and, as it were, portable elements of performance: the elements that can indeed be extractible and reproducible (and ultimately enscribable?) as text. It is true that some opaqueness perhaps remains and we may also need to be cautious about presupposing an exclusively *verbal* model of both the performed 'now' and the enduring 'that'. As Goldhill among others has pointed out (in Goldhill and Osborne 1999: 13), the linguistic paradigm sometimes used to underpin performance studies can obscure the complexities of multi-modal realisation – partly the result, perhaps, of the insidious scriptist connotations of the term 'text' which constantly and quietly turn one's gaze from non-verbal dimensions. What is significant, however, is the move away from the more extreme and mutually opposed models of both performance and text – from 'performance' as either, on the one hand, the mere contingent embellishment of abiding 'text' or on the other the essential reality behind it; and from 'text' as either existentially prior to performance or, more recently, merely a (doomed) attempt to capture or prescribe the reality of the performed event.

These recent perspectives lead into more subtle attempts to grasp the overlapping dimensions of entextualised performance, performed textuality – and with them the complex ways people draw on diverse modes to actualise the past in the present, external and internal, uniqueness and recurrence, the ephemeral and the durable, as they creatively enact and interweave words (and perhaps more than words). The multi-layered quality of performed textualisations and their intertwinedness with *both* the durability of something (more, or less) objectivated *and* the evanescent moment of performance and participation adds yet further complexity to the once simple-sounding notion of oral text.

Across academic divides

When I was first developing my interest in African forms, studies of 'literature' (implicitly defined as written) were largely conducted in arenas separated from the anthropological or folklore departments where, together with 'African Studies', the analysis of 'oral' 'African' genres seemed appropriately to reside. With the changed interdisciplinary reach of today, studies are being brought into conjunction which would once have been separated under such heads as (for example) theatre studies, dance, music, performance studies, folklore, anthropology, oral history, ethnomusicology, sociolinguistics, oral-formulaic studies, cultural studies, interviewing methodologies, narrative, life histories, cultural identity, information technology, comparative literature, media studies and popular culture. The study of oral texts has benefited from and fed into this conjunction, linked both to changing moves in literary theory and, perhaps even more emphatically, to the overlapping interests of linguistic, literary and performance anthropology.

196

African scholars have been thoroughly involved in challenging earlier compartmentalisations as inappropriate for many African forms. Steve Chimombo for example interacted with University of Malawi colleagues from Linguistics, Fine and Performing Arts, French, Chichewa, and English to complete his fine analysis of Chichewa oral literature and aesthetics (Chimombo 1988) while David Coplan's book on the word music of South Africa's Basotho migrants explicitly drew on cultural anthropology, literary criticism, sociology, ethnomusicology and history (1994 see esp. p. xvii). Duncan Brown's interdisciplinary *Oral Literature and Performance in Southern Africa* (1999) spans literary studies, anthropology, sociology, ethnomusicology and history, and Jonathan Draper (2003) brings biblical studies, too, into the interdisciplinary reach. There are comparable transdisciplinary trends in the study of personal narratives and life histories as scholars move on from 'testimonies' and 'facts' to greater emphasis on literary and performative qualities with mutual crossovers between history, life stories and the study of oral literature (evident for example in Roberts 2002, Tonkin 1992, Vail and White 1991, White et al. 2002). History, literature and narrative are brought together in Wilson-Tagoe and Kwadwo Osei-Nyame's *Literature and History* (1999) which straddles oral and written forms and spans pre-colonial, colonial and post-colonial periods. Isabel Hofmeyr (2002) draws creatively on history, literary theory, and studies of reading and of performance to throw light on the reception of John Bunyan's *The Pilgrim's Progress* in Europe and Africa. A similarly synoptic and comparatively informed vision pervaded the workshops and publications emanating from the 'Literature and performance' strand in the University of London's wide-ranging 'Centre for Asian and African Literatures' which ran equally across oral and written, danced and pictured, present-day and mediaeval, bringing together scholars from literary theory, linguistics, technology, anthropology, psychology, dance studies, ethnomusicology, art history, communication, popular culture, and areas and languages from five continents.[12]

The result is both a less ring-fenced concept of oral texts and a richer image of African oral performances. These are no longer either just one-line textual products or far-away arts of only marginal interest to those outside the continent and its study but (no different from European literature) complex cultural productions created and reproduced in specific conditions whose analysis rightly involves a range of mutually interacting and comparative disciplinary perspectives. This brings to the fore not only the complexities of terms like 'the oral' or 'the performed' but also, in a sense, their pervasiveness as ubiquitous dimensions of cultural activity, transcending the once-accepted contrasts of 'oral'/'written' or European/other.

The apparent boundary between scholar and practitioner has at the same time been dissolving. This partly goes along with the widespread questioning of the once dominant 'objective research' model – of the 'researcher' as sitting apart from the subject-of-investigation. 'Participation' is no longer an auto-matically derogatory term and the once standard opposition between 'researcher' and 'researched' now looks over-simple. So, too, with the once

---

[12] www.soas.ac.uk/literatures/, see also Gerstle et al. 2005.

seemingly clear contrasts of 'scholar/subject', 'interviewer/informant', 'observer'/'actor'. One need only recall the multiple roles people may play in the creation and consolidation of texts to see the inadequacy of these simplifying contrasts. The exploration of 'identity', 'cultural revival', 'tradition' or 'our own culture' has been undertaken not just by 'the academics' but participants from many positions and educational backgrounds, illustrated among many other cases by the local historians in Nigeria who are narrowing the gap between 'university' and 'community' historians (Alagoa 2001, see also Okpewho 1998a&b). At the same time there are new possibilities for local and independent dissemination through desktop pub-lishing, new typographies and the web, channels which do not have to rely on the established forms – and gatekeepers – of costly hard copy publishing. This has enabled a multiplicity of public and reflective voices: not just the scholarly hegemony of accredited specialists or of outsiders charged with the responsibility of interpreting local meanings but an increasing acknowledge-ment of voices previously defined out of existence by elitist or establishment ideologies.

This blurring of the once established scholar/enactor and researcher/ subject division is arguably especially salient in Africa. The traditional image of the foreign scholar coming from outside to research 'on' or, at best, direct the efforts of, uneducated colonised locals no longer carries the same credence. Not that the practice probably ever totally matched that picture. Isabel Hofmeyr's *The Portable Bunyan* (2004b) is just one among many studies to explode decisively the over-simple view which saw earlier African intellectual endeavours as inevitably driven by external forces. Even in colonial and missionary settings 'performers' and 'informants' were not always clearly separate from 'collectors', or 'researchers' from scribes and 'assistants', and whether or not recognised by outside scholars there were of course many notable African intellectuals. But the balance, or at least the perception, has certainly shifted over the last decades. There is now an acknowledged plenitude of scholars from and of Africa, often themselves established actors in the fields they study and able to build on first-language expertise and personal involvement.

But in any case reflection, analysis or explication is not just some separate action by demarcated 'scholars' or an activity directed only to the past, but also something that to an extent runs through all cultural activity, one dimension of people's present actions. One of the wonderful things about doing things with words, one might say, is the potential it offers for detach-ment and self-consciousness in the very act of uttering, and the capacity of participants to comment verbally on what they do. Speakers, composers and audiences can themselves be reflective meta-analysts. The examples of indigenous exegesis referred to earlier bring home the same point. Even Bubu Dema's conclusion to his Limba tug-of-war story was as much commentary and interpretation as part of the plot, simultaneous and concurrent processes. Accounts of West African popular theatre do not confine themselves to the plays but also convey the views and interpretations of the players – 'reminiscing, explaining, philosophising, and grumbling' (Barber 2000, Barber et al. 1997: blurb); while Hunter and Oumarou's study of Hausa language about using language depicts how 'when Hausa verbal artists take ordinary language and craft it, manipulate it, transform it to create extraordinary language they are functioning not only as artistic creators but as analysts and critics as well' (1998: 169). The significance of local interpretations and conceptualisations, whether on-going or in some way detached from the event, is increasingly visible in studies of African verbal arts, reinforcing the ramifying interest in local exegeses.

Here again we find a bridging of what once seemed obvious divides – not just across disciplines or across the older dichotomies between 'traditional-local-African' as against 'modern-international-European', but also of the distinction between analyst and performer, 'us' and 'them'. In some circles at least the stress on 'objectivity' and scientific detachment is now complemented by an acknowledgement of participatory research and the co-creation of knowledge. Getting away from a presupposed contrast between scholar/subject or external analyst/participant reveals a more complex spectrum of roles and conceptualisations, perhaps overlapping and co-operating, perhaps contending, sometimes simultaneous, sometimes sequential. 'Oral texts' are no less rich in potentially conflicting interpretations and approaches than other forms of human cultural production, and the validation of knowledge is surely not just in the hands of one single group (much though some scholars – or politicians – might wish that to be so). Some analyses will be considered wrong-headed by certain groups of scholars, arguing for instance that particular interpretations are (for example) influenced by outdated Eurocentric views or by simplistic and poorly evidenced appeals to 'tradition' or cultural revival. But then there is the other side of the coin – that approaches considered misguided by some parties may indeed form part of the situation for others. Oral genres, from Africa or from anywhere, are complex enough to thrive amidst the elaboration of an infinity of diverse interpretations from a host of participants coming from varying perspectives, all arguably in one way part of the full picture. Whose conceptualisations ultimately prevail, if any, is no longer (if it ever was) a foregone conclusion.

Current conceptualisations of oral texts, then, have moved us towards more complex and problematic issues than the simplex uniform one-line text that was once the influential framework for outside scholars' analysis and reflection. And even that apparently innocent phrase of 'oral texts' – adequate as a starting point – can now be seen to carry its own implications. It is founded in two concepts each of which is both elusive and diverse: in 'oral' with its problematic and ambiguous overtones; and in 'text' with its far from neutral emphasis on the verbal, the linear, the writably permanent. Words do indeed form a major medium through which humans encapsulate the more enduring and external dimensions of performance. But 'oral texts', and the concepts and practices widely associated with that general phrase, have now to be increasingly recognised as composite, multi-voiced, multi-modal, ambiguous, dynamic, multi-dimensional, situationally formulated, multiply interpreted, and often co-created by multiple – and possibly conflicting – parties. They are not confined to the past but equally part of modern urban life, the commercial world and youth culture. Nor does the 'oral' dimension hold them separate, for modern novels or modern poetry go in and out of the oral and along various dimensions. The established – and still valuable – awareness of 'context' and 'performance' has been enlarged by new perspectives on entextualisation and the integral if riddling interrelation of performance and text. To understand what have in the past been regarded as 'oral texts' we have to go beyond just the 'words' and just the evanescent moment, into a host of multiplexities.

And we also have to go beyond the 'external' researchers (myself included) to bring in the many people who have worked with entextualised words in other capacities too. There is hopefully now more push to incorporate the actions of that full complement of interested and reflective parties who have in their multifarious ways created, formulated, stood back from, interpreted, reflected on, and worked with verbal or partially verbal productions and the multiplex forms in which they are embodied. All are ways that people deal reflectively with linked chains of words, with conventions for structuring and displaying words, for attending to them, for going beyond them, working with them, and, in their various ways, conceptualising them. These are indeed among the many things that humans do with words whether in Africa or elsewhere.

IV

Epilogue

12

Words,
the Human Attribute?[1]

Words amidst words, words in play, words turning back around themselves, words winding together in complex interacting meta-spirals and exegeses, actively and creatively wielded to formulate and reformulate imagination and experience, and both to enact and transcend the bounds of the everyday: small wonder that verbal language has been regarded as *the* typical human attribute, the crucial evolutionary achievement which divides humans from animals and provides the comprehensive medium for our communication needs. This linguistic model of humankind has a long history and a strong hold in the present. It is not uncontested however. This final chapter re-examines this debate and brings it back to the context of Africa.

Human history as the history of language

What makes us human is our possession of language – that has long been the refrain of both popular wisdom and academic exposition. Language is the specific human character, 'the essence of our humanity' (Keesing and Strathern 1998: 26), 'the quintessential human attribute' (Pilbeam 1992: 4), 'the funda-mental difference between human and animal societies' (Elias 1991: 114), 'the most distinctive single criterion for defining what sets us apart from our closest relatives in the animal world' (James 2003: 142). The 'qualitative leap' between humans and apes came in 'the development of language as a referen-tial, time- and space-transcending sign system' (Luckmann 1995: 176). The same theme is echoed across otherwise diverse disciplines and theoretical perspectives, from general books on communication asserting that 'only with language did we become really human' (Rosengren 1999: 28) or 'when

---

[1] Written for this volume (some themes and examples have also figured (variously) in Finnegan 2002, 2003, 2005, 2006).

humans crossed the threshold of language ... [they] distanced themselves from the rest of creation' (Finch 2003: 1) to Chomsky's insistence on the faculty of language as 'a true "species property"' (2000: 3). Whether it originated in some momentous event, in a wired-in language instinct or inbuilt 'language organ', or through gradual development from more primitive stages, the distinctiveness of humankind, it seems, lies in our possession and practice of language.

This tale of human division from animals through language, repeated and repeated both now and in earlier centuries, is sometimes asserted as a truism, sometimes recounted with an air of originality and profundity, a deep wisdom to be constantly rediscovered. Jack Goody is categorical, seeing a shift 'from gesture to language' as fundamental to the human condition.

> The most significant elements of any human culture are undoubtedly channelled through words, and reside in the particular range of meanings and attitudes which members of any society attach to their verbal symbols. ... Language is the specific human attribute, the critical means of interaction between individuals, the foundation of the development of what we call 'culture' and of the way in which learned behaviour is transmitted from one generation to the next. (Goody 1968: 28, 1987: 3)

For I. A. Richards language is 'the instrument of all our distinctively human development, of everything in which we go beyond the other animals' (1936: 161). Or again, in the resounding words of Thomas Astle, eighteenth-century Keeper of Records at the Tower of London, 'Without speech we should scarcely have been rational beings' (Astle 1784: 2).

The tale is further elaborated to portray the two great forms through which this mark and fulfilment of humanity has been manifested in human history. There is, first of all, speech – oral language. And then came written language. In the language-based story this advent of writing is critical for the unfolding of human history. This theme rings time and time again through the centuries. The fifteenth-century author of one of the earliest European vernacular grammars, Antonio de Nebrija, saw writing as the greatest invention of humankind:

> Among all the things that human beings discovered through experience, or that were shown to us by divine revelation in order to polish and embellish human life, nothing has been more necessary, nor benefited us more, than the invention of letters. (Nebrija 1926 [1492]: 234 Book I, chapter 2, as translated in Mignolo 1994: 95)

Two centuries later Thomas Astle was expressing parallel ideas on writing and human progress:

> The noblest acquisition of mankind is SPEECH, and the most useful art is WRITING. The first, eminently, distinguishes MAN from the brute creation; the second, from uncivilized savages. ... [Writing is] an invention which hath contributed more than all others to the improvement of mankind. (1784: 1, 10)

A century on saw remarkably similar sentiments being enunciated by the anthropologist Edward Burnett Tylor.

The invention of writing was the greatest movement by which mankind rose from barbarism to civilization. How vast its effect was, may be best measured by looking at the low condition of tribes still living without it, dependent on memory for their traditions and rules of life, and unable to amass knowledge as we do by keeping records of events, and storing up new observations for the use of future generations. (Tylor 1881: 179)

The tale resounds through more recent years too. For the mid-twentieth century sociologist Talcott Parsons writing was a 'watershed' in social evolution, 'the focus of the fateful development out of primitiveness' (Parsons 1966: 26), while the long-running UNESCO position set writing as the dividing line that separated 'those who master nature, share out the world's riches among themselves, and set out for the stars' from 'those who remain fettered in their inescapable poverty and the darkness of ignorance' (UNESCO 1966: 29): literacy is the 'prerequisite for citizenship and for human and social development' (UNESCO 2001). Jack Goody's strikingly influential publications over nearly half a century have similarly told of 'the transforming effects of literate activity on human life' and its 'primary importance in the history of human cultures' (Goody 2000: 2, 3–4), where the differences between primitive and advanced cultures are attributable to the advent of writing and writing underpins civilization (Goody 1987: 291, 300). 'The emergence of writing and literate activity some five thousand years ago transformed human life', he writes, 'a quantum jump in human consciousness, in cognitive awareness' (Goody 2000: blurb, 1998: 1).

These accounts, far-reaching and emotive, correlate the ideologies and technologies of language with modernity and the mission of the west. They feed on that same familiar paradigm of the powerful binary oppositions that divide humankind and demarcate the great eras of its history: orality versus literacy, primitive versus civilised.

The linguistically driven narrative has been so pervasively and consistently deployed that it might indeed be described as a foundational myth of the west. Like other myths that set out the nature and destiny of humankind it is no doubt differentially believed, at times contested (some contrary voices are considered below) and certainly turned to many different purposes. But it indubitably presents a profoundly evocative and compelling account. Europe fulfils the foreordained human destiny through its attainment of writing, and above all of print, buttressed by the successes of modernising science and rationality to which this led. Human history is to be read through the glass of language and its technologies.

A more multiplex story?

The language-centred story is told and retold, overtly a descriptive and incontrovertible account formulating shared assumptions about the nature and destiny of humankind. But it is a tendentious one after all. It projects a tale of language and alphabetic literacy moving humanity onward into the scientific and democratic regimes of the west. The actions and structures of the west over the centuries of expansion nestle well within this encompassing tale, mutually intertwined with the social arrangements and ideologies of education, socialisation, science, expansion, empire, social mobility, modernity ... . Language, not least in the extensive projects of biblical translation, was a primary vehicle in the missionary conversion process and crucial for the civilising vision of the west: Simon Gikandi well notes 'the central role accorded literary texts in the project of colonial modernity by both the colonizer and the colonized' (2004: 385). Language and writing fed into and out of the power structures with 'language [as] the means of the spiritual subjugation' as Ngugi wa Thiong'o (1986: 9) famously had it. The alphabetic script – 'universally employed by civilized peoples' (Diringer 1968, Vol. 1: 13) – was the 'ultimate tool of conquest' (Griffiths 1997: 144).

The linguistic myth of human history, for all it looks universal, is no neutral account. The essence of human-ness is posited as language; and language in its two predestined modes, first oral then written, as unrolling the stages of human history. The tale echoes that Enlightenment ideology in which language, and especially written language, is the condition of rationality, civilisation and progress, attaining its apotheosis in the alphabetic writing of the west. Music, dance and drama fall out of the picture. So do the gestural, pictorial, sculptural, sonic, tactile, bodily, affective and artefactual dimensions of human life. What we have is a cognitive language-centred model of the nature and destiny of humanity.

Over the last centuries this account has without doubt inspired and authorised many precious actions, experiences and understandings. But it is not inevitably subscribed to in all traditions or times, nor does it necessarily provide a trusty cross-cultural guide. It is not only the 1960s Limba who, for all their interest in language, might resist the notion that verbal language is self-evidently *the* distinctive and leading human attribute. Many others would now query the once-unquestioned practice, sanctioned by that same myth, of translating multisensory African performances into thin textual lines and as Steve Chimombo points out classifications of African art that prioritise 'the *verbal*, exclude other art forms (e.g. the visual) which are inextricably interrelated with all the rest' (Chimombo 1988: 2 [emphasis in original]). The linguistic focus may indeed chime well with certain aspects of western history, but is less felicitous for illuminating other dimensions of human cultural experience and scarcely a universal or comprehensive account of human destiny.

The tale has indeed functioned as a kind of mythical charter, enunciating and validating a western vision and at the same time projecting an image of 'Africa' as, in its essence, 'oral', 'pre-literate' and (by that very lack of writing) not fully civilised. It is over-simple, however, just to castigate it as *the* self-interested western tale. 'The west' after all is scarcely monolithic in its geography, history or varied social experiences and there have been recurring alternative themes too. The powerful Lockean version for example, in which language is rational, referential, decontextualised, the key to scientific progress, is countered in the tradition of Herder and his followers where the emphasis on language is complemented by an interest in the role of feeling and imagination and the scope for intertextuality, context and sensory celebration (see especially Bauman and Briggs 2000, 2003, Briggs 2002). And it was western writers after all like Bakhtin (1968) and Huizinga (1949) who highlighted the realities of carnival and of play, and the philosopher R. G. Collingwood who emphasised non-verbal communicative modes like bodily gesture, dance and music (1938: 242 and his chapter 11 *passim*).

The present seems to be one of those periods when alternative perspectives to the (still prevalent) linguistic myth are becoming more visible. They are articulated not just in the by-now commonplace critiques of ethnocentric grand narrative, but across many disciplines and backgrounds. The practices of language are coming to be recognised as processes for empirical study rather than primarily as uplifting tokens of human destiny or prescriptive ideals; so too, if as yet less prominently, are the ideologies surrounding language.[2] Current moves in cultural history, sociology, material culture and studies of 'the body' are between them undermining the assumed centrality of the word to human life – indeed it has been proposed that a 'sensual revolution' is now supplanting the so-called linguistic turn in the human sciences (Howes 2005: 1). In anthropology (though not just there) there has been a flowering of studies of sensual forms: 'of the visual, of art, of aesthetics; of "performance", of body language; and of the aural – the interpretation of sound, of music and song' (James 2003: 74).[3] The resulting appreciation of the multiple modes of human life – touches, sounds, sights, smells, movements, material artefacts – and of shared experiences, dynamic interactions and bodily engagements at once takes us beyond the purely verbal and cognitive and uncovers the partiality of the narrow linguistic tale.

The challenge is also coming through our changing communication technologies. It has to be said of course that their 'impact' has often been much exaggerated, seriously over-simplifying the complexity of human action and of cultural and political controls and ideologies. And in any case 'new' communication media long precede the present generation. But with all the caveats, recent technological developments may indeed be playing some part in cajoling our sensibilities to realities beyond (spoken and written) words.

The technology of writing and the practices of enscription privilege the substantiality of written words. It was these, whether composed on the page or transcribed from performance, that once seemed to give the 'real thing' – the durable and materialised text. But audio-technology has enabled attention to realities missed by pen-and-paper recording. Parry and Lord's phonograph revealed variability and challenged the assumption of abiding verbal texts (Lord 1960), just as audio recordings have uncovered acoustic subtleties in African oral genres and opened our ears to once unappreciated facets of performance.

Audio is part of popular usage and perception too. In Africa as elsewhere people employ audio technologies for their own purposes – composing, performing, listening, and more. Radio has long been a medium for dissemination and publication, from story, song and performed poetry to oratory,

---

[2] See Chapter 1, p. 6 n. 5.

[3] Among the explosion of cross-disciplinary works on the senses and related issues, see for example Burke 1997, Classen 1993, 1998, 2005, Classen et al. 1994, Geurts 2002, Harvey 2003, Howes 2003, 2005, Matera 2002, and the new journal *The Senses and Society*; also on multi-modality more generally Finnegan 2002, Kress and Van Leeuwen 2001, Norris 2004.

plays and talk shows (Fardon and Furniss 2000, Spitulnik 2004) and for years now tape and cassette recorders have been readily used devices for composition and recordings; decades ago they were already a regular part of Somali camel-riders' gear as they criss-crossed the desert. Cassettes of Haya epics are on sale from street vendors in Tanzania (Mbele 2004: 105), dub poetry grew from the complex intermixture of creative poetic composition with sound recording technology, and recordings on disc or web are a regular part of the popular culture scene. As Russell Kaschula comments

> Those extralinguistic elements, which are often lost in the transmission of orality into literacy, can again be re-captured through technology. The reaction of the audience, the performer's intonation, voice quality and emphasis, the effects of rhythm, context and the speed of performance are lost in the written version, but can once again come alive in the technologized version. (Kaschula 2003: 8–9)

Audio-technologies enable us not only to hear but to document and embody music, volume, tempo, sonic structures, dynamics, intonation or intensity, and multiple ensembles as well as solo performer – and bring to notice elements that had before been defined out of existence by the prioritising of the verbal.[4]

The visual is being more clearly revealed too. Certain visual dimensions have of course long been capturable in still images like the illuminating photographs, mentioned earlier, of Tuareg and Xhosa narrative performances (Calame-Griaule 1985, Scheub 1997a, Scheub and Zenani 1992). But it is the moving-image technologies that have truly enlarged our awareness. They can make real the sequential deployment of gesture, display, material symbols, spacing and dance, supplementing still photography by encapturing movement, dynamic development and the seen dialectics of audience and performer interactions. They do so, furthermore, in temporal flow with a sense of immediacy and personality – a counter both to the single-voice text and to the anonymous 'tradition' sometimes purveyed through more distanced written representations.

In Africa as elsewhere people are now well acquainted with the realities of moving images in television, film and video, and of how performers can disseminate their creations more widely than in the immediate moment and place of live performance. Christian video narratives interfused with 'indigenous imaginations' circulate in Nigeria (Obododimma 2001), a Yoruba popular theatre group performs on television and video as well as on tour (Barber 2000), video technologies are familiarly drawn on in a host of contexts to capture the realities of performance and experience, and film is an established form in and about Africa which is turned to many purposes (both 'research' and other). With all their well-known problems of cost or unequal access the enlarged perspective of video technologies has unquestionably given new insight not just into some secondary dimension at the margin but into the solidity of the visual acts and arts of performance.

---

[4] Some hard copy books – still a minority but more than in the past – now include audio-recordings (and occasionally video) and/or links to multi-media material on the web to convey a greater sense of what is 'really' there in the texts (for example Askew 2002, Bourgault 2003, Conrad and Condé 2004, Görög-Karady and Seydou 2001, Johnson 2003, Mack 2005).

The multi-media opportunities increasingly (if unequally) offered by computers have further extended the narrower focus on words. CD-ROMs and web displays, with their facility for the vivid multi-media combinations of colour, shape, movement, image, graphic and sound interlaced with individual creativity and playful dynamics, can move between, around and beyond oral/written boundaries, presenting multiplex performance modes in both real and transferred time. Such resources are now exploited not just by scholars or activists but by African artists and their admirers. Performances by the Xhosa praise poet Zolani Mkiva, for example, are available for a world-wide audience on the web (www.makingmusic.co.za – Kaschula 2003: 2). Such media give a new kind of reality to dimensions that once seemed (at best) peripheral to the firm centrality of print.

The 'new' technologies have their limitations. They may have marvel-lously alerted us to aural, visual and moving elements but leave other dimensions uncaptured (smell, touch, bodily presence), nor, as Tedlock points out for earlier technologies, do they automatically and immediately affect people's sense of reality (Tedlock 1985: 341). Nevertheless they are taking us beyond one-line verbalised text to greater awareness of co-creators, multiple voices and multiple media, giving substance to dimensions screened out in the technology of writing – to realities that could before too easily be presumed to be either, on the one hand, merely ephemeral and tangential or, on the other, only truly existent when translated into verbal text. A recent international conference of the Society for Oral Literature in Africa (held in Banjul 2004) is symptomatic of this newer perspective, embracing as it did such topics as music, theatre, dance, textile oracy, contemporary song, audio, video, film, radio, hyper media and multi-media archiving. The take on what oral forms 'are' is being stretched from writable one-voice texts into the multifacetness of multi-modal enactment.

From this angle, too, the once apparently clear concepts of orality and literacy – of speech and writing – have become cloudier. Speech may have been pictured as the essential human attribute but it does not stand on its own: it is inextricably intertwined with other modes of human interaction, gestural, bodily, visual, artefactual, tactile. Nor are the echoes and overtones of either performance or text purely verbal either. Proverbs are not just spoken and written but drummed, carved, miniaturised in gold weights, or repre-sented in figurines, masks and cloth, carrying multi-modal evocations what-ever their immediate medium. Verbal language is both complemented and interpenetrated by multi-sensory products and practices – by the great textile arts of Africa, so notable for their range of graphic and figurative expression, by representations in wood or beadwork, by music and dance, no less than by the more recent arts of film, video and electronic communication, between them all eroding and extending the ostensibly comprehensive categories of oral and written.[5]

The image of some single (west-generated) 'Writing' ushering in the second act of the great human drama has also been muddied by our gathering appreciation of the diverse forms of literacy. Not all writing systems are

[5] For examples of interactions and overlaps between verbal and other media in Africa see esp. Schipper 2000, and, for an earlier discussion, Calame-Griaule 1965: part 4.

alphabetic, nor can they necessarily be analysed as merely the transparent transliteration of spoken language – of language pure and simple. Pictorial and decorative dimensions can play a prominent role and even the familiar alphabetic scripts are not made up just of words but also of such other – integral – elements as layout, space, colour, shape or texture. And it is not just in form but also in practice that 'literacy' varies, for people use writing and reading in a multiplicity of ways and through a huge diversity of systems, situations and social arrangements – not so much literacy as multiliteracies.[6] The once-hard concept of 'writing' has turned into something more fluid and unstable: manifest in diverse shapes and deployments and, with the contemporary development of 'soft' text and visual display, itself often both multimodal and evanescent. 'Language as oral' and 'language as written' no longer look clearly distinct from each other in attributes or usages, nor to be the only players in the destiny of humankind.

The linguistic myth has not gone away, intertwined as it is with powerfully entrenched social institutions. But there is now perhaps a greater inclination across a series of social and humanistic disciplines to draw away from the assumption that *the* way to pin down reality in durable form must naturally be through language. This in turn is to question the presupposition, perhaps held above all by intellectuals, that only verbally captured elements truly exist and are worthy of academic study. The challenges now coming from many different directions, not least in people's lived practices, are unveiling the multiple dimensions and diversities screened out in the account that accords the central role to language and its two epiphanies in orality and literacy. The tale of humanity goes beyond the verbal and to focus on the fortunes of language is to leave out a vast proportion of human reality.

Words in their place

That is not to say there is no place for words and language – if nothing else, the contents of this volume tell otherwise. My point is rather that getting rid of the over-ambitious claims for 'language' in fact allows a clearer perspective on humans' active use of words – but words now seen, more modestly, as set in the context of, and intermingled with, the array of other communicative modes of which verbal language is only one.

And it *is* still a wonderful mode. The nodes of human cultural production in which the verbal in some sense plays a prominent role – from Greek or Japanese drama, European mediaeval song or epic narrative to personal life stories, praise poetry, rap or popular song on the web – are indeed among the stupendous achievements of humankind. Throughout the world and the centuries human creations in verbalised narrative, in poetic performance, in all the many forms of oral engagement touched on in this volume and elsewhere are not just for some limited utilitarian purpose – though they can

---

[6] See for example Barton et al. 2000, Boyarin 1993, Cavallo and Chartier 1999, Collins and Blot 2003, Cope and Kalantzis 1999, Olson and Torrance 2001, Saenger 1997, Street 1993.

include that – but among the central realities and glories of human living. English-language terms like 'poetry', 'story', 'literature', or indeed 'orature' or 'oraurality', may be culture-bound indeed but for all their limitations they alert us to a continuing and striking dimension of human activity.

Just what is covered by those loosely linked terms 'language', 'words', 'the verbal' admittedly continues to be elusive, more so than may seem implied throughout this volume (or, indeed, in most analyses of human cultural activity). Defining 'language' may look a relatively neutral process of pinning down something with some kind of autonomous existence, an assumption that chimes well with the linguistic tale. Some recent accounts would argue however that the notion of 'language' is in fact irretrievably rooted in particular social and historical phases and ideologies; not, after all, 'an object that exists prior to and independently of efforts to study it' (Briggs 2002: 493).[7] Amidst such debates I am not aspiring to carve out some precise demarcation for this inescapably complex and loaded term but I do need to return briefly to the issues about boundaries raised both at the start and by the further discussion and topics throughout the volume.

The growing interest in context and dialogic interaction that has increasingly emerged over recent decades is challenging the narrower model of language as single-voiced, abstract and referential. The boundaries have become more fuzzy, if only because of the shift of gaze onto the complicated and diverse ways people act and interact, where the verbal dimension becomes more verb or adverb than demarcatable noun. The current emphasis on the multi-sensory has led in the same direction, with the further suggestions that multi-modality may be not a secondary feature of language but central to its usage. Speech includes, at the least, non-verbal acoustic elements like volume, intensity, speed, timbre, emphasis, intonation, pacing, sequence, length, cadence, together perhaps with laughter, shrieks, sighs, hesitations, silence ... the multi-dimensionality of oral expression has been a constant theme of this volume, as of other recent writing. Written formulations, too, are shot through with non-verbal features, predominantly visual (space, layout, picture, colour, texture, shading, graphics), but also sometimes tactual and auditory. Non-verbal elements brushed aside in traditional grammars and dictionaries by the focus on words and their grammatical and syntactical interrelations are arguably now receiving more attention, instanced in the 1994 *Encyclopedia of Language and Linguistics'* conclusion that 'the central element of [language] is verbal but [it] contains as an essential component a substantial non-verbal element, e.g. intonation, stress, punctuation, etc.' (Asher and Simpson 1994 Vol. 10: 5137 [Glossary entry for 'language']).

In this larger view of language which extends it beyond the restricted bounds of dictionary-defined writable words the question of just where the frontiers are to be set becomes a culturally variable and far from self-evident

---

[7] On such issues see especially recent work on the ideologies and practices of language which, unlike the more common prescriptive and often ethnocentric literature, take a broad comparative perspective: Bauman and Briggs 2003: 265ff (and *passim*), Briggs 2002, Dalby 1999/2000 Vol. 1: 22, Schieffelin et al. 1998, also works referred to elsewhere in this section.

matter. Where 'language' ends and 'music' begins is a moot point for example, perhaps differently construed in different traditions. There is the question of gesture, too, in standard definitions often set apart from language – but recent studies of the intimate ways it is systematically co-ordinated with speech have led some to urge that the boundaries of language should perhaps be widened to encompass this visual, dynamic and embodied mode of communicating.[8] The broader perspectives on 'language' bring out its intrinsically multi-dimensional and culturally diverse features.

A contrasting but ultimately complementary approach is to retain a relatively narrow demarcation of language – but with two provisos. First, it is not a matter of some separate entity or activity but a somewhat vague, overlapping and ragged-at-the-edges sector within the multifarious constellation of human arts and activities. Whatever boundaries we suggest are unlikely to be either stable or cross-culturally neutral (even 'words', those apparently hard entities, do not everywhere have the same independent and delimited existence that can seem self-evident to those socialised into recent alphabetic traditions[9]). Second, since a full account of language must surely include looking at both usage and context, we have to bring into the picture the other modes and media with which it is in practice variously intermingled. From this perspective language is only one of several communicative-expressive modes: it works together with them and cannot be properly understood alone.

Whether we take the wider or the narrower delineation we need to go beyond just words. Language has to be envisaged as either, on the one hand, made up of more than just spoken and written words; or, on the other, as one mode among many, working in multi-modal settings where the verbal element may or may not play the primary role. Either way this leads to a more questioning approach to language than in the apparently unproblematic linguistic myth, relating it not to prescribed ideal forms or single cultural-linguistic traditions, but to actual human practices and their diverse settings.

Parallel dilemmas face us in delineating terms like 'oral texts', 'oral literature', 'oral performance', or more general concepts like 'orality' or 'orature'. One strategy, consonant with the larger picture of language, is to define the 'oral' as itself multi-modal, essentially broader and more multiple than just 'the verbal'. The alternative is to use the term 'oral' (and its composites) as just *one* of many modes – not as clearly delimited as it once seemed, admittedly, nor to be understood in isolation, but as a roughly recognisable, if fuzzy, sector to do with the vocalised and (in some vague sense) verbal dimensions within the overlapping fields of human arts and communication.

In this volume I suspect that, perhaps like some other authors, I have wavered between these two perspectives on the 'oral' – the broader and the narrower – perhaps at times simultaneously drawing on both; but have probably mostly presupposed the second, the somewhat narrower sense. This

---

[8] For example Haviland 2004, Kendon 1997, 2000, McNeill 2000, Scollon 2001, Streeck and Knapp 1992, Tracey 1999, see also Poyatos 1992.
[9] See Saenger on the varying traditions to do with 'space [and non-space] between words' (1997) and Greenberg (1996) on the 'word-paradigm model' of language (a model reinforced by the European dictionary tradition of pinning down individually demarcated written units).

arguably has advantages for certain purposes, to be pursued in a moment. But let me first re-emphasise that it has to go along with a recognition that the term is indeed problematic and to an extent culture-bound, its delimitation and interrelationships inescapably ragged. The ideas of 'oral', 'orality' etc. need to be used with some modesty rather than taken for granted as transparent and independent concepts, far less with the unquestioned priority in human affairs projected in the grand linguistic myth. Equally important, a proper understanding of the actual practice of human communication and expression, both 'artistic' and 'ordinary', must include setting words in the context of the other modes and media used alongside them. Often enough it is a matter of interpenetrating and inextricably interwoven dimensions in which the verbal is just one – and not necessarily, in any given situation or genre, the most salient.

Looking at language as only one among several dimensions goes some way towards putting words in their place. It pushes us towards recognising the full range of modes present in any given case rather than taking for granted – the temptation intellectuals can so readily fall into – that the crucial element is verbal. It still needs saying that, as Okpewho put it of oral performance in Africa, 'the words spoken are only part of a general spectacle designed to please the ears and the eyes' (Okpewho 1992: 48), that African, Caribbean and African American drama is characterised by 'the interdependence of music/dance/gesture to language' (Morales 2003: 151), or, even more pertinently since it is applied to one very specific genre, that Kpelle epic performances from Liberia involve the intermingling of singing, narration, dramatic enactment and instrumental accompaniment, with 'sounds and movements textured with the voice ... an aural type of texture augmented with dramatic gestures ... The epic is heard, seen and felt' (Stone 1998: 135, 137).

Differentiating the verbal – and in this sense the oral – for analytic purposes, however roughly, can alert us both to the combinations of modes in any given instance, and to the ideologies and social arrangements that may lie behind them. The pre-eminence conceptually accorded to the verbally textualised in (much) western tradition does not automatically apply everywhere, and dimensions recognised in one set of conventions as irretrievably coming together in particular genres may not do so in others, or may be prioritised or conceptualised differently. As David Coplan points out for Basotho migrants' songs

> To a Western observer like myself, the melodic declamation of literally hundreds of lines in a *sefela* [Basotho migrants' song] performance made these songs appear powerfully text-driven. Yet in discussions and interviews, performers repeatedly advised me to focus on rhythm and melody as keys to the understanding of compositional creativity. As the singer-poet Makeka Likhojane – in Sesotho one of the *likheleke*, 'eloquent ones' – explained firmly in deflecting the exegesis of an opaque metaphorical passage: 'If you want to understand my song, mister, just listen to the music.' ...
>
> [My preferred] term 'auriture' ... makes no claim for the universality of intersense modalities in African performance but rather insists that empirical ethnoaesthetic categories be investigated rather than assumed. (Coplan 1994: 8–9)

We have to recognise the *diverse* ways that such 'intersense modalities' are used in and by different genres, traditions, occasions, interested parties, registers, linguistic practices. The verbal element may *or may not* play a leading part. At any rate its centrality is a question to be investigated rather than conclusion to be taken for granted.

Such an approach does not come easily. It runs counter to the still power-ful myth assigning the central reality to language. It may also, paradoxically, recall one of the sub-plots within that same linguistic myth in which 'lower' peoples are supposed to be nearer to animals as possessing only some 'primitive' language, limited in vocabulary and powers of abstraction and thus more reliant on non-linguistic modes. The reaction against this was wholly justified. As Sapir summed up what is still essentially the standard scholarly position:

> There seems to be no warrant whatever for the statement which is sometimes made that there are certain people whose vocabulary is so limited that they cannot get on without the supplementary use of gesture. ... The truth of the matter is that language is an essentially perfect means of expression and communication among every known people. (Sapir 1956: 1)

It was similarly roundly asserted in the authoritative 1996 *Encyclopedia of Cultural Anthropology*, 'All known languages are full and complete; no language lacks anything essential or central to human speech' (Witkowski 1996: 687–93).

In some circles this insistence is still needed. There is still some inclina-tion to refer to certain languages – especially languages of once-colonised areas – as 'rudimentary', 'restricted', 'dialect', or 'patois'. Hallpike's contin-uingly influential *Foundations of Primitive Thought* (1979) chimed in with once-conventional wisdom in suggesting that 'primitive' cultures (which for him indubitably included Africa) had only marginally attained the human destiny of fully developed language. 'Most primitive societies are distin-guished from our own by the greater prominence of non-linguistic symbolic representations', he asserts, and 'the higher the level of thought, the more dependent it becomes on verbal representation' (Hallpike 1979: 135, 487).

So to suggest that the verbal element may sometimes be less important than other modes may seem to be reverting to these uninformed prejudices. But, whether we are considering Africa or anywhere else, verbal language is not in fact deployed in the same ways or the same roles in all situations, groups or genres – any more than the plastic arts are always and everywhere developed in the same manner. Language and its usages are neither an enduring natural bedrock nor some status symbol in the ranked achievements of human cultures but have to be recognised as differently practised, developed, experienced, conceptualised and battled over in different cultures, ages, groups or situations – and, especially relevant to this volume, as intermingling in varying ways with other modes and media.

In oral forms such as those that make up the main focus of this volume the verbal is indeed often prominent. The intellectual creativity of Nzema *ayabomo* women's songs in Ghana for example assigns priority to the words: they have neither instrumental nor dance accompaniment and 'although the performance is intended to dramatize a text-music fusion, its emphasis is clearly on the message of the text' (Agovi 1989: 2). In Somali classical poetry it is again verbal text rather than the drama of delivery that seems to the fore. In many Limba songs, by contrast, especially those performed by acclaimed experts, the words were by most people regarded as esoteric and, as far as I could see, not especially attended to; for most participants (but perhaps not all?) the prime focus seemed to be the sung, instrumental and partly chorused music, the embodied, rhythmic and circularly spaced dynamic of dance, and perhaps the visual glamour of costume. Or take the performances of Ichegbeh and his ensemble quoted in the last chapter – the moral and political messages did indeed matter to participants but at the same time 'dance, music and masquerades were an integral part of the event' (Ogede 1993: 53). Where there *is* some verbal element it is of course tempting for those many analysts who, like myself, have been socialised in textual traditions, to take *that* as the central reality. And yet it might be only one component among several, and not necessarily the most important. Dan Ge masked performances in contemporary Côte d'Ivoire for example do indeed include words – the proper song texts sung at the appropriate moment activate spiritual power (Reed 2003: 108) – but as Daniel Reed's study makes clear it is music that is central (2003: 2 and *passim*). Whether for Africa or elsewhere, questions of this kind need raising rather than closing down in advance.

Separating the verbal for analytic purposes, however unbounded at the edges it must continue to be, also has the virtue of directing our attention to the overlapping (sometimes contrasting) roles that can be simultaneously or sequentially played by differing modes. Adam Kendon pertinently signals the complementary roles of gesture and speech in conversation – an approach that might also in principle be applied to other oral genres:

> Participants in conversation ... use gesture and speech in partnership and can shift the respective roles of gesture and speech in the utterance from one moment to the next in ways that seem rhetorically appropriate. ... The two modes of expression employ different media which have different possibilities. ... Gesture can be useful as a way of exhibiting overarching units of meaning, as a way of keeping visible an aspect of meaning throughout the course of a spoken utterance or even after the speech has finished. Gesture and speech ... serve different but complementary roles. (Kendon 2000: 61)

As has emerged time and again in earlier examples the dynamics and subtleties of gesture and bodily posturing are often key dimensions of oral performance that can only too easily be missed if we take the verbal text as the whole of what needs to be attended to. The complementarity of word and gesture may in fact be salient to the action. Thus for Shona story telling Doreen Klassen portrays gestures working together with words to not only make the story visible by re-enacting actions and characters or gesturing 'abstract concepts like *silence* or *darkness'*, but also to locate the narrative in space and time, and reveal its form and moral dimensions (Klassen 2004: 150). In classical Greek tragedy, to take a different but no less revealing example, Charles Segal comments on 'the complex reciprocal relation between what we see acted out before us on the stage and what we hear from actors and chorus. Verbal statements are always qualified or supplemented by visual action' (Segal 1985: 212). Nketia makes a comparable point about the complementary contributions of differing arts in the dynamic of a performance.

> What seems for a moment static in the music may be relieved by the text or the dynamic quality of the movements that accompany it. Similarly, the appearance of a masked dancer in a performing arena may reinforce the essence and intention of the occasion and give added meaning to the musical and dance forms. (Nketia 1996: 126)

Differentiating the verbal analytically so as to appreciate how it is interacting with other media illuminates the roles of each. For different modalities do not necessarily just substitute for or reinforce each other on parallel lines but by their differing, even at times contradictory, contributions add to the rich complexity of the whole.

Attempts to disentangle such composite mixtures reveal the complementary but not necessarily equal or consistent roles played by different expressive media. For popular music Simon Frith points out how good song lyrics 'score' the performance not 'in the words themselves ... [but] by the music' (Frith 1996: 181), just as for women singers in late twentieth-century Zimbabwe it was 'not the script of the songs that mattered most but rather the sound coming over radio waves, on a cassette, or live, and staying in people's memories and their consciousness' (Gunner 1994: 2). Kelly Askew's study (2002) of popular bands and ensembles 'performing the nation' in Tanzania brings out the importance of music and dance, not just the song texts, while with the contemporary South African urban rap band 'Prophets of Da City' the ruptured lyrics do indeed receive great attention but at the same time not only have to be *heard* ('it is crucially rhythm, rhyme, verbal inflection, and the syncopation of these with sound and beat') but are also articulated through 'music, dance, style, and the associated activities of hip-hop culture, including graffiti or spray-can art' (Brown 2003: 159, 145). In radio words jostle with music, co-operating and at times competing, and no doubt sometimes carrying differing priorities for differing listeners and situations. In film – by now a familiar medium in Africa – spoken or sung verbal dimensions may be relatively prominent, in this sense comparable to other genres of verbal art; but language may not always lie at its heart for crucial roles may be played by variegated visual manifestations, by music and other sonic input, sometimes by dance – all of which make it possible, as with the popular indigenous films in Nigeria, to communicate polyvocally across linguistic boundaries (Okome 1995). The web now offers further striking examples of multi-dimensional expression, coming in a host of different combinations, sometimes privileging the verbal (though seldom perhaps exclusively), more often intershot with the visual and sonic dimensions now increasingly deployed by performers both from Africa and beyond (Kaschula 2003).

Exploring the roles of different elements within such composite ensembles is no easy task. Over and above the expectations for specific genres there are the dynamics of particular performances; of differential and unfolding balances within a particular event; and of varied participants perhaps weighting their experiences in diverse ways. Individual choices and talents may be in play too, or the particular circumstances of performance – thus Hausa story-telling conventions allow for personal initiative in voice, gesture and facial expression, but narrators accustomed to performing for radio 'use more verbal details' whereas in live performances a narrator who 'uses his body effectively draws a larger audience' (Ahmad 1989: 119). It is not always a simple matter to assess reports from the field, even from those most intimately involved. How are we to read comments on the priority of verbal text in some particular performance given that the linguistic myth can still so readily screen other dimensions out of conscious awareness? And then again how far have *these* – or other – ideologies and interpretations themselves become part of people's expectations and lived reality? But difficult or not, such questions are now emerging as necessary both for comparative analysis and for a greater understanding of the many African – and other – ways of doing things with words.

All this can only emphasise yet again how narrow it is to chain our central reality to the encompassing myth of language. Representations and re-presentations in a multiplicity of media, both sequential and simultaneous, are common human practices. And far from the (supposedly) fundamental categories of 'oral' or 'written' being the 'normal' context for verbal arts – or arts in which the verbal plays some part – we find instead an infinitude of possibilities, of multiple parties and modes in a spectrum of established, changing, contested and innovative processes. Once again words must be set in their place – which is to say there *is* no settled place, far less an automatic priority for words, rather a plethora of variegated possibilities that, again, need investigation rather than assumption.

Decentring linguistic expression and seeing it as only one mode within a complex, humanly controlled and multi-dimensional diversity in fact helps us better to recognise the role(s) of the verbal, to give due attention to language, to put words in their place. Words, voiced or other, are indeed a wonderful and wonderfully exploited human resource. But, however we choose finally to define them, there is no way we can fully understand them except in conjunction with the other modes with which they are so often inextricably intertwined and among which they do not always take the leading or the defining role.

Literature, performance and words in their place in Africa and beyond

This finally brings us back to the image evoked at the start: Africa as the home of orality and the word. How does that now look in the light of the discussions and examples of this volume?

There is certainly much to be said for it. And much *has* been said both within and beyond Africa, and by commentators coming from otherwise differing perspectives. Terms like 'orature', 'aurality', 'auriture', 'speech', 'verbal arts', 'auditory arts', 'the power of the word', and 'the voice' bring out the oral and acoustic qualities of African expression. We hear of 'the power of words and the primacy of auditory aspects of the world for ... African peoples' (Peek 1994: 475), of the 'compelling power of the word in African verbal art ... [which] help[s] to constitute African social life' (Haring 1994: 3, 12), of African cultures as 'cultures par excellence de la voix' (Zumthor 1983: 41) and, from a film scholar, of 'the profound reverence that [in Africa] traditionally surrounds the spoken word' (Thackway 2003: 55). Edward Brathwaite's *History of the Voice* (1984) gave a moving take on the role of voice in the Afro-centred diaspora, while more recently Abiola Irele has written of the 'one common denominator' in the traditional imagination: 'an oral mode of realization. ... The tradition of orality remains predominant and serves as a central paradigm' (Irele 2001: 9, 11).

Nor are such terms just backward-looking nostalgia. They are also prominent in discussions of contemporary practices. Ngugi wa Thiong'o speaks not only of 'our formative roots in *orature*' (1997: 134) but of current dialogue among the literatures of the pan-African universe where 'the voice of orality from the Caribbean [can meet] with the voices of orality from rural Kenya' (Ngugi wa Thiong'o 1997: 135). For Molefi Kete Asante

> The contemporary black disc jockey, rap musicians, and the deejay rockers of Jamaica all operate out of the same collective Afrocentric response to words. ... It is precisely the power of the word, whether in music or speeches, that authentically speaks of an African heritage. (1998: 60, 97)

Orature and orality is heard through written forms too, whether as residue, as spice, as creative inspiration, or in the cadences of poetry.[10] And now 'technauriture' both takes us back to 'auriture' and forward into contemporary poetic arts through the web and the most modern of modern technologies. It is in 'the diverse, modern world', writes Liz Gunner, 'that African orality has its place' (2004: 14).

So Philip Peek and Kwesi Yankah speak for many when they emphasise the significance for Africa of 'sound' rather than 'sight' and preface their authoritative encyclopaedia of African folklore 'In the beginning was the Word ... the primacy of the human voice' (Peek and Yankah 2004: xi, xii).

Such insights have undoubtedly brought fresh understandings of human culture, and not just in Africa. The stress on this complex of speech, orality, voice, the verbal arts, sound and audition has uncovered dimensions of human life and creation that those socialised into the prioritising of writing often simply overlook. It has revealed a wealth of forms and genres, of verbal arts and actions, discussed to impressive depth and extent by numberless scholars and practitioners over the last decades. It has drawn attention to subtleties of sonic expressiveness commonly passed over in both the spatial representations of print and the analyses of conventional western criticism, and allowed a fuller appreciation of the voice, 'the embodied locus of spoken and sung performance' (Feld et al. 2004: 341).

Equally important it has revealed the oral as something worthy of analysis in its own right, countering that long dominant paradigm that accords prior ontology to written forms and dismisses the non-written as, at best, inferior (if not defined out of existence altogether). The validity of the 'oral', it could be

[10] See Chapter 11, p. 187.

said, has been one of the great re-discoveries of the twentieth century. Terms like 'orature', 'auriture', 'voice', 'oraurality', 'auditory arts', 'oral literature', 'oral texts'– terms which roughly coincide with much of the coverage of this volume – reclaim the status of the great arts of Africa. They rightly challenge the damaging ethnocentric myths that, on the one side, 'traditional' Africa had not yet attained fully developed human language, and, on the other, that the true destiny of humankind can only be fully achieved through writing. Taking serious account of the oral, the spoken, the non-written has been a notable step forward – and not just for African forms – over the last half century.

Against this background and amidst this chorus of such eloquent and authoritative voices how could one raise problems? And yet – does it follow that Africa is distinctive in its recognition of the word and the primacy of sound? That Africa above all stands out by its orality?

There is good reason to revisit these fertile but eventually problematic assumptions.

To start with, as has repeatedly emerged in the volume, to understand oral expression we have to look to *more* than words, even more than just 'sounds'. To that we must add the points rehearsed earlier in this chapter: the partiality (in several senses) of the linguistic myth, the rewards of a more multi-sensory approach, and the diverse and relative roles of words as they interweave with other modes. This multidimensionality applies in Africa no less than else-where. To focus just on the verbal and voiced or to assume – and reify – the primacy of the 'oral' is to utilise what is ultimately a tendentious myth to impose a pseudo-uniformity on a notably diverse, changing continent and its people. It is also to sell short the other wondrous resources deployed in African genres whether relatively separate or intertwined with the oral: visual, graphic, kinetic, choreographic, textile, plastic ....

And it is not just for Africa that the linguistic myth is insufficient. The history of human communication and expression is surely not confined to the treatment of language – or to just two alternatives called 'orality' and 'writing'. To take 'language' as the key spine of human destiny gives only a blinkered view onto the sparkling constellation of multi-modal and multi-media human arts. It is to screen out the astonishing array of communicative forms developed by human beings and used so exuberantly in their multiplex practices throughout the world. A more complex and more realistic view of the human arts and of the human world – and of Africa not apart but within it – is long overdue.

The same could be said of focusing too exclusively on 'sound'. This unavoidably recalls the sweeping contrasts posited by scholars like McLuhan (1964) and Ong (1967, 1977, 1982) and their view of vision as privileged over audition in the modern west as 'an eye for an ear' supersedes a more primaeval emphasis on sound (McLuhan 1964: 91). Such theories are now justly criticised as both too generalised and too elusive to fit the diversities of human cultures and history, underplaying both the continuing – and crucial – role of audition in the modern world and the cross-cultural presence of the visual in human cultures across space and time.[11] It seems blinkered indeed

[11] See further in Finnegan 2002: 82ff, 172ff.

to yet again divide up the cultures of the world, opposing the supposedly visual modern west to the auditory rest, or to use the unquestioned role of audition in Africa to close off a recognition of the other modes, often visually enacted, which in Africa as elsewhere play such a large part in the complex multi-dimensional productions of human art and expression.

This then returns us to that continuing binary paradigm that has been raising its head throughout this volume: of the great divisions between 'primitive' and 'civilised', 'age-old' and 'modern', 'African' and 'western'. Here cultures characterised by modern ways – literate, urban, creative, scientific, rational, western – are set against those steeped in tradition – oral, communal, non-reflective, unchanging, participatory, close to nature. As repeatedly emphasised in this volume, these sweeping dichotomies are now widely and rightly challenged. But whether in romantic or denigratory tone they still surface. The Latin poet Horace was right. 'You can throw nature out with a pitchfork but it keeps coming back'. So too here: however often refuted, those same beguiling oppositions keep reappearing. Even when not explicitly stated or, perhaps, intended, they interpenetrate and structure people's understandings of the peoples of the world and of how they act.

And 'orality' is the guise in which this long-told tale of opposites is nowadays most often clad. Seemingly innocuous, it is 'oral', 'orality' and their associated terms that now serve to evoke those loaded binary resonances that divide humankind.

Thus Leroy Vail and Landeg White (1991: 1–39) have given a striking – and convincing – account of how 'Oral Man' was constructed out of the background of Lévy-Bruhl's 'primitive mentality' and on through the armchair generalisations of such writers as Walter Ong, Marshall McLuhan, Eric Havelock and, if in somewhat roundabout ways, Milman Parry and Albert Lord. Emevwo Biakolo (1999: 61) has similarly drawn attention to the equation of Ong's 'oral man' with 'primitive man'. It is notable that Jack Goody, whose writings have played such a central role over many decades, aligns his key contrast of 'oral' versus 'literate' with the earlier dichotomies of 'simple'/'complex', 'domesticated'/'savage', or 'primitive'/'advanced' (e.g. 1987: 290–1, 2000: 5, 24–5). His 'oral culture' equates with 'features that are commonly regarded as characteristic of the "primitive mentality"' (Goody 1992: 10). This interlocks in turn with the powerful linguistic myth where to say 'oral' has long been one shorthand way of setting Africa and its works into the box associated with primitive, early, undeveloped – existentially 'pre'-literate.

Africa above all has been taken to stand for the primordial 'non-literate experience' which McLuhan pictures as 'the Africa within' and where Africa represents that 'empathic involvement, natural to the oral society and the audile-tactile man' (1962: 46, 45, 39). It is 'Black orality' as against 'White literacy and technocracy' as the *Times Literary Supplement* had it (Anon 1973: 1323). In the mythic linguistic story of human development Africa plays its role as the epitome of wild untutored primitiveness signalled precisely by its lack of writing, that accepted mark and condition of civilisation. Nowadays the tale may be recounted with more positive spin, prizing the age-old, authentic, deeply oral dimensions of African experience – a more generous interpretation certainly but still with associations of generalised exoticising, of attributing some special status to 'the oral', even, as Karin Barber puts it, of falling into a 'sentimental valorization of "orality"' (Barber et al. 1997: xiii). But whatever the evaluation, 'orality' seems central. A recent volume on mass media in Africa asserts confidently that the communication norms of Black Africa 'did not call for the critical distanced postures typical of literate societies' and that 'although the press in Black Africa *appears* in printed form, it has inherited little of the reasoned discourse associated with the printed tradition of post-Reformation Europe. Rather, [it] displays "pre-empirical" stylistics typical of oral discourse' characterised by the 'situational thinking typical of oral societies' (Bourgault 1995: 181, 196). More sympathetically but still evocatively, we hear how 'Orality ... promotes social cohesion, consensus and transmits social consciousness. ... Africans are primarily an oral people, and it is that tradition that has dominated their cultural norms' (Mphande 2005: 71, 70).

The resonating echoes of the long-entrenched polar oppositions still bring an entrancing air of familiarity and credibility to generalised claims that seem to chime in with them. 'Oral Africa' is the projected image which by its contrast defines (from one angle) progressive modernity or (from another) the intrusive heartless west – Africa still exploited, in Mudimbe's telling phrase, as 'a paradigm of difference' (1994: xii). Isabel Hofmeyr speaks of the 'idea of orality' as 'an implicit last redoubt where Africa's "difference" lurks' (Hofmeyr 2002: 78).

The 'orality' of Africa seems by now to have become established as the most enduring of all these generalised stories of difference. The long-running stereotype of oral-Africa as against literate-Europe is seemingly still with us. But setting the 'orality' of Africa against the 'literacy' of Europe is of course to miss not only the rich – and essential – oral dimensions of 'European culture' but also the long practice of writing in Africa; and in so doing to overlook much of Africa's past and present. For even if we ignore the earlier histories of north Africa and Ethiopia or the multiple scripts invented in Africa (large exceptions indeed), Arabic has been written and circulated in Africa for well over a millennium, and from at least the early eighteenth century written works in Swahili, Hausa, Fulani and (increasingly) other African languages have been produced in a variety of Arabic scripts, often preserved and transmitted through the private manuscript collections of families and religious leaders. By the early nineteenth century printed works were being produced and disseminated in African and European languages, often linked to a flourishing intellectual and literate tradition – sometimes in relatively small numbers certainly (scarcely an unknown phenomenon anywhere ...) but influential and real nonetheless, a vibrant world in its own right not just a peripheral offshoot from some foreign culture. The printing press has long been active in Africa, churning out hymn books, bibles, *The Pilgrim's Progress,* school texts, newspapers, announcements, administrative matter, histories, folktales, proverbs, poetry, popular novels, and much else (and, it ought to be needless to add, in African not just European languages). Written forms appear everywhere, not just on paper but on lorries, on clothing, as body decoration, in advertisements, with little hint that this is somehow antipathetic to some entrenched authentic 'orality' or that there is anything strange about the 'interpenetration', as Ranger well puts it, of oral and literate (2003: 238). It is true that, as we are constantly being told, the 'literacy rates' of many parts of Africa have been and are below those of some other countries – but that, though certainly deplorable in its inequitable incidence, is a matter of degree and scarcely alters the fact that a general familiarity with writing is often a regular part of much everyday experience.[12] Doing things with written words is emphatically an 'African' not just a 'European' practice.

These oral-Africa versus literate-Europe stereotypes receive much of their backing from that same powerful myth discussed earlier, of human destiny as equated with the history and unfolding transformations of language. It is that myth that narrows the gaze onto language, making it reasonable to apply the (presumed) two alternative manifestations of language – oral and written – as *the* markers of difference, to ignore the complexities introduced by considering other modes, and to simplify as 'oral' any situations or genres where writing seems (or can be presumed to be) absent or inconspicuous. The linguistic tale too easily leads to the conclusion that if some area or people are not notably literate then they must be characterised by 'oral culture', something which can be both reified and mystified, fitted into the recurring binary oppositions within humankind. Exotic cultures, and above all Africa, are 'the oral'.

It is time to reject this set of associations. With its evocations of the primitive, and of 'Africa' as a continent with an enduring badge of difference, it cannot be allowed to stand as a fair or an illuminating image of the variegated actions and diversities of all those people who might in some sense or other be referred to as Africans. But the conclusion has to be not that we give up our interest in oral forms within Africa (or anywhere else) or deny the insights brought by stretching our imagination beyond a prime focus on the linguistic; rather that we must now approach such concepts with a full critical awareness of their limiting and perhaps ethnocentric connotations and see them in the perspective of the full range of human media. We can and should still consider the verbal dimension of human action. We must always, of course, see it in its (limited) place – as only one dimension and always in practice intermingled with others, not clearly demarcated, doubtless carrying inescapable culture-bound connotations, and, finally, *not* inevitably the most important or the most quintessentially 'human'. But, given all that, it *is* still a dimension of profound significance for human experience, enactment and celebration. The reflective practice of speech, the performative utterances illustrated in Chapter 3, the narratives, poetry, oral literary forms in later chapters or the working with oral and written texts by scholars and others in Part III – here, and in so many other instances, words have a fine place in the active experience of humanity.

So as I end let me recall again the way that unwritten as well as written words can be deployed to realise that element of reflectiveness and detachment once seen as distinctive of the modern west. It is not just the Limba but many others who use words both to 'objectivate' and somehow set away from oneself – to treat something as object for attention and reflection – and at the

---

[12] For references on writing in Africa see Chapter 1, p. 2 n. 1.

same time to bring it close in that charmed moment of performance and performancing. Peculiarly effective in the double-sided 'me-and-they' of human performance, people marshal verbal enactments – do things with words – for the widest range of human ends: for voicing something, owning it, distancing it, perhaps rejecting and arguing with it, drawing frames around it, demonstrating it, singling it out for attention, participating in it, evoking others' words, or somehow detaching it as held-out display. Engaging in verbal art is both 'object' *and* 'action', both making strange and making one's own.

And here the concept of 'literature' in its broader more generous sense still has something appropriate about it. For all its limitations for cross-cultural analysis, it nonetheless points to a broadly recognisable dimension of human artistic production, in which verbal formulations are in some way set apart, the focus of special attention. So we have the multitude of deliberately artful verbal genres and performances considered throughout much of this volume as something rich and real, to be prized rather than explained away. All this feeds, too, into the resumption of interest in 'text' and exegesis and into 'comparative literature', now arguably reinventing itself as a cross-cultural discipline with an openness to African and Asian literatures, to a spectrum of media, and to the unwritten and performed as much as the written.[13] Far from undermining the study of literature and performance a recognition of the multiplicity of media and of voices provides a firmer grasp on the multiplex and varying modalities in which they exist, whether in traditional western literary canon or popular performances in contemporary European or African towns. It can uncover literary art in unexpected places, arenas where the verbal artistry has been rendered invisible by folk or scholarly ideologies which look only to certain settings or a limited circle of enactors. It imposes the obligation to get beyond an assumption of some foreordained ontological priority for words: to see words in their place.

The wonderful examples emanating from Africa and the ways these have been utilised and studied can indeed illuminate how people do things with words: both en-performanced in the moment but also to one degree or another framed as somehow enduring, with associations of both present and past, intimate and shared, inner and externalised, contemplation intermixed with action. In asserting throughout this chapter that words must be demoted from the unique and unproblematised centrality of the linguistic myth, we must still come back to recognising them, set in wider perspective, as one fertile mode through which humans do indeed enact and formulate their art, their reflection and their participant creativity.

So we can see Africa as indeed the rich home of words – but emphatically not of words separate from their multiplex multi-modal settings or of some mysterious and distinctive 'orality'. And it is not just in Africa that words find their home, nor is Africa devoid of all those other arts to which too devoted a celebration of words might blind us. Even while we go on reminding ourselves that it is not sufficient to focus only on the auditory arts or just on words or voice, the study of Africa has indeed revealed rich ways of

[13] For some recent debates and a variety of viewpoints see Bassnett 1993, 2003, Gerstle, Jones and Thomas 2005, Spivak 2003, Traoré 2000 (esp. 101ff).

doing, reflecting and artfully creating with words. We can best benefit from such lessons not by setting Africa in a special 'orality' category or as steeped in some past or present 'oral culture' or 'oral mentality', but rather by approaching it as a locale in which as in any other area of the world, people amazingly exploit the beauties and potentialities of words *together* with the resources of a shimmering multi-modal and multi-media constellation of arts.

The boundaries of 'the oral', of 'performance' and of 'literature' may have come to dissolve, together, hopefully, with the judgmental binary categorisations or ethnocentric linguistic narratives into which they were once bound. But at the same time such notions, treated both critically and imaginatively, can lead into a deeper understanding of people's creative and reflective ways with words, more sophisticated and more richly intermingled into intricately meshed modalities than we once realised. The insights they offer surely transcend the once-presumed 'difference' of Africa and Europe, taking us beyond just 'words' and beyond just 'Africa'.

References

Abdulkadir, Dandatti (1975) 'The role of an oral singer in Hausa/Fulani society: a case study of Mamman Shata', doctoral thesis, Folklore Institute, Indiana University.

Abraham, W. E. (1962) *The Mind of Africa*, London: Weidenfeld and Nicolson.

Abrahams, Roger D. (1966) 'Some varieties of heroes in America', *Journal of the Folk-Lore Institute* 3, 3: 341–62.

—— (1968) 'Introductory remarks to a rhetorical theory of folklore', *Journal of American Folklore* 81: 143–58.

—— (1976) 'The complex relations of simple forms', in Ben-Amos.

Abrahamsson, H. (1951) *The Origin of Death: Studies in African Mythology*, Uppsala: Studia Ethnographica Upsaliensia 3.

Abu-Haidar, Farida (ed.) (1997) *Arabic Writing in Africa*, special issue, *Research in African Literatures* 28, 3.

Achebe, Chinua (1964) 'Foreword', in Whiteley 1964.

Adedeji, J. A. (1977) 'Trends in the content and form of the opening glee in Yoruba drama', in Lindfors.

Adu-Gyamfi, Yaw (2002) 'Orality in writing: its cultural and political significance in Wole Soyinka's *Ogun Abibiman*', *Research in African Literatures* 33, 3: 104–24.

Agovi, Kofi Ermeleh (1989) 'Sharing creativity: group performance of Nzema ayabomo maiden songs', *The Literary Griot* 1, 2: 1–41.

Ahmad, Aijaz (1992) *In Theory. Classes, Nations, Literatures*, London: Verso.

Ahmad, Saidu B. (1989) 'Stability and variation in Hausa tales', *Journal of African Languages and Cultures* 2: 113–31.

Ajayi, J. F. Ade (1968) 'The continuity of African institutions under colonialism', in Ranger, T. O. (ed.) *Emerging Themes of African History*, Dar es Salaam: East African Publishing House.

—— (1974) 'The impact of Europe on African cultures and values', unpublished conference paper, African Studies Association of United

Kingdom, Liverpool.

Alabi, Adetayo (2005) *Telling Our Stories: Continuities and Divergences in Black Autobiographies*, New York: Palgrave-Macmillan.

Alagoa, E. J. (2001) 'The dialogue between academic and community history in Nigeria', in White et al.

Alexander, M. (1966) *The Earliest English Poems*, Harmondsworth: Penguin.

Amodio, Mark C. (ed.) (2005) *New Directions in Oral Theory*, Tempe: Arizona Center for Medieval and Renaissance Studies.

Anderson, William (1983) *Dante the Maker*, London: Hutchinson.

Andrzejewski, B.W. (1965) 'Emotional bias in the translation and presentation of African oral art', *Sierra Leone Language Review* 4: 95–102.

—— (1981) 'The poem as message: verbatim memorization in Somali poetry', in Ryan, Peter (ed.) *Memory and Poetic Structure*, London: Middlesex Polytechnic.

—— (1985) 'Oral literature', in Andrzejewski, Pilaszewicz and Tyloch.

—— and Innes, G. (1975) 'Reflections on African oral literature', *African Languages* 1: 5–57.

—— and Lewis, I. M. (1964) *Somali Poetry: An Introduction*, Oxford: Clarendon Press.

—— Pilaszewicz, S. and Tyloch, W. (eds) (1985) *Literatures in African Languages: Theoretical Issues and Sample Surveys,* Cambridge: Cambridge University Press, and Warszawa: Wiedza Powszechna.

Anon (1973) 'Black fusing White', *Times Literary Supplement* 26 Oct: 1323.

Anyumba, H. O. (1964) 'The nyatiti lament songs', *East Africa Past and Present,* Paris: Présence africaine.

Appiah, Kwame Anthony and Gates, Henry Louis (eds) (2005) *Africana. The Encyclopedia of the African and African American Experience,* 5 vols, Oxford: Oxford University Press.

Archibald, S. and Richards, P. (2002) 'Converts to human rights: popular debate about war and justice in rural central Sierra Leone', *Africa* 72: 339–67.

Asante, Molefi Kete (1998) *The Afrocentric Idea*, revised edn, Philadelphia: Temple University Press.

Ashcroft, B., Griffiths, G. and Tiffin, H. (1998) *Key Concepts in Post-Colonial Studies*, London: Routledge.

Asher, R. E. and Simpson, J. M. Y. (eds) (1994) *The Encyclopedia of Language and Linguistics*, 10 vols, Oxford: Pergamon.

Askew, K. M. (2002) *Performing the Nation. Swahili Music and Cultural Politics in Tanzania*, Chicago: Chicago University Press.

Astle, Thomas (1784) *The Origin and Progress of Writing*, London: The Author.

Austen, Ralph A. (ed.) (1999) *In Search of Sunjata. The Mande Oral Epic as History, Literature, and Performance,* Bloomington: Indiana University Press.

Austin, J. L. (1962) *How to Do Things with Words,* Oxford: Clarendon Press.

Avorgbedoe, Daniel (1990) 'The preservation, transmission, and realization of song texts: a psycho-musical approach', in Okpewho.

Ayer, A. J. (1946) *Language, Truth and Logic,* 2nd edn, London: Gollancz.

Ayittey, George B. N. (2005) *Africa Unchained. The Blueprint for Africa's Future*, New York: Palgrave Macmillan.

Baaz, M. E. and Palmberg, M. (eds) (2001) *Same and Other: Negotiating African Identity in Cultural Production*, Uppsala: Nordic Africa Institute.

Babalọla, S. A. (1966) *The Content and Form of Yoruba Ijala*, Oxford: Clarendon Press.

—— (1973) ' "Rárà" chants in Yoruba spoken art', in Jones, Eldred D. (ed.) *African Literature Today*, 6, *Poetry in Africa,* London: Heinemann.

Bakhtin, Mikhail (1968) *Rabelais and his World*, Eng. transl., Cambridge MA: MIT Press.

Barber, Karin (1984) 'Yoruba oriki and deconstructive criticism', *Research in African Literatures* 15, 4: 497–518.

—— (1987) 'Popular arts in Africa', *African Studies Review* 30, 3: 1–78, 105–32.

—— (1991) *I Could Speak Until Tomorrow: Oriki, Women and the Past in a Yoruba Town*, Edinburgh: Edinburgh University Press.

—— (1995a) 'Literacy, improvisation and the public in Yorùbá popular theatre', in Brown.

—— (1995b) 'African-language literature and postcolonial criticism', *Research in African Literatures* 26, 4: 3–28.

—— (1997a) 'Preliminary notes on audiences in Africa', *Africa* 67: 347–62.

—— (ed.) (1997b) 'Audiences in Africa', special issue, *Africa* 67, 3: 347–499.

—— (ed.) (1997c) *Readings in African Popular Culture*, Oxford: James Currey.

—— (1999) 'Obscurity and exegesis in African oral praise poetry', in Brown 1999a.

—— (2000) *The Generation of Plays. Yorùbá Popular Life in Theater,* Bloomington: Indiana University Press.

—— (2003) 'Text and performance in Africa', *Bulletin of School of Oriental and African Studies* 66, 3: 324–33.

—— (ed.) (2006) *Africa's Hidden Histories: Everyday Literacy and Making the Self*, Bloomington: Indiana University Press.

—— (forthcoming) *Texts, Persons and Publics in Africa and Beyond*, Cambridge: Cambridge University Press.

——, Collins, John and Ricard, Alain (1997) *West African Popular Theatre*, Oxford: James Currey.

—— and Farias, P. F. de Moraes (eds) (1989) *Discourse and its Disguises: The Interpretation of African Oral Texts*, Birmingham: Birmingham University African Studies Series, 1.

—— and Furniss, Graham (eds) (2006) *Writing in African Languages*, special issue, *Research in African Literatures* 37, 3.

Barker, F., Hulme, P., and Iversen, M. (eds) (1994) *Colonial Discourse/Postcolonial Theory*, Manchester: Manchester University Press.

Barton, David, Hamilton, Mary and Ivanic, Roz (eds) (2000) *Situated Literacies: Reading and Writing in Context,* London: Routledge.

Bassnett, Susan (1993) *Comparative Literature. A Critical Introduction*, Oxford: Blackwell.

—— (ed.) (1997) *Translating Literature*, Cambridge: D. S. Brewer.

—— (2002) *Translation Studies*, 3rd edn, London: Routledge.

References

—— (2003) 'Note on comparative literature', *AHRB Centre for Asian and African Literatures Newsletter* (SOAS/UCL) 9: 1.

—— and Trivedi, Harish (eds) (1999) *Post-Colonial Translation. Theory and Practice*, London: Routledge.

Bastide, R. (1968) 'Religions africaines et structures de civilisation', *Présence Africaine* 66: 98–111.

Bauman, Richard (1977) *Verbal Art as Performance,* Rowley, MA: Newbury House.

—— (1989) 'American folklore studies and social transformation: a performance-centered perspective', *Text and Performance Quarterly* 9, 3: 175–84.

—— (ed.) (1992) *Folklore, Cultural Performances, and Popular Entertainments: A Communications-Centered Handbook*, New York: Oxford University Press.

—— (2004) *A World of Others' Words. Cross-Cultural Perspectives on Intertextuality*, Oxford: Blackwell.

Bauman, Richard and Briggs, Charles (1990) 'Poetics and performance as critical perspectives on language and social life', *Annual Review of Anthropology* 19: 59–88.

—— and Briggs, C. L. (2000) 'Language philosophy as language ideology: John Locke and Johann Gottfried Herder', in Kroskrity, P. (ed.) *Regimes of Language. Ideologies, Polities, Identities*, Oxford: James Currey.

—— and Briggs, Charles L. (2003) *Voices of Modernity. Language Ideologies and the Politics of Inequality*, Cambridge: Cambridge University Press.

Bauman, Richard and Sherzer, Joel (eds) ([1974] 1989) *Explorations in the Ethnography of Speaking*, 2nd edn, London: Cambridge University Press.

Becker, Howard S. (1974) 'Art as collective action', *American Sociological Review* 39: 767–76.

Belcher, Stephen (1999) *Epic Traditions of Africa*, Bloomington: Indiana University Press.

—— (2004) 'Epics: overview', in Peek and Yankah.

Belinga, Eno (1977) *Introduction générale à la littérature orale africaine,* Yaounde: Université de Yaounde.

—— (1978) *L'épopée camerounaise mvet, Moneblum ou l'homme bleu,* Yaounde: Université de Yaounde.

Ben-Amos, Dan (1975) *Sweet Words. Storytelling Events in Benin,* Philadelphia: Institute for the Study of Human Issues.

—— (ed.) (1976) *Folklore Genres,* Austin: University of Texas Press.

—— (1977) 'Introduction: folklore in African society', in Lindfors.

—— (ed.) (1983) *Epic and Panegyric Poetry in Africa*, special issue, *Research in African Literatures* 14, 3: 277–400.

—— and Goldstein, Kenneth S. (eds) (1975) *Folklore: Performance and Communication*, The Hague: Mouton.

Bendix, Regina (1997) *In Search of Authenticity. The Formation of Folklore Studies*, Madison: University of Wisconsin Press.

Benson, L. D. (1966) 'The literary character of Anglo-Saxon formulaic poetry', *Publications of the Modern Language Association* 81: 334–41.

Berry, J. (1958): 'Nominal classes in Hu-Limba', *Sierra Leone Studies,* New

Series, 11: 169–72.

—— (1960) 'A note on voice and aspect in Hu-Limba', *Sierra Leone Studies, New Series,* 13: 36–40.

Besnier, N. (1990) 'Language and affect', *Annual Review of Anthropology* 19: 419–51.

Biakolo, Emevwo (1999) 'On the theoretical foundations of orality and literacy', *Research in African Literatures* 30, 2: 42–65.

Biebuyck, Daniel P. (1972) 'The epic as a genre in Congo oral literature', in Dorson.

—— (1978a) 'The African heroic epic', in Oinas, F. J. (ed.) *Heroic Epic and Saga,* Bloomington: Indiana University Press.

—— (1978b) *Hero and Chief. Epic Literature from the Banyanga,* Berkeley: University of California Press.

—— and Mateene, Kahombo C. (eds) (1969) *The Mwindo Epic from the Banyanga,* Berkeley: University of California Press.

Biesele, Megan (1999) ' "Different people just have different minds". A personal attempt to understand Ju/'hoan storytelling aesthetics', in Brown 1999a.

Bird, C. S. (1972) 'Heroic songs of the Mande hunters', in Dorson.

Black, M. (ed.) (1961) *The Social Theories of Talcott Parsons,* Englewood Cliffs: Prentice-Hall.

Bledsoe, Caroline H. and Robey, Kenneth M. (1993) 'Arabic literacy and secrecy among the Mende of Sierra Leone', in Street.

Bleek, W. H. I. (1864) *Reynard the Fox in South Africa; or, Hottentot Fables and Tales,* London: Trübner.

Boahen, A. Adu (1987) *African Perspectives on Colonialism,* London: James Currey.

Boelaert, E. (1949) 'Nsong'a Lianja. L'épopée nationale des Nkundo', *Aequatoria* 12: 1–75.

Boone, E. H. and Mignolo, W. D. (eds) (1994) *Writing without Words. Alternative Literacies in Mesoamerica and the Andes,* Durham: Duke University Press.

Bourdieu, P. (1977) 'The attitude of the Algerian peasant toward time', in Pitt-Rivers, J. (ed.) *Mediterranean Countrymen,* Westport: Greenwood Press.

Bourgault, Louise (1995) *Mass Media in Sub-Saharan Africa,* Bloomington: Indiana University Press.

—— (2003) *Playing for Life. Performance in Africa in the Age of AIDS,* Durham: Carolina Academic Press.

Bowra, C. M. (1963) *Primitive Song,* New York: Mentor Books.

Boyarin, J. (ed.) (1993) *The Ethnography of Reading,* Berkeley: University of California Press.

Brathwaite, Edward (1984) *History of the Voice,* London: New Beacon Books.

Briggs, Charles L. (1985) 'Treasure tales and pedagogical discourse in Mexicano New Mexico', *Journal of American Folklore* 98: 287–314.

—— (1986) *Learning How to Ask. A Sociolinguistic Appraisal of the Role of the Interview in Social Science Research,* Cambridge: Cambridge University Press.

—— (1993) ' "I'm not just talking to the victims of oppression tonight – I'm talking to everybody": rhetorical authority and narrative authenticity in an African-American poetics of political engagement', *Journal of Narrative and Life History* 3: 33–78.

—— (2002) 'Linguistic magic bullets in the making of a modernist anthropology', *American Anthropologist* 104: 481–98.

Bright, William (1981) 'Literature: written and oral', in Tannen, D. (ed.) *Georgetown University Round Table on Languages and Linguistics,* Washington DC: Georgetown University Press.

Brown, Duncan (1998) *Voicing the Text. South African Oral Poetry and Performance,* Cape Town: Oxford University Press.

—— (ed.) (1999a) *Oral Literature and Performance in Southern Africa,* Oxford: James Currey.

—— (1999b) 'Orality and Christianity: the hymns of Isaiah Shembe and the Church of the Nazarites', in Brown 1999a.

—— (2003) ' "Where shall I wonder under the thunder who's that black boys making that black noise step a little closer to the mic": Prophets of Da City and urban (South African) identity', in Draper.

Brown, P. and Levinson, S. C. (1987) *Politeness. Some Universals in Language Usage,* Cambridge: Cambridge University Press.

Brown, Stewart (ed.) (1995) *The Pressures of the Text: Orality, Texts and the Telling of Tales,* Birmingham: Birmingham University African Studies Series, 4.

Bruner, Jerome (1986) *Actual Minds, Possible Worlds,* Cambridge MA: Harvard University Press.

—— (1987) 'Life as narrative', *Social Research* 54: 11–32.

—— (1991) 'The narrative construction of reality', *Critical Inquiry* 18: 1–21.

Bryant, Jerry B. (2003) *'Born in a Mighty Bad Land'. The Violent Man in African American Folklore and Fiction,* Bloomington: Indiana University Press.

Bubu, Malami and Furniss, Graham (1999) 'Youth culture, *bandiri*, and the continuing legitimacy of debate in Sokoto town', *Journal of African Cultural Studies* 12: 27–46.

Buchan, David (1972) *The Ballad and the Folk,* London: Routledge and Kegan Paul.

Burke, P. (1997) *Varieties of Cultural History,* Cambridge: Polity.

Calame-Griaule, G. (1965) *Ethnologie et langage: la parole chez les Dogon,* Paris: Gallimard.

—— (1985) 'La gestuelle des conteurs: état d'une recherche', in Gentili and Paione.

—— (écrits pour) (1989) *Graines de parole: puissance du verbe et traditions orales. Textes offerts à Geneviève Calame-Griaule.* Paris: Éditions du Centre National de la Recherche Scientifique.

Cancel, Robert (1989) *Allegorical Speculation in an Oral Society: the Tabwa Narrative Tradition,* Berkeley: University of California Press.

—— (2004) 'Oral performance dynamics', in Peek and Yankah.

Carey, Margret (1970) *Myths and Legends of Africa,* Feltham: Hamlyn.

Carrier, James G. (ed.) (1995) *Occidentalism. Images of the West,* Oxford: Clarendon Press.

Cassidy, F. G. (1965) 'How free was the Anglo-Saxon scop?', in Bessinger, J. B. and Creed, R. P. (eds) *Medieval and Linguistic Studies,* London: Allen and Unwin.

Cassirer, E. (1953) *The Philosophy of Symbolic Forms,* Vol. I, Eng. transl., New Haven: Yale University Press.

—— (1954) *An Essay on Man,* New York: Doubleday.

Cavallo, G. and Chartier, R. (eds) (1999) *A History of Reading in the West,* Eng. transl., Cambridge: Polity.

Chabal, Patrick (ed.) (1996) *The Post-Colonial Literature of Lusophone Africa,* Johannesburg: Witwatersrand University Press.

Chabal, Patrick and Daloz, Jean-Pascal (1999) *Africa Works. Disorder as Political Instrument,* Oxford: James Currey.

Chadwick, H. M. and N. K. (1932–40) *The Growth of Literature,* 3 vols, Cambridge: Cambridge University Press.

Chadwick, N. K. (1939) 'The distribution of oral literature in the Old World', *Journal of the Royal Anthropological Institute* 69: 77–94.

Chatelain, H. (1894) *Folk-Tales of Angola,* Boston and New York: American Folk-Lore Society.

Chaytor, H. (1945) *From Script to Print. An Introduction to Medieval Literature,* Cambridge: Cambridge University Press.

Childs, G. T. (1994) 'African ideophones', in Hinton, L., Nichols, J. and Ohala, J. J. (eds) *Sound Symbolism,* Cambridge: Cambridge University Press.

Chimombo, S. (1988) *Malawian Oral Literature: The Aesthetics of Indigenous Arts,* Zomba: Centre for Social Research and Department of English, University of Malawi.

Chinweizu, Onwuchekwa, Jemie and Madubuike, Ihechukwu (1985) *Toward the Decolonization of African Literature,* London: KPI.

Chomsky, N. (2000) *New Horizons in the Study of Language and Mind,* Cambridge: Cambridge University Press.

Clark, H. H. (1992) *Arenas of Language Use,* Chicago: University of Chicago Press.

Clark, J. P. (1977) *The Ozidi Saga,* Ibadan: Ibadan University Press.

Classen, C. (1993) *Worlds of Sense. Exploring the Senses in History and Across Cultures,* London: Routledge.

—— (1998) *The Color of Angels. Cosmology, Gender and the Aesthetic Imagination,* London: Routledge.

—— (ed.) (2005) *The Book of Touch,* Oxford: Berg.

Classen, C., Howes, D. and Synnott, A. (1994) *Aroma. The Cultural History of Smell,* London: Routledge.

Cole, Catherine (2001) *Ghana's Concert Party Theatre,* Bloomington: Indiana University Press.

Coleman, J. (1996) *Public Reading and the Reading Public in Late Medieval England and France,* Cambridge: Cambridge University Press.

Colleyn, J-P (2004) 'Films on African folklore', in Peek and Yankah.

Collingwood, R. G. (1938) *The Principles of Art,* Oxford: Clarendon Press.

Collins, James and Blot, Richard K. (2003) *Literacy and Literacies. Texts, Power, and Identity,* Cambridge: Cambridge University Press.

Commission for Africa (2005) 'Commissioners declaration', 11 March 2005,

http://www.commissionforafrica.org/english/report/commissiondeclaratio
n11march05eng.pdf/

Conrad, David C. and Condé, Djanka Tassey (2004) *Sunjata: a West African Epic of the Mande People*, Indianapolis: Hackett.

Conteh-Morgan, J. and Olaniyan, T. (eds) (1999) *Drama and Performance*, special issue, *Research in African Literatures* 30, 4.

Cooper, Carolyn (1995) *Noises in the Blood; Orality, Gender, and the 'Vulgar'*, Durham: Duke University Press.

Cooper, Frederick (2002) *Africa since 1940. The Past of the Present*, Cambridge: Cambridge University Press.

Cope, B. and Kalantzis, M. (2000) *Multiliteracies. Literacy Learning and the Design of Social Futures*, London: Routledge.

Cope, T. (ed.) (1968) *Izibongo. Zulu Praise-Poems*, Oxford: Clarendon Press.

Coplan, David B. (1978) '"Go to my town, Cape Coast!": the social history of Ghanaian highlife', in Nettl, B. (ed.) *Eight Urban Musical Cultures*, Urbana: University of Illinois Press.

—— (1987) 'The power of oral poetry: narrative songs of the Basotho migrants', *Research in African Literatures* 18: 1–35.

—— (1994) *In the Time of Cannibals. The Word Music of South Africa's Basotho Migrants*, Chicago: University of Chicago Press.

—— (2001) 'Orature, popular history and cultural memory in Sesotho', in Kaschula.

Cosentino, Donald J. (1980) 'Lele Gbomba and the style of Mende baroque', *African Arts* 13, 3: 54–5, 75–8, 92.

—— (1982) *Defiant Maids and Stubborn Farmers: Tradition and Invention in Mende Story Performance,* Cambridge: Cambridge University Press.

Coupez, A. and Kamanzi, Th. (1962) *Récits historiques rwanda, Annales (sciences humaines)* 43, Tervuren: Musée Royale de l'Afrique centrale.

Crosby, R. (1936) 'Oral delivery in the Middle Ages', *Speculum* 11: 88–110.

Curschmann, M. (1967) 'Oral poetry in mediaeval English, French, and German literature: some notes on recent research', *Speculum* 42: 36–52.

Czekelius, A. R. (1993) 'Of "meaning" and "significance": the emic interpretation of a West African tale', *African Languages and Cultures* 6: 121–32.

Dalby, David (1965) 'The Mel languages: a re-classification of Southern "West Atlantic"', *African Language Studies* 6: 1–17.

—— (1967–9) 'A survey of the indigenous scripts of Liberia and Sierra Leone: Vai, Mende, Loma, Kpelle and Bassa', 'The indigenous scripts of West Africa and Surinam: their inspiration and design', 'Further indigenous scripts of West Africa: Manding, Wolof and Fula alphabets and Yoruba "holy" writing', *African Language Studies* 8: 1–52; 9: 156–97; 10: 161–81.

—— (1999/2000) *The Linguasphere Register of the World's Languages and Speech Communities,* 2 vols, Hebron: Linguasphere Press.

Dauphin-Tinturier, A-M. (2001) 'AIDS and girls' initiation in Northern Zambia', in Kaschula.

Deng, F. M. (1973) *The Dinka and their Songs*, Oxford: Clarendon Press.

Derive, Jean (1985) 'Oralité, écriture et le problème de l'identité culturelle en Afrique', *Bayreuth African Studies* 34, 3: 5–36.

232

—— (1989) 'Le jeune menteur et le vieux sage. Esquisse d'une théorie "littéraire" chez les Dioula de Kong', in Calame-Griaule.

Diabate, Lansina (1995) *L'Épopée de Sunjara, d'après Lansine Diabate de Kela (Mali)*, Leiden: Research School CNWS.

Diamond, Elin (ed.) (1993) *Performance and Cultural Politics*, London: Routledge.

Diop, Samba (ed. and transl.) (2004) *Épopées africaines: Ndiadiane Ndiaye et El Hadj Omar Tall*, Paris: L'Harmattan.

Diringer, D. (1968) *The Alphabet. A Key to the History of Mankind*. 2 vols, 3rd edn, London: Hutchinson.

Dlali, Mawande (2004) 'The speech act of apology in IsiZhosa educational contexts', *South African Journal of African Languages* 24, 2: 118–31.

Doleželová-Veleringerová, M. and Crump, J. I. (transl.) (1971) *Ballad of the Hidden Dragon*, Oxford: Clarendon Press.

Dorson, R. M. (ed.) (1972) *African Folklore*, Bloomington: Indiana University Press.

Draper, Jonathan A. (ed.) (2003) *Orality, Literacy, and Colonialism in Southern Africa*, Atlanta: Society of Biblical Literature.

Drewal, Margaret Thompson (1991) 'The state of research on performance in Africa', *African Studies Review* 34, 3: 1–64.

—— (2004) 'Performance studies and African folklore research', in Peek and Yankah.

Driberg, T. (1932) *Initiation: Translations from Poems of the Didinga and Lango Tribes,* Waltham St. Lawrence: Golden Cockerel Press.

Du Bois, J. W. (1986) 'Self-evidence and ritual speech', in Chafe, W. and Nichols, J. (eds) *Evidentiality: The Linguistic Coding of Epistemology*, Norwood: Ablex.

Duggan, J. J. (1973) *The Song of Roland. Formulaic Style and Poetic Craft,* Berkeley: University of California Press.

Dumestre, Gérard (ed.) (1974) *La Geste de Ségou. Textes des griots bambara,* Abidjan: Université d'Abidjan, Institut de Linguistique Appliquée.

Duranti, Alessandro (1997a) *Linguistic Anthropology*, Cambridge: Cambridge University Press.

—— (1997b) 'Universal and culture-specific properties of greetings', *Journal of Linguistic Anthropology* 7: 63-97.

—— (ed.) (2001) *Key Terms in Language and Culture*, Oxford: Blackwell.

—— (ed.) (2004) *A Companion to Linguistic Anthropology*, Oxford: Blackwell.

Duranti, Alessandro and Goodwin, Charles (eds) (1992) *Rethinking Context. Language as an Interactive Phenomenon*, Cambridge: Cambridge University Press.

Egudu, R. and Nwoga, D. (ed. and transl.) (1973) *Igbo Traditional Verse*, London: Heinemann.

Elias, N. (1991) 'On human beings and their emotions: a process-sociological essay', in Featherstone, M., Hepworth, M, and Turner, B. (eds) *The Body. Social Process and Cultural Theory,* London: Sage.

El-Shamy, Hasan M. (ed.) (1980) *Folktales of Egypt,* Chicago: University of Chicago Press.

Evans-Pritchard, E. E. (1967) *The Zande Trickster,* Oxford: Clarendon Press.

Ezeigbo, T. A. and Gunner, Liz (1991) *The Literatures of War,* special issue, *Journal of African Languages and Cultures* 4, 1.

Ezenwa-Ohaeto (1994) 'Orality and the craft of modern Nigerian poetry: Osundare's *Waiting Laughters* and Odechuwu's *What the Madman Said'*, *African Languages and Cultures* 7: 101–19.

Faber, Paul (2004) 'Popular culture', in Peek and Yankah.

Fabian, J. (1998) *Moments of Freedom. Anthropology and Popular Culture,* Charlottesville: University of Virginia Press.

Fanthorpe, Richard (1998) 'Limba "deep rural" strategies', *Journal of African History* 39: 15–38.

Fardon, R. and Furniss, G. (eds) (2000) *African Broadcast Cultures. Radio in Transition,* Oxford: James Currey.

Farias, P. F. de Moraes (2003a) *Arabic Medieval Inscriptions from the Republic of Mali,* Oxford: Oxford University Press.

—— (2003b) 'Afrocentrism: between crosscultural grand narrative and cultural relativism', *Journal of African History* 44: 327–40.

Featherstone, Simon (2005) *Postcolonial Cultures,* Edinburgh: Edinburgh University Press.

Feeley-Harnik, Gillian (1991) *A Green Estate. Restoring Independence in Madagascar,* Washington: Smithsonian Institution Press.

Feld, S., Fox, A. A., Porcello, T. and Samuels, D. (2004) 'Vocal anthropology: from the music of language to the language of song', in Duranti.

Fikry-Atallah, M. (1972) 'Oral traditions of the Wala of Wa', in Dorson.

Finch, Geoffrey (2003) *Word of Mouth. A New Introduction to Language and Communication,* Basingstoke: Palgrave Macmillan.

Fine, E. C. (1984) *The Folklore Text: From Performance to Print,* Bloomington: Indiana University Press.

Finnegan. Ruth (1963) 'The Limba of Sierra Leone, with special reference to their folktales or "oral literature"', doctoral thesis, University of Oxford.

—— (1965) *Survey of the Limba People of Northern Sierra Leone,* London: HMSO.

—— (1967) *Limba Stories and Story-Telling,* Oxford: Clarendon Press.

—— (1969) 'Attitudes to the study of oral literature in British social anthropology', *Man* 4: 59–69.

—— (1970) *Oral Literature in Africa,* Oxford: Clarendon Press.

—— [1977] (1992) *Oral Poetry: Its Nature, Significance and Social Context,* Cambridge: Cambridge University Press (2nd edn, Bloomington: Indiana University Press).

—— (1988) *Literacy and Orality: Studies in the Technology of Communication,* Oxford: Blackwell.

—— (1989) *The Hidden Musicians. Music-Making in an English Town,* Cambridge: Cambridge University Press.

—— (1992) *Oral Traditions and the Verbal Arts: A Guide to Research Practices,* London: Routledge.

—— (1998) *Tales of the City: A Study of Narrative and Urban Life,* Cambridge: Cambridge University Press.

—— (2001) 'Oral and literate expression', *International Encyclopedia of the Social and Behavioral Sciences,* Amsterdam: Elsevier, Vol. 16: 10887–91.

—— (2002) *Communicating. The Multiple Modes of Human Interconnection*, London: Routledge.

—— (2003) 'Orality and literacy: epic heroes of human destiny?' *International Journal of Learning* 10: 1551–60.

—— (2005) 'The how of literature', in Gerstle et al.: 164–87.

—— (2006) 'Not by words alone: reclothing the oral', in Olson, D. R. and Cole, M. (eds), *Technology, Literacy and the Evolution of Society: Implications of the Work of Jack Goody*, Mahwah: Erlbaum.

Foley, John Miles (1988) *The Theory of Oral Composition. History and Methodology*, Bloomington: Indiana University Press.

—— (2002) *How to Read an Oral Poem*, Urbana: University of Illinois Press.

—— (ed.) (2003) *Oral Tradition: State of the Art*, special issue, *Oral Tradition* 18: 1–2.

Fox, Adam (2000) *Oral and Literate Culture in England 1500–1700*, Oxford: Oxford University Press.

Fox, Robert E. (1980) 'Review of Wole Soyinka *Poems of Black Africa*', *African Literature Today* 11: 209–12.

—— (1999) 'Diasporacentricism and black aural texts', in Okpewho et al.

France, Peter (ed.) (2000) *Oxford Guide to Literature in English Translation*, Oxford: Oxford University Press.

Francis, D. J. and Kamanda, M. C. (2001) 'Politics and language planning in Sierra Leone', *African Studies* 60, 2: 225–44.

Fraser, Robert (1986) *West African Poetry. A Critical History*, Cambridge: Cambridge University Press.

Fretz, Rachel I. (1994) 'Through ambiguous tales: women's voices in Chokwe storytelling', in Haring.

—— (2004) 'Dialogic performances: call-and-response in African narrating', in Peek and Yankah.

Frith, Simon (1996) *Performing Rites: Evaluating Popular Music*, Oxford: Oxford University Press.

Frobenius, Leo (1921–28) *Atlantis: Volksmärchen und Volksdichtungen Afrikas*, 12 vols, Jena: Dietrichs.

Furniss, Graham (1996) *Poetry, Prose and Popular Culture in Hausa*, Edinburgh: Edinburgh University Press.

—— (1998) 'Hausa creative writing in the 1930s: an exploration in post-colonial theory', *Research in African Literatures* 29, 1: 87–101.

—— (2001) 'Language, truth and rhetoric in the constitution of orality', in Kaschula.

—— (2004) *Orality. The Power of the Spoken Word*, Basingstoke: Palgrave Macmillan.

Furniss, Graham and Gunner, Liz (eds) (1995) *Power, Marginality and Oral Literature in Africa*, Cambridge: Cambridge University Press.

Gayibor, Lodjou and Ligier, Françoise (1983) *Foli Bébé, ou l'épopée des Gâ du Togo*, Libreville: Lion.

Gbadamosi, B. and Beier, U. (1959) *Yoruba Poetry*, Ibadan: Ministry of Education.

Gecau, R. N. (1970) *Kikuyu Folktales,* Nairobi: East African Literature Bureau.

Gelaye, Getie (2001) *Peasants and the Ethiopian State. Agricultural Producers'*

Cooperatives and their Reflections in Amharic Oral Poetry, Munster: LIT Verlag.

Gentili, B. and Paione, G. (eds) (1985) *Oralità. Cultura, Letteratura, Discorso*, Roma: Ateneo.

Gérard, Albert S. (1981) *African Language Literatures. An Introduction to the Literary History of Sub-Saharan Africa*, Harlow: Longman.

—— (1990) *Contexts of African Literature*, Amsterdam: Rodopi.

—— (1996) *Afrique plurielle. Études de littérature comparée*, Amsterdam: Rodopi.

Gerstle, Andrew, Jones, Stephanie and Thomas, Rosalind (eds) (2005) *Performance Literature*, special issue, *Oral Tradition* 20, 1–2.

Geurts, K. L. (2002) *Culture and the Senses. Bodily Ways of Knowing in an African Community*, Berkeley: University of California Press.

Gikandi, Simon (2004) 'African literature and the colonial factor', in Irele and Gikandi, Vol. 1.

Giles-Vernic, Tamara (2001) 'Lives, histories, and sites of recollection', in White et al.

Goldhill, Simon and Osborne, Robin (eds) (1999) *Performance Culture and Athenian Democracy*, Cambridge: Cambridge University Press.

Goldstein, K. S. (1964) *A Guide for Field Workers in Folklore*, Hatboro: Folklore Associates.

Goodwin, Marjorie H. (2001) 'Participation', in Duranti.

Goody, Jack (ed.) (1968) *Literacy in Traditional Societies*, London: Cambridge University Press.

—— (1972) *The Myth of the Bagre*, Oxford: Clarendon Press.

—— (1977) *The Domestication of the Savage Mind*, Cambridge: Cambridge University Press.

—— (1987) *The Interface between the Written and the Oral*, Cambridge: Cambridge University Press.

—— (1998) *Food and Love. A Cultural History of East and West*, New York: Verso.

—— (1992) 'Oral culture', in Bauman.

—— (1999) 'The implications of literacy', in Wagner et al.

—— (2000) *The Power of the Written Tradition*, Washington: Smithsonian Institution Press.

Görög-Karady, Veronika (1980) *Histoires d'enfants terribles (Afrique noire): études et anthologie*, Paris: G. P. Masonneuve et Larose.

—— (1981) *Littérature orale d'Afrique noire: bibliographie analytique*, Paris: Maisonneuve et Larose.

—— (ed.) (1982) *Genres, Forms, Meanings: Essays in African Oral Literature*, Oxford: JASO.

—— (ed.) (1984) *African Oral Narrative*, special issue, *Research in African Literatures* 15, 2: 161–288.

—— (1990) *D'un conte ... à l'autre. From One Tale ... to the Other: Variability in Oral Literature*, Paris: Editions du Centre National de la Recherche Scientifique.

—— (1992) *Bibliographie annotée: littérature orale d'Afrique noire*, Paris: Conseil International de la Langue Française.

—— (ed.) (1994) *Le Mariage dans les contes africains*, Paris: Karthala.

—— (1997) *L'Univers familial dans les contes africains. Liens de sang, liens d'alliance*, Paris: L'Harmattan.

Görög-Karady, Veronika and Seydou, Christiane (2001) *La Fille difficile: un conte-type africain*, Paris: CNRS Editions.

Graham, Laura R. (1995) *Performing Dreams. Discourses of Immortality among the Xavante of Central Brazil*, Austin: University of Texas Press.

Greenberg, Joseph (1996) 'Linguistics', in Kuper, A. and J. (eds) *The Social Science Encyclopedia*, 2nd edn, London: Routledge.

Greenway, J. (1953) *American Folk Songs of Protest*, Philadelphia: University of Pennsylvania Press.

Griffiths, G. (1997) 'Writing, literacy and history in Africa', in Msiska and Hyland.

Gumperz, J. J. and Levinson, S. C. (eds) (1996) *Rethinking Linguistic Relativity*, Cambridge: Cambridge University Press.

Gunner, Elizabeth (1986) 'A dying tradition? African oral literature in a contemporary context', *Social Dynamics* 12, 2: 31–8.

—— (1991) 'Mixing the discourses: genre jumping in popular song', in Sienaert et al.

—— (ed.) (1994) *Politics and Performance Theatre, Poetry and Song in Southern Africa*, Johannesburg: Witwatersrand University Press.

—— (2000) 'Wrestling with the present, beckoning to the past: contemporary Zulu radio drama', *Journal of Southern African Studies* 26: 223–37.

—— (2004) 'Africa and orality', in Irele and Gikandi, Vol. 1.

Hadas, M. (1954) *Ancilla to Classical Learning*, New York: Columbia University Press.

Hale, Thomas (1998) *Griots and Griottes*, Bloomington: Indiana University Press.

—— (ed.) (1994) *Politics and Performance Theatre, Poetry and Song in Southern Africa*, Johannesburg: Witwatersrand University Press.

—— (2003) 'Oral tradition in the context of verbal art', *Oral Tradition* 18: 91–2.

Hallpike, C. R. (1979) *The Foundations of Primitive Thought*, Oxford: Clarendon Press.

Hanks, W. F. (1989) 'Text and textuality', *Annual Review of Anthropology* 18: 5–127.

—— (1996) *Language and Communicative Practices*, Boulder: Westview Press.

Harding, Frances (ed.) (2002) *Performance Arts in Africa*, London: Routledge.

Haring, Lee (ed.) (1994) *African Oral Traditions*, special issue, *Oral Tradition* 9, 1.

Harries, L. (1962) *Swahili Poetry*, Oxford: Clarendon Press.

—— (1970) 'Review of D. Biebuyck and K. C. Mateene, *The Mwindo Epic*', *Research in African Literatures* 1: 98–100.

Harvey, E. D. (2003) (ed.) *Sensible Flesh. On Touch in Early Modern Culture*, Philadelphia: University of Pennsylvania Press.

Hatto, A. T. (ed.) (1980) *Traditions of Heroic and Epic Poetry*, Vol. 1, *The Traditions*, London: Modern Humanities Research Association.

Haviland, J. B. (2004) 'Gesture', in Duranti.

Hermans, Theo (2003) 'Cross-cultural translation studies as thick translation', *Bulletin of School of Oriental and African Studies* 66, 3: 380–89.

Herrick, Robert (1869) *Hesperides. The Poems and Other Remains of Robert Herrick*, (ed. W. Carew Hazlitt), London: John Russell Smith.

Herskovits, M. J. and F. S. (1958) *Dahomean Narrative*, Evanston: Northwestern University Press.

Hill, Jane H. and Irvine, Judith T. (eds) (1992) *Responsibility and Evidence in Oral Discourse*, Cambridge: Cambridge University Press.

Hiskett, M. (1964–5) 'The "Song of Bagauda": a Hausa king list and homily in verse', *Bulletin of the School of Oriental and African Studies* 27: 540–67; 28: 112–35, 363–85.

Hofmeyr, Isabel (2002) 'John Bunyan, his chair, and a few other relics. Orality, literacy, and the limits of area studies', in White et al.

—— (2004a) 'Orality and literacy in Africa', in Peek and Yankah.

—— (2004b) *The Portable Bunyan. A Transnational History of The Pilgrim's Progress*, Princeton: Princeton University Press.

Honko, Lauri (2000a) 'Text as process and practice: the textualization of oral epics', in Honko 2000b.

—— (ed.) (2000b) *Textualization of Oral Epics*, Berlin and New York: Mouton de Gruyter.

Horovitz, M. (ed.) (1969) *Children of Albion: Poetry of the 'Underground' in Britain*, Harmondsworth: Penguin.

Horton, Robin (1969) Personal communication, Ibadan.

Howe, Stephen (1998) *Afrocentrism: Mythical Pasts and Imagined Homes*, London: Verso.

Howes, David (2003) *Sensual Relations: Engaging the Senses in Culture and Social Theory*, Ann Arbor: University of Michigan Press.

—— (ed.) (2005) *Empire of the Senses. The Sensual Culture Reader*, Oxford: Berg.

Hughes-Freeland, F. (ed.) (1998) *Ritual, Performance, Media*, London: Routledge.

Huizinga, J. (1949) *Homo Ludens*, London: Routledge and Kegan Paul.

Hunter, Linda and Oumarou, Chaibou Elhadji (1998) 'Towards a Hausa verbal aesthetic: aspects of language about using language', *Journal of African Cultural Studies* 11, 2: 157–70.

Hunter, Monica (1961) *Reaction to Conquest*, 2nd edn, London: Oxford University Press.

Hunwick, J. O. (1974) *Literacy and Scholarship in Muslim West Africa in the Pre-Colonial Period*, Nsukka: University of Nigeria, Institute of African Studies.

Hunwick, J. O. and O'Fahey, R. S. (eds) (1994–) *Arabic Literature of Africa*, 6 vols (in process), Leiden: Brill.

Hymes, D. H. (1979) 'Tonkawa poetics; John Rush Buffalo's "Coyote and Eagle's Daughter"', in Maquet, J. (ed.) *On Linguistic Anthropology: Essays in Honor of Harry Hoijer*, Malibu: Undena Publications.

—— (1981) *'In Vain I Tried to Tell You': Essays in Native American Ethnopoetics*, Philadelphia: University of Pennsylvania Press.

—— (1996) *Ethnography, Linguistics, Narrative Inequality*, London: Taylor and Francis.

Ibrahim, Abdullahi A. (2002) 'The birth of the interview: the thin and the fat of it', in White et al.

Innes, Gordon (1973) 'Stability and change in griots' narrations', *African Language Studies* 14: 105–18.

—— (1974) *Sunjata. Three Mandinka Versions,* London: School of Oriental and African Studies.

—— (1976) *Kaabu and Fuladu. Historical Narratives of the Gambian Mandinka,* London: School of Oriental and African Studies.

—— (1978) *Kelefa Saane. His Career Recounted by Two Mandinka Bards,* London: School of Oriental and African Studies.

Innes, Lyn (2002) Cover comment, Newell, Stephanie (ed.) (2002) *Readings in African Popular Fiction,* Oxford: James Currey.

Irele, Abiola F. (2001) *The African Imagination: Literature in Africa and the Black Diaspora,* Oxford: Oxford University Press.

Irele, Abiola F. and Gikandi, Simon (eds) (2004) *The Cambridge History of African and Caribbean Literature,* 2 vols, Cambridge: Cambridge University Press.

Jackson, Bruce (1972) *Wake up Dead Man: Afro-American Worksongs from Texas Prisons,* Cambridge MA: Harvard University Press.

Jackson, M. (1982) *Allegories of the Wilderness: Ethics and Ambiguity in Kuranko Narratives,* Bloomington: Indiana University Press.

Jahn, Janheinz (1961) *Muntu: An Outline of Neo-African Culture,* Eng. transl., London: Faber and Faber. [first pub. in German 1958]

Jahoda, Gustav (1999) *Images of Savages. Ancient Roots of Modern Prejudice in Western Culture,* London: Routledge.

James, Deborah (1999) *Songs of the Women Migrants. Performance and Identity in South Africa,* Edinburgh: Edinburgh University Press.

James, Wendy (2003) *The Ceremonial Animal. A New Portrait of Anthropology,* Oxford: Oxford University Press.

Jansen, Jan (2001a) *Épopée, histoire, société, le cas de Soundjata: Mali et Guinée,* Paris: Karthala.

—— (2001b) 'The Sunjata epic – the ultimate version', *Research in African Literatures* 32, 1: 14–46.

Johnson, John William (1971) 'The development of the genre *heello* in modern Somali poetry', M.Phil. thesis, University of London.

—— (1974) *Heellooy Heelleellooy. The Development of the Genre Heello in Modern Somali Poetry,* Bloomington: Indiana University Publications, African Series 5.

—— (1978) 'The epic of Sunjata: an attempt to define the model for African epic poetry', doctoral thesis, Indiana University.

—— (1980) 'Yes, Virginia, there is an epic in Africa', *Research in African Literatures* 11, 3: 308–26.

—— (ed.) (2003) *Son-Jara: The Mande Epic. Performance by Jeli Fa-Digi Sisoko,* Audio CD, Bloomington: Indiana University Press.

—— (ed.) (2004) *Son-Jara: The Mande Epic Mandekan/English Edition with Notes and Commentary,* Bloomington: Indiana University Press.

Johnson, John William, Hale, Thomas A. and Belcher, Stephen (eds) (1997)

Oral Epics from Africa: Vibrant Voices from a Vast Continent, Blooming-ton: Indiana University Press.

Jones, A. M. (1943) *African Music*, Livingstone: Rhodes-Livingstone Museum Occasional Papers, 2.

Jones, Eldred Durosimi, Palmer, Eustace and Jones, Marjorie (eds) (1992) *Orature in African Literature Today*, London: James Currey.

Jorholt, Eva (2001) 'Africa's modern cinematic griots – oral tradition and West African cinema', in Baaz and Palmberg.

Jousse, M. (1925) 'Le style oral rhythmique et mnémotechnique chez les verbo-moteurs', *Archives de Philosophie* 2, 4: 1–240.

Julien, Eileen (1992) *African Novels and the Question of Orality*, Blooming-ton: Indiana University Press.

Junod, H. A. (1912–13) *The Life of a South African Tribe*, 2 vols, Neuchâtel: Attinger Frères.

Jury, B. (1996) 'Boys to men: Afrikaans alternative popular music 1986–1990', *African Languages and Cultures* 9: 99–109.

Kagame, A. (1951) *La Poésie dynastique au Rwanda*, Mémoires 22, 1, Brussels: Institut Royal Colonial Belge.

Kane, Mohamadou (1974) 'Sur les formes traditionelles du roman africain', *Revue de littérature comparée* 48: 536–68.

Kaschula, Russell H. (1997) 'Exploring the oral-written interface with particular reference to Xhosa oral poetry', in Ricard and Swanepoel.

—— (1999) '*Imbongi* and griot: toward a comparative analysis of oral poetics in Southern and West Africa', *Journal of African Cultural Studies* 12: 55–76.

—— (ed.) (2001) *African Oral Literature. Functions in Contemporary Con-texts*, Claremont: New Africa Books.

—— (2002) *The Bones of the Ancestors are Shaking: Xhosa Oral Poetry in Context*, Cape Town: Juta.

—— (2003) '*Imbongi* to slam: the emergence of a technologized auriture', paper for African Languages Association of Southern Africa Conference, University of Stellenbosch.

—— (2004) 'Southern Africa: contemporary forms of folklore', in Peek and Yankah.

Kaunda, Kenneth D. (1966) *A Humanist in Africa*, London: Longmans.

Kavari, Jekura U. (2002) *The Form and Meaning of Otjiherero Praises*, Köln: Rödiger Köppe Verlag.

Kawada, Junzo (1996) 'Human dimensions in the sound universe', in Ellen, R. and Fukui, K. (eds) *Redefining Nature*, Oxford: Berg.

Keesing, R. M. and Strathern, A. J. (1998) *Cultural Anthropology. A Contem-porary Perspective,* 3rd edn, Fort Worth: Brace College.

Kendon, Adam (1997) 'Gesture', *Annual Review of Anthropology* 26: 109–28.

—— (2000) 'Language and gesture: unity or duality?', in McNeill 2000.

Kesteloot, L. (1989) 'The African epic', *African Languages and Cultures* 2: 203–14.

—— (1993a) *Oral Literature*, special issue, *Research in African Literatures* 24, 2.

—— (ed. and transl.) (1993b) *L'Épopée bambara de Ségou,* 2 vols, Paris:

L'Harmattan.

Kesteloot, L. and Dieng, B. (1997) *Epopées d'Afrique noire*, Paris: Karthala.

Kesteloot L. and Dumestre, G. (eds) (1975) *La Prise de Dionkoloni. Episode de l'épopée bambara, raconté par Sissoko Kabine*, Paris: Armand Colin.

Kilson, Marion (1976) *Royal Antelope and Spider: West African Mende Tales*, Cambridge MA: Langdon Associates.

Kirk, G. S. (1965) *Homer and the Epic*, Cambridge: Cambridge University Press.

Kishani, Bongasu Tanla (2001) 'On the interface of philosophy and language in Africa: some practical and theoretical considerations', *African Studies Review* 44, 3: 27–45.

Klassen, Doreen Helen (2004) 'Gestures in African oral narrative', in Peek and Yankah.

Knappert, Jan (2000) 'The textualization of Swahili epics', in Honko (2000b).

Knoblauch, H. and Kotthoff, H. (eds) (2001) *Verbal Art Across Cultures. The Aesthetics and Proto-Aesthetics of Communication*, Tübingen: Narr.

Koelle, S. W. (1854) *African Native Literature; Or, Proverbs, Tales, Fables, and Historical Fragments in the Kanuri or Bornu Language*, London: Church Missionary House.

Kress, Gunther (2003) *Literacy in the New Media Age*, London: Routledge.

Kress, Gunther and Van Leeuwen, T. (2001) *Multimodal Discourse. The Modes and Media of Contemporary Communication*, London: Arnold.

Krieger, Milton (2004) 'The formative journals and institutions', in Irele and Gikandi, Vol. 1.

Kromberg, S. (1991) 'The role of audience in the emergence of Durban worker izibongo', conference paper, 'Oral Tradition and Innovation', University of Natal.

Kubik, Gerhard (1977) *Recording and Classification of Oral Literature in Tanzania and Some Other Parts of Africa*, Dar es Salaam: Goethe-Institut.

Kuyk, Betty M. (2003) *African Voices in the African American Heritage*, Bloomington: Indiana University Press.

Laws, G. M. (1957) *American Ballads from British Broadsides*, Philadelphia: American Folklore Society.

Lévi-Strauss, C. (1949) *Les Structures élémentaires de la parenté*, Paris: Presses Universitaires de France.

Lévy-Bruhl, L. (1926) *How Natives Think*, Eng. transl., London: Allen and Unwin.

Lindblom, K. G. (1928–35) *Kamba Folklore*, 3 vols, Uppsala: Applebergs Boktryckeri Aktiebolag.

Lindfors, B. (ed.) (1977) *Forms of Folklore in Africa*, Austin: University of Texas Press.

Lord, Albert B. (1960) *The Singer of Tales*, Cambridge MA: Harvard University Press.

—— (1965) 'Oral poetry', in Preminger, A. (ed.) *Encyclopedia of Poetry and Poetics*, Princeton: Princeton University Press.

Luckmann, T. (1995) 'Interaction planning and intersubjective adjustment of perspective by communicative genres', in Goody, E. N. (ed.) (1995) *Social Intelligence and Interaction. Expressions and Implications of the Social*

Bias in Human Intelligence, Cambridge: Cambridge University Press.

Lucy, John A. (2001) 'Reflexivity', in Duranti.

—— (ed.) (1993) *Reflexive Language: Reported Speech and Metapragmatics,* Cambridge: Cambridge University Press.

Lüpke, F. (2004) 'Language planning in West Africa – who writes the script?', *Language Documentation and Description* 2: 90–107.

Ly, Amadou (1991) *L'Épopée de Samba Guéladiégui: version orale peul de Pahel,* Paris: UNESCO.

Mack, Beverly B. (2005) *Muslim Women Sing: Hausa Popular Song,* Bloomington: Indiana University Press.

Magoun, F. P. (1953) 'The oral-formulaic character of Anglo-Saxon narrative poetry', *Speculum* 28: 446–67.

Makang, Jen-Marie (1997) 'Of the good use of tradition: keeping the critical perspective in African philosophy', in Eze, Emmanuel Chukwudi (ed.) *Postcolonial African Philosophy. A Critical Reader,* Oxford: Blackwell.

Makward, E., Ravell-Pinto, T. and Songolo, A. (eds) (1998) *The Growth of African Literature. Twenty-Five Years after Dakar and Fourah Bay,* Trenton and Asmara: Africa World Press.

Malinowski, B. (1923) 'The problem of meaning in primitive languages', in Ogden, C. K. and Richards, I. A. (eds) *The Meaning of Meaning,* London: Routledge and Kegan Paul.

Mannheim, Bruce and Tedlock, Dennis (1995) (eds) *The Dialogic Emergence of Culture,* Urbana: University of Illinois Press.

Mapanje, Jack and White, Landeg (eds) (1983) *Oral Poetry from Africa,* Harlow: Longman.

Marivate, C. T. D. (1991) Personal communication.

Matera, Vincenzo (ed.) (2002) *Antropologia delle sensazioni,* special issue, *Enreffe, La Ricerca Folklorica* 45: 1–160.

Mauss, M. (1954) *The Gift: Forms and Functions of Exchange in Archaic Societies,* London: Cohen and West.

Mbele, Joseph L. (2004) 'East African folklore: overview', in Peek and Yankah.

Mbiti, John S. (1966) *Akamba Stories,* Oxford: Clarendon Press.

McLuhan, M. (1962) *The Gutenberg Galaxy. The Making of Typographic Man,* London: Routledge and Kegan Paul.

—— (1964) *Understanding Media. The Extensions of Man,* London: Routledge and Kegan Paul.

—— (1969) *Counterblast,* London: Rapp and Whiting.

McNeill, David (ed.) (2000) *Language and Gesture,* Cambridge: Cambridge University Press.

Meeker, Michael E. (1979) *Literature and Violence in North Arabia,* Cambridge: Cambridge University Press.

Meyer, G. (1991) *Récits épiques toucouleurs. La vache, le livre, la lance,* Paris: Karthala.

Mignolo, W. D. (1994) 'Literacy and the colonization of memory: writing histories of people without history', in Keller-Cohen, D. (ed.), *Literacy. Interdisciplinary Conversations,* Cresskill: Hampton Press.

Mitchell, W. J. T. (ed.) (1981) *On Narrative,* Chicago: University of Chicago Press.

Mofokeng, S. M. (1945) 'Notes and annotations of the praise-poems of certain chiefs and the structure of the praise-poems in southern Sotho', honours dissertation (Bantu Studies), University of the Witwatersrand.

Morales, D. M. (2003) 'The pervasive force of music in African, Caribbean, and African American drama', *Research in African Literatures* 34, 2: 144–54.

Morris, H. F. (1964) *The Heroic Recitations of the Bahima of Ankole*, Oxford: Clarendon Press.

Moyo, S. P. C. (1986) 'The aesthetic structure of oral poetry: the media of a complex form', in Moyo, S. P. C. et al. (eds) *Oral Traditions in Southern Africa*, Lusaka: University of Zambia Institute of African Studies, 4: 482–515.

Mphande, L. (2005) 'African oral literature', in Appiah and Gates, Vol. 1: 70–5.

Msiska, M. H. and Hyland, P. (eds) (1997) *Writing and Africa*, London: Longman.

Muana, Patrick Kagbeni (1998) 'Beyond frontiers: a review of analytical paradigms in folklore studies', *Journal of African Cultural Studies* 11: 39–58.

Mudimbe, V. Y. (1994) *The Idea of Africa*, London: James Currey.

Mulokozi, Mugyabuso M. (2002) *The African Epic Controversy: Historical, Philosophical and Aesthetic Perspectives on Epic Poetry and Performance,* Dar es Salaam: Mkuki na Nyota Publishers.

Mumin, Hassan Sheikh (1974) *Leopard among the Women. Shabeelnaagood. A Somali Play,* London: Oxford University Press.

Munday, J. (2001) *Introducing Translation Studies*, London: Routledge.

Mutembei, A. K. (2001) *Poetry and AIDS in Tanzania; Changing Metaphors and Metonymies in Haya Oral Traditions*, Leiden: CNWS Publications.

Nagler, M. N. (1967) 'Towards a generative view of the oral formula', *Transactions of the American Philological Association* 98: 269–311.

Ndong Ndoutoume, Tsire (1970, 1975) *Le Mvett,* 2 parts, Paris: Présence africaine.

Nebrija, E A. de (1926 [1492]) *Gramática de la Lengua Castellana*, London: Oxford University Press.

Neethling, S. J. (2003) 'Graduation poetry: a comparative view of two Xhosa oral poets', *South African Journal of African Languages* 23, 4: 199–207.

Newell, Stephanie (2002a) *Literary Culture in Colonial Ghana: 'How to Play the Game of Life'*, Manchester: Manchester University Press.

—— (ed.) (2002b) *Readings in African Popular Fiction*, Oxford: James Currey.

Ngandu Nkashama, Pius (1992) *Littérature et écriture en langues africaines*, Paris: L'Harmattan.

Ngugi wa Thiong'o (1986) *Decolonising the Mind. The Politics of Language in African Literature,* Oxford: James Currey.

—— ([1981] 1997) *Writers in Politics: A Re-engagement with Issues of Literature and Society*, 2nd edn, Oxford: James Currey.

—— (1998) *Penpoints, Gunpoints, and Dreams,* Oxford: Clarendon Press.

Nichols, S. G. (1961) *Formulaic Diction and Thematic Composition in the Chanson de Roland*, Chapel Hill: University of North Carolina Press.

Niles, John D. (1999) *Home Narrans. The Poetics and Anthropology of Oral Literature*, Philadelphia: University of Pennsylvania Press.

Niranjana, Tejaswini (1992) *Siting Translation. History, Post-Structuralism, and the Colonial Context*, Berkeley: University of California Press.

Nketia, J. H. Kwabena (1955) *Funeral Dirges of the Akan People*, Achimota [printed by James Townsend and Sons, Exeter].

—— (1963) *Drumming in Akan Communities of Ghana*, Edinburgh: Nelson.

—— (1996) 'National development and the performing arts of Africa', in Altbach, P. G. and Hassan, S. M. (eds) *The Muse of Modernity. Essays on Culture as Development in Africa*, Trenton and Asmara: Africa World Press.

Norris, Sigrid (2004) *Analyzing Multimodal Interaction. A Methodological Framework*, New York: Routledge.

Noss, P. A. (1970) 'The performance of the Gbaya tale', *Research in African Literatures* 1: 41–9.

Notopoulos, J. A. (1964) 'Studies in early Greek oral poetry', *Harvard Studies in Classical Philology* 68: 1–77.

Obododimma, Oha (2001) 'Yoruba Christian video narrative and indigenous imaginations', in Kaschula.

Ochs, Elinor. (1979) 'Transcription as theory', in Ochs, Elinor and Schieffelin, Bambi B. (eds) *Developmental Pragmatics*, New York: Academic Press.

—— (2001) 'Socialization', in Duranti.

Ochs, Elinor and Capps, Lisa (1996) 'Narrating the self', *Annual Review of Anthropology* 25: 19–43.

—— (2001) *Living Narrative: Creating Lives in Everyday Storytelling*, Cambridge MA: Harvard University Press.

Ochs, Elinor, Schegloff, E. A. and Thompson, S. A. (eds) (1996) *Interaction and Grammar*, Cambridge: Cambridge University Press.

Ogede, Ode S. (1993) 'The role of the Egede poet. Micah Ichegbeh's *Adiyah* songs in the political and moral education of his local audiences', *African Languages and Cultures* 6: 49–68.

Okome, Onookome (1995) 'The character of popular indigenous cinema in Nigeria', conference paper, 2nd International Conference on Oral Literature in Africa, Legon: University of Ghana.

Okpewho, Isidore (1977) 'Does the epic exist in Africa? Some formal considerations', *Research in African Literatures* 8: 171–200.

—— (1979) *The Epic in Africa. Toward a Poetics of the Oral Performance*, New York: Columbia University Press.

—— (1983) *Myth in Africa. A Study of its Aesthetics and Cultural Relevance*, Cambridge: Cambridge University Press.

—— (ed.) (1990) *The Oral Performance in Africa*, Ibadan: Spectrum Books.

—— (1992) *African Oral Literature. Backgrounds, Character and Continuity*, Bloomington: Indiana University Press.

—— (1998a) 'African mythology and Africa's political impasse', *Research in African Literatures* 29, 1: 1–15.

—— (1998b) *Once upon a Kingdom*, Bloomington: Indiana University Press.

—— (2003) 'The art of *The Ozidi Saga*', *Research in African Literatures* 34, 3: 1–26.

References

Okpewho, Isidore (2004a) 'Oral literary research in Africa', in Peek and Yankah.

—— (2004b) 'African oral epics', in Irele and Gikandi, Vol. 1.

Okpewho, Isidore, Davies, Carole Boyce, and Mazrui, Ali A. (eds) (1999) *The African Diaspora. African Origins and New World Identities*, Bloomington: Indiana University Press.

Ọlajubu, Oludare (1974) 'Iwè Egúngún chants – an introduction', *Research in African Literature*s 5, 1: 31–51.

Olaniyan, Tejimola (2004) 'Festivals, ritual, and drama in Africa', in Irele and Gikandi, Vol. 1.

Olson, D. R. and Torrance, N. (eds) (2001) *The Making of Literate Societies*, Oxford: Blackwell.

Ong, W. J. (1967) *The Presence of the Word*, New Haven: Yale University Press.

—— (1977) *Interfaces of the Word*, Ithaca: Cornell University Press.

Ong, Walter (1982) *Orality and Literacy: the Technologizing of the Word*, New York: Methuen.

Opland, J. (1980) 'The development of the epic in Xhosa', unpublished paper for Modern Languages Association.

—— (1983) *Xhosa Oral Poetry*, Cambridge: Cambridge University Press.

—— (1998) *Xhosa Poets and Poetry*, Cape Town: David Philip.

—— (2005) *The Dassie and the Hunter. A South African Meeting*, Scottsville: University of KwaZulu-Natal Press.

Orwin, Martin (2003) 'On the concept of "definitive text" in Somali poetry', *Bulletin of School of Oriental and African Studies* 66, 3: 334–47.

Orwin, Martin and Topan, F. (eds) (2001) *Islamic Religious Poetry in Africa*, special issue, *Journal of African Cultural Studies* 14, 1.

Ottenberg, S. (1996) *Seeing with Music. The Lives of Three Blind African Musicians,* Seattle: University of Washington Press.

Owomoyele, Oyekan (2004) 'Tricksters in African folklore', in Peek and Yankah.

Paredes, A. and Bauman, R. (eds) (1972) *Toward New Perspectives in Folklore*, Austin: University of Texas Press.

Parry, A. (1966) 'Have we Homer's *Iliad*?', *Yale Classical Studies* 20: 177–216.

Parry, M. and Lord, A. (1954) *Serbocroation Heroic Songs. I. Novi Pazar; English Translations*, Cambridge MA: Harvard University Press.

Parsons, Talcott (1966) *Societies. Evolutionary and Comparative Perspectives,* Englewood Cliffs: Prentice-Hall.

Paulme, D. (1972) 'Morphologie du conte africain', *Cahiers d'études africaines* 12: 131-63.

—— (1976) *La Mère dévorante: Essai sur la morphologie des contes Africains,* Paris: Gallimard.

Peek, Philip M. (1994) 'The sounds of silence: cross-world communication and the auditory arts in African societies', *American Ethnologist* 21, 3: 474–94.

Peek, Philip M. and Yankah, Kwesi (eds) (2004) *African Folklore. An Encyclopedia*, New York: Routledge.

Pelton, Robert D. (1980) *The Trickster in West Africa. A Study of Mythic Irony and Sacred Delight*, Berkeley: University of California Press.

Pepper, H. and de Wolf, P. P. (eds.) (1972) *Un Mvet de Zwè Nguéma, chant épique fang*, Paris: Armand Colin.

Phelan, Peggy (1993) *Unmarked. The Politics of Performance*, London: Routledge.

Pilaszewicz, S. (1985) 'The rise of written literatures in African languages', in Andrzejweski et al.

Pilbeam, D. (1992) 'Introduction: what makes us human?', in Jones, S., Martin, R. and Pilbeam, D. (eds), *The Cambridge Encyclopedia of Human Evolution*, Cambridge: Cambridge University Press.

Pongweni, Alec J. C. (1997) 'The Chimurenga songs of the Zimbabwean war of liberation', in Barber 1997c.

Potter, J. (1996) *Representing Reality. Discourse, Rhetoric and Social Construction*, London: Sage.

Poyatos, F. (ed.) (1992) *Advances in Nonverbal Communication*, Amsterdam: Benjamins.

Prahlad, Sw. Anand (ed.) (2005) 'Africana folklore', special issue, *Journal of American Folklore* 118: 469.

Propp, V. (1958) *Morphology of the Folktale*, Eng. transl., Bloomington: Indiana University.

Radlov, V. V. (1885) *Proben der Volkslitteratur der nördlichen türkischen Stämme*, vol. 5, St. Petersburg: Commisionäre der Kaiserlichen Academie der Wissenschaften.

Ramamurthy, Anandi (2003) *Imperial Persuaders. Images of Africa and Asia in British Advertising*, Manchester: Manchester University Press.

Ranger, Terence (2003) 'Commentary', in Draper.

Reed, Daniel B. (2003) *Dan Ge Performance. Masks and Music in Contemporary Côte d'Ivoire*, Bloomington: Indiana University Press.

Ricard, Alain (1974) 'The concert party as a genre: the happy stars of Lomé', *Research in African Literatures* 5, 2: 165–79.

—— (2004) *The Languages and Literatures of Africa: The Sands of Babel* Oxford: James Currey.

Ricard, Alain and Swanepoel, C. F. (eds) (1997) *The Oral-Written Interface*, special issue, *Research in African Literatures* 28, 1.

Ricard, Alain and Veit-Wild, Flora (eds) (2005) *Interfaces Between the Oral and the Written: Versions and Subversions in African Literature*, Amsterdam: Rodopi.

Richards, I. A. (1936) *The Philosophy of Rhetoric*, London: Oxford University Press.

Richards, Paul (1998) *Fighting for the Rainforest. War, Youth and Resources in Sierra Leone*, revised edn, Oxford: James Currey.

Ricoeur, P. (1984) *Time and Narrative,* Vol. 1, Chicago: University of Chicago Press.

Roberts, Brian (2002) *Biographical Research*, Buckingham: Open University Press.

Roberts, John W. (1989) *From Trickster to Badman. The Black Folk Hero in Slavery and Freedom*, Philadelphia: University of Pennsylvania Press.

Rogers, H. L. (1966) 'The crypto-psychological character of the oral formula',

English Studies 47: 89–102.

Rollins, H. E. (1919) 'The black-letter broadside ballad', *Publications of the Modern Language Association* 34, 2: 258–339.

Rosenberg, Bruce A. (1987) 'The complexity of oral tradition', *Oral Tradition* 2: 73–90.

Rosengren, K. E. (1999) *Communication. An Introduction*, Thousand Oaks: Sage.

Russo, Joseph A. (1974) Planning notes, Conference on 'Oral Literature and the Formula', Center for the Coordination of Ancient and Modern Studies, University of Michigan.

Saenger, Paul (1997) *Space Between Words. The Origins of Silent Reading*, Stanford: Stanford University Press.

Sammons, K. and Sherzer, J. (2000) *Translating Native American Verbal Art*, Washington: Smithsonian Institution Press.

Sapir, Edward (1956) *Culture, Language, and Personality. Selected Essays*, Berkeley: University of California Press.

Sayers, E. F. (1927) 'Notes on the native language affinities in Sierra Leone', *Sierra Leone Studies* (old series) 10: 112–14.

Sbisà, Marina (2001) 'Act', in Duranti.

Scharfe, D. and Aliyu, Y. (1967) 'Hausa poetry', in Beier, U. (ed.) *Introduction to African Literature*, London: Longmans.

Schechner, Richard (1988) *Performance Theory*, New York: Routledge.

—— (2002) *Performance Studies. An Introduction*, London: Routledge.

Scheub, Harold (1971) 'Translation of African oral narrative-performances to the written word', *Yearbook of Comparative and General Literature* 20: 8–36.

—— (1975) *The Xhosa Ntsomi*, Oxford: Clarendon Press.

—— (1977a) 'Body and image in oral narrative performance', *New Literary History* 8: 345–67.

—— (1977b) *African Oral Narratives, Proverbs, Riddles, Poetry and Song: An Annotated Bibliography*, Boston: G. K. Hall and Co.

—— (1985) 'A review of African oral traditions and literature', *African Studies Review* 28, 2/3: 1–72.

—— (2002) *The Poem in the Story. Music, Poetry and Narrative*, Madison: University of Wisconsin Press.

—— (2004) 'Storytellers', in Peek and Yankah.

—— (ed. and comp.) (2005) *African Tales*, Madison: University of Wisconsin Press.

Scheub, Harold and Zenani, Nongenile Masithathu (1992) *The World and the Word. Tales and Observations from the Xhosa Oral Tradition*, Madison: University of Wisconsin Press.

Schieffelin, E. L. (1998) 'Problematizing performance', in Hughes-Freeland.

Schieffelin, B. B., Woolard, K. A. and Kroskrity, P. V. (eds) (1998) *Language Ideologies. Practice and Theory*, New York: Oxford University Press.

Schipper, M. (ed.) (2000) *Poetics of African Art*, special issue, *Research in African Literatures* 31, 4.

Schousboe, K. and Larsen, M. T. (eds) (1989) *Literacy and Society*, Copenhagen: Akademisk Forlag.

Schultz, D. E. (2001) 'Music videos and the effeminate vices of urban culture in Mali', *Africa* 71: 345–72.

Scollon, Ron (2001) *Mediated Discourse. The Nexus of Practice,* London: Routledge.

Searing, James F. (2002) *'God Alone is King'. Islam and Emancipation in Senegal,* Oxford: James Currey.

Segal, Charles (1985) 'Tragedy, orality, literacy', in Gentili and Paione.

Seidel, A. (1896) *Geschichten und Lieder der Afrikaner,* Berlin: Schall und Grund.

Seitel, Peter (1980) *See So That We May See: Performances and Interpretations of Traditional Tales from Tanzania,* Bloomington: Indiana University Press.

Senghor, Léopold Sédar (1956) 'L'esthétique négro-africaine', *Diogène* 16, Oct: 43–61.

—— (1961) *Nation et voie africaine du socialisme,* Paris: Présence africaine.

Seydou, Christiane (ed.) (1972) *Silâmaka et Poullori, récit épique peul raconté par Tinguidji,* Paris: Armand Colin.

—— (1982) 'Comment définir le genre épique? Un exemple: l'épopée africaine', in Görög-Karady.

—— (2004) 'Epics: West African epics', in Peek and Yankah.

Seydou, Christiane, Biebuyck, Brunhilde, and Bekombo, Manga (eds) (1997) *Voix d'Afrique, Anthologie,* 1, *Poésie,* Paris: Classiques africains.

Sherzer, Joel F. (1977) 'Cuna *ikala*: literature in San Blas', in Bauman.

Shippey, T. A. (1972) *Old English Verse,* London: Hutchinson.

Sienaert, E., Bell, N. and Lewis, M. (eds) (1991) *Tradition and Innovation. New Wine in Old Bottles?* Durban: University of Natal Oral Documentation and Research Centre.

Shuman, Amy (2005) *Other People's Stories. Entitlement Claims and the Critique of Empathy,* Urbana: University of Illinois Press.

Silverstein, M. and Urban, G. (eds) (1996) *Natural Histories of Discourse,* Chicago: University of Chicago Press.

Sithebe, Zodwa (1997) 'The dynamics of oral and written transmission processes in SiSwati oral poetry', in Ricard and Swanepoel.

Smith, E. W. and Dale, A. M. (1920) *The Ila-Speaking Peoples of Northern Rhodesia,* 2 vols, London: Macmillan.

Smith, M. G. (1957) 'The social functions and meaning of Hausa praise-singing', *Africa* 27: 26–45.

Spencer, J. S. (2002) 'Storytelling theatre in Sierra Leone: the example of Lele Gbomba', in Harding.

Spitulnik, D. (2004) 'Electronic media and oral traditions', in Peek and Yankah.

Spivak, G. C. (2003) *Death of a Discipline,* New York: Columbia University Press.

Stein, R. A. (1959) *Recherches sur l'épopée et le barde au Tibet,* Paris: Presses universitaires de France.

Stone, Ruth M. (1988) *Dried Millet Breaking. Time, Words and Song in the Woi Epic of the Kpelle,* Bloomington: Indiana University Press.

—— (1998) 'Time in African performance', in *The Garland Encyclopedia of World Music,* Vol. 1, *Africa,* New York: Garland.

Streeck, J. and Knapp, M. L. (1992) 'The interaction of visual and verbal features in human communication', in Poyatos.

Street, Brian (ed.) (1993) *Cross-Cultural Approaches to Literacy*, Cambridge: Cambridge University Press.

Swanepoel, C. F. (1983) *Sotho Dithoko tsa Marena: Perspectives on Composition and Genre*, Pretoria: The Author.

—— (1997) 'An exploration of J. J. Moiloa's *Thesele, Ngwana Mmamokgatjhane*, the epic tradition, and the oral-written interface', in Ricard and Swanepoel.

Swann, B. (ed.) (1992) *On the Translation of Native American Literatures*, Washington and London: Smithsonian Institution Press.

Sweet, J. H. (2003) *Recreating Africa. Culture, Kinship, and Religion in the African-Portugese World 1441–1770*, Chapel Hill: University of North Carolina Press.

Tedlock, Dennis (1972) 'On the translation of style in oral literature', in Paredes and Bauman.

—— (1977) 'Toward an oral poetics', *New Literary History* 8: 507–19.

—— (1980) *Finding the Center. Narrative Poetry of the Zuni Indians*, 2nd edn, Lincoln: University of Nebraska Press.

—— (1983) *The Spoken Word and the Work of Interpretation*, Philadelphia: University of Pennsylvania Press.

—— (1985) 'Phonography and the problem of time in oral narrative events', in Gentili and Paione (also as conference paper, 1980).

Tempels, Placide (1959) *Bantu Philosophy*, Paris: Présence africaine. [first pub. in Flemish 1945]

Thackway, M. (2003) *Africa Shoots Back. Alternative Perspectives in Sub-Saharan Francophone African Film*, Oxford: James Currey.

Thomas, Nicholas (1994) *Colonialism's Culture. Anthropology, Travel and Government*, Cambridge: Polity.

Thomas, N. W. (1910) *Anthropological Report on the Edo-speaking Peoples of Nigeria*, London: Harrison and Sons.

Thomas, Rosalind (1989) *Oral Tradition and Written Record in Classical Athens*, Cambridge: Cambridge University Press.

—— (2003) 'Performance and written literature in classical Greece: envisaging performance from written literature and comparative contexts', *Bulletin of School of Oriental and African Studies* 66, 3: 348–57.

Thoyer, A. (ed. and transl.) (1995) *Récits épiques des chasseurs bamanan du Mali*, Paris: L'Harmattan.

Tonkin, Elizabeth (1992) *Narrating our Pasts: The Social Construction of Oral History*, Cambridge: Cambridge University Press.

Torrend, J. (1921) *Specimens of Bantu Folk-lore from Northern Rhodesia*, London: Kegan Paul, Trench, Trubner.

Tracey, Hugh T. (1929) 'Some observations on native music in Southern Rhodesia', NADA 7: 96–103.

—— (1948) *Chopi Musicians. Their Music, Poetry, and Instruments*, London: International African Institute.

—— (1967) *The Lion on the Path and other African Stories*, London: Routledge.

Tracey, K. (ed.) (1999) *Language and Social Interaction at the Century's Turn*, special issue, *Research on Language and Social Interaction* 32, 1/2.

Traoré, Karim (2000) *Le jeu et le serieux. Essai d'anthropologie littéraire sur la poésie épique des chasseurs du Mande*, Köln: Rudiger Köppe.

Tsohatzidis, S. L. (ed.) (1994) *Foundations of Speech Act Theory: Philosophical and Linguistic Perspectives*, London: Routledge.

Tuchscherer, K. (1995) 'African script and scripture: the history of the *kikakui* (Mende) writing system for Biblical translation', *African Languages and Cultures* 8: 169–88.

—— (2005) 'Writing, history of, in Africa', in Appiah and Gates, Vol. 5: 476–80.

Tylor, E. B. (1881) *Anthropology. An Introduction to the Study of Man and Civilization*, London: Macmillan.

UNESCO (1966) *World Congress of Ministers of Education on the Eradication of Illiteracy, Teheran, 1965, Speeches and Messages,* Paris: UNESCO.

—— (2001) *Discussion Paper on the United Nations Decade of Literacy*, online, http://www.unesco.org/education/litdecade/discussion.html/

Vail, Leroy and White, Landeg (1991) *Power and the Praise Poem*, Charlottesville: University of Virginia Press; Oxford: James Currey.

Vambe, Maurice (2000) 'Popular songs and social realities in post-independence Zimbabwe', *African Studies Review* 43, 2: 73–85.

Vanderveken, Daniel and Kubo, Susumu (eds) (2002) *Essays in Speech Act Theory*, Amsterdam: Benjamins.

Venuti, L. (ed.) (2004) *The Translation Studies Reader*, 2nd edn, London: Routledge.

Wagner, D. A., Venezky, R. L. and Street, B. V. (eds) (1999) *Literacy. An International Handbook*, Boulder: Westview.

Walker, C. E. (2001) *We Can't Go Home Again: An Argument about Afrocentrism*, Oxford: Oxford University Press.

Watts, A. C. (1969) *The Lyre and the Harp. A Comparative Reconsideration of Oral Tradition in Homer and Old English Epic Poetry*, New Haven: Yale University Press.

Wauthier, C. (1966) *The Literature and Thought of Modern Africa: A Survey*, Eng. transl., London: Pall Mall Press.

Weate, J. (2003) 'Achille Mbembe and the postcolony: going beyond the text', *Research in African Literatures* 34, 4: 27–41.

Wellek, R. and Warren, A. (1949) *Theory of Literature*, London: Cape.

Werner, A. (1918) 'Swahili poetry', *Bulletin of School of Oriental Studies* 1, 2: 113–27.

White, Luise, Miescher, Stephen, and Cohen, David William (eds) (2002) *African Words, African Voices: Critical Practices in Oral History*, Bloomington: Indiana University Press.

Whiteley, W. H. (1958) *The Dialects and Verse of Pemba*, Kampala: East African Swahili Committee.

—— (ed.) (1964) A *Selection of African Prose. 1. Traditional Oral Texts*, Oxford: Clarendon Press.

Wilgus, D. K. (1983) 'Collecting musical folklore and folksong', in Dorson, R. M. (ed.) *Handbook of American Folklore*, Bloomington: Indiana University Press.

Williams, P. and Chrisman, L. (eds) (1993) *Colonial Discourse and Post-Colonial Theory. A Reader*, New York: Harvester Wheatsheaf.

Wilson-Tagoe, Nana and Osei-Nyame, Kwadwo (eds) (1999) *Literature and History*, special issue, *Journal of African Cultural Studies* 12, 2.

Witkowski, S. R. (1996) 'Language', in Levinson, D. and Ember, M. (eds) *Encyclopedia of Cultural Anthropology*, New York: Holt, Vol. 2: 687–93.

Wolff, H. (1962) 'Rárà: a Yoruba chant', *Journal of African Languages* 1: 45–56.

Woodley, Krista (2004) 'Let the data sing: representing discourse in poetic form', *Oral History* 32, 1: 49–58.

Yankah, Kwesi (1985) 'Risks in verbal art performance', *Journal of Folklore Research* 22: 133–53.

—— (1995) *Speaking for the Chief. Okyeame and the Politics of Akan Royal Oratory*, Bloomington: Indiana University Press.

—— (2004) 'The folktale and its extensions', in Irele and Gikandi, Vol. 1.

Zumthor, Paul (1983) *Introduction à la poésie orale*, Paris: Éditions du Seuil.

—— (1989) 'Préface', in Calame-Griaule.

Index